Y0-CJH-671

GOD AND SPACE-TIME

GOD AND SPACE-TIME

Deity in the Philosophy of
Samuel Alexander

BY

ALFRED P. STIERNOTTE, Ph. D. (Harvard)
Research Fellow in Philosophy, Yale University

With a Foreword by
HENRY NELSON WIEMAN

PHILOSOPHICAL LIBRARY
NEW YORK

Copyright, 1954, by the
PHILOSOPHICAL LIBRARY, INC.
15 East 40th Street, New York 16, N. Y.

PRINTED IN THE UNITED STATES OF AMERICA

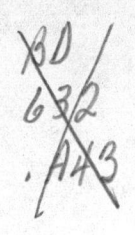

TO MY WIFE

TO MY WIFE

This nisus not only leads to the formation of things and to the sustainment of them, but impels the world forward towards new creations, bringing forth the new out of the bosom of the old. It creates chemical bodies and keeps up their form by the stability of their functions; but also, and this is perhaps more striking, drives on 'the chemic lump,' in Emerson's words, to 'ascend to man.'

One of the elements of religious feeling is the sense of mystery . . . which is other than anything we know by our senses or our reflection. . . . Mr. Otto calls this the 'numinous' element in the world. . . . In recognising the existence in real fact of this numinous element in the world, I follow him, and . . . profess myself in this respect an Otto-man.

SAMUEL ALEXANDER

FOREWORD

This book is an analysis of a typical case of religious thought. The study of the religious thinking of Samuel Alexander is incidental to a larger purpose. The larger purpose is to analyze the intellectual problem which underlies all religion. To be sure religion is not merely an intellectual problem, any more than getting food for the body or establishing a home. But these all involve intellectual problems of great importance. If the intellectual problem is misunderstood in such wise that the proposed solution is confused or false, disaster may ensue whether it be a religion or food for the body or a home that is under consideration. The problem treated here by way of this study of Samuel Alexander might be stated, thus: What is the question that must be answered correctly if religion is to attain the end it seeks?

This study of the religious thought of Samuel Alexander indicates that the source of confusion so widely prevalent in religious thinking is failure to locate and analyze the problem which underlies religion and failure to keep it steadfastly in mind throughout the inquiry.

What is the primary concern of religion as it appears in the supreme exemplars of religious living and what is the basic intellectual problem involved in this concern? This question must be answered with clarity and in truth before ever we can begin to avoid the confusions and bypaths which lead astray. Dr. Stiernotte's analysis

FOREWORD

of Alexander's religious thought reveals the confusion and error resulting from failure to get this question clearly and truly formulated. But, as said before, it is not Alexander alone who is under examination. He is simply taken as one sample, exemplifying the confusion which prevails in religious thinking. The writer of this Foreword does not exempt himself from this indictment.

Perhaps this failure to reach any clarity and agreement on the basic question to be answered by religious thinking will be more apparent if we glance at some of the different ways in which the question seems to have been stated. All these different ways of interpreting the religious question are more or less implicit or explicit in the religious thinking of Alexander. Alexander's failure to settle on one of these questions as basic, treating the others as incidental to it, seems to have been the reason his answers to the religious question are often confusing and misleading. Some of these different questions, each of which seems at times to be treated as though it were the primary question which religion is concerned to answer, can be listed in the following way.

1. Is the primary concern of religion as seen in the supreme exemplars of religious living timeless Being which sustains and controls all temporal existence and from which all temporal existence has come forth? Is this the primary concern of Jesus and St. Paul, of Buddha and Ramakrishna Paramahansa, of Mahomet and Gandhi, of Lao-Tzu and Confucius? Or were these supreme exemplars of religious living most concerned with a process of change by which men are delivered from evil and transformed into the best they can ever become? These great religious leaders disagree on what the final outcome of human destiny may be. Buddha thought it was timeless Being but he refused to pass into Nirvana be-

FOREWORD

cause his primary concern seems to have been that process of change by which men are saved from the illusion of change and absorbed into the timeless Being of Nirvana. This statement is paradoxical but the philosophy of Buddhism makes paradox unavoidable.

2. Is the primary concern of religion as seen in its supreme exemplars a certain kind of experience called by Alexander the religious sentiment? Or is this experience quite incidental to a primary concern, namely, devotion to that process of transformation by which men are saved from evil and delivered over to the highest attainment of human destiny?

3. Is the primary concern of religion as seen in the supreme exemplars a certain coherent body of doctrine embodied in a close-knit religious fellowship molding the mind and the devotion of all its members? Was this the chief concern of these supreme persons or was it again rather the process of change aforementioned, the fellowship being incidental to this larger end?

4. Is the primary concern of religion as seen in the great exemplars the affirmations common to all the great religions? Or again must we say that these religious giants considered these affirmations as quite incidental to bringing about that transformation in the life of man which is the way of salvation?

5. Is the primary concern of religion as seen in the great exemplars some other exemplar of religious excellence, living at some earlier date? For example, was the primary concern of Jesus the great Hebrew prophets, for St. Paul was it Jesus and the prophets, for St. Augustine was it Paul and Jesus and the prophets, and so on? Similar examples could be taken from religions other than Christianity. Here again we must compare this concern for a predecessor with the concern these men

FOREWORD

showed for the salvation of their fellow men. Which was dominant and primary and which subordinate and secondary?

6. Is the primary concern of religion as seen in the great exemplars the self-giving of man to what has such character and power that man must commit himself to it to be saved from the worst and transformed into the best that he can ever become? For example, when Jesus said, Thou shalt love the Lord thy God with all thy heart and with all thy mind and with all thy soul, was he referring to a way of living? If so, he was referring to a process.

Here we have six different ways in which the basic and generative question is being interpreted. If the first interpretation is correct, the primary question that religion must answer is a metaphysical one, and the method of inquiry must be metaphysical speculation. The point under consideration is not whether the metaphysical question enters into religion. It certainly does. No one is denying that. But the point at issue is this: Is the metaphysical question the basic, ruling concern of religion or is it incidental to another problem which is the primary one? For example, if the primary concern of religion is the process of change by which man is saved, then timeless Being enters into the problem only to the measure that it is an agent in causing this saving process to occur. Some may think that this way of understanding the religious problem represents man to be more important than the ultimate reality of timeless Being. But such is not the case. Even supposing that man is utterly insignificant as compared to timeless Being, still the primary problem of religion would be to bring about that change in men whereby they

FOREWORD

recognize their insignificance compared to the absolute majesty of Being. I am not endorsing this view of the matter, but only analyzing the religious problem.

If the second interpretation of the religious question is correct, then the primary concern of religion is psychological. First of all this special kind of experience called by Alexander the religious sentiment must be distinguished from every other kind. This in itself is exceedingly difficult because we ordinarily distinguish experiences by naming the object being experienced. We might distinguish the religious experience as Dr. Stiernotte does for the purposes of this study and say that it is "man's whole response to the whole universe." But this raises very difficult questions. One must then ascertain in what sense this experience involves the whole person more than some other experiences. Also in what sense does it involve the whole universe more than some other experiences. This experience becomes clear when one restates the issue by speaking of a certain kind of experience which accompanies a certain belief, on condition that the belief is held passionately. But an experience caused by a belief must be sharply distinguished from an experience indicating encounter with an objective reality. It is very difficult if not impossible to disentangle experience from belief, especially when the reality which one is supposed to experience is neither a physical thing under direct impact nor a living organism using signs that convey communicable meanings. In the two latter cases, simple experiments can ordinarily assure us that we are dealing with objective reality and not an illusory belief. But how can we tell if our experience is of the whole universe and not merely of some part of it mistakenly believed to be the whole? Here again I am only

FOREWORD

analyzing the problem with a view of indicating what is the basic question for religion and most promising way of seeking a true answer to it.

If the third interpretation of the religious question is correct, the true answer must be a confessional one. In such case the area of inquiry must be the special tradition inherited by the individual and no answer can be accepted which is not a part of the tradition shaping the minds and the devotion of the religious fellowship to which the individual belongs. Christians who interpret the religious question in this manner appeal to what they call the Jewish-Christian tradition as their final authority. But examination reveals that they refer not to this tradition in its entirety but only to that part and form of it that is embodied in their own religious fellowship. For example, some appeal to the Hegelian idealists as the best interpreters of this doctrine while others, just as truly and devoutly Christian, repudiate the absolute idealists as falsifiers of this tradition and misleaders of their fellow men.

If the fourth interpretation of the religious question is correct it becomes an historical problem. The answer must be sought by studying the great religions and finding those points on which they seem to agree, or can be made to agree by mediating between them. This approach is not prominent in Alexander but he follows it along with all the others. It appears in his attempt to reconcile theism and pantheism by a mediating interpretation. However, as Dr. Stiernotte shows, this only leads to confusion. Yet this historical interpretation of the religious question seems to be accepted by an increasing number today in the field of religious thought. The primary concern for them seems to be to study and understand appreciatively all the great religions and then to mediate between them to bring about some maximum agreement. But is this in truth the primary concern of religion as seen in the great exemplars of religious living? Were they concerned to mediate and reconcile the great religious affirmations found in history? It seems to me most decidedly this was not their ruling concern. Something much more vital, intimate and revolutionary engaged their lives namely, the process of change by which the individual, society and history are transformed from evil ways into the best that can ever be attained.

If the fifth interpretation of the religious question is correct, the religious problem is a biographical one. The answer must be sought by intensive study of certain individuals, what they said, did, enjoyed and suffered and what their lives may signify. In the recent past this seemed to be the interpretation of the religious question implicitly adopted by the great majority of Christian thinkers in the field of religion. "Back to Jesus" was the slogan, and the whole issue of religion seemed to rest upon what might be discovered by studying the life and work and teachings of Jesus. To broaden the study to include the supreme exemplars of other religions than the Christian is not to alter the approach. One is still interpreting the religious question as primarily concerned with certain outstanding individuals. Here again the issue is not whether the study of such individuals can be excluded from religious inquiry. Such study must certainly be included. But is the basic question which religion tries to answer primarily about any one or more of these individuals or is it about something else, the study of these individuals being merely incidental to finding the answer to this other question? That is the issue before us.

FOREWORD

Throughout this analysis it is plain that I am defending the sixth interpretation of the religious question. According to this sixth view the basic question which religion tries to answer is about that process of transformation by which man is saved from the worst and unto the best. Metaphysics may provide help in finding the answer to this question but the history of thought indicates that no knowledge is so precariously established and so likely to be mistaken as knowledge concerning that reality from which all the temporal forms of existence have come forth, by which they are sustained in being and by which their final destiny is determined. The two outstanding Christian theologians of our time, Paul Tillich and Karl Barth, disagreeing as they do on many other points, are agreed in saying that ultimate reality is utterly beyond the reach of human inquiry. Yet both insist that ultimate reality, unknowable as it is to metaphysics, is the ultimate concern of the religious man. Barth claims that revelation, faith and the grace of God can provide us with what we need to know about this ultimate reality for our salvation. But all the teaching, writing and working of these two men, despite what they say about the ultimate concern of religion, seems to be devoted to the process of transformation by which they themselves as individuals and all other men can be sustained and transformed into the best that man can become whether in this life or beyond the grave.

There is still a seventh way of interpreting the religious question which I have not yet mentioned. I have postponed its consideration to the last because of its crucial importance in this study of the religious thinking of Samuel Alexander. Also it is a crucial issue in current religious thinking. According to this seventh interpretation the basic question that concerns religion is about some ideal future state of being to be brought into existence by human striving. Here again the critical issue is not whether some ideal future state of being shall be a matter of religious concern along with much else. Of course the future is a matter of human concern in everything we do and not least in religion. But the critical issue is this: Which is primary? Which is basic? Which should command the ultimate commitment of man? Should it be the ideal future or should it be the actual present process transforming man and his world into the best they can ever become?

The question at issue in this last interpretation of the religious question is this: Is the primary concern of religion an ideal or a process? To put the issue in terms used by Alexander and Dr. Stiernotte in his analysis: Is it the nisus which brings forth the best or is it the future state of being as yet unknown to us in its distinctive character to which we should give ourselves in supreme devotion and worshipful commitment? In the language of Alexander, the alternatives are nisus versus Deity, since Deity for Alexander is a future state of Being.

This term "nisus," referring to a process, can be applied to the other alternatives which we have been considering, looking at each of these alternatives in the way Alexander treats it. Is it the nisus, or is it the primordial Being of space-time which should command our ultimate religious commitment? Is it the nisus or is it the Jewish-Christian tradition that we must understand to find the answer to the religious question? Is it the nisus or is it the reconciliation of the great religious affirmations such as theism and pantheism which must guide to find the answer to the religious question? Is it the nisus

FOREWORD

or is it the supreme exemplars of religious living to which we must give ourselves in religious devotion?

These are the questions raised by this study of Samuel Alexander's religious philosophy. Their importance extends far beyond the philosophy of Alexander, great as his philosophical achievement may have been. These are questions which religious thinking throughout the world and through the years to come must answer. We must reach some agreement on what the question is that we are trying to answer when we engage in religious inquiry and exposition. If we cannot agree on this most elementary first step, confusion in religious thought and religious striving will become worse confounded as the isolation of long established and coherent traditions comes to an end under the impact of their intermingling.

We have come to the time when we must find our way by religious inquiry and not alone by the single tradition which our forefathers may have handed down to us. But religious inquiry cannot be cooperative if we cannot agree on the question we are trying to answer. Neither can we hope to find any answer to the religious question if our search is directed to seeking an answer to the wrong question.

The religious philosophy of Samuel Alexander is peculiarly well fitted to expose these problems involved in religious inquiry; and Dr. Stiernotte's analysis has caused these issues to stand forth in striking clarity.

HENRY NELSON WIEMAN

PREFACE

In an article evaluating philosophic trends toward Neo-Realism in Britain and the United States in the early decades of the twentieth century, R. F. Alfred Hoernlé stated:

> To make a Neo-Realist, very little is needed; least of all any excursions into the realm of religion.[1]

Hoernlé implied that British and American Neo-Realism had occupied itself with epistemological discussions challenging the older idealistic conceptions of knowledge, but had done little to elaborate a distinctive philosophy of religion beyond the "marriage of Naturalism and Philanthropy which was characteristic already of Comte and Mill and the 'religion of humanity.' "[2] Ralph Barton Perry may be presumed to agree with Hoernlé in his general estimate of the services rendered to the philosophy of religion by idealism:

> Indeed, during the last century, idealism has almost alone defended the citadel of religious philosophy from this most powerful and vicious adversary.[3]

Perry's reference to "this most powerful and vicious

---

1. R. F. Alfred Hoernlé, "Neo-Realism and Religion," *Harvard Theological Review*, Vol. XI, No. 2 (April, 1918), 149.
2. *Ibid.*, 148.
3. Ralph Barton Perry, *Present Philosophic Tendencies* (New York, Longmans, Green & Co., 1929), 192.

PREFACE

adversary," by which he means Naturalism, would involve us very far in a discussion of the mutual relevance of Idealism and Naturalism, which is beyond the scope of this work. At this point we merely wish to state the fact that at the time of writing, Hoernlé had grounds for his assertion that Neo-Realism (a variety of Naturalism) had made little exploration of religion. Perry's discussion of the various types of Idealism. and his refutation of the argument from the ego-centric predicament in his *Present Philosophic Tendencies* are indeed illuminating, but one must come to the conclusion that his contributions to a philosophy of religion, at least in this volume, consist of little more than the assertion that Realism means to take life "realistically" in the common sense meaning of the term "realism" as merely "a sense of things as they are." The concluding paragraph of *Present Philosophic Tendencies* is a fitting expression of this modest and mundane orientation of Neo-realism:

> There is nothing dispiriting in realism. It involves the acceptance of the given situation as it is, with no attempt to think or imagine it already good. But it involves no less a conception of the reality and power of life. It is opposed equally to an idealistic anticipation of the victory of spirit, and to a naturalistic confession of the impotence of spirit. In this sense all bold and forward living is realistic. It involves a sense for things as they are, an ideal of things as they should be, and a determination that, through enlightened action, things shall in time come to be what they should be.[4]

It may be remarked, however, that such vague expres-

4. *Ibid.*, 347.

PREFACE

sions as "a sense for things as they are, an ideal for things as they should be" cry aloud for fuller development in terms of a full-blown metaphysic of Realism in which the universe and the ethical and spiritual aspirations of man shall be related in such a close-knit system that a philosophy of religion shall perhaps be elaborated that will rival in comprehensiveness and adequacy the older theological and idealistic systems. We make bold to assert that Samuel Alexander's *Space, Time, and Deity*[5] is such a system, and we shall be concerned in this work —not primarily with the full, detailed, discussion of this system—but rather with the peculiar conceptions of God and deity which are involved in it. However, it would be inadvisable to consider the various ideas of the divine contained in Alexander's system without giving a rapid summary of the epistemological and metaphysical ingredients. Alexander's direct realism may have strong similarities with Scholastic realism (as well as some divergences) but since this work is not primarily an epistemological discussion, we shall not explore this fascinating vista. Again, though we shall express Alexander's metaphysical views on the categorial structure of his universe of Space-Time, we are not primarily interested in a cosmological system, except in so far as it bears on the conception of deity. Also, Alexander's value theory presents certain facets which invite comparison with both objective and subjective theories of value, but since we are not writing a work on ethical theory or value theory, we shall limit our discussion to value as it bears on Alexander's idea of deity. In short, without dealing too cavalierly with the earlier portions of Alexander's Gifford Lectures, we wish to proceed to

---

5. Samuel Alexander, *Space, Time, and Deity* (New York, The Humanities Press, 1950), two volumes, hereafter designated as *STD*.

PREFACE

a fuller examination of deity and to work out our analysis on two grounds:

1. The philosophical justification of Alexander's conception of deity, to be understood, however, not as a colorless presentation of Alexander's views, but to include critical evaluations and objections.

2. The religious availability of Alexander's "deity." Here we wish to point out that we are primarily concerned with the philosophical issues involved, and not particularly with the question how far Alexander's deity reflects, or does not reflect, any specific denominational theology. At the same time, it will be discovered that there are broad relationships between Alexander's system and certain types of empirical and realistic theology now current in the United States.

One way of approaching this discussion would be to present a step-by-step exposition and criticism of Alexander's views. The objection to such a procedure is that full justice might not be done to the comprehensiveness and elegance of Alexander's system which might well dissolve in the welter of minute analysis of separate and disparate points. We propose rather to follow the pattern adopted by Milton R. Konvitz in his *On the Nature of Value*. That is to say, the first part of this work will attempt to "convey the spirit and logic of Professor S. Alexander's enquiry"[6] into the nature of deity, calling attention, however, to certain inconsistencies and obscurities in his treatment. The second part will endeavor to give expression to more radical criticism raised by others—as well as our own—on specific points of Alexander's system bearing on his views of God and deity.

For my reluctance to accept modern subjectivist

6. New York, King's Crown Press, 1946, 1.

PREFACE

theories of value, I am greatly indebted to Dr. Brand Blanshard who lectured at Harvard Divinity School in 1948, and to Dr. John Wild, Department of Philosophy, Harvard University—both of them wise philosophic counselors and friends. I wish to thank Professor Theodore M. Greene, Yale University, and Dr. R. I. Aaron, chairman, Department of Philosophy, University of Wales, and Visiting Professor, Yale University, 1952-53, for reading this work. Professor Aaron was personally acquainted with Samuel Alexander and I value his reminiscences of the great philosopher and his assurance that the idea of deity was an integral part of Alexander's system. I am grateful to Dr. W. H. Sheldon, Professor Emeritus, Yale University, for the opportunity of reading the manuscript of his forthcoming volume, *God and Polarity,* to be published by Yale University Press, but regret pressure of time did not enable me to utilize his brilliant insights into the relationships of Process philosophy and Neo-Thomism. I appreciate the suggestions made by Dr. Donald Williams, Chairman, Department of Philosophy, Harvard University, directing me to criticism of Alexander by Bernard Bosanquet, and I rejoice in recalling the emphasis which Dr. Williams placed, in his course on the philosophy of religion, on Otto's *mysterium tremendum*—an emphasis which Alexander shared and from which I have profited. I am most indebted to Professor John Wild for his patient criticism and illuminating comments generously given at a time when his academic duties were particularly heavy. For an enlightening Foreword on the issues arising from this study I thank Professor Henry Nelson Wieman, University of Houston, whose exposition of empirical theism has important relations to Alexander's ontology of levels. I am grateful to the Department of

PREFACE

Philosophy, Yale University, for a Visiting Fellowship, 1952-54, which enabled me to make important revisions in this work. However, I remain responsible for the opinions expressed and for the degree to which I have incorporated, or failed to incorporate, suggestions received. Finally, mention should be made of Professor John A. Irving, Chairman, Department of Philosophy, Victoria College, University of Toronto, and Visiting Fellow, Yale University, in 1953, who urged me to revise and publish this work—a work some of whose conclusions may not be shared by Professor Irving. Nevertheless, I must emphasize that without the stimulus which he provided, this study would not have seen the light of day for several years.

I cannot adequately express my thanks to my wife who read all the proofs, completed part of the index, removed obscure expressions, and who has endured with infinite patience for many years the cadences of a "noiseless" typewriter, a fit symbol of the unsubstantial values of the academic life.

ALFRED P. STIERNOTTE

New Haven, Conn.

TABLE OF CONTENTS

	PAGE
FOREWORD by Dr. Henry Nelson Wieman	ix
PREFACE	xix

PART I — EXPOSITION

CHAPTER I — ALEXANDER'S REALISM ... 1
Introduction ... 1
Epistemology ... 5
Space-Time and the Categories ... 12
A Formula for Space-Time — Emergence ... 28
Is Total Space-Time an Absolute? ... 45
Alexander and Eternity ... 47

CHAPTER II — DEITY AND GOD ... 53
The God of Metaphysics and the God of Religion ... 53
Deity and Spirit ... 58
God as the Universe Possessing Deity ... 59
Deity is a Nisus and not an Accomplishment ... 66
The World-soul ... 77
Is Space-Time an Absolute Spirit? ... 80
Mind, Nisus, and Deity ... 85

CHAPTER III — DEITY AND THE RELIGIOUS CONSCIOUSNESS ... 92
The Religious Sentiment and Its Object ... 92
Religious Criteria of the Concept of God ... 100
Theism and Pantheism ... 111
Is God a Creator? ... 126
God's Supposed Timelessness ... 133
Summary ... 136

CHAPTER IV — DEITY AND VALUE ... 140
The Uniqueness of the Religious Sentiment ... 140
Deity and Goodness ... 144

TABLE OF CONTENTS

	PAGE
Truth, Goodness, and Beauty as Human Inventions	147
Deity on the Side of Goodness	156
Good and Great Men	163
The Problem of Evil	166
The Question of Immortality	175
Deity and Feeling	179
Summary	182

PART II — EVALUATION AND CRITICISM

CHAPTER I — THE SYSTEM AS A WHOLE ... 187
Space-Time as Mathematical Abstraction or Physically Real?	187
Are Space and Time intimately united in Space-Time?	192
Is Space-Time a Changeless Whole or Historical Through and Through?	199
Is Alexander's Metaphysics Materialism?	209
Prediction in Alexander's System	221
Summary	228

CHAPTER II — GOD, DEITY, NISUS ... 230
The Four Conceptions of the Divine in Alexander's System	230
The "Body" and the "Mind" of God	235
Theism and Pantheism in Alexander's System	244
John Laird's Criticisms	250
Dean Inge's Criticisms	264
A Radical Criticism of Alexander's Deity	266
The Vindication of the Nisus	279
Summary	288

CHAPTER III — DEITY, VALUE, PERSONS ... 290
A Criticism of Alexander's Theory of Value	290
Deity and Value	316
Alexander's Theory of Evil	320
The Uniqueness of the Religious Sentiment	325
The Problem of Immortality in Alexander's System	330
A Reconstruction of Alexander's System to Include the Objectivity of Value	334
Alexander and Hylomorphism	348
Alexander and Wieman	351
Has Alexander overlooked Personality?	359

TABLE OF CONTENTS

	PAGE
CHAPTER IV – CONCLUSION: WHAT IS LEFT OF ALEXANDER'S SYSTEM?	364
What Elements are Rejected	364
Elements of Lasting Value in Alexander's System	371
The Justification of Alexander	382
Notes Part I	404
Notes Part II	419
Acknowledgments	439
Index	441

PART I
EXPOSITION

CHAPTER I

ALEXANDER'S REALISM

Introduction—Alexander's Gifford Lectures, *Space, Time, and Deity,* were first published in 1920, and represent the culmination of Alexander's metaphysical thought, unifying in a comprehensive synthesis his epistemology, his categorial system, his views on the tertiary qualities of truth, goodness, and beauty, and finally his novel study of the time-honored conceptions of God and "deity." The philosophical climate in British universities has now turned to precise analytic studies of logic and mathematics, but one may be pardoned for attempting to recapture the general impression of Alexander's eminence from his evaluation by Rudolf Metz:

Next to Whitehead, Alexander is in his work and influence the strongest philosophical force which Anglo-Saxon thinking has produced since the war. What Bergson means for French philosophy, that Alexander means in many respects for British philosophy. But he stands less conspicuously above his environment and has been much later in coming to maturity and in attaining an influential position than his more famous French contemporary, born in the same year. The influence of Alexander's doctrine, moreover, has been so far confined to the Anglo-Saxon world, and

1

within this to professional philosophical circles. ... Among British philosophers he is one of the greatest and boldest system-makers, and among the moderns Whitehead, Bradley, and McTaggart are the only men to compare with him in respect of the impulse to the formation of a comprehensive world-system.[1]

John Laird testifies to the friendly reception of *Space, Time, and Deity* by foreign critics:

The foreign reviews—Italian, French, and Belgian—also attained a high standard and showed the keenest interest. Some may have betrayed a tendentious aim. The neo-scholastics in Belgium and elsewhere find neo-realism in harmony with neo-Thomism.[2]

It is clear that Alexander as a system-builder displays the metaphysical orientation concerned for the comprehensive character of existing things which are studied by the separate sciences. Nothing but a long quotation will make apparent Alexander's profound agreement with the metaphysical tradition of Western philosophy:

Philosophy, by which I mean metaphysics, differs from the special sciences, not so much in its method as in the nature of the subjects with which it deals. They are of a peculiarly comprehensive kind, and are revealed to the most superficial glance cast at the things or existences in the world. These things fall into groups distinguished from one another by specific characters which some have and others have not. Thus there are material bodies, ranging from ordinary things like stones down to molecules and ions, if these may be called material; there are living things; and there are beings with minds. What is the relation of these different orders of existence to one another? Is there any fundamental nature which they have in common, of which they are specific examples, and what meaning can we attach to such specification? What is the primary form of being, and how are different orders of being born of it? ... Metaphysics is thus an attempt to study these very comprehensive topics, to describe the ultimate nature of existence if it has any, and these pervasive characters of things, or categories. If we may neglect too nice particulars of interpretation we may use the definition of Aristotle, the science of being as such and its essential attributes.[3]

Alexander's whole metaphysical orientation, however, is in the direction of a pronounced realism rather than the idealism of Bradley and Bosanquet. The issue between idealism and realism has been stated many times[4] but we shall let Alexander speak for himself in the following:

The real difference between idealism and realism lies in their starting-point or the spirit of their method. For the one, in some form or other, however much disguised, mind is the measure of things and the starting-point of inquiry. The sting of absolute idealism lies in its assertion that the parts of the world are not ultimately real or *true* but only the whole is *true*. For realism, mind has no privileged place except in its perfection. The real issue is between these two spirits of inquiry; and it is in this sense that the following inquiry is realistic. But no sane philosophy has ever been exclusively the one or the other, and where the modern antithesis has hardly arisen, as with Plato, it is extraordinarily difficult to say under which head the philosophy should be classed.[5]

A realistic philosophy, then, differentiates itself from philosophic idealism especially that idealism which implies that appearance is a deceptive presentation of the Real,[6] as well as from that idealism which regards all existences as manifestations of cosmic mind. But it is worthy of note that Alexander apparently omits any reference to a materialistic metaphysic in which mind is reduced to the status of a material existent. All existents, whether sticks and stones, animals and men, or minds with their ethical and spiritual qualities, are equally real in the democracy of things. This notion is again accentuated in *The Basis of Realism*:

> The temper of Realism is to de-anthropomorphize: to order man and mind to their proper place among the world of finite things; on the one hand to divest physical things of the colouring which they have received from the vanity or arrogance of mind; and on the other to assign them along with minds their due measure of self-existence. . . . Realism strips mind of its pretensions but not of its value or greatness. On the contrary, in leaving to other things their rights mind comes into its own. It is as in a democracy where all men are equal. . . . Realism is the democratic spirit in metaphysics, and if it dethrones the mind, it recognizes mind as chief in the world it knows.[7]

ALEXANDER'S REALISM

The conception of all existing things as belonging to a "democracy" leads directly to Alexander's view of compresence which is an integral part of his epistemology. We turn, therefore, to a brief examination of his theory of knowledge, and since this work is not primarily concerned with epistemology, it lies beyond its scope to give a full discussion of Alexander's views on this subject.

Epistemology.—The starting point of this epistemology is the notion of compresence:

> Bury yourself, we say, in the fact of experiencing an object like a table, feel yourself into the whole situation, and you will realize that this situation is the compresence of two things of which one, the act of mind, enjoys itself and, in that act of enjoying itself, contemplates the other. To be aware of a thing is to be caught in the common web of the universe, to be an existence alongside of other existences. . . . But it is this very peculiarity of mind, that it enjoys and does not contemplate itself, which conceals from us if we do not keep careful guard against prepossessions, the experienced fact that a common world unites us both—the one, the thing contemplated; the other the thing enjoyed.[8]

In fact, Alexander seems to extend his doctrine of compresence to an extreme position especially in those passages in which he seems to find no difference between our compresence with physical things and the compresence of physical things with one another, for instance, an ash-tray's compresence with the table on which it lies. Such an extremely elementary view of compresence is apparent in the following quotation:

our compresence with physical things, in virtue of which we are conscious of them, is a situation of the same sort as the compresence of two physical things with one another. To recognize that my consciousness of a physical object is only a particular case of the universal compresence of finites is in fact the best way to realize the analysis which has been given.[9]

We feel that Alexander is a little precipitate in using such an expression as "a situation of the same sort as the compresence of two physical things with one another" when he is referring to our awareness of external objects. The easiest way to refute such a view is to give the elementary illustration that a dead man is surely compresent with the objects about him, but surely does not know them, or is not conscious of them as he indeed was conscious of them in his lifetime. In other passages, Alexander seems to redeem his epistemology from this extreme simplicity by accentuating the distinction between the mental and the non-mental, and the two aspects of the cognitive relation as enjoyment of the mind and contemplation of the object:

Experience varies from that of 'something or other' through all the grades of mental life, sensation, perception, imagination, memory, thought. In each case the -*ing* and the -*ed* are distinguishable and the -*ed* is non-mental, and in some cases patently physical.[10]

This stress on the non-mental and physical character of the objective pole of experience is one which is challenged particularly by Berkeley's famous doctrine of *esse* is *percipi*, to be is to be perceived. But in agreement with the various schools of realism, Alexander states that sensations are not utterly dependent on mind but are felt immediately to refer to external and non-mental existents:

> The externality and physical nature of sensations is a particularly disputable matter; for to some they appear to be immediate experiences utterly dependent on mind, though objective in their reference as distinguished from subjective acts like desiring or attention. I will only say that to me every mental act is equally immediate, thinking as much as sensation, and the sensum no less external and non-mental than the thought.[11]

Without going into a full exposition of Alexander's theory of knowledge, it is necessary to refer to an important doctrine of his, the objectivity of both primary and secondary qualities. The primary qualities of things "are the empirical modes of categorial characters, such as size, shape, number, motion of various sorts,"[12] while the secondary qualities, "colour, temperature, taste, and the like,"[13] are usually ranged in a class different from that of the primary qualities. This distinction—with amplifications which are beyond the scope of this work—runs through the empiricism of Locke, Berkeley, and Hume, and reappears in some forms of critical realism, but is challenged by theories of direct realism, such as that of Alexander and neo-Thomism. Alexander, in fact, is fond of "defending the thesis that secondary qualities do not owe their character to the mind, but only owe to it the fact that they are seen or tasted."[14] For him, colors, tastes and smells are fully objective and are not manufactured by the mind:

There is in fact something unintelligible in the idea that out of heterogeneous material the mind could fabricate a colour or taste or smell.[15]

He continues:

Our plain experience is that we do not see colours in our eyes, but only *with* our eyes and *in* the rose or apple. Further, if we are aware of colour as an affection of the body, why is it more difficult to suppose that we see it in the rose?[16]

His conclusion is fundamental:

We are compelled then to deny that either mind or the living sense organs give to secondary qualities their being, and to affirm that these reside in the material things themselves.[17]

Without expanding on detailed elaborations of the epistemology of Alexander and that of other realists, it is interesting to note the objectivity of secondary qualities in the epistemology of recent realists. For instance John Wild asserts:

Thus Locke held that sensations of the primary qualities are "resemblances" of something really in the extra-mental thing, whereas sensations of the secondary qualities do not resemble anything outside the mind at all. The first part of this assumption is definitely false and the second, if true, must lead to an unmitigated subjectivism which is incompatible with the existence of knowledge.[18]

Again, J. E. Turner prefaces his work on direct realism with the observation:

ALEXANDER'S REALISM

The first part of this volume is an attempt to formulate a realistic theory of Perception and of the physical world which is more realist than any of the current realism with which I am acquainted, with the exception, it may be, of Dr. Alexander's position. Subject to this qualification, it appears to me that all recent systems concede far more than is logically necessary to either subjectivism, phenomenalism, or noumenalism.[19]

The full objectivity of Alexander's neo-realism—as well as that of the other realists whom we have quoted—is also apparent in the rejection of that theory of knowledge known as "critical realism" in which what is known is not the external object but a presentation regarded as a revelation, or as Sellars asserts, a "disclosure"[20] of the object. As Alexander states:

> For that theory the presentation is still psychical though it is the revelation of its underlying ground or condition.[21]

Under such a theory, a mysterious jump from psychical presentation to object is assumed, but since the object is not directly known, the epistemology of critical realism remains within the confines of an irremediable subjectivism in which the object is not known at all. Alexander's conclusion is quite forthright on this point:

> the whole statement that in presentation we refer to its condition is open to the old objection brought against the Lockeian doctrine, which it resembles that our ideas are copies of their originals. How can experience warrant a reference to this something conditioning presentation which we never experienced and which is only a symbol

for the non-mental? . . . But the supposed condition of presentation cannot be further known for it is not known at all.[22]

J. E. Turner's examination of critical realism is similar to that of Alexander:

> This dilemma faces Critical Realism. If it maintains its universal distinction between physical things themselves beyond our consciousness, and their perceived or apparent sense-character, then it becomes a noumenalism. But if on the other hand it founds its affirmations on instinctive belief, it forfeits all title to be regarded as a philosophic system, whatever other merits it may possess. Or at best it can become a philosophy only of the content of perception as distinct from physical reality itself.[23]

As we are not primarily concerned with a full investigation of Alexander's epistemology, nor of that of other recent direct realists, we shall not develop his valuable doctrine of real appearances, mere appearances, and illusions. The point we wish to stress is the integrity of the independent object and its qualities, an integrity which is fundamental in Alexander's philosophy. The world of nature appears as a "democracy" of things and these things are not the mere hurrying to and fro of dead material but are in a most emphatic manner possessors of their own qualities. And in view of Alexander's epistemology of "enjoyment" of the mind which "contemplates" the external object and its qualitative aspects, the qualitative nature of the world is directly apparent to the mind to the measure of the mind's capacity.

In this elementary stage of our presentation of Alexander's system and conception of deity, it is necessary to point out that such a realism is a first step towards a religious view of reality. Pringle-Pattison is quite justified in stressing—as does Alexander—the objectivity of the secondary qualities in the course of developing a philosophic approach to theism:

> Just consider for a moment what the world would be if it were stripped of the secondary qualities; remove the eye and the other senses and what remains? As Stirling vividly puts it, taking as his instance the astronomical spectacle of the heavens: 'All that is going on, all these globes are whirling in a darkness blacker than the mouth of wolf, deeper than the deepest pit that ever man has sunk—all that is going on, all that is taking place in a darkness absolute; and more . . . in a silence absolute; in a silence that never a whisper . . . never the most momentary echo breaks. . . It is in a cave, in a den, blacker than the blackest night, soundless and more silent than the void of voids, that all those intermingling motions of the globes go on—but for us, that is; but for an eye and an ear and a soul behind them.' It is enough to make this simple reflection to recognize the helpless unreality of the abstraction. As Professor Bosanquet says, 'If the world apart from knowledge has no secondary qualities, it has hardly anything of what we care for. It is not recognizable as our world at all.'[24]

If we adopt provisionally a definition of religion as man's whole response to the whole universe,[25] and if we further accept Alexander's view that the universe is objectively qualitative, the religious response is then liberated from a merely "subjective" interpretation and is given an object in a universe characterized by richness of content—a point of no mean significance when we consider and criticize Alexander's view of "deity."

Space-Time and the Categories.—Alexander's epistemology is not the most distinctive part of his philosophy, but was held repeatedly subordinate to his major interest—metaphysics. He was pained when critics did not appreciate that

> for me the doctrine of the categories, taken along with the notion of S-T, is central; ... Anger is not my master passion; but I have felt something approaching irritation when my first volume, which is fundamental, has been passed over with a word ... and exclusive attention directed to the theory of knowledge, and even in some cases the whole doctrine is declared to depend on the theory of knowledge which I expressly declare to be derivative.[26]

The ultimate metaphysical realities for him are Space and Time, and it is important to note that these are not subjective notions but are considered as existing objectively in their totality, their infinity, and their mutual involvement. The continuity and infinitude of Space and Time are "presented in experience" as "crude, original characters of them."[27] Space is continuous and infinite in its three dimensions.

Time is also continuous and infinite and possesses the characters of succession, irreversibility, and duration. Alexander has here obviously been influenced by Bergson's doctrine of *durée réelle,* though we shall observe presently there are major differences between Alexander and Bergson in their conceptions of Space and Time. Likewise, he appeared to take encouragement from the mathematical studies of relativity by Einstein and Minkowski to support his doctrine of the intimate union of Space and Time, but it is important to realize that while for Minkowski time is simply one dimension added to the three dimensions of space, in Alexander's system

> Time with its distinctive features corresponds to the three dimensions of Space, and in a manner of speech Time does with its one-dimensional order cover and embrace the three dimensions of Space, and is not additional to them. To use a violent phrase, it is, spatially, not temporally, voluminous.[28]

This is the characteristic and fundamental feature of Alexander's system, the intimate union of Space and Time, so that Space and Time considered apart from one another are abstractions. Moreover, Alexander characterizes Space and Time as wholes of parts, the parts being point-instants. Since it is important to realize just what Alexander means by the expression "continuous wholes" we shall give several quotations bearing on this point:

> When we proceed to speak of Space and Time as continuous wholes and distinguishable into points or instants, we are going beyond what we learn through sense and employing ideas, or what are sometimes called intellectual constructions, and are employing also thoughts in the special and proper sense of concepts.[29]

But we must not imagine that the points and instants are unreal, for "Space and Time are so constituted."[30]

> We must not imagine that the elements are unreal because they are ideal constructions, as the word construction is apt to suggest, any more than we must imagine that a man's back is unreal because I do not see it but only imagine it or have it in idea.[31]

Other references to Space and Time as wholes follow:

> The infinitude of Space and Time ... express not their uninterruptedness but their single wholeness.[32]

> Space and Time then are presented to us as infinite and continuous wholes of parts. I shall call these parts points and instants.[33]

> Space-Time as a spatial whole.[34]

> selection from the whole of Space-Time.[35]

Let us examine what Alexander means by Space-Time as a whole of parts, the parts being point-instants. Space is made of points, and every point has a time-coefficient, and it would seem that Alexander's view of Space-Time is a combination of what is static and what is dynamic:

> Points do not of course move in the system of points, but they change their time-coefficient. What we ordinarily call motion of a body is the occupation by that body of points which successively become present, so that at each stage the points traversed have different time-values when the line of motion is taken as a whole. Thus Space-Time is a system of motions.[36]

In this passage, Alexander seems to envisage a static element in that the points of Space are motionless, but each point has a time-coefficient and these coefficients are changed through the advance of an enduring body in Time in so far as this body includes fresh points in its advance. The combination of the static and the dynamic is again implied in his view that

> Space of itself has no movement. The corresponding proposition is that Time as it moves from past through present to future (from earlier to later) is the occupation of a stretch of Space.[37]

An important question has to do with the advance in Time and whether we shall consider fresh Space as being swept out in Time, as if Time were to generate new Space through a succession of present moments. In such a conception, the present moment determines a section along the advance of Time, and

> We then have the idea of an infinite spatial present sweeping forward in Time. Space is defined as the assemblage of events at one moment.[38]

The movement of Time is not to be understood as a succession of presents mysteriously recreated at each moment, for this would imply nothing more than bare Time:

> If it were nothing more than bare Time it would consist of perishing instants. Instead of a continuous Time, there would be nothing more than an instant, a now, which was perpetually being renewed. But Time would then be for itself and for an observer a mere now, and would contain neither earlier nor later.[39]

Alexander, however, is a philosopher who takes Time

seriously, and we must inquire precisely what he means by this favorite expression of his. Does he mean the bare successive character of Time, a series of perishing "nows," or does he mean the infinite continuity of Time in which this succession takes place? It would appear that he means the latter, especially when he discusses the reality of the past:

> The objection may be made, how can reality contain at this moment the past, for the past is past and exists no longer? But the difficulty is only apparent. It arises from identifying reality with the present or actual reality; it assumes in fact that Time is not real. The past event, it is true, does not exist now, and if existence is taken to be present existence, the past clearly does not exist. But if we avoid this error and take Time seriously, the past possesses such reality as belongs to the past, that is, to what is earlier than the point of reference; it does not exist now but it did exist then, and its reality is to have existed then. As to the later or future, there is at bottom no greater difficulty in speaking of the future as being real and existing really than there is in respect of the real existence of the past.[40]

The reality of Time for Alexander has these two important implications: the successiveness and irreversibility of Time, and its character as an infinite and uninterrupted whole. Space is not to be considered "as a mere instantaneous section"[41] of an advance of successive "nows" in Time. The conception of an advancing column must be abandoned for we must think of lines of advance not in terms of fresh recreations of the universe at every moment but rather as displacements of Time over positions in Space. It is important to grasp Alexander's thought in this connection, as it will enable us to understand more clearly how Space can be full of Time and Time can be full of Space:

> We have to think of lines of advance as displacements of the present in relation to past and future over positions in Space. In this way we conceive of growth in Time, or the history of the Universe as a whole, or any part of it, as a continuous redistribution of instants of Time among the points of Space. There is no new Space to be generated as Time goes on, but within the whole of Space or the part of it the instants of Time are differently arranged, so that points become different point-instants and instants become also different point-instants.[42]

Alexander admits that this is a very abstract though simple conception of the world, and in order to clarify the discussion of Space-Time and its point-instants, we have drawn the diagram on the following page to suggest the continuous rearrangement or redistribution of instants among the points of space. The present is indicated by the line LM, and the observer is at position O along this line. With reference to the observer at O, points and their instants are characterized by both positions and time-coefficient, and are denoted by the notation $A_1 t_{-3}$, $A_2 t_{-2}$, $A_3 t_{-1}$, $A_4 t_0$, $A_5 t_1$, $A_6 t_2$, $A_7 t_3$. The A's indicate the positions of points in Space along the line of advance from $A_1 t_{-3}$ to $A_7 t_3$. Using the same letter A with various subscripts signifies that the points are repeated in time, and their repetition is indicated by time-

GOD AND SPACE-TIME

$$\begin{array}{c}
\text{L} \\
| \\
-A_1t_{-3} - A_2t_{-2} - A_3t_{-1} - A_4t_0 - A_5t_1 - A_6t_2 - A_7t_3 - \\
| \\
-B_1t_{-3} - B_2t_{-2} - B_3t_{-1} - B_4t_0 - B_5t_1 - B_6t_2 - B_7t_3 - \\
| \\
-C_1t_{-3} - C_2t_{-2} - C_3t_{-1} - C_4t_0 - C_5t_1 - C_6t_2 - C_7t_3 - \\
| \\
\text{M}
\end{array}$$

Past   Future

⟵―――   ―――⟶

Time

―――⟶

O

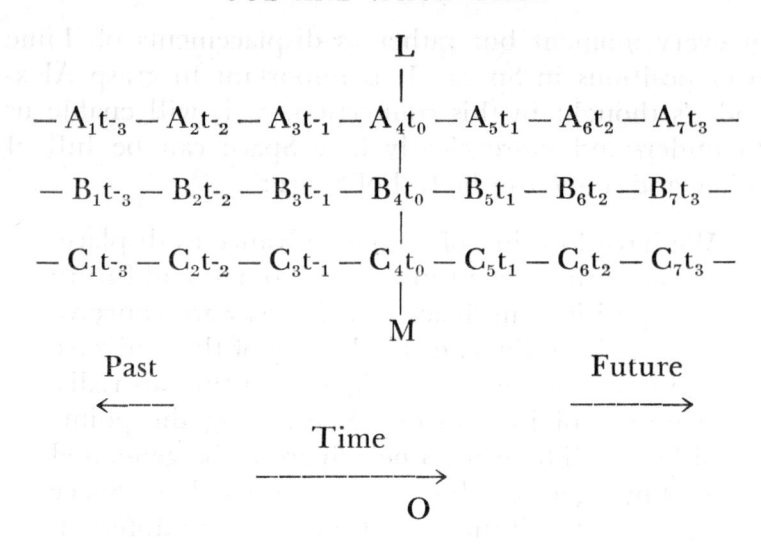

coefficients from t_{-3}, indicating the past, to t_0, on the line of the present, LM, and the line of advance of these points proceeds to the future indicated by the coefficients t_1, t_2, and t_3. Similar lines of advance are shown for points B_1t_{-3} to B_7t_3 and for points C_1t_{-3} to C_7t_3, and in this way it is easy to understand Alexander's statement:

> We have to think of lines of advance as displacements of the present in relation to past and future over positions in Space.[43]

As we picture the advance of Time by the movement of the line of the present LM from time t_0 to time t_1, the time-coefficients are redistributed since all the points in the past have now become older by one unit, and all the points in the future have decreased in temporal distance from the present by one unit. The irreversible flow of Time implies this constant redistribution of instants among points and points among instants. But it is important to note that every point has its instant, and every instant has its point. We may imagine the point-instants multiplied to infinity in the Past and in the Future, as shown on the diagram, and in this infinite multiplication of points and instants, it still remains true that every point has its instant, or time-coefficient, and every time-coefficient has its point. In this way do we understand Alexander's explanation of his difference from Bergson:

> The main result of our discussion has been to show that Time is really laid out in Space, and is intrinsically spatial. The representation of Time as spatial, Mr. Bergson regards as depriving Time of its real character. What he regards as a habit founded upon the weakness of our imagination has now been shown to be vital to the nature of Time.[44]

Another important divergence from Bergson may be mentioned at this point:

> No one has rendered such service to metaphysics as he has done in maintaining the claims of Time to be considered an ultimate reality....With Mr. Bergson... Space is a sort of shadow or foil to Time, and not co-equal. It implies degradation and unreality, relatively to Time. Time remains the unique and ultimate reality. We have seen reason to regard them as so implicated in each other that each is vital to the other's existence.[45]

Since both Alexander and Bergson are philosophers who take Time seriously, it was thought necessary to indicate briefly their principal disagreement. Alexander here stresses Space and Time as being co-equal partners, and it remains to be seen whether Alexander is consistent in this respect. We shall find in due time that he is not.

Returning to our diagram on page 18, it is possible to clarify the manner in which Alexander believes that Space and Time are implicated in each other. From the observer at O, in the present moment LM, points A_4, B_4, and C_4 are perceived at the time t_0. The points can be imagined multiplied infinitely to indicate the whole universe of Space at moment t_0. Such a section indicates some event at every point of Space at this moment t_0. Shall we suppose, then, that at the next moment t_1 the universe is made of a section at this particular time, and that the universe of Space and Time is made by an integration of such sections?[46] While such a section is a "legitimate selection" it "does not represent what Space-Time is at any moment of its history."[47] We find once more Alexander's objection to a recreation of the universe at every moment:

> It does not matter whether the instant occupies a point or the whole of Space; the universe cannot be composed in reality of such sections. An integration of such sections does not represent the history of the world. The world would need to be recreated at every moment. . . .For the moment which is now would be a now which perished utterly and was replaced by another now. Time would cease to be duration and would be nothing but a now, for the different nows would have no continuity. We would vanish utterly at each moment and be replaced by something like ourselves but new.[48]

Referring once more to our diagram, a perspective is to be distinguished from a section in that when we consider Space-Time with reference to the observer at the instant of time t_0, we shall find, not a section at this instant t_0, but rather

> the whole of Space, not occurring at one instant but filled with times of various dates. There is a continuum of events filling Space but divided by the point of reference into earlier and later.[49]

An example which may make clear our perception of a past event is the fact that we perceive Sirius not as it is at the moment of perception but as it was nine years ago, since it takes nine years for the light to reach us from Sirius. Referring to astronomical events occurring at various distances from us, it is therefore correct to state that they are "filled with times of various dates," that is, the time-coefficients of these events are different with respect to the point of reference which is the observer at time O. It is a persistent conception with Alexander that events are located in place and time, for

> we realise that in thinking of the history of the past or divining the future, the events are located not in one place and still less in no place at all, but in the places where they occurred or will occur, however inaccurately we may apprehend their positions.[50]

Such a conception explains why it is possible for Alexander to use the metaphor in which

> having regard to the differing dates of its points with reference to the centre, which is the present of that perspective, we may say that Space at any moment is full of memory and expectation.[51]

Total Space-Time is the synthesis of all perspectives,

each perspective being "historical phases"[52] of Space-Time. Perspectives are synthesized when we imagine not merely one center of reference but an infinity of such centers, one for every instant. In such imagined totality of centers as points of reference

> any point of Space is occupied, not as in the single time-perspective by some one moment of Time but by the whole of Time. The whole of Time in the totality of such perspectives streams through each point of Space. . . .in total Space-Time each point is in fact repeated through the whole of Time and each instant over the whole of Space.[53]

An important question with respect to total Space-Time which includes infinite Space and infinite Time, is whether such a vision, which obviously is not possible to finite human beings, is a vision of Space-Time *sub specie aeternitatis*. After due reflection, we must conclude that it is not, for it is not a vision of Space-Time with the time-coefficients removed from the points as if total Space-Time were viewed as an eternal present, the *totum simul* of theology. The time-coefficients are never removed by Alexander for the very meaning of his taking Time seriously includes both the successive order of Time as well as the infinity of Time. But this infinity is a historical infinite series, or an infinite historical series, for Alexander states:

> The physical universe is thus through and through historical, the scene of motion.[54]

Total Space-Time is through and through historical because its Space is occupied by Time of various dates, and in no instance can these various dates be ignored:

In other words, the reality of Space-Time may be resolved into the elements total Space and total Time, provided only it be remembered that in their *combination* Space is always variously occupied by Time and Time spread variously over Space.[55]

We have felt it important to quote profusely from Alexander in delineating his conception of Space-Time through his insistence on taking Time seriously in order to indicate that in no case does he conceive of Time moving into fresh Space, like an advancing column. On the contrary Time is not merely irreversible movement, it is an infinite continuum laid over the whole of Space so that each point has a time-coefficient denoting its position in the infinite past, present, or infinite future. Total Space-Time is Space-Time in its total historicity, not a vision of eternity.[56]

Nor is Space-Time merely the hypostatization of universal volatility or universal vacuity. This would be to misconstrue Alexander's stress on physical Space-Time as being much more than a mere vacuum:

> Space is full of Time and Time is full of Space, and because of this each of them is a complete or perfect continuum. If this might seem a quibble of words, which it is not, let us say that Space-Time is a *plenum*. Its density is absolute or complete. There is no vacuum in Space-Time, for that vacuum would be itself a part of Space-Time.[57]

In keeping with this conception of Space-Time as a *plenum* is the vindication of the ancient term *hyle* (substrate) as its most appropriate description:

> In truth, infinite Space-Time is not the substance of substances, but it is the stuff of substances. No word is more appropriate to it than the ancient one of hyle (ὐλη). Just as a roll of cloth is the stuff of which coats are made but it is not itself a coat, so Space-Time is the stuff of which all things, whether as substances or under any category, are made.[58]

The startling idea in this philosophy is that all existents are not merely immersed in the fullness of Space-Time, but are made of it. This is an original conception of Alexander, though it had been expressed a few years previously by the Hungarian thinker Palágyi.[59] There is no evidence, however, that Alexander borrowed his doctrines from the Hungarian. All existents from the simplest electron or proton to the most complex, man himself, are configurations of Space-Time, complexities of Space-Time, or, to use a term of Bosanquet, "complications of Space-Time."[60] Space-Time is a creative being, a matrix containing whirlpools of motion, groupings of motion within finite elements of space and time, but sustained by the all-encompassing total Space-Time and intimately connected with it. These structures of motion are not all alike, obviously. They vary from the simple "lines of advance" among point-instants in primordial Space-Time to the complex motions associated with the qualities of mind. The correlation of motion with quality is an intrinsic feature of this metaphysical system:

> Primarily, therefore, empirical existents are spatio-temporal and remain so to the end. But with

certain groupings of motion, certain spatio-temporal complexes, there are correlated what we call qualities, such as materiality, life, colour, consciousness.[61]

It is clear that these groupings are associated with variable, empirical characters of things, but there are also pervasive characters which belong to all existents whatever—the categorial, *a priori* or non-empirical patterns of things.[62] Since they are pervasive characters of things, they are in a wider sense also empirical. They are "fundamental properties or determinations of Space-Time itself, not taken as a whole, but in every portion of it."[63] Space-Time itself in its totality is beyond any categorial determination, but any portion of Space-Time, finite or infinite, possesses categorial characters. Devaux interprets with more precision than did Alexander the non-historical nature of the categories, which exist at any time, past, present, or future, but at the moment—wherever it may be in Time's succession—wherever they may be required to give the necessary categorial structure to any existent:

> Les catégories sont les conditions intrinsèques de tout devenir. . . .Les catégories ne peuvent donc pas avoir d'histoire, tout en n'ayant d'actualité que du fait de leur apparition au cours même d'un devenir quelconque. Elles n'évoluent nullement comme les êtres dont elles constituent l'armature essentièlle. Elles sont régulatrices de toutes les distributions variées, actuelles, passées, et futures s'opérant au sein de l'Espace-Temps.[64]

Alexander's realism is apparent not merely in his epistemological doctrine of the objectivity of the secondary qualities, but also in his insistence on the objectivity of categories in existents. He is here opposed to Kant for the latter said categories were used by the mind "as planes or chisels are used in carpentering wood."[65] For Alexander, the categories do not belong to the understanding (except in so far as the understanding itself is a complex of Space-Time), are not imposed on empirical existents by the mind, but belong intrinsically to any existent and are permanent patterns in the whirlpools of Space-Time.

The simplest categories are existence, diversity, and identity. By existence he means the determinate nature of any configuration of Space-Time which is identical with itself and different from any other configuration of Space-Time.[66] Being is therefore determinate being in a specified configuration of Space-Time, and not-being

> is not the bare absence of being, not in the language of the logicians a privative conception, but is equivalent to other-being, that is occupation of a different space-time.[67]

Alexander acknowledges that these notions "are ancient considerations derived from Plato's *Sophistes*."[68]

It is interesting to note that Alexander's emphasis on the Space-Time matrix enables him to interpret the metaphysical laws, or the so-called laws of thought, in a thoroughly objective manner. The law of identity merely signifies that to occupy Space-Time is to occupy it—that is, a thing actually occupies that finite portion of Space-Time which it is. The law of the excluded middle signifies in its metaphysical interpretation that given a specific occupation of Space-Time, every specific occupation of Space-Time is either this given specific occupation, "or belongs to the rest of Space-Time,"[69] or, stated more precisely, belongs to a particular occupation within the rest of Space-Time.

The category of universality is possessed by every group of finites characterized by identity of kind simply because each of the finites in this group admits of repetition in Space-Time without distortion. It is because Space-Time is uniform that its finites possess universality and not the other way around.[70] Universals exist in their particulars but have greater significance in that they are constitutive plans of things. The universal may be said to have the reality of existence which is called subsistence, but subsistence is not to be understood in terms of neutral being as distinct from spatio-temporal existence.

> The universal is nowhere and nowhen in particular but anywhere and anywhen, and in Hume's language is in readiness to start into being (which is existence) when the occasion calls.[71]

Moreover, universals are spatio-temporal, physical, biological, mental, according to the level of existence to which their particular individuals belong in the evolutionary process.

Other categorial characters are relation, order, substance, causality, reciprocity, quantity, number, and finally motion, which presupposes the other categories. It is beyond the scope of this work to deal exhaustively with all these categories.

Substances may be simple or complex, the latter being what we usually refer to as "things."

> A thing or complex substance is then a contour of space (*i.e.* a volume with a contour) within which take place the motions correlated to the qualities

of the thing; and the complex substance of thing is the persistence in time of this spatial contour with its defining motions.[72]

The identity of a substance refers to its individual identity as persisting through a duration of time, and such changes as are compatible with a persistence of identity involve a question for empirical investigation. All empirical existents, whether atoms, molecules, plants, animals, human beings, are configurations of Space-Time with varying degrees of motion and complexity, and their different qualities are rigidly correlated with different types of motion. The mind of man is itself a spatio-temporal existent[73] with qualities peculiar to its eminent status and functions. Indeed, it would not be unjust to summarize Alexander's metaphysics by stating that all existents are complexities of Space-Time, constructed according to categories which are potential plans of organization pervading these existents; and, further, that these existents are themselves "spatial-historicities"[74] which carry not only a special configuration but a time-impression just as an old New England church informs us of its structure and of its age, perhaps through the date engraved on a cornerstone, or more directly through the erosion of the stone.

A Formula for Space-Time: Emergence—From the preceding discussion, it is apparent that Space and Time are equal partners in the total reality which is Space-Time. Alexander, however, in the second volume of *Space, Time, and Deity,* introduces a new conception in which Time is given a pre-eminent function with reference to Space. This is the so-called "formula for Space-Time" according to which Time is the mind of Space. In order that this formula be not read in terms

ALEXANDER'S REALISM

of panpsychism, we shall quote directly from Alexander:

> It is that Time as a whole and in its parts bears to Space as a whole and its corresponding parts a relation analogous to the relation of mind to its equivalent bodily or nervous basis: or to put the matter shortly that Time is the mind of Space and Space the body of Time.[75]

Alexander here makes a vast extrapolation from our construction as personal unions of mind and body. This same formula he applies to point-instants in the sense that the instant is the mind of its point; that a group of points has its "mind," and that finally "total Time is the mind of total Space."[76] He believes that there is nothing strange in such a formula for "The conception of a world-soul is an old one."[77] He further attempts to disengage himself from accusations of panpsychism by declaring that "mind is mind and Time is Time,"[78] and that the Time formula is a functional one:

> I mean that in the matrix of all existence, Space-Time, there is an element Time which performs the same function in respect of the other element Space as mind performs in respect of its bodily equivalent. The points of Space have no consciousness in any shape or form, but their instants perform to them the office of consciousness to our brains.[79]

From our previous discussion it is clear that all empirical existents are configurations, or constellations, of Space-Time. We now wish to add the further qualification, namely, that they are emergents from Space-Time. As the doctrine of emergence is proverbially vague, and has certainly not won universal assent in philosophical literature, it will be necessary to set forth Alexander's view of it, reserving critical comment for the second part of this work.

The reality of Time signifies that no existents are given from all eternity, but that they come into existence in the course of that real succession which is the character of Time with which we are most intimately connected. It is clear that Alexander has been influenced by that evolutionary trend of thought which owes a good deal of its impetus to Darwinism. But, obviously, he is not concerned merely with Darwinian evolution, but with evolutionary change as a real character of existing things in so far as they partake of the temporal quality of Space-Time. It is not merely that out of the Space-Time matrix, complexities of motion of varying character arise side by side, so to speak, but that out of simpler motions new and more complicated motions arise with new qualities. These new qualities did not previously exist. The fact that they exist now is called "emergence." This term does not mean a mysterious emergent force which pushes new and complex qualities through simpler space-time collocations. Its significance is descriptive rather than explanatory. It describes a process rather than explains it:

> The emergence of a new quality from any level of existence means that at that level there comes into being a certain constellation or collocation of the motions belonging to that level, and possessing the quality appropriate to it, and this collocation possesses a new quality distinctive of the higher complex.[80]

That is to say, a certain level of existence is characterized by *a* processes. When these *a* processes increase in complexity so as to be *ab* processes, a new quality B is present with the process *ab* and this quality did not exist when the process was merely *a*.[81]

In order to penetrate as closely as we can to Alexander's theory of levels of existence, we shall quote another formulation:

> Using symbols we may put the case briefly thus. A complex of processes on a level L with the distinctive quality l becomes endowed, within the whole L-thing or body with a quality l' and the whole thing characterised by this quality rises to the level L'. The processes with the emergent quality l' constitute the soul or mind of a thing or body which is on the level L. The mind of a thing is thus equivalent only to a portion of that thing. . . . Another corollary is the obvious one that a thing or body at the level L' is as it were stratified and, besides containing processes which have the quality l', is built up on processes of all the lower levels down to the spatio-temporal one itself.[82]

We have here the cardinal doctrine of emergent evolution, the theory that nature is stratified, for at critical points in the history of nature, a new quality arises, such as l', and the existent previously characterized by l processes and the correlated quality, is now characterized by both l and l', and the existent is now on the level L'. The existent on this level may emerge on a higher level L'' through the addition of a higher quality L'' which now characterizes the existent in question. But it is to be noted that the quality l'' in no sense destroys qualities l and l' so that the object—no less than nature—is stratified along these qualities. We are not inquiring at present as to the "why" or "how" of this process; we are merely stating that nature seems to display critical points in the course of Time:

> Nature is rather a history of organic growth of species, in which the new type of organism is the outgrowth of the older type, and continues the earlier life into a form at once more complex and more highly simplified. As there is in the animal world or the plant world a hierarchy of forms, so in nature there is hierarchy of qualities which are characteristic of various levels of development. There are, if I may borrow a metaphor used by Mr. Sellars of Michigan in his recent book [*Evolutionary Naturalism*], 'critical points' in the unfolding of nature when she gathers up her old resources for a new experiment and breeds a new quality of existence.[83]

These levels are, in Alexander's system, first, the level of Space-Time itself during that part of its history which lies before any qualitied emergents have arisen; the level of matter; the level of physico-chemical changes including the simplest chemical change as well as the most complex reaction of highly organized molecules, such as the proteins; the level of life; the level of mind, and finally the level of deity, which is the quality next in order of emergence and complexity to that of mind. Each level is characterized by its specific quality, and the quality is not merely added but depends upon the complexity of integration of the lower levels. Such terms as "integration," "organization," or "form of combination," are just as significant as the elements which are integrated, organized, or combined, for as Alexander states:

> So important is it to remember that besides elements there is the form of their combination, and that the form is as much a reality as the elements and gives them their significance.[84]

Thus life is not *merely* physico-chemical though it is *also* physico-chemical. That a higher quality l' emerges from the organization of lower qualities l is illustrated by Alexander when he quotes from Browning's poem, *Abt Vogler*, and refers to the musician in these terms: "out of three sounds he frames not a fourth sound but a star."[85]

Let us now consider in greater detail the process of emergence up to life and mind from Space-Time itself. One of the earliest emergents from Space-Time is matter, and "material existence is possibly closest to Space-Time and the stuff of reality may therefore most easily be conceived on the material analogy."[86]

Alexander was aware of recent developments in atomic theory involving the discovery of sub-atomic particles, such as the proton and the electron (more have been discovered since), and he was open to the view that there might be several intermediary stages or levels of existence between primordial Space-Time and that complex of motion which is an electron. The question was one for the physicist to settle, but whatever might be involved in future discoveries of further sub-atomic particles, Alexander felt sure they could be incorporated within his metaphysical system of Space-Time.[87]

Matter apprehended as a configuration of atoms and molecules reveals the primary qualities of things, which are the empirical modes of the categorial characters: shape, size, number, and the motions associated both with the thing as a whole and its internal molecular, atomic, and electronic vibrations.[88] In a sense, these are not qualities but determinations of the thing. The secondary qualities are color, temperature, taste, odor, sound; and, as previously indicated in our discussion of Alexander's epistemology of direct realism, these secondary qualities are in no sense merely mental, but are intimately correlated with specific disturbances in the material particles in which they originate. These disturbances are communicated to the intervening medium between observer and the thing in which they arise. It is important to note that it is not the medium which possesses these qualities but the material thing which originates the motion correlated with the qualities in question. Thus it is the ochre which is yellow, the vibrating string which has the quality of sound, the column of air in the organ pipe which has a distinct pitch, the bell which sounds.[89]

Without embarking on an extended analysis of various types of Realism, it is important to point out in this connection that other realists disagree with Alexander when he states that the medium does not carry the secondary quality, such as color. For instance John Wild asserts that the color yellow is combined inseparably with the light energy of which it is an aspect:

> I must not fall into sensationalism and suppose that the pure yellow I sense exists in the air outside my eye precisely as I sense it, for outside my apprehension it exists materially in a different way, inseparably combined with the light energy of which it is only a distinguishable aspect.[90]

Again, Boodin, referring to the transmission of the human voice through an electric current, is in agreement with Wild rather than with Alexander:

> The electric current carries the living voice and will of the speaker over distances of hundreds of miles and communicates them in kind to the human instrument at the receiver.[91]

Similarly, a phonograph record may lie unused for months or years, but imbedded in its grooves is the living voice or symphony which may be reproduced at any time when the record is played. In this case we do indeed have a medium which carries the secondary quality. But as this work is not primarily concerned with the details of epistemology, though favoring realism, we return to the further development of Alexander's theory of levels.

The level of materiality which includes primary and secondary qualities is understood by Alexander to be followed by the next higher level which is that of life:

> Life then would be an emergent quality taken on by a complex of physico-chemical processes belonging to the material level, these processes taking place in a structure of a certain order of complexity, of which the processes are the functions.[92]

It is readily observed that this method of interpretation is in keeping with the description of previous levels of existence as emerging from fundamental Space-Time. Not all vortices or whirlpools of Space-Time are matter, but some do have the quality of materiality because of an additional mode of motion supervening upon the primordial motions of Space-Time. Not all physico-chemical processes are vital, but some do have the quality of life because of an additional mode of motion supervening upon the more primitive physical and chemical processes which are involved in living forms. This additional mode of motion is a deceptively simple manner of describing those extremely complex collocations of physico-chemical processes which carry those organic responses which we term life. The emphasis here is on a doctrine of immanence. Life is not some factor which intervenes *ab extra,* but something which supervenes at a certain degree of complexity of physico-chemical motions, and is borne by these motions. But the specific constellation of processes which we call vital in no way negates the lower levels of existence which are characterized by the motions appropriate to biochemistry, physical laws, and the secondary and primary qualities of the living organism. That is to say, man is a living organism, with mind as emergent from a particular brain organization, but this highest emergent rests on a large number of intermediary organizations or "forms," such as biochemical laws, the laws of more elementary physics and chemistry, the laws of mechanics in the movements of arms and legs, and finally the law of gravitation. To use a vivid example, the most individualized and refined artistic spirit has admittedly aesthetic and spiritual qualities which are peculiarly features of the individuality he represents, but this "summit character" (to use a term of Henry Nelson Wieman) in no way negates, but is fully integrated with, the more elementary levels of existence involved in his personality. For instance, his brain structure has the qualities which are present in all human brains, his metabolism is that associated with human organisms; the chemical reactions involved in his muscles can be reproduced in the laboratory, and he observes as rigidly as the most senseless stone the laws of gravitation. Not all his artistic eminence can prevent him from obeying the laws of gravitation which hold sway over the lowest material existent.

Life is intermediary between matter and mind, and Alexander pursues a model of description which is midway between sheer mechanism and vitalism. He rejects the explanations of Hans Driesch which rely on a directing principle, such as "entelechy" or "psychoid";

> Instead of straightway postulating an entelechy to act as a guide, it would seem to me more reasonable to note that a given stage of material complexity is characterized by such and such special features, and that these are part and parcel of the nature of the principle or plan of the new order of complex.[93]

This new order of complex, by which he means life, is no longer purely material, since it has many new qualities—such as that of reproduction—not possessed by the most complex chemical compound—but it is nonetheless material. To those who may be doubtful of such a non-vitalistic interpretation, he throws out a question which is also a challenge:

> Why should not matter whose quality has budded out from Space-Time bud out in its turn into a new quality, the ultimate stuff being throughout the same and the proximate stuff of life being matter.[94]

This is not a doctrine of reductive materialism, for the emphasis on emergence of new qualities distinctly implies that they involve a collocation of structure, configuration, and organization which cannot be reduced to merely physical or chemical reactions, though these are involved in the total activity of the living organism. Thus, mind is a quality of living process, life is a quality of complicated chemical-biological processes, sense-qualities like color are collocations of movements of matter; and finally matter itself has the quality of "materiality" as a specific complexity of motion nearest the behavior of primordial Space-Time. The more selective qualities such as life and mind rest on the broader pyramid of more elementary movements which ultimately find their structure in Space-Time itself.

It is necessary to recall at this point the pregnant metaphor of Alexander to the effect that the human self as an intimate union of body and soul is but an example of a more fundamental cosmic plan which is Space with its "mind" or "soul," Time. He suggests the fruitful analogy that this pattern is applicable to all emergents according to the following equation of analogy which he does not give in this precise form, but which we have deduced from his more elaborate explanations:

$$\frac{\text{Mind}}{\text{Body}} \text{ as } \frac{\text{Time}}{\text{Space}} \text{ as } \frac{\text{instant}}{\text{point}} \text{ as } \frac{\text{primary qualities}}{\text{elementary motion of primordial matrix of Space-Time}}$$

$$\text{as } \frac{\text{secondary qualities}}{\text{primary qualities}} \text{ as } \frac{\text{qualities expressive of life}}{\text{secondary qualities}}$$

$$\text{as } \frac{\text{qualities of mind}}{\text{qualities of life}} \text{ as } \frac{\text{quality of deity}}{\text{quality of mind}}$$

All existents are ultimately complexities of Space-Time, but throughout the hierarchy from lowest to highest level, there is an aspect which performs to the level immediately below it the office of mind. Such a vast process of multi-levelled emergence is not the senseless rushing to and fro of dead material, but is the whole universe of Space-Time in its myriad complexity sustaining ever-richer qualities, and is animated—is alive. Alexander's own words summarize adequately the substance of his comprehensive process philosophy which we have all too sketchily abbreviated in this introductory chapter:

> Beginning with spatio-temporal finites, there is a continual ascent to newer and more developed existents, so that the course of Time issues in the growth of ever new types of 'soul,' and in this way all existence is linked in a chain of affinity, and there is nothing which does not in virtue of its constitution respond to ourselves, who are but the highest known illustration of the general plan; so that there is nothing dead, or senseless in the universe, Space-Time being itself animated.[95]

A further note is necessary to give more precision to the notion of primordial Space-Time. It might be assumed that, since all qualitied existents are emergents from primordial Space-Time whose sole quality—if it can be called a quality—is motion, Space-Time as such is a negative concept derived by successive abstraction of the qualities pertaining to each level so that we are left finally with an abstraction of extreme simplicity devoid of any characterization. But this would be to forget that Space-Time in its primordial form possesses the real potentiality which blossoms out in all its existents:

> All the wealth of qualities which makes things precious to us belongs to existents which grow within it, and which are in the first instance characterised by the categories.[96]

The categories and the richness of qualities, however, in no sense exhaust the infinite potentiality of Space-Time. It is not exhausted by any richness of quality, nor by any category which may be ascribed to any finite portion of it. It is not possible to state definitely that even the highest emergent exhausts the potentiality of Space-Time, and that no emergent, finite, or infinite, can emerge beyond the mind of man. Devaux has a lucid passage which makes clearer than Alexander has done the view that Space-Time in its immensity transcends any categorial character which may be ascribed to its finite portions or collocations of motion:

> L'Espace-Temps . . . est, si l'on peut dire, *infra-catégoriel*. Son apriorité éminente n'en fait ni une existence, ni une substance, ni un universel, ni un ensemble, ni un système de relations définies, ni une cause, ni un ordre, ni une quantité. Considéré comme la condition élémentaire de toute "forme" et de toute "matière" l'Espace-Temps intrinsèque continu et infini ne peut figurer à titre de donnée ultime *épuisée* dans *aucun* de ses produits immédiats ou médiats.[97]

In other words, Space-Time in its intrinsic character of infinitude and continuity is not exhausted by any of its products. As Alexander has stated, this method of interpretation

> is a method which redounds to the honour of Space-Time in the same sense as it redounded to the honour of Cornelia to be named as the mother of the Gracchi.[98]

There is a further word of observation which we feel is necessary in order to separate the various meanings

ALEXANDER'S REALISM

which may be given to Space-Time and which we think Alexander has not separated too precisely.

1. There is primordial Space-Time, the matrix whose motion is defined by lines of advance in Time from point-instant to point-instant, these primitive motions, however, not yet emerging into more complicated motions correlated with their appropriate qualities. Potentially, as we have just observed, primordial Space-Time contains all its emergents with their qualities, and all their categorial characters as patterns of the matrix which are available anywhere and anywhen they may be required. This primordial Space-Time is the parent of all its existents, be they finite or infinite, and as such is greater than them all:

> It is greater than all existent finites or infinites because it is their parent.[99]

A further question suggests itself: Has Space-Time itself a parent? Alexander acknowledges that this is a perennial question but regards it as a futile metaphysical inquiry since he believes that the infinite becoming which is Space-Time cannot begin to become:

> Space-Time does not exist but is itself the totality of all that exists. Existence belongs to that which occupies a space-time. There is a perennial question which is stilled by no assertion of its futility, how the world came to exist or what made the world? We can see at once the answer to the question, and how far it is futile. The world which is Space-Time never and nowhere came into existence, for the infinite becoming cannot begin to become. It could only do so in a larger Space and Time and at the order of some cause exterior to

it. Now all existence arises within Space-Time, and there is no cause which is not itself a part of it.[100]

Equally futile would be the question how much Time elapsed before the simplest emergent arose. The only possible answer seems to be an infinite Time.

2. There is actual Space-Time, or Space-Time at any moment of its existence, the present moment in which the matrix of Space-Time has crystallized into existents of various levels and qualities, from stone to man, all equally real and fundamentally bits of space and time. At such a moment, do we perceive the whole of Space-Time from the infinite past to the present? Obviously, such a vision is not given to man, and while Alexander has used the term "whole" to designate infinite Time and infinite Space, as we indicated on page 14, he gave a more precise elaboration of his meaning in Chapter X, Book II, Volume I, entitled, "The One and the Many." Here Alexander states that the term "whole" which may be applied to a stone and its parts when it disintegrates cannot be applied to Space-Time. The stone is given all at once, whether as a whole or crushed to its smallest fragments. But this is not the case with Space-Time:

> If Space-Time were such a whole it would be given all at once. But being Time (or indeed Space, which is the same thing) it is not, as Mr. Bergson rightly says, given altogether. To suppose so is to ignore the reality of Time, to fail to take Time seriously. At any one moment the universe is the whole of its existent parts, but at any one moment the universe is not the whole universe of parts. For in the redistribution of dates among

> places, new existents are generated within the one Space-Time. It may indeed be called not a whole of parts, but the whole or system of all existents.[101]

That is to say, at any one moment the universe is the whole of its parts which happen to exist at that moment. But the universe at one moment is merely a section of the universe of Space-Time extending to the infinite past and also to the future. This total universe of Space-Time is not given as a whole precisely because Alexander and Bergson take Time seriously, and, obviously, we do not perceive the infinity of Time but Time at a moment. It is clear, then that at a moment, we "see" the universe as the whole of its existing parts, but we do not "see" the existents which emerged in the past and ceased to exist, nor do we have any knowledge of those which will exist in the future. This signifies that the universe as the whole of its existing parts at this moment is not the universe as the whole of parts which existed or will exist in infinite Time.

Another way in which we may understand that Space-Time is not given as a whole lies in the consideration of the question that

> Since Time is infinite, it might seem that every form of existence must have existed in the past. Every form of motion must have been tried, and therefore in the strictest sense the universe is not an evolution at all, but the whole of its varied riches exists already, no matter at what point in the history we are imagined to stop.[102]

In this view, the universe of Space-Time taken at any moment of its existence has already contained all its varied riches of existence, and there is no evolution of anything new. But such a conception is rejected by Alexander for two reasons:

(a) It misunderstands the notion of infinity, for an infinity of negative integers which ends at -1 does not yet include 0 and plus 1. Hence, an infinity of events in the past history of Space-Time does not mean that there are no new events possible in the present and future history of the world.

(b) It neglects "the distinctive character of Time which is to be a succession within duration; it conceives of Time as given all at once as if it were a line."[103] But Time is not given all at once as if it were a line or extension for it is essentially successive, and patterns are traced out in time, and do not exist from all time. Alexander's argument is so cogent here that we shall give it in full:

> The time which has elapsed down to man is infinite, but it is an infinity which has been occupied with the generation of other forms. Though Time is infinite, experience as registered in historical records tells us that in times before the birth of man there was no man. That pattern had not yet been traced which is the condition for the emergence of human mind.[104]

This quotation clearly indicates that not only existents, such as man, emerge at a certain historical epoch in the world's history, but also the categories and universals, which are potential patterns of the Space-Time matrix, actually exist at the particular times and places where they are required to define the individuals to which they pertain.

3. There is total Space-Time or infinite Space-Time

in the infinity of its Space and Time. Let us imagine that this conception includes the whole of Time from the infinite past to the infinite future. Obviously such a vision is not possible to man, though it has traditionally been ascribed to God. It is, in the words of Dean Inge, "the time-honoured solution that God surveys the whole temporal process as present—as a *totum simul*."[105] Such a conception is not without its difficulties, as Dean Inge points out, but even if it were imagined, Alexander would probably stress the fact that the infinite becoming, because of the reality of Time, carries its time-coefficients from the infinite past to the infinite future. Since he takes Time seriously, Alexander would probably not allow the possibility of such a vision in which time-coefficients would be removed so as to present events in the whole temporal process as an extended present. The vision of total Space-Time—were it possible, which it is not—is not then the vision of the world *sub specie aeternitatis*, but rather the vision of the world in its full historicity, since Alexander has repeatedly stated that the world is historical through and through.

Is Total Space-Time an Absolute?—Alexander has so frequently used the expression "whole" to denote infinite Space, and infinite Space-Time, that the question is pertinent whether total Space-Time is the Absolute of certain types of idealist philosophy. The nature of such an Absolute is briefly characterized by Miss Calkins:

> the strictly absolute being is literally *all*-inclusive, complete being. Nothing can be either conceived or imagined as existing beyond or outside it, consequently nothing can be future to it, or irrevocably past; and change—implying passage from what has been to what is not yet—simply

cannot be attributed to Absolute Being.[106]

It is true that total Space-Time is also all-including for Alexander, and that there is nothing outside of it, since "infinite Space has no contours,"[107] and "its Space is always full."[108] But the important qualification which Alexander applies to Space-Time immediately after the last quoted words is:

> it grows older through internal rearrangements, in which new orders of empirical finites are engendered.[109]

A more forceful statement of the same meaning is the following:

> It has become a commonplace to say that the world and everything in it is historical, that the world is a world of events. Instead of space *and* time, a world laid out in space and moving forwards in time, we have space-time, time entering into the very constitution of things; a four-dimensional and no longer a three-dimensional world.[110]

The contrast between the world as historical, which is Alexander's conception, and the world as a changeless Absolute could not be indicated more sharply. It is true that in an earlier article, when Alexander was probably still under the influence of Bradley, his sense of the historicity of the world was not so pronounced, for he wrote:

> Though time is a real form of the universe, and the universe therefore has a history, it is not the universe which can be said to grow, but only its parts.[111]

ALEXANDER'S REALISM

If Alexander means a growth of the world in Space, he is correct in stating that it does not grow, for Space-Time includes all the Space there is, and there is no Space outside of it. But if by growth he means the process of becoming, then in later years Alexander applied the process of becoming to the universe as a whole. For instance, he writes of "the infinite becoming":

> The world which is Space-Time never and nowhere came into existence, for the infinite becoming cannot begin to become.[112]

It is clear that a careful analysis of Alexander's use of the term "whole" for the totality of Space-Time does not mean the Whole or Absolute of idealistic philosophy, such as we find it in Bradley or Bosanquet. Indeed, Alexander's system is a rebellion against Bradley's system in which change is unreal.

Alexander and Eternity.—If total Space-Time is an "infinite becoming" what becomes of eternity for Alexander? He states that "eternity as something different from Time and superior to it" is "a misconception."[113] for

> the only eternity which can be construed in terms of experience is infinite Time. If it is different from this it is out of all relation to Time, and if attributed to the world requires justification on its merits, and not because it may be thought to derive its nature from contrast with the alleged defects of ordinary empirical and mathematical Time. Space-Time therefore is neither in Time nor in Space; but it *is* Time and it *is* Space.[114]

Again, he states,

If everything is historical, including the world itself as a whole, it follows that we can no longer interpret eternity as timelessness. To be out of relation to time can belong to no character of things, nor as we have noted, even to the whole universe.[115]

In his rejection of the concept of eternity as timelessness, and in his retention of it only under the meaning of "infinite Time," it may be observed that Alexander makes a distinct departure from the meaning of eternity in Platonic philosophy and in traditional Christian thought. Roger Hazelton, in a recent article, makes clear the derived, created, character of Time:

> As in Christian, so in Platonic thought the question about time is fundamentally a question about the world's relation to God. For Plato, in the mature if somewhat tortuous conception of the *Timaeus,* God is the originator of the eternal forms in which all temporal facts participate. He is the "Maker and Father of all things" who wishes to make the world "as like Himself as possible." Time, no less for Plato than for the Bible, is a creature—something made by a will not its own and bearing on its face the marks of likeness to its Maker.[116]

Platonic and Christian thought emphasize the creatureliness of Time while Alexander emphasizes the creativity of Time. The relevant passage in Plato which has had an incommensurable influence in Christian thought is in the *Timaeus*:

> Time, then, and the heaven came into being at the same instant in order that, having been cre-

ated together, if ever there was to be a dissolution of them, they might be dissolved together. It was framed after the pattern of the eternal nature, that it might resemble this as far as was possible; for the pattern exists from eternity, and the created heaven has been, and is, and will be, in all time.[117]

But even though the "created heaven" exists in all time, or in infinite time, the meaning of Plato is that eternity belongs to God and is qualitatively different from time. This qualitative difference is emphasized also by Welldon, as quoted by Dean W. R. Inge:

> St. Augustine's point, in discussing the meaning of *saecula saeculorum,* is that the eternity of God is no mere unifying or synthesizing of the time-process, but something different in kind, to which the moments of the time-series stand as subjects.[118]

Augustine stresses the view that the eternity of God is not a mere synthesis of infinite Time, but is radically different in quality. And "eternity is not simply timelessness or changelessness . . . eternity is not only the unending prolongation of time."[119] Eternity is a mode of reality which includes time but transcends it, is different from it in quality, and is traditionally ascribed to the very being of God. It is clear that Alexander's conception of eternity as simply infinite time is a greatly watered down meaning from the historic significance of the term in Christian thought.

And yet Alexander has another meaning for eternity which he seems to derive from Whitehead, though it is not free from obscurity:

> It would be better to avoid altogether the word

eternal, which raises notions of time; but regarded as a name for that element which is distinct from lapse of time, eternal may be applied to the qualities, colour or taste or life or consciousness, which are the surd or irreducible or unexplainable character of things. We cannot ask why things have their qualities, why, for instance, a certain complexity of chemical and physical process possesses life. We accept these qualities. In this sense we may accept Mr. Whitehead's designation of them as eternal objects."[120]

We feel, however, that Alexander is not sufficiently precise in his use of the term "eternal object." To him, "eternal object" means:
1. Any quality, such as color, or taste, or life, or consciousness.
2. Any such quality is irreducible and beyond explanation as it defies the "ultimate why" as to the reason why it should be possessed by a particular complexity of physico-chemical processes, or by a complication of Space-Time.
3. Any such quality is distinct from the lapse of time, in the sense that consciousness has existed in animals and men, in varied degrees to be sure, for millions of years; or the color red may be perceived in a distant galaxy millions of light years away and may also be perceived at this moment in a near-by red object.

It is clear that the first meaning of Alexander's "eternal object" is what is qualitative; the second meaning is what is inexplicable; and the third is what is distinct from the lapse of time. It would seem that only the third meaning approaches in some way the Platonic conception of eternity since eternity is certainly distinct from time, and time and the world are in the *Timaeus* held to be created according to a pre-existing eternal pattern. But on closer inspection the third meaning of Alexander's "eternal object" is not at all the Platonic or the Christian meaning of eternity, for, strictly speaking, the color red emerges at a distinct critical moment in the history of Space-Time, and may appear at any time thereafter. We must assume, on Alexander's emergent system, an elementary stage in the development of Space-Time before the color red or any secondary quality had as yet been formed. Hence any of the qualities mentioned by Alexander are not even eternal in the sense of the whole of infinite Time, much less are they in the Platonic sense.

Furthermore, is Alexander correct in borrowing Whitehead's term "eternal object" in the manner we have just explained, or rather, explained away? Whitehead gives the following definition:

> I use the phrase 'eternal object' for what in the preceding paragraph of this section I have termed a 'Platonic form.' Any entity whose conceptual recognition does not involve a necessary reference to any definite actual entities of the temporal world is called an 'eternal object.'[121]

It is clear Whitehead's meaning is much more Platonic than Alexander's. And it is equally clear that Alexander's use of the term "eternal object," when he speaks of color, life, consciousness, necessarily refers to actual entities possessing these objects or qualities. Hence there seems to be a contradiction between Whitehead and Alexander at this point.

It would appear that Alexander is not successful in applying the term "eternal" to what is qualitative, or to what is inexplicable. The only way to do justice to him is to accept provisionally the meaning of eternity which he gives as "infinite Time."[122]

We thus conclude this elementary discussion of Alexander's emergent system prior to the fuller discussion of the nature of deity. In order to cast into sharper relief his conception of Space-Time, it was necessary to distinguish his system from that of Absolute Idealism and to indicate that total Space-Time is not a whole, nor is it changeless. It is through and through historical. Also, it was necessary to distinguish Alexander's various meanings for the term "eternity," examine them, and conclude that his meaning of "infinite Time" is quite distinct from the more traditional concept of eternity.

A central aspect of Alexander's system is the reality of Time both in the sense of succession, and of an infinite continuum. This is real Time, physical Time, if you please, and is never to be equated with merely subjective Time or mathematical Time, for it is the objective Reality of which these are derived.

> Real Time hints, by analogy with the past, the movement towards higher empirical qualities of existence. On this is founded the possibility of understanding deity.[123]

CHAPTER II

DEITY AND GOD

The God of Metaphysics and the God of Religion.—
There are two ways of approaching God, the religious approach and the metaphysical approach. They are incomplete in themselves, but may be brought in closer relationship—the very task Alexander sets himself in this final section of his work.

In the practical, religious approach

God must be defined as the object of the religious emotion or of worship. He is correlative to that emotion or sentiment, as food is correlative to appetite. What we worship, that is God. This is the practical or religious approach to God.[1]

This approach to God, however, may be incomplete and even defective for it may center on an imaginative and inspiring being but one whose reality is not correlated with the realities of the world with which we were familiar. And yet the religious sentiment is averse to the idea that it is merely a spiritual fancy or "a dream of perfection."[2] The religious sentiment insists on the reality of its object, and the practical experience of this reality as external—just as food satisfies the appetite and is external—needs to be supplemented by a metaphysical inquiry just what is the being which possesses the divine quality or deity, and whether this being corresponds with the being which elicits religious emotion.

It is necessary, however, to emphasize the reality of the religious sentiment as distinct from metaphysical inquiry into the foundation for this sentiment. For instance, Spinoza's intellectual love of God would not strike us with the religious quality unless it were based on a more inclusive religious passion of which the metaphysical passion is but a part. Alexander insists on this priority of the religious passion for he returns to it on many occasions in his writings. For instance, referring to Spinoza, he states:

> Unless the religious passion were already lit, it is hard to see how the intellectual love would rise above a supreme intellectual satisfaction, and this is not the religious but the scientific sentiment. Suppose the passion for God, and this scientific sentiment blazes into religion. But the religious passion must be there to begin with.[3]

Intellectual passion, metaphysical contemplation, no matter how satisfying, are not religion but may blaze into the religious sentiment which is more fundamental than intellectual satisfaction. Nevertheless, religion and metaphysics support each other:

> Religion leans on metaphysics for the justification of its indefeasible conviction of the reality of its object; philosophy leans on religion to justify it in calling the possessor of deity by the religious name of God. The two methods of approach are therefore complementary.[4]

How shall we begin the philosophical quest for God? In conceptual terms? But Alexander contends that God defined in such conceptual terms as perfect being, sum of reality, or first cause is merely an abstraction, and if we start with an abstraction, we shall end with one. As to the traditional theological arguments for God's existence, he states, perhaps a little too hastily: "No one now is convinced by the traditional arguments for God's existence."[5]

Alexander's discussion of the traditional arguments is exceedingly brief and unsatisfactory, but it seems to reduce itself to the following considerations: The traditional arguments introduce *a priori* conceptions in the bad sense of the term, a use of analogy which he finds unpersuasive. The ontological argument merely proves that the totality of things is real, which he regards as a tautology, for "my idea can be nothing but that reality, and there can be no difference between my object and the reality."[6]

The argument from design Alexander admits is persuasive—but apparently not to him for it implies the unwarranted use of analogy from a finite designer to an infinite Designer. If this infinite Being is regarded under the notion of immanent design, the process so assumed still presents great difficulties, for how could we "forget or possibly explain the wastefulness and destruction involved in the process."[7]

Alexander's more modest approach involves the rejection of an attempt to define God directly but insists on the investigation of just what is the reality in the world which possesses the quality of deity. This investigation proceeds from the point at which we left the description of the all-embracing structure of Space-Time which is a matrix giving birth to existents with the successive empirical qualities of materiality, life, and mind. Mind or spirit is the highest empirical quality of which we are aware, but there is no reason to suppose that Time which brings new empirical qualities at certain times in the process of emergence, would end with mind. On this supposition, Alexander asserts:

> There is an empirical quality which is to succeed the distinctive empirical quality of our level; and that new empirical quality is deity.[8]

Time is the soul of Space and performs towards Space the office of soul to its body. Furthermore, Time is the principle of growth and cannot be regarded as ceasing with the arrival of existences which carry the empirical quality of mind. At this point, Alexander makes a shift in his presentation, for the office of Time as the soul of Space, or the principle of growth of the whole emerging structure of existents in Space-Time, is replaced by the hitherto not mentioned principle of the "nisus in Space-Time,"[9] which bears the creatures of the primordial matrix not only to the levels so far experienced, but "will bear them forward to some higher level of existence."[10]

It is important to emphasize that the nisus of Space-Time, or driving impulse, is not mentioned prior to Alexander's consideration of deity in his famous two-volume work, *Space, Time, and Deity*. In the previous sections of this study, we were led to believe that Time was the creative agency with a function superior to that of Space, since Time was held to be the mind of Space. In other sections, the co-partnership of Space and Time was stressed. Alexander is apparently inconsistent as to precisely what is the creative agency. In his discussion of God and deity, however, increasing importance is given to the nisus, and though not precisely defined, it would appear to be a fundamental character or category of

Space-Time, more fundamental than other categories.

Whatever it be, the nisus of Space-Time is engaged in bringing to birth the next empirical quality higher than mind, which is deity. On the basis of the theory of levels summarized in the previous chapter, that of higher levels emerging at critical points in Nature when a complexity of integration is attained on the level immediately below, we are speculatively assured that the universe is pregnant with the quality of deity. We cannot, however, know its nature, nor enjoy it, nor contemplate it directly, so that in a real sense, "Our human altars still are raised to the unknown God."[11] By analogy it may be pictured as the color of the universe, "a soul of things which is their last perfection; whose relation to our soul is that of bridegroom to bride."[12]

Alexander, however, is not content with the presentation of deity as the next empirical quality after the emergence of mind. He extends the notion to mean that

> For any level of existence, deity is the next higher empirical quality. It is therefore a variable quality, and as the world grows in time, deity changes with it. On each level a new quality looms ahead, awfully, which plays to it the part of deity.[13]

Such a generalization of the conception of deity introduces a complication so that we must differentiate what is deity at our particular level or moment in Space-Time from what is deity at any other level in the past or future. If we imagine the infinite past, then primordial Space-Time has deity as its next empirical quality to arise in Time, and this deity is materiality, for Alexander supposes no level of existence nearer the spatio-temporal than the material.[14] Likewise, if we consider Space-Time at the moment—or during the period—when matter has emerged, then the next empirical quality is life, and this is the "deity" of the material universe. Again, if we consider the Space-Time matrix with all existents up to the level of living forms, but not man, then the next empirical quality is mind, and this is the "deity" of the forms of life not yet including mind. Finally, if we consider the Space-Time matrix at the moment in which we find ourselves then the next empirical quality is the "deity" of our level of mind. In every case, deity is a mysterious something which is more than the level at which it is apprehended and felt, though Alexander admits that he cannot describe the "feeling" of matter for its deity.[15]

Deity and Spirit.—It is clear that Alexander's conception of deity is based on the theory of levels which is the crucial part of his metaphysical system. Each level implies the addition of a complication of Space-Time with its corresponding quality which is higher than the quality on the next lower level, but presupposes it. We can, then, approach the meaning of "our deity."[16] It is not mind or spirit, since it must be a quality beyond mind or spirit. However, it includes mind or spirit for by analogy with levels of existence of lower quality, mind is not life but presupposes life; life is not merely physico-chemical processes but presupposes them; and physico-chemical material processes presuppose primordial Space-Time. The possessor of the quality of deity presupposes, therefore, the possession of the lower qualities: spatio-temporality, materiality, life, *and* mind.

At this point Alexander introduces another conception, that of the body of God and its relation to deity. The "body" of God includes all the qualities below deity, such as spatio-temporality, materiality, life and mind, while the "mind" of God is his deity. However, deity is more than mind or spirit, though next to mind or spirit in the emerging future. It is not strange, then, that religious consciousness has interpreted this mysterious quality in terms of spirit. But this is a mere device of "our pictorial cravings" for God's deity is different from spirit not merely in degree but in kind.[17]

God as the Universe possessing Deity.—Alexander at this point in his exposition is not concerned with religious views of God, but with the metaphysical inquiry of what is the being which possesses the quality of deity. He seems to give answers from two points of view, not as precisely differentiated as they might be. The first point of view is implied in his definition of God:

> God is the whole world as possessing the quality of deity. Of such a being the whole world is the 'body' and deity is the 'mind.'[18]

In what sense is Alexander using the verb "is" as a present tense when we have insisted previously that he conceives of the whole of Space-Time as historical through and through? Is it a reversion to a vision of the universe under the aspect of eternity? It is rather the vision of the universe under the aspect of its complete historicity as implied in the following sentence:

> Within the all-embracing stuff of Space-Time, the universe exhibits an emergence in Time of successive levels of finite existences, each with its characteristic empirical quality.[19]

It is an all-embracing vision of Space-Time, but the emergence in Time of successive levels and qualities, including deity, is never lost, for Alexander emphasizes "for us deity is like all other empirical qualities a birth of Time and exists in Time, and timelessness is for us a nonentity."[20]

One answer of Alexander as to what deity is has to do with the view of Time as an infinite continuum and the successive births of emerging qualities in Time, of which deity is the highest. But the other answer he gives implies a change of view from Time as an infinite continuum to Time as a succession and our present moment of existence in that succession. Accordingly, he gives us an answer based on "actuality":

> But this possessor of deity is not actual but ideal. As an actual existent, God is the infinite world with its nisus towards deity, or, to adapt a phrase of Leibniz, as big or in travail with deity.[21]

In order to clarify Alexander's exposition, it is necessary to keep definitely contrasted, wherever possible, these two views of the universe, first, that implied by the phrase, "within the all-embracing stuff of Space-Time," and second, the view of the universe at a moment in Time, the moment in which we find ourselves. It is, of course, within the second view that we find our experience, and the first view is only imaginatively and speculatively envisaged.

One objection to Alexander's exposition of God might well be: "Why not identify God with Space-Time"[22] Why should we seek to go beyond the present development of Space-Time to include the travail to generate deity? Here Alexander returns from his metaphysical orientation to an awareness of religious need. No one could worship Space-Time though it may fill our mind with mathematical or intellectual enthusiasm. Space-Time evokes from us intuition; Space-Time in travail with deity evokes from us worship. On the one hand, we have the totality of the world which is formed of Space-Time; on the other hand the world is not merely spatio-temporal, but includes the successive series of empirical qualities, materiality, life, mind, and the forecast of the next empirical quality, deity.

> These two features are united in the conception of the whole world as expressing itself in the character of deity, and it is this and not bare Space-Time which for speculation is the ideal conception of God.[23]

It seems clear that in stressing the development within Space-Time, and not bare Space-Time, as the character which evokes religious response, Alexander has advanced from an earlier conception in which he had not made this distinction:

> The religious idea of the world as a whole is the response which the mind sets up when the actual world as a whole operates on us through feeling, revealing itself in this indirect way.[24]

In the more adequate conception, the universe as in travail with deity evokes the religious response. While deity is not apprehended by sight or by sense, it is felt through speculative and religious faith. It may be imaginatively pictured through the visualization of a finite being possessing the quality deity, such as "a god of a polytheistic system, or what we have called an angel."[25] While we do not know whether such beings exist, should they exist, on the pattern of the successive births of existents and qualities in Time, we can conceive that the finite being possessing deity will have a "body" constructed of mind, life, matter, in fact a special configuration of finite Space-Time bearing as its "mind" the quality deity. In the case of the human body, a part of living substance—neural processes in the brain—sustains the mind. In the case of the mysterious finite god whom we imagine to exist, a part of Space-Time which is mental is differentiated so as to bear the quality deity. This deity, it is to be noted, is sustained by all the configurations and lower qualities which make up its divine life, that is to say, mind, life, physico-chemical processes, materiality—all of them qualities intimately associated with their corresponding complications of the movement of a particular portion of Space-Time. The mental part of this "body" of the divine being would sustain the "deisings"[26] or enjoyments of the divine mental life. But Alexander warns us that this mental part must not be thought of as a human mind, as if this finite god were a superhuman or a supernatural person. Such an assumption would be as unfounded as if a race of seaweeds held that mind, which is the quality higher than the "life" of seaweeds, must be strictly established on the life of seaweeds. In other words, the quality of "deity" in the finite god envisaged is a more complex aggregation of the mental order, but not necessarily a human mind.[27] Whether there are such finite gods, composed of material bodies, and carrying life, mind, and "deity" "in regions of the universe beyond our ken . . . is a scholastic and trivial question."[28] Actually, of course, at the present moment of Time, in our own immediate earthly environment, such finite gods do not presumably exist, and in the words of Alexander:

> We use the picture merely in order to understand how the whole world can be thought of as possessing deity.[29]

DEITY AND GOD

The whole of infinite Space-Time, with all the emergent levels of existence with their appropriate empirical qualities, sustains the deity of God, just as a portion of Space-Time, whether it be finite person or finite god, sustains its highest quality, mind in the case of the finite person, "finite deity" in the case of the finite god. But there are two differences. The first is that our experience is partly internal (vital feelings within the body) and partly external, the contemplation of external objects. But the experience of God, if we may be so bold as to use such a phrase, is wholly internal, since the body of God is the whole universe of Space-Time, and there is nothing outside of it, nor does it grow in Time, but all movements are redistributions of point-instants within the Space-Time matrix according to categories and the driving forces of the nisus. Space-Time is always full, and it does not grow bigger in extent with the lapse of Time, for this lapse is marked by "internal rearrangements"[30] in which new empirical finites grow of various degrees of complexity.

On the analogy that our mind occupies the neural processes of the brain and is thus only a portion of the space-time of our body, the deity of God which is the "mind" of God, occupies only a "portion"[31] of total Space-Time, but this portion is "infinite in extent and duration."[32] Within an all-comprehending view, God's body, being the whole of Space-Time, is "omnipresent and eternal,"[33] due note being taken of Alexander's meaning of eternity as infinite Time. God's deity is infinite in extent though of a lower degree of infinity than the whole of Space, and it is also infinite in time though again of a lower degree of infinity than the whole of Time.[34] At this point Alexander makes a daring analogy between "memory and expectation in ourselves"[35] and memory and expectation in God's deity which is "infinite in both directions."[36] It is not clear whether Alexander means that God's deity has infinite memory and infinite expectation for the notion is not developed further. In any case, both God's "body" and "mind" are infinite, spatially and temporally.

A further distinction between all finites and God is that we are finitely infinite while God is infinitely infinite. We are finitely infinite because, as finites, we occupy a finite portion of Space-Time, but as infinite we are related to all of Space-Time and to all things in it, so that "from our point of view, our place or date, we mirror the whole universe."[37] Obviously, we do not apprehend all things in the universe, but only "a limited range of distinct things" fringed with relations to other existents beyond them. The things with which we are actually compresent are "islands rising out of an infinite circumambient ocean,"[38] while the whole of which they are parts is apprehended as "a vague object of feeling"[39], and may be conceptualized into that system of levels of existence which is the heart of Alexander's metaphysics.

Furthermore, we participate in two sorts of infinity, internal and external. The external infinite is obviously Space-Time which is apprehended through its objects and our organs of sense. The internal infinite is our mind which is capable, as a portion of Space-Time, of an infinite number of neural structures and patterns which make up the brain, for

> within the brain there is room for multitudinous combinations initiated from within and enjoyed as imaginations and thoughts, and, for all I know, these are infinitely numerous in their possibilities of combination.[40]

DEITY AND GOD

There is thus room in the brain for an increasingly accurate and qualitied apprehension of the objects of the universe, and our brain-mind is assumed by Alexander to be internally infinite though finite in being confined within a very limited portion of Space-Time.

God, however, is infinitely infinite because his body, or "spatio-temporal organ"[41] is the whole of Space-Time, and there is nothing outside of it. But the spatio-temporal organ of God which is his deity, and which is analogous to our minds, and which is in fact called "the mind" of God by Alexander, is infinite, but as we have just observed, an infinite of a lower order than infinite Space-Time. The mind of God which is his deity is therefore infinite internally, while the body of God which is the whole world is infinite externally. Hence God is both internally and externally infinite, and his deity is infinitely infinite, while our human minds are finitely infinite.

God's deity is, then, "lodged in an infinite portion only of this whole infinitude"[42] which is total Space-Time. A very interesting question is: Are there other infinites contained within total Space-Time besides the infinite which is deity? Alexander replies in the affirmative, for these are "infinite lines in Space and infinite numbers"[43] and "infinite number is the number belonging to classes containing infinite members."[44] But these infinites are without quality, while God as the possessor of deity is a qualitied infinite. The conception of realized deity is difficult to visualize, Alexander admits, but assuming it were realized, it would be "the whole of Space-Time on a reduced scale,"[45] and just as the categories cannot be applied to total Space-Time, neither can they be applied to the "deity" part of Space-Time. Alexander clearly states: "this breakdown of the attempt to apply to it the categories."[46] We are therefore challenging Anna Forbes Liddell's interpretation on this point for she writes:

> They [the categories] apply to everything that is a part of Space-Time, including the empirical infinites, like infinite numbers, or . . . infinite deity, because they are not the whole of Space-Time.[47]

Also, realized deity cannot be a universal, since representing the whole, it admits of no repetition.

Deity is a Nisus and not an Accomplishment.—It might appear that our exposition has overlooked the concept of the nisus which we introduced at the beginning of this chapter. The notion of the nisus is re-established by Alexander after his long discussion of what deity might be were it realized, for he admits that the "infinite God is purely ideal or conceptual."[48] Such an assertion should be qualified, however, by the correction that the infinite God in so far as it is "body" is the whole of Space-Time inclusive of qualitied existents up to the mind of man, while the infinite God in so far as it is "mind" does not yet exist for the "mind" of God, his deity, is a future emergent. What can be asserted as actual, then? The nisus of the universe which strains towards deity:

> But the infinite God is purely ideal or conceptual. The individual so sketched is not asserted to exist; the sketch merely gives body and shape, by a sort of anticipation, to the actual infinite God whom, on the basis of experience, speculation declares to exist. As actual, God does not possess the quality of deity but is the universe as tending to that quality. The nisus in the universe,

though not present to sense, is yet present to reflection upon experience. Only in this sense of straining towards deity can there be an infinite actual God.[49]

Again, he confirms his exposition:

> The actual reality which has deity is the world of empiricals filling up all Space-Time and tending towards a higher quality. Deity is a nisus and not an accomplishment. This, as we shall note, is what prevents the conception from being wholly theistical.[50]

Actually, therefore, infinite deity is not yet realized. In fact, if it were realized, it would take the form of the empirical quality of finite gods or angels, a multiplicity of higher beings, and any finite realization of deity in turn presupposes a new quality of a yet higher deity. Let Alexander present his conception in his own words:

> Beyond these finite gods or angels there would be in turn a new empirical quality looming into view, which for them would be deity—that is, would be for them what deity is for us.[51]

Such a race of finite gods or angels would be "merely a higher race of creatures than ourselves with a God beyond."[52] Alexander is inexact here, for elsewhere he seems to reserve the term "God" as actual for the body of total Space-Time as straining towards deity, so that what these higher creatures have beyond them is not "a God beyond" but a new empirical quality, a higher degree of deity. As existents with higher empirical qualities than mind emerge, each new empirical quality is "deity" to the preceding one, and the process of the development of ever-higher qualities of "deity" never ends. Alexander calls this the "notion of a variable God, which is, as it were, projected in front of each successive level of existents."[53] However, to be more exact, it is not this variable God which is projected in front of each successive level, but a new quality of deity which is so projected:

> Deity is subject to the same law as other empirical qualities, and is but the next member of the series. At first a presage, in the lapse of time the quality comes to actual existence, animates a new set of creatures, and is succeeded by a still higher quality. God as an actual existent is always becoming deity but never attains it. He is the ideal God in embryo. The ideal when fulfilled ceases to be God, and yet it gives shape and character to our conception of the actual God, and always tends to usurp its place in our fancy.[54]

Again, it seems possible to give the meaning of this passage with greater precision. "Deity" may be understood as a general name for the successive empirical qualities which emerge in Time; it may also be understood as the name of the next empirical quality at any stage of the emergent process in Time. For instance, the deity of x is assumed to be realized. Another deity looms in view, the deity of the deity of x. Is this second deity also the deity of x? No, for Alexander states: "The ideal when fulfilled ceases to be God," which we believe is an inexact way of stating that when the deity of x is realized, it becomes an empirical quality in a new being, X, and since Alexander always stresses deity as "the next empirical quality," when Time has formed the being, X, its deity is "the next member of the series", and is not the deity of x but the deity of X. That is to say, as soon as this "next member of the series" is realized, it ceases to be deity, but becomes the "mind" of the highest being then in existence, and another deity, the "next member of the series" then looms into view.

The expression, "The ideal when fulfilled ceases to be God" is also inexact in another sense, for God does not cease to be God, but at any stage in the internal development of Space-Time, God is the universe up to that stage in its striving towards the next empirical quality. The body of God is further rearranged in complexity by fresh additions of deity. The diagram on this page makes clear these complicated relationships.

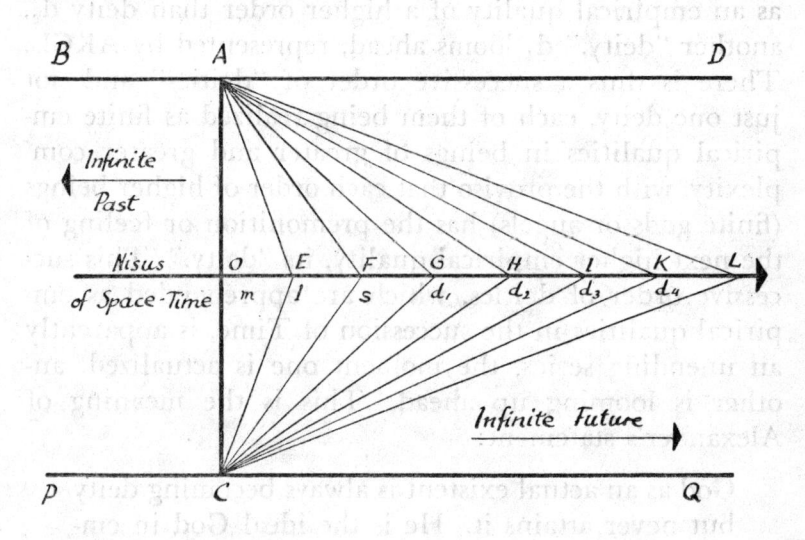

It is obviously impossible to represent Infinite Space-Time and this is indicated by the fact that diagram BADPCQ is left open in both directions of infinite past and infinite future. The portion BAOCP represents primordial Space-Time, that is to say, the universe manifesting only the most primitive motions before the rise of the material level which is represented by the segment AOCE, indicated by m. The nisus of Space-Time brings to birth successive empirical qualities, such as l, the level of life, indicated by the segment AECF; s, the level of mind or spirit, indicated by the segment AFCG; the next empirical quality deity, d_1, indicated by the segment AGCH. But when this next empirical quality of deity is realized, a new deity, d_2, looms ahead, represented by the segment AHCI. When d_2 is empirically realized through the motion impelled by the nisus of Space-Time, another "deity," d_3, looms ahead, represented by the segment AICK. When deity d_3 is realized as an empirical quality of a higher order than deity d_2, another "deity," d_4 looms ahead, represented by AKCL. There is thus a successive order of "deities" and not just one deity, each of them being realized as finite empirical qualities in beings of greater and greater complexity, with the proviso that each order of higher beings (finite gods or angels) has the premonition or feeling of the next higher empirical quality, its "deity." This successive order of deities, which are apprehended as empirical qualities in the succession of Time, is apparently an unending series, the moment one is actualized, another is looming up ahead. This is the meaning of Alexander's statement:

> God as an actual existent is always becoming deity but never attains it. He is the ideal God in embryo. The ideal when fulfilled ceases to be God, and yet it gives shape and character to our conception of the actual God, and always tends to usurp its place in our fancy.[55]

And yet there seems to be some confusion between Alexander's conception of God and deity, especially when he refers to the next "deity" as a "God beyond." It would be much clearer to retain his usage of God's body as the whole of Space-Time up to the last empirical quality, and the next quality as the "deity" of God. When this next quality changes from being ideal (that is, anticipated) to actual, it becomes a finite empirical quality, it becomes part of the "body" of God, and the "deity" of God is then the next empirical quality. It is always the next quality in the series, no matter what moment of the movement of the nisus we happen to choose as our point of reference.

It would be incorrect, however, to deduce from this explanation that the body of God grows with each successive incorporation of future qualities of "deity" into empirical characters. At any stage of development the body of God is always the whole of Space-Time plus the hierarchy of existents up to that stage, striving to bring forth deity. Alexander, as we have indicated in the first chapter, stresses his view that Space does not grow, for there is no Space outside of Space-Time, but there is a succession in infinite Time, and a growth of existents in Time. Accordingly, one may interpret our diagram and the various segments m, l, s, d_1, d_2, d_3, d_4, etc., in it, not as actual growths of the total matrix of Space-Time, but as actual growths of finite existents in it. There are "internal rearrangements"[56] within the matrix of point-instants, but we understand these to be the combination and integration of a number of these point-instants to form qualitied complexes through the action of the nisus of Space-Time. There is a growth of complicated finites in Space-Time, but no growth of total Space-Time in Space, though there is a growth in Time since Space-Time is historical through and through.

By means of this diagram we are able to state just what is God's body and what is God's deity at various stages of development. At the level of primordial Space-Time, when there is merely the most primitive motion but no qualitied existent, the body of God is this primordial matrix, and the unrealized deity is the level of materiality, m. At the level of materiality, the body of God is primordial Space-Time with the internal rearrangement AOCE which is the level of materiality, and the as yet unrealized deity is the level of life, l. At the level of life, the body of God is primordial Space-Time with internal rearrangements AOCE and AECF, representing matter and life respectively, and the as yet unrealized quality of deity is the level of mind, s. At the level of mind, which we occupy as physical-mental creatures, as intimate unions of mind and body, the "body" of God is once more primordial Space-Time plus the internal rearrangements representing materiality, life, and mind, segments AOCE, AECF, AFCG, respectively, and the as yet unrealized quality of deity is represented by segment AGCH, d_1. If we suppose by imaginary extrapolation the emergence of finite gods or angels, at that level the body of God is again primordial Space-Time plus all emergent qualities of materiality, life, mind, and the first empirical quality of deity, and the "deity" looming ahead is the second successive quality of deity, represented by the segment AHCI, d_2. This process may be continued for any level of emergent beings higher than man and finite gods, but, of course, when we make such extrapolations, we are dealing with highly hypothetical entities. We have no knowledge of such higher beings, and Alexander regards this question as "trivial," though he has labored to indicate the metaphysical hierarchy under which they could be produced.

DEITY AND GOD

At any rate, actually, at the level of humanity, deity does not exist, but is mysteriously perceived as the next empirical quality.

The interpretation which we have given clarifies, we believe, the following exposition of Alexander:

> Since God's deity is different for plants and men and angels, and varies with the lapse of time, how can we declare him to be the whole universe? Must not God be different at each level? I answer that the variation lies in the empirical development within the universe, and therefore not in God's totality, but, first of all, in his deity, and secondly, and in correspondence therewith, in the orders of existents within his body which have as yet been reached. It is still one Space-Time within which grows up deity in its successive phases, and within which the body of God varies in its internal composition. Yet God's body is at any stage the whole Space-Time, of which the finites that enter into God's body are but specialized complexes. . . . It is thus always the one universe of Space-Time which is God's body, but it varies in its empirical constitution and its deity. For we are not to think of the matrix, Space-Time, as something which grows bigger in extent with the lapse of Time; its Space is always full and it grows older through internal rearrangements, in which new orders of empirical finites are engendered. No matter therefore what quality the deity of God may be, his body is always the whole Space-Time.[57]

In this passage, Alexander refers to "deity in its successive phases" and these phases we have called in our diagram, d_1, d_2, d_3, etc., and while Alexander emphasizes internal rearrangements, there are at each stage the addition of the qualities pertaining to the level attained, such as the qualities of materiality, life, mind, and the various phases of deity. As to the portion of the infinite future of Space-Time represented in our diagram by DALCQ, it signifies the matrix of simple point-instants which have not yet been organized into complex existents because at the time considered, the nisus of Space-Time has *not yet* energized these complexes into existence. Obviously, not the whole matrix is used up to form existents since these rise like islands from a circumambient sea, but at any time, no matter what hierarchical order of existents is generated in Time, the matrix continues as their enveloping medium.

We believe that our diagram more correctly represents Alexander's conception than the one given by C. Lloyd Morgan[58] and reproduced on this page, as a triangle in which ST, the base, is space-time, and apex, D, is deity. N with the arrow represents the nisus. Morgan's diagram does not do justice to the successive phases of

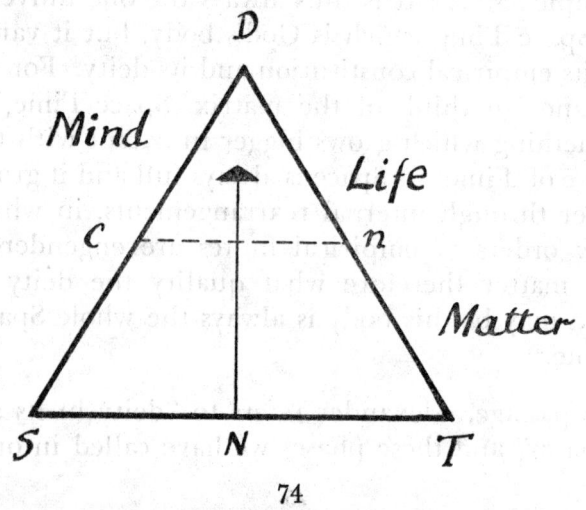

DEITY AND GOD

deity which are an integral part of Alexander's metaphysics, and he is decidedly wrong in interpreting Alexander's conception of deity in the following manner:

> an emergent quality that characterises only certain persons at the highest and latest stage of evolution along a central line of advance.[59]

In Alexander's system, deity does not at all characterize "certain persons" for it is the next empirical quality to mind or spirit, and thus characterizes the hypothetical beings which Alexander calls finite gods or angels. However, if we use the term "deity" in its general meaning of *any* subsequent quality to one just realized, and if we take our point of reference as the level of animal life, then this quality of "deity" is mind which is found not merely in certain persons but in all persons. Morgan has not paid sufficient attention to the successive phases of deity in Alexander's system, and we believe that we have given them the emphasis they deserve for more accurate evaluation.

After discussing his elaboration of the constitution of finite gods and of infinite God, Alexander seems to indicate that in speculative metaphysics these two conceptions are mutually exclusive. We wish to examine whether this is really so on the basis of his metaphysical system. He writes:

> For as we have seen, in speculation, either there is an infinite God, which is an ideal, and there are then no angels or finite deities, or if there are finite gods, the infinite or supreme ideal has ceased to be God.[60]

If Alexander means by speculation the type of metaphysical investigation which postulates the existence of various phases of deity, there is no contradiction between an infinite God which is the primordial matrix inclusive of the finites up to the moment when these finites have been engendered, even if we assume that the highest of these finites are finite gods or angels. Since the body is total Space-Time up to any moment of reference in Time, any finite gods postulated to exist would do so not merely "along with" Space-Time but within Space-Time since all existents are within the universe. God as the whole universe straining towards the quality of deity necessarily includes its highest existents, if and when these are postulated to be finite gods. Alexander could have prevented this apparently unusual inclusion of limited gods within the "body" of God had he rejected any description of possible beings higher than men in terms of finite gods but had called them by some such cumbersome phrases as "existents of the first higher order," "existents of the second higher order," etc. Alexander's essential conception is the reality of God as the whole world straining to realize the quality deity, and the partial realization of this quality in finite existents is not to be called "a finite god."

If Alexander, however, means by "speculation" the religious imagination of primitive peoples, then it is clear that at the stage when primitive imagination postulates the divine in terms of polytheism, monotheism especially in its ethical form is not even attained. On the other hand, when monotheism is accepted, it presupposes the definite rejection of polytheism. In the history of religions, therefore, there is a true "either . . . or" in the development of a religious tradition. But there need not be, as we have attempted to show, such an exclusion between finite gods and the infinite God in Alexander's metaphysics. This admittedly strange metaphysical implication is perhaps merely a problem in terminology, for Alexander could have been more precise in not calling these hypothetical beings higher than man, "finite gods."

The World-soul.—Having thus clarified the various meanings of the "body" of God, and the successive phases of the "deity" of God through the notion of successive addition of ever-higher qualities to finites through the energizing activity of the nisus, Alexander considers in what sense the philosophic conception of a world-soul may be applied to his metaphysics of Space-Time. In order to bring out more clearly his several answers, we shall consider Space-Time under various aspects:

1. *Primordial Space-Time,* which is Space-Time before the emergence of any qualitied existents. In this conception, Time is the soul of the world:

> The world whose soul is Time is the world which precedes quality.[61]

The world which precedes the emergence of any qualitative existent is then the world in a purely spatio-temporal character and consisting of an infinity of point-instants, the instants being coextensive with the points. The following quotation apparently applies to this conception of primordial Space-Time:

> When we take Space-Time as a whole in its purely spatio-temporal character, its soul is coextensive with its body.[62]

There may be an ambiguity due to the expression "as a whole," but in order to make Alexander consistent, we shall consider the whole here mentioned not total Space-Time, but Space-Time up to any moment prior to the emergence of any qualitied existent. Total Space-Time up to this moment is made up of Time which is full of Space, and Space which is full of Time. Accordingly, it is correct for Alexander to say that the soul of the world is Time and is co-extensive with Space.

2. *Actual Space-Time* which is

> this same Space-Time but with qualitied finites evolved within it up to the level for which deity is the next empirical quality in advance.[63]

This is Space-Time at a moment, or actual Space-Time in which we find ourselves, and in this case the soul of Space-Time is not the whole of Time but deity as the next empirical quality to be realized in the evolutionary process. The world-soul so conceived is a variable quality, as it is always the next quality in the succession and hierarchy of qualities. If we visualize Space-Time at any moment in the development of these qualities, we must be aware of the fact that this next quality, "deity," once realized, becomes simply an empirical quality, and ceases to be deity, for a higher deity is then the next quality ahead. We have explained these successions of deities sufficiently without stressing the point again. It would seem that deity as such is never realized as deity. We might modify slightly a line from Pope's *Essay on Man* and state: "Deity never is but always to be blessed." In Alexander's own words, deity is always prophetic:

> But it [deity] is never realised and remains prophetic only—in the immortal phrase, "the soul of the wide world dreaming of things to come." There is thus no true world-soul, but only a soul of Space-Time and a nisus in the world to deity.[64]

What is actually perceived, then, in actual Space-Time is not an actual "soul" of the world but the nisus of Space-Time urging the finites of Space-Time in their evolution to deity. It seems strange that when we consider primordial Space-Time before the emergence of any finites with qualities, there is a soul and this soul is Time "coextensive with its body"; but once finites emerge and we consider actual Space-Time, then there is no actual "soul" but merely a nisus in the world to deity. Why should primordial Space-Time, which Alexander calls "the world in its simplest expression"[65] be given a soul and actual Space-Time be deprived of one? There is a difficulty here in Alexander's exposition, and we do not think he has clarified it by merely calling attention to a different qualification:

> Whether we think of Time or deity, in either case we may use the designation of a world-soul, but in either case with a qualification which is different in the two cases.[66]

Actually, when finites have emerged from the primordial matrix, "Soul and body are distinctions within finite things."[67]

3. *The world in which deity is realized.* This is a supposition for we have already discussed the fact that if soul is equated with deity, deity is never actually realized as deity. If deity were realized, there would be a true world-soul:

> If the ideal God could be actual, and his deity realised, deity would truly be the soul of the world in strict analogy with the human soul or the colour of things to which it has been compared, lodged like our soul or like colour in a

GOD AND SPACE-TIME

> portion of the body whose soul it is. We should have to remember that the world-soul so conceived is a variable quality, according to the level for which it is the next in the hierarchy of qualities.[68]

It is always "the next in the hierarchy of qualities." Is it then ever realized? Alexander accordingly corrects his supposition of a realized world-soul by stating frankly:

> But it is never realized and remains prophetic only.[69]

This is the point we have emphasized repeatedly, for soul as the next empirical quality called "deity" is never realized as deity or as soul. Rejecting this supposition of a world-soul, the actual situation is this:

> There is thus no true world-soul, but only a soul of Space-Time and a nisus in the world to deity.[70]

The soul of primordial Space-Time which is Time is here referred to, as in the first meaning of the term "soul" considered on page 77. Time is then the "soul" of Space, and we shall return to this notion at the end of this chapter to determine whether this is not really a metaphorical, rather than a metaphysical, use of the word "soul."

Is Space-Time an Absolute Spirit?—A further consideration involves the question as to whether we may

> profitably compare the conception of empirical deity with that of the Absolute Spirit of the current doctrine of idealism.[71]

In the philosophy of Absolute Idealism, finites are not real in their own right but are merely appearances of the one Absolute. The God of religion is a real appearance of the Absolute, but not ultimately real.[72] Alexander rejects such an Absolute:

> For it is clear that Space-Time takes for us the place of what is called the Absolute in idealistic system. It is an experiential absolute. All finites being complexes of space-time are incomplete. They are not the sum of reality. But their absorption into the One does not destroy their relative reality.[73]

Also,

> The One is the system of the Many in which they are conserved not the vortex in which they are engulfed.[74]

Alexander's system is then neither an extreme monism nor an extreme pluralism. This is necessarily so, for all finites are ultimately pieces of Space-Time with that intrinsic complexity of configuration of the motions of the matrix within themselves that makes them the bearers of empirical qualities. Both the finites and their qualities and the circumambient matrix of Space-Time are real. The finite parts and the infinite whole are ultimately homogeneous, and the reality of the one in no way detracts from the reality of the other.[75] Finites of a lower order are transformed into finites of a higher order when a complex carries a quality of a higher order. "Thus physiological complexes of a sufficient complexity carry mind or consciousness."[76] But the elements which make up the physiological complex retain their identity: "the water in our bodies remains water still."[77] Similarly, the parts of the human organism are not absorbed or obliterated in the whole which is the organism, but subserve the life of the whole organism. Hence, whether we think of total Space-Time in its complete historicity, or the finites which are themselves wholes of parts, "the parts . . . are not altered or superseded but subserve."[78]

The fact that the lower life subserves the higher is perverted by Absolute idealism:

> The well-attested fact that the lower life subserves in the course of time the higher is perverted into the erroneous doctrine that there is a higher something or Absolute in which all lower life is submerged and transformed, and this Absolute is spirit, which is not even the highest empirical quality. Dowered with this empirical quality, the Absolute claims to be above the empirical, but would be itself empirical.[79]

When Alexander writes: "this Absolute is spirit, which is not even the highest empirical quality" he is referring to his own system, in which deity, higher than the human spirit, is held to be the next empirical quality, and we have seen that there are many grades of deity.

A further question is: Is total Space-Time, including its finites, to be called spirit? This question has already been answered in part in our discussion of the world-soul, but further considerations are offered by Alexander. If we attempt to equate Absolute Spirit with the deity of God, there are two difficulties: (1) Deity, as we have seen, is not the total Space-Time but only a portion of Space-Time, though this portion is infinite. If we provisionally identify deity and spirit, then spirit is applied not to the totality of existence as in some types of idealistic metaphysics, but only to a portion of this totality; (2) We cannot think of spirit as the highest

DEITY AND GOD

quality in the universe, since under Alexander's assumption of a successive order of ever-higher empirical qualities born in Time, the quality spirit which is met in man will be followed by a higher quality in the order of beings next in complexity to that of man. Obviously, we face the objection of the successive phases of deity, to which we have referred repeatedly, and none of these successive phases can be called spirit, since they are all higher than the spirit of man. These phases could not be called spirit, "unless it means something not merely different in degree but in kind from the human spirit."[80]

While we have indicated how seriously Alexander's conception of total Space-Time diverges from the Absolute of idealistic philosophy, there are passages where Alexander uses the term "Absolute," and we feel that such an unguarded use of the term is confusing, and may easily lead his readers to imagine that his system is merely a variant of Absolute Idealism, forgetting his emphasis on the full historicity of the world, which idealism denies. Such a misleading passage is the following:

> Deity is located only in a portion of the infinite whole of Space-Time, and therefore God, though infinite both in respect of his body and his deity, is only in respect of his body co-extensive with the absolute whole of Space-Time, while his deity is empirical and belongs only to a part of the Absolute. Thus the Absolute is not deity as if it were permeated with that quality, any more than the human organism is mind, but only that part of the organism has mind which is equivalent to it.[81]

The only way to reduce the ambiguity of this passage and remove it from associations with Absolute Idealism is to keep in mind that Alexander uses the word "absolute" as synonymous for "total":

> Thus, where we are dealing with what is absolute or total, the parts are neither lost nor are they transformed; where we are dealing with transformation, we are referring to what is not absolute but empirical.[82]

While he contends that Absolute Idealism is right in regarding God's deity and finites as appearances, it is important to note that they are not deceitful appearances, but real appearances, and this remains the significant difference between Absolute Idealism and Alexander's historical system:

> Thus it is true, as absolute idealism contends, that God is (at least in respect of his deity) on the same footing as finites and if they are appearances so is he, though an infinite appearance. But both God and finites are appearances only in the proper interpretation of that term, as parts of the things to which they belong, and in which they are not submerged but retained.[83]

The retention of the finites and infinites and not their submergence is the constant reiteration of Alexander over against Absolutism in metaphysics. As to the question as to whether total Space-Time is a spirit, Alexander summarizes the conclusions already elaborated:

> It still remains that neither is God a spirit, nor far less is the whole or Absolute which includes spirit itself spirit; nor is it deity but includes deity.[84]

DEITY AND GOD

This is one of the typical short-hand statements of Alexander which requires a little elucidation. In this passage "God" must be the "mind" of God, or else there would be no reason to distinguish him from "the whole or Absolute" which is his body. The mind of God, which is deity, as indicated above, is not spirit, since it includes phases of emerging empirical qualities higher than man's spirit. And the Absolute, or total Space-Time which includes the spirit of man is not itself spirit, since it also includes primordial Space-Time, plus all finites lower than man, and obviously not possessing man's spirit, and there may be finites higher than man, whose "mind" is higher than man's spirit. Hence the total Absolute of Space-Time cannot be comprehended under one quality, such as spirit, since spirit is a finite quality of a finite order among many such orders in the universe. Alexander could possibly have added that neither can total Space-Time be reduced to matter, since matter is but a finite quality, and one of the lowest, if not the lowest, in a hierarchy of qualities which emerged to undetermined heights above the material level. But whatever be these finites, they possess reality and are not submerged in an Absolute, though we contend that Alexander should have avoided using the term "Absolute" to give added relief to his difference from Absolute Idealism.[85]

Mind, Nisus, and Deity.—In summarizing this chapter on God and deity, we wish to return to his conception of Time as the mind of Space, or Time "as the soul of Space-Time."[86] Time seemed to be given a superior function to that of Space, while in the earlier books he considered Space and Time as equal co-partners of the universe. Yet, when he came to Book IV, "Deity" in Volume II of *Space, Time, and Deity,* Time as the mind of Space did not seem to provide the necessary driving force, and Alexander utilized the conception of the nisus, or dynamic impulse, in addition to that of Time as the directing agency of the whole process. It is not clear whether nisus is subsidiary to Time, or Time subsidiary to nisus. In our interpretation we shall be so bold as to suggest that it is not necessary for Alexander to consider Time as the soul of Space, for we believe this terminology to be metaphorical and not strictly metaphysical. It is possible to make an exposition of Alexander's system without including his analogy of Time as the mind of Space. This is precisely what Devaux has done:

> Nous avons écarté autant que possible l'argument par analogie, et l'inévitable métaphore du Temps se muant au sein de chaque étendue en une qualité originale.[87]

And Devaux adds in a footnote:

> la *métaphore* d'un Temps moteur par rapport à l'Espace se reproduisant à chaque émergence se trouve inutilement proposée puisque nous savons bien que la spatio-temporalité est intrinsèque à toute médiation.[88]

In other words, Time as a motive power is a useless metaphor since every existent is ultimately contructed of space and time in intimate union, such a close union of space and time being intrinsically required for finite existents. We would make the suggestion that the factor responsible for the creative advance of finites into finites of higher hierarchical order, responsible in fact for the whole emergent process in total Space-Time, is the nisus. In this interpretation, the nisus may be understood as a

DEITY AND GOD

category of Space-Time, perhaps the most fundamental category of all, penetrating all other categories, and perhaps more fundamental than motion, since motion, whether simple in primordial Space-Time, or complex in qualitied existents, would in some sense come under the creative sway of the nisus. Or again, the nisus may be understood as a metaphysical factor independent of Space-Time but active in Space-Time.

In this modification of Alexander's system which reduces the office of Time to that of equal partner with Space, and which exalts the function of the nisus, it is no longer required to state that Time is the soul of Space, but it is permissible to state that the soul of Space-Time, whether considered in its simplest form or at any moment at which qualitied finites have emerged, is deity, the next empirical quality.

At this point, however, a further difficulty presents itself, for at times Alexander writes as if deity, in the vision of total Space-Time, were realized, and at other times, he writes as if deity would never be realized. The following passage previously quoted, represents this confusion:

> If the ideal God could be actual, and his deity realised, deity would truly be the soul of the world in strict analogy with the human soul or the colour of things to which it has been compared, lodged like our soul or like colour in a portion of the body whose soul it is. We should only have to remember that the world-soul so conceived is a variable quality, according to the level for which it is next in the hierarchy of qualities.[89]

It is true that in this quotation, Alexander uses the conditional, "if the ideal God could be actual," but there are passages where he is no longer conditional but affirmative:

> Deity is located only in a portion of the infinite whole of Space-Time, and . . . his deity is empirical and belongs only to a part of the Absolute.[90]

Let us attempt to clarify these statements. Alexander writes: "If the ideal God could be actual" but there is an actual God which is the whole universe straining towards deity. What Alexander means is: If deity could be actualized, as he himself indicates when he states: "deity would truly be the soul of the world . . . lodged like our soul . . . in a portion of the body whose soul it is." But if Alexander implies that deity could be realized, or at other times states that "it is located in a portion of the infinite whole of Space-Time," it is incorrect for him to state in other contexts:

> the world-soul so conceived is a variable quality, according to the level for which it is next in the hierarchy of qualities.[91]

Alexander cannot have it both ways: either the world-soul, or deity, "is located" or "is realized" or else "it is next in the hierarchy of qualities." He apparently confuses the vision of Space-Time at a moment with the vision of total Space-Time. But this vision of total Space-Time is still Space-Time in its historical character through and through, with successive phases of deity still emerging. Is the succession of these phases infinite? Alexander does not discuss this point, but on the basis of his statements that deity is infinite, we may postulate that the number of these successive phases is infinite. A phase of deity is realized in the next empirical quality, and ceases to be deity. A phase of deity is then finite.

DEITY AND GOD

The next phase is then realized, again finite, and the process apparently goes on ceaselessly. Since it takes an infinite number of finites to make an infinite, we must conclude that the totality of deity includes an infinity of "phases of deity," or an infinity of successive phases of existents higher than man as suggested by the segments in our diagram on page 69.

We are, of course, extrapolating Alexander's system of levels beyond the development which he gave, but we insist that this extrapolation is carried out with rigid attention to his formulation. It seems clear, however, that this supposition of an infinity of existents in which the various phases of deity are realized, but as such cease to be deity, is highly speculative. We have no evidence that they do exist.

Furthermore, since "God as an actual existent is always becoming deity but never attains it,"[92] Alexander is forced to return to one of his basic conceptions, that of the nisus:

> It remains to observe that the conception of an infinite world contains nothing which does not follow the lines of experience. The nisus in the world which drives it, because of Time, to the generation of fresh empirical qualities is a verifiable fact. Its extension from mind to deity is an application of analogy.[93]

It appears that the nisus of the world is factual, the creative impulse is actual, while deity in its successive phases is based on analogy, and the analogy becomes highly hypothetical when the successive phases are multiplied indefinitely in order to do justice to Alexander's assertion that deity is infinite.

In order to summarize adequately Alexander's speculative scheme, we shall clarify the various conceptions he uses. The simplest formulation is this:

> God is the whole world as possessing the quality of deity. Of such a being the whole world is the 'body' and deity is the 'mind.'[94]

On closer examination of Alexander's metaphysical system, we have discovered that it is necessary to be clear as to just what we mean by God, the whole world, and by deity. It is then possible to further subdivide Alexander's various conceptions of the divine:

1. The "body" of God is the whole of Space-Time, whether we think of primordial Space-Time before any qualitied existents have arisen, or whether we think of the primordial matrix at any moment at which qualitied existents are present. This body always occupies the same Space, but a hierarchical order of finite existents grows within it and this order displays a variety of qualities. This is the immanent strain in Alexander.

2. The "deity" of God, or the "mind" of God, is the empirical quality to be realized, whether we think of primordial Space-Time, or Space-Time at any moment of its historical existence. This is the transcendent strain in Alexander.

3. The "successive phases of deity," for as we have explained at length, once deity is realized in a finite existent, it becomes the highest quality of that existent, and a new deity looms ahead. This is the conception of the multiple transcendence of deity.

4. Deity is a nisus, not an accomplishment. The key quotation is the following:

> The actual reality which has deity is the world of empiricals filling up all Space-Time and tending

towards a higher quality. Deity is a nisus and not an accomplishment.[95]

Another description of the nisus, and one fuller than those already given is the following:

> This impulse of creativeness I call the nisus of the universe, borrowing an idea from Spinoza and agreeing, as I think, with the spirit though not all the details of Mr. Bergson's *élan vital*. This nisus not only leads to the formation of things and to the sustainment of them, but impels the world forward towards new creations, bringing forth the new out of the bosom of the old.[96]

The nisus, or vital impulse, is not the whole of the universe, but is the nisus of the universe. Since not all living forms exhibit a hierarchical growth of qualities in Time, some species dying out, and some scarcely indicating any change in the vast evolution of life on the earth, for instance, the amoeba, we may conclude that the nisus is less than a fully pantheistic concept. We shall coin the word "infra-pantheism" to mean the conception of God as nisus of the universe, the creativity of the universe which impels portions of the universe forward towards new creations through the emergence of ever higher levels in Space-Time.

The metaphysical conception of the divine in Alexander's system may then be subdivided into four divisions: the immanent or pantheistic: the transcendent; the analogical conception of multiple transcendence; and finally the infra-pantheistic conception of the nisus. We shall investigate in the following chapter to what degree these various conceptions fulfill, if at all, the religious sentiment.

CHAPTER III

DEITY AND THE RELIGIOUS CONSCIOUSNESS

The Religious Sentiment and its Object.—Having discussed the metaphysical conception of the universe of Space-Time which through internal rearrangements of finite beings manifests a hierarchy of existents with the quality of deity ahead of them in Time, it is necessary to continue our investigation of the relationship between this novel conception of deity as engendered in Space-Time with the conceptions of God as presented by the religious consciousness and by the intellectual elaboration of religious consciousness in theology. Alexander indicates the breadth of mind with which he approaches this study when he remarks:

> Since the religious experience varies from people to people and from age to age, there will be special Jewish or Christian or Buddhist theologies within the general ambit of theology as a whole; or, rather, it is these particular theologies from which theology in general might be gathered.[1]

He shows more interest, however, in the consideration of the religious sentiment in general than of theology in general. While this sentiment varies, as he has stated, from people to people and from age to age, and contains a diversity of emotions, Alexander vindicates its unique character in these words:

> Various emotions enter into the full constitution of the religious sentiment—fear, admiration, self-abasement—but its distinctive constituent is the feeling of our going out towards something not ourselves and greater and higher than ourselves, with which we are in communion, a feeling whose object is not that of any of these subsidiary or suggesting emotions, nor of any combination of them.[2]

The religious sentiment is, then, a distinctly religious appetite which may be compared to the more rudimentary appetite for food which discovers its object, or the impulse of love which discovers its mate. Each impulse implies its specific object which satisfies the outgoing emotion, and the task of intellectual reconstruction is secondary to the primary sentiment or impulse which expresses the outgoing of our whole personality, be it in quest of food or drink, in quest of a mate, or in quest of the religious object. That is to say, the idea of God as presented through metaphysical interpretation, whether it be Alexander's "or any other metaphysical interpretation of God, is as far as possible from being an original discovery of knowledge; it is only possible to reflection working upon primitive notions already acquired."[3] These primitive notions may be as rudimentary as "fear of the thunderstorm,"[4] or they may be as elevated as the theological conceptions of God which we shall examine presently to compare them with Alexander's metaphysics. In any case, whether it be taken in its primitive or elevated form, religious emotion is not merely something subjective corresponding to no external reality. On the contrary, it is of the very essence of Alexander's religious philosophy that this emotion is provoked in us by the nature of reality, by the world itself:

> it is because the world itself provokes in us a specific response which makes us aware, no matter in how primitive a form, of God, and this specific reaction is what has been described above as a going out to something in the world with which we are in communion.[5]

In an attempt to sustain this conception, Alexander draws upon William James' study in *Varieties of Religious Experiences,* and quotes with approval James' conclusion, that "the conscious person is continuous with a wider self through which saving experiences come."[6] The "wider self" is, however, merely one of James' formulations, and Alexander could have used a formulation much closer to his own thought:

> The only thing that it [religious experience] unequivocally testifies to is that we can experience union with *something* larger than ourselves and in that union find our greatest peace.[7]

Since Alexander has nowhere indicated that the object of religious sentiment is a "self," James' formulation of "something larger than ourselves" rather than a "self" is in greater agreement with Alexander's fundamental conception that

> The world as a whole in its forward tendency acts upon our bodily organism and that the religious sentiment is the feeling for this whole. Parts as we are of Space-Time we throw out feelers to-

wards the rest of it and we are accessible to its influences.[8]

The body of the universe, which is the whole of Space-Time up to the moment of our existence, affects our body, which is nothing but a configuration of Space-Time sustaining the qualities of our personality, and our personality is characterized by the religious hunger which returns to the whole which has elicited it into overt manifestation. Our religious conation is our groping to the reality which is God.[9] This religious impulse may be experienced as a need of our nature, indeed the profoundest need. Or it may be directly stirred in us by the impact of the universe of Space-Time with its tendency to deity. Actually, since we are immersed in the world of Space-Time, it is the nisus of this world "that grips the finite conative complex which is fitted to it."[10] The world in its essential metaphysical structure of a nisus striving for deity excites in us a peculiar emotion which is the religious emotion. Other emotions or appetites have specific organs through which they are satisfied, but the religious emotion has no such specificity for it is based upon our whole personality, "upon the whole make-up or constitution of the mind and body."[11]

Rather than emphasizing Space-Time as "the body" of God, or deity as "the mind" of God, Alexander at this point in his development stresses "the whole of reality in its nisus towards a new quality."[12] All existents are caught in this nisus "due to the onward sweep of Time,"[13] and since we are finite existents the nisus penetrates our body and that part of the body which sustains the mind. The religious response is both the penetration, or the "ingression" of this nisus (to use a phrase of Whitehead) and our response to it, and our response is actually a contribution towards the nisus.[14] The nisus, however, bears existents to a new empirical quality higher than mind, but "we know not what it is"[15] though we are aware of it through the religious sense. The world is not what is actually present to our senses and intellect. The nisus of Space-Time enters into our very constitution; in fact both the world and ourselves are impregnated with this universal tendency which manifests itself in our personalities in ways other than cognition. It is not a cognition but rather "a vague endeavour or desire" as Alexander indicates:

> The whole world with its real tendency to deity stirs in us from the depths of our nature a vague endeavour or desire which shadows forth its object.[16]

But this vague endeavor is not to be interpreted as a confused sentiment which is dispelled on fuller investigation. It is due to "a real tendency to deity" and when the intellect is brought to play upon our inner striving, endeavor, or desire, it is "shadowed forth", or better still, it is illumined philosophically by the conception of "the tendency of the world forwards towards a new quality."[17]

A consequence of Alexander's insistence that the religious sentiment is a response to the pervasive tendency of the universe to a higher quality than expressed in humanity, that of deity, is the realism of his religious conception which is, for this very reason, unalterably opposed to subjective views or interpretations of religion as mere illusion. In this way

> the ground is cut from the feet of any attempt to treat religion as a mere practical necessity of

man's nature, which might have no foundation in fact and yet might be precious because of the contentment it brings, or as some have thought, because of the usefulness of the belief for securing morality.[18]

Religion as civil theology for social convenience and the security of the state was given this reduced status by enlightened circles in the Periclean age as we are informed by A. E. Taylor:

> Civil theology is knowledge of the various feasts and fasts of the State Calendar and the ritual appropriate to them, such as is imparted, for six months of the year, by Ovid's *Fasti*. The whole of this cultus, it was held, is the manufacture of legislators aiming at social utility and convenience.[19]

Alexander's concern is not with the question of the sociology of religion, or the social utility of doctrines not founded on rigorous analysis. His emphasis is rather on what A. E. Taylor calls *"philosophic* or *natural,* theology"* as "the doctrine of God and the divine seriously taught by scientific philosophers as an integral part of a reasoned theory of $\phi\upsilon\sigma\iota\varsigma$, *natura,* the reality of things."[20]

The reality of things is for Alexander the world pregnant with deity, the new quality higher than anything we know and which cannot be seen or understood, though its presence is felt through the feeling evoked in us by the nisus which produces deity. The religious sentiment differs, of course, among various persons. Some may be insensitive or only faintly sensitive to its "peculiar flavor"[21] just as some may be tone-deaf, but most men are suggestible to it in some degree, from the lowest degree to the highest response and exemplification found in the religious giants of the race. The religious sentiment, moreover, corresponds to the impulse generated in us by the nisus of the universe, and is thus an effect of that forward tendency in reality. It is in a sense a verification of the speculative notion of the universe emerging to deity, just as the effect of the existence of ions in chemistry is a verification of their existence, or the observation of a planet through a telescope is a verification of the predicted position and existence of this planet.[22]

The speculative development of the nisus of Space-Time striving to deity thus completes the religious sentiment of our total response to some mysterious quality greater than we are and in which we share our existence and find rest and peace. There is one puzzling feature which Alexander admits in this account of deity, and it is the fundamental character of deity as a future quality to which we have paid so much attention in the previous chapter:

> Deity is some quality not realised but in process of realisation, is future and not present. How then, may be asked, can the future make itself felt energetically in our minds, draw them towards itself and satisfy them?[23]

But deity as such is not an object of cognition or of contemplation. Alexander at this point shifts his exposition from deity as a future existent to deity as a present potentiality. In the actual evolution of forms of Space-Time in which we find ourselves, the world does not as yet contain deity, but it contains the seed of its future, which will be the "various phases of deity" which we elaborated in the previous chapter. "What acts upon us is what is to bring forth deity."[24] The vague future quality of deity is felt in religious experience, not as an intrinsic essence of deity, but as "giving a flavour to the experience of the whole world which it does not possess as merely an object of sense or thought."[25] This flavor of experience is one of the assurances of the reality of deity. The other assurance is the speculative one that

> we become familiar with levels of different quality, and we may by analogy conceive a higher type unfolded by the onward pressure of Time. There is no invention here, but only extension of a series whose principle is known, to another term.[26]

The more direct assurance, however, is the religious emotion itself, which precedes the elaboration of a speculative metaphysical system such as is here presented by Alexander. Religious assurance of deity is given through the emotion appropriate to deity, the distinctive religious emotion and not a mere composite of other emotions. Social assurance of the reality of other minds is given through the emotion appropriate to this assurance which is social instinct. There is this difference between these two emotions which brings into sharp relief a very significant difference between Alexander's conception of God and the traditional religious view of God as personality. The social instinct is satisfied by the reciprocal action of others, but "There is no such reciprocal action from God."[27] When we speak in human terms of God's response to us, we have no direct experience of that response in any other terms than our own feeling of devotion to God, or that worship carries in itself its own intrinsic satisfaction. There is no answer to prayer through any intervention of God or through any suspension of the laws of nature, as is sometimes envisaged by the religious orthodox. Alexander is clear on this point:

> The universe does not answer to our prayers by overt external actions as our fellows respond to our social approaches to them, but in the strength and sustainment which in its tendency to deity it gives to our minds.[28]

There are thus two poles in Alexander's orientation to the reality of God. One is the emotional pole, the distinctly religious emotion which is deeper than cognition or contemplation and stirs our whole being in the ardent search for that reality which it calls God. The other is the speculative pole, the result of speculative reflection upon this religious emotion and which gives the speculative assurance that the universe of Space-Time which has produced a hierarchy of existents up to man and his mind cannot be presupposed to stop with man, but through the nisus of the world carries its creativity to the next empirical quality, deity, higher than man. It is now necessary to inquire further into the religious criteria of the God idea in order to indicate whether Alexander's conception of deity meets them; and to what degree and with what modification of these criteria, Alexander's conception of deity is congruent with the more articulate conceptions of theology.

Religious Criteria of the Concept of God.—The religious sentiment requires four criteria for God:

1. God should be greater than men. The testimony of primitive as well as modern religion is the "conviction of some overpowering thing in the world."[29] The point is so obvious that it needs no elaboration. Even

modern conceptions of a finite God[30] present God as greater than man.

2. God as "a 'universal' or all-inclusive being."[31] By this brief expression, Alexander means that God's

> empire, whether directed by a single God or put into commission as in polytheism, is extended over the whole universe. In some sense God acts through the whole—we have said that the whole of Space-Time with its finites engendered within it is the body of God.[32]

Alexander has little to say on this notion of all-inclusiveness which he believes to be a second requirement of the religious consciousness beyond quickly and hastily interpreting it in terms of his pantheistic notion of the body of God being the whole of Space-Time. His argument is faulty in several respects. First, to say that God's empire is extended over the whole universe is quite different from the statement that God is an all-inclusive being, for God's rule may extend over the whole universe, while his being is not limited by the universe. Traditionally, theism has never been pantheistic but most decidedly theistic, and the following brief definition of theism indicates that Alexander was mistaken in stating that the religious sentiment regarded God as "all-inclusive being":

> According to theism, God is a Person who is responsible for the changing world but not identical with it; his activity is engaged in the world, but his own being and perfection are not part of it.[33]

3. God as different in quality from man. This is a requirement that religious consciousness has stressed in the sense that God's divinity is not merely a "higher

humanity but something different in kind."[34] Popular imagination and religious reflection have indicated this difference in such terms as omniscience, omnipotence, infinite goodness, eternity, but Alexander relies on Hegel's judgment that these terms represent figurative disguises of a faith in something of a different order from man.[35] After examining these "disguises" one by one, Alexander seems to accept eternity as a characteristic of deity:

> Now we have seen that deity in a monotheistic God, though lodged in a portion only of the universe, is lodged in an infinite portion and is therefore eternal, but that this conception is valid only so long as deity is in process and not actually realized.[36]

We have already discussed in the first chapter the great difference between Alexander's view of eternity and the traditional Platonic-Christian view of eternity, so that we need not repeat this discussion here.[37] His conception is the following:

> the only eternity which can be construed in terms of experience is infinite Time.[38]

The only way in which we can justify Alexander's ascription of eternity to his conception of deity is to have recourse to the mathematical notion that there are different orders of infinites, some being parts of others. Hence the infinity of Time which characterizes deity is but a part of the total infinity of Time when Time is considered not as succession but as a continuum extending to the infinite past and to the infinite future. But we do not understand how Alexander can state that this conception of infinite deity "is valid only so long as deity is in process and not actually realized." The previous chapter rather laboriously indicated that when deity is in process, it is being gradually realized in finite existents as their highest qualities, but ceases to be deity, and becomes a finite quality. This conception of a futuristic infinite deity is one which presents special difficulties to be discussed further in the second part of this work.

As to the other qualities traditionally attributed to God, omniscience and perfect goodness, Alexander is quite clear in his statement that they "do not belong to deity at all." Referring to omniscience, for instance, he gives a passage which requires further elaboration to be fully understood:

> Deity does not know, but only the minds know which are included in the body of God. Deity knows only in the extended sense of knowing which is not human knowing nor any extension of it. God's 'knowing' is his contemplation of things, his 'knowledge' the objects of his acts of enjoying his deity. Moreover, infinitely as his deity is extended in space and time, and though he contemplates the whole of Space-Time, even deity contemplates only those qualities which have been hitherto developed within Space-Time, and he cannot foretell the quality which shall in good time supersede his deity, any more than we humans can fortell what qualities shall supersede mind. There is always impending over him the menace which Prometheus levels against Zeus of supersession by a higher God. In this way God's 'knowledge' is limited and it is something higher than knowledge.[39]

We shall have to interpret this difficult passage at some

length, as Alexander has not presented it in the clearest fashion. In the first place, it seems incorrect to state that deity has over him the menace of supersession by a higher God. As we have repeatedly stated, God is as "body" the whole of Space-Time considered in any of its three principal aspects, whether as primordial Space-Time, Space-Time at any moment of the flow of Time, or total Space-Time. There is no supersession of God by a higher God, therefore, but merely the development of various phases of deity as empirical qualities are added to finites so that their hierarchy of empirical qualities is increased with ever higher qualities above mind, these various phases of deity being possessed by finite existents rooted in portions of Space-Time. Deity then knows in two senses: (1) through the minds of men which know the qualities developed in Space-Time up to the level of man, but have no knowledge of higher qualities; (2) through the "mind" portion of existents higher than men, this "mind" portion being constituted of a part of realized deity. It is in this sense of a being higher than man and possessing as its highest quality a finite portion of "deity" that Alexander can state that

> deity contemplates only those qualities which have been hitherto developed within Space-Time, and he cannot foretell the quality which shall in good time supersede his deity, any more than we humans can foretell what qualities shall supersede mind.[40]

It is necessary to transform Alexander's apparent conception of the knowledge possessed by the abstract quality of deity (which is not what he means) to that knowledge which in the extension of his speculative, hierarchical scheme, we presume is possessed by those grades of finite beings higher than man, and in which a portion of infinite deity is realized as the highest type of finite consciousness, or what corresponds at this high level of finite existence to our human consciousness. Such beings of a higher order than man, then, in accordance with Alexander's exposition, know all the empirical qualities up to the quality of their higher consciousness. In fact they contemplate the external world up to their level, and enjoy their higher consciousness. But they do not know, nor can they predict, what new and higher quality of deity shall supersede that quality of deity which they enjoy as the highest empirical quality so far realized. But as higher existents are engendered in Space-Time, these existents contemplate a greater hierarchy of empirical qualities and complexities of motion than is contemplated by existents of the next lower order. Yet they contemplate a hierarchy of empirical qualities less rich and involved and integrated than existents of a still higher order yet to be evolved through the nisus of Space-Time. We are obviously extrapolating the exposition of Alexander's speculative emergent scheme, but it is the only way in which we can make clear Alexander's statement: "In this way God's 'knowledge' is limited and it is something higher than knowledge."[41]

To put the same thought more precisely, God's knowledge at any moment in the development of finites in Space-Time is possessed by his deity, but it must be remembered that this deity is not represented by one conscious being but by possibly an infinity of beings of large hierarchical dimensions, in which deity is fragmented as the highest conscious "mental acts" of these beings. These beings, through that highest quality of theirs which corresponds to our "mental" quality, know all existents in Space-Time (within the limits of observation) up to their level, but they do not know nor can they predict just what is the next empirical quality to them—which is "deity" to them. All these existents of a higher order than we are, are included in the body of God, since the body is the whole of SpaceTime inclusive of all existent finites up to the moment at which we are considering the development of these finites in Space-Time. It is thus that deity as an abstract quality does not know, but only our minds and the "mind" of the existents higher than man, know, and all of these are, obviously in the body of God.

We might at this point make a slight digression into the question of predictive knowledge in Alexander's metaphysics. In his speculative scheme each new creation is not just a chance creation but is determined by existents of a lower level. Does this determination mean exact prediction? We shall give *in extenso* Alexander's answer:

> if the world is a determinate growth, each new creation determined by its predecessors on a lower level, the history of the world must be capable of prediction, according to the famous assertion of Laplace. But this conclusion does not follow. Laplace's calculator might foresee that at a certain point a certain complexity might arise, whose actions were capable of measurement and would be those of living things. He could never affirm that this form of action would have the quality of life, unless he lived to see. He might predict ethereal waves but could not predict them to be light; still less that a material body would be material or when touched by light would be red, or

even merely look red to a living body with eyes. All known forms of action could be predicted in their measurable characters, but never in their emergent ones. Not even God, if we suppose a God presiding over the birth of the world, in accordance with the conception of the crudest theism, could predict what these emergent qualities would be; he could only accept them like ourselves when the world he made had originated them.[42]

We have quoted Alexander at length on this question to indicate that his concept of the knowledge of God in his metaphysics is quite different from the traditional conception of God as omniscient. We have seen that God only "knows" through the finites which form part of his body, and which are compresent with the hierarchy of finites up to their highest quality, but that these finites, no matter how elevated they may be in the development of Space-Time through its nisus, cannot know and cannot predict higher qualities than theirs. All living finites, from man up to the highest, view the universe with that "natural piety" which forms a large element in Alexander's natural religion. He is so bold as to indicate that God himself in the traditional theistic sense of a creator God could view emergent qualities only through "natural piety." In Alexander's speculative scheme, we are all natural religionists, including God himself!

As to the quality of infinite goodness traditionally ascribed to God, Alexander limits it through rigid adherence to his emergent speculative scheme:

> In the same way all goodness is included in the body of God, for goodness belongs to the minds which are within that body. But for those minds

there is no perfect goodness, no limit to perfection in conduct; while on the other hand deity being raised above willing is not goodness at all.[43]

Just as in the previous discussion of the degrees of knowledge possessed by the hierarchy of beings through their minds as the highest quality in them which corresponds to our "minds," so Alexander posits degrees of goodness possessed by the "minds" which exist in the "body" of God, though goodness is not to be equated with deity. We shall follow Alexander's suggestion that a full discussion of the relationship between goodness and deity be reserved for the following chapter on deity and value.[44]

It is clear, in any case, that the usual conceptions of traditional theology of the infinite knowledge and infinite goodness of God are given radical reinterpretations to make them consonant with Alexander's emergent metaphysics of Space-Time.

4. God as responsive to man is the most vital feature of religious consciousness, though it has appeared in many different forms in the history of religion. Primitive religion interprets God in terms of fear, awe, and dependence of man upon God. The more advanced stages of Brahmanism and the absolute idealism of T. H. Green emphasize the identity of God and man, or, more precisely, the absorption of man in God.

> This is the pantheistic sense of the divine response, and it tends towards the feeling of absorption in the divine.[45]

In theistic forms of religion, however, no such radical absorption is involved, but rather the conception of the fatherhood of God, whose mystery is somehow pierced by the sense of sustaining love to his children who return this love in an attitude of trustful dependence. The higher religious stress this affinity between man and God, so that man does the work of God in assuming his most distinctive human qualities in the apprehension of his passion for truth, beauty and goodness as the meaning of God in human experience.[46] Alexander is aware that religion does not present man's worship of God as homage paid to a static reality. On the contrary it involves a community of co-operation, for man depends upon God, and in a sense God would seem to be dependent on man for the realization of some divine goals. Indeed, man's dependence on God has been stressed to an extreme degree by Schleiermacher, and Alexander agrees with Höffding's criticism of this doctrine of dependence which assumes the character of helplessness:

> he does not sufficiently emphasise the point that this dependence is conditioned by an activity, and that it appears at the limits of this activity. Nor does he make it sufficiently obvious that this dependence makes itself felt in the struggle for those values which appear to man to be the highest.[47]

Our dependence is not to be interpreted as utter helplessness or feebleness which is relieved by God, but as the completion of an activity which fulfills our needs by one who "is perfect where we are imperfect."[48] Alexander claims that man has apparently the temerity to require that God shall satisfy his deepest needs, and even the mystical experience does not mean the obliteration of man but the satisfaction of man's deepest need so that a self-abandonment in which there was on one side complete loss and on the other side no gain is scarcely conceivable.[49]

Hence, in the higher religions, man's obedience to God is a "dignified obedience" given by man with his limited standards of what is great and highest to a higher being who sustains him and whom he regards as worthy of trust. Our attitude is not one of silent resignation but active co-operation with a divine partner. In the higher religions our trust is not given in an attempt to placate God or win him over but is given because "we desire" him:

> It appears in the consciousness that goodness or even a certain ritual is not merely demanded by God but pleasing to him.[50]

If Alexander assumes that this is the religious consciousness in the higher religions, it would seem that he has not sufficiently distinguished prophetic religion which stresses the ethical demands of God from the ritualistic which tends to placate God by means of a proper ritual.[51] He is in agreement, however, with certain modern conceptions of God which assert:

> that we also help to maintain and sustain the nature of God and are not merely his subjects; that God himself is involved in our acts and their issues, or, as it was put above, not only does he matter to us, but we matter to him.[52]

Thus does Alexander summarize the religious requirements for the conception of God which he claims traditional religion has found valid: That God should be greater than man; an all-inclusive being; different in quality from man; and, finally, responsive to man. We have seen that Alexander's own metaphysics of God as the body of Space-Time straining after deity in some respects agrees with and in other respects differs from, these requirements of the religious consciousness. There is still necessary a comparison of Alexander's own view of deity with doctrines of God made familiar by the philosophy of religion. To this examination we now give our attention.

Theism and Pantheism.—These two conceptions of God belong to the philosophy of religion rather than to the religious consciousness because they involve reflective thought as to God's relation to the world and to his creatures. They are in a sense metaphysical[53] and by that very fact invite comparison with Alexander's own doctrines.

Alexander defines theism as that doctrine in which "God is an individual being distinct from the finite beings which make up the world,"[54] disregarding for the moment whether God is regarded as the creator of the finites, or as in Aristotle's philosophy he moves the finites "from without."[55] In any case, theism implies the transcendence of God while pantheism implies that "God is immanent in the universe of finite things."[56] Moreover, pantheism has two forms: a less exalted and satisfying form in which God is considered as the mere presence which animates the world; and a more exalted form in which the world consists of fragments which owe their real existence to him.

> Hegel expressed the difference between these two varieties of pantheism in the phrase that in true pantheism God is not merely in everything, but everything is in God. Whatever form pantheism

assumes, there is no room for God outside the world, and immanence in the philosophical sense does not mean residence in this, that, or other, part of the world, but throughout, so that the immanent being is coextensive with the world which he indwells.[57]

There is a metaphysical system which might be mistaken for pantheism and this is Absolute Idealism, for the Absolute takes the place of a pantheistic God, while God in such a system of idealism becomes merely an appearance. Alexander establishes his point here by quoting the following from Bradley:

> We may say that God is not God till he has become all in all, and that a God which is all in all is not the God of religion. God is but an aspect, and that must mean an appearance of the Absolute.[58]

But to return to theism, Alexander emphasizes the idea of theism as that of a transcendent being outside the material world. To be sure this transcendent being includes our own life primarily as embodied spirit, as well as the "spirit" part of any creatures higher than ourselves, but the transcendent aspect of God means existence beyond any beings, no matter how high they may be with reference to man. Among examples of transcendent Gods, Alexander finds the Jewish God though in this case the transcendence is thought of in terms of moral considerations and not primarily in terms of metaphysics. Judaism, at least in its prophetic period, did not include much attention to an after-life, so pressing was the emphasis on the ethical life on earth.[59] Theism is differentiated from Deism in that the transcendent

DEITY AND THE RELIGIOUS CONSCIOUSNESS

God of theism is held to possess moral attributes, to enter into personal relations with his human creatures, and to manifest himself through revelation. Deism differs from theism for the most part in accentuating the externality of God and rejecting the notion of Christian revelation.

> Deism, in fact, is opposed not so much to theism as to revelation. Its God and his attributes and goings-on are discoverable by the light of nature only.[60]

As Deism is not a live doctrine, Alexander concentrates his attention on theism and pantheism. The strength of theism lies in the fact that it appeals to the personal or even egotistic side of the religious consciousness. Just as the truth-seeker puts aside prejudices and pettiness and achieves the fulfilment of his personality by the impersonal pursuit of truth, so the worshipper by putting aside his imperfections and surrendering to God achieves his individualilty which remains separate from God since God is always transcendent of man. God is awfully distant from man, possessing a quality which man does not have, and yet the God of theism does not absorb man as does the God of pantheism, but stands by man as a helper and sustains him as a father.[61] Hence God is both continuous and discontinuous with man. The continuous element is the pantheistic tendency in theism, but the discontinuous element is usually so prominent that the detachment of God from the world and his creatures is, for Alexander, a distinct speculative weakness.

This detachment of God may be thought of in a number of ways. God may be conceived as existing in his perfection before the creation of the world. A more profound meaning is that in which God creates both time and the world in the same moment, so that it is not exact to assume that there was a time in which God existed before he created the world. In theism as historically defined in the Christian tradition—though Alexander does not mention this point—time does not apply to God since time is a creature of God. In Alexander's conception of the body of God being the whole of Space-Time, however, infinite time *is* in Space-Time.

Another way to express the detachment of the transcendent God of theism from the world is in Plato's *Timaeus* in which

> God becomes then an artificer shaping or imposing form upon what is not a part of himself; he is what Kant, speaking of this conception, called aptly but slightingly an architect-god.[62]

The weakness of transcendent theism lies in the fact that it is difficult to reconcile with the immanence which is held to be somehow implied in it. The difficulty, as it appears in Alexander's mind, is as follows:

> If God's word is at the same time the coming into being of the material as well as the form of his creatures; if the theism becomes according to the current phrase an immanent one, we are at a loss to understand how this God, whose acts are his creatures, can also lead an existence separate from them, and can ever have, as he is supposed to have been, without them. The transcendence and immanence of God are postulated together without reconciliation.[63]

One may well inquire whether this is a correct rendering of traditional theology, for the phrase, "this God, whose acts are his creatures" is not found in traditional

Christian theology. In such theology, the actions of God are his from all eternity, and his creatures are created in time and the *result* of his actions. Also, may we not say that Alexander has emphasized the immanence of traditional theism to the point of pantheism, all the while recognizing that pantheism is utterly foreign to traditional theism? R. G. Collingwood appears to express traditional thought better than Alexander:

> Christianity . . . is equally hostile to a theism which restricts God's power, that is, makes him only one of the number of limited or finite beings, for the sake of preserving his goodness, and to a pantheism which denies his goodness in the interest of his infinitude.[64]

Returning to Alexander's argument, we find that he believes that the transcendence and immanence of God endeavor to satisfy two aspects of the religious consciousness: 1. that God shall be higher than man; 2. the "demand for unity of substance of man with God."[65] Again, he re-asserts the difficulty of a transcendent and immanent view of God, "if his deity at once permeates his creatures and transcends them."[66] But this permeation of God into his creatures is not a correct interpretation of traditional theism. Once more, Collingwood seems to be a better interpreter:

> Christian theology regards God as spirit, exercising creative power, however conceived, over the world of matter. This material world is supposed truly to exist, that is, to be no mere illusion: but yet to be not self-existent but to depend for its existence and nature on will.[67]

It seems clear that a material world, as creature of

God, depends for its existence on the will of God, so that it is sustained by God, and this is a different concept from Alexander's view of God's permeation of his creatures.

Alexander, however, continues his objection and, with reference to Leibniz's system of monads, asserts:

> The monads at once mirror God and are his creations. Thus the so-called immanent theism has never, so far as I know, been clearly distinguished from pantheism; there is always lingering about the conception a suspicion that without much regard for consistency it seeks to combine the religious attraction of theism with the speculative attraction of pantheism.[68]

The orthodox theist might object that immanent theism is still to be distinguished from pantheism, since the theory of the monads as creatures of God does not mean that God is immanent in them, but rather that God sustains them without being identified with them.

Another reconciliation of immanence and transcendence is sought through the familiar doctrine of the God-man, a doctrine present especially in Christianity:

> We may even conceive a special being, a God-man, in whom God is historically revealed, in whom divinity has taken human shape; and in such a person God would really be immanent. But if we pretend that in this way theism and pantheism are combined, we expose ourselves to that besetting danger of theology to which I have alluded above; we divert our conceptions from their proper use. . . . Supposing that the highest religious consciousness demands a historical per-

sonage, who is a man but really God . . . that experience is not to be described in rational terms as a synthesis of immanence and transcendence or of pantheism and theism; but if it can be rationalised at all, demands different conceptions.[69]

Alexander is adamant in his view of the impossibility of a reconciliation between divine immanence and d'vine transcendence: "If God is coextensive with the world, he does not transcend it. If he transcends it, he is not immanent in it."[70]

But the very transcendence of the God of theism signifies for Alexander an artificial relation to his creatures for he does not share their lives. He remains outside them, ruling them through wisdom and attracting them to him through love. Hence theology feels the need to bridge the gap[71] between man and God through the postulation of a perfect type of manhood in which God is embodied. This doctrine is called the incarnation, but Alexander, as we have observed, finds it artificial.[72] Equally artificial is the connection of the God of theism with nature for his control over nature seems to be arbitrary and obeys no principle. The God of undiluted theism becomes merely the greatest thing in a universe of things, and is dowered with finite qualities through the mythologizing imagination of man.[73]

This criticism of the transcendent God of theism seems to be corroborated by A. S. Pringle-Pattison:

> Primitive man was insured to an arbitrary despotism which uses power for selfish aggrandizement and luxury, and sees in the subject populations only the instruments of its own pomp and glory; and the attitude of the Oriental ruler to his people is half-unconsciously transferred by the wor-

shipper to his god. And although the relationship became purged in time of its baser features, and might be characterized, as in the case of Israel and Jahve, by a singular intimacy and depth of feeling, still the conception of God remains that of a purely transcendent Being, whose own life is not involved in the fortunes of mankind.[74]

Furthermore, Alexander perceives fresh difficulties for theism in its various doctrines of creation, regarding these problems as aspects of the general question of immanence and transcendence. He introduces a very brief discussion of doctrines of creation as follows:

> Their religious significance lies in the belief that somehow God and his world are not disjoined, and that at least God, if not the cause or ground of the world, is its last and supreme meaning.[75]

For pantheism, God is not a creator since all things are within the one reality which is God. God is the cause of all things, as Spinoza expressed it, only in the sense that a triangle is the cause that the sum of its three angles is equal to two right angles.[76]

While the pantheistic God does not create in a real sense of the term, the transcendent God does create, "and creates out of a pre-existent material,"[77] whether this be chaos which he fashions into specific forms, or whether these forms come into being out of the chaos ("the face of the waters") by his word. Alexander finds validity in Kant's remarks concerning a God who creates in the sense of fashioning previously existing material:

> It is hardly necessary, after Kant, to labour the point that a God who creates the world out of materials which he finds is no creator but an arti-

ficer; it is more useful to add that the material upon which he works limits his power.[78]

Alexander here hints at a finite God doctrine, but he does not develop the point at all. He jumps to the idea of an omnipotent God:

> An omnipotent God cannot create, except from himself, and he ceases then to be transcendent. And yet if he is regarded as a creator, and in some sense a person, he cannot but be transcendent.[79]

Here we see the pantheistic *motif* which runs through Alexander's interpretation of theism. Is it a correct interpretation? Is he right in suggesting that God creates from himself, so that he is immanent in his creation, and thus ceases to be transcendent, while at the same time God as a creator is held to be transcendent? Upon closer examination of doctrines of creation held in traditional theology, the head-on collision which Alexander seems to visualize between transcendence and immanence does not occur. Bertocci in interpreting the traditional doctrine of creation makes clear the view that God is not to be identified with his creatures, nor is the world created out of himself:

> *What is meant by creation?* God, we have said, is not to be identified with his creatures: what we call matter, life, and finite mind is not to be considered a part of God or the continuous overflow or emanation of his Being.... All that is not God depends for its existence upon God—this is the fundamental thought in the doctrine of creation. But if God did not create the world "out of" himself, and if he did not create it "out of something

not himself," how did he create it? Many theologians and philosophers reply: Out of nothing![80]

Alexander, in fact, considers the concept of creation out of nothing, but dismisses it as one more instance of his favorite illustration of the conflict between theism and pantheism:

> 'Creation out of nothing' is to speak the language of immanence while using the idea of transcendence, to speak pantheism and to think theistically.[81]

This is all he says. He does not explain how "creation out of nothing" refers to the language of immanence, or of pantheism. But it would appear that those who use the expression "creation out of nothing" did it to prevent any possibility of pantheism:

> By saying that God created 'out of nothing' we are simply denying (a) that he made it out of something, and (b) that the creation is to be identified with him. Frankly, we do not know what is actually involved in God's creation.[82]

It would seem that Alexander is not as well informed as he might be on the meaning of certain orthodox doctrines, quite apart from the question as to whether these doctrines are ultimately valid.

Turning to pantheism, Alexander finds that it is not the ideal solution for it "is strong where theism is weak and weak where that is strong."[83] Its chief defect is the difficulty of retaining the independence and freedom of the worshipper. The individual is lost in God, and the religious feeling of trustful dependence is replaced by that of mystical ecstasy. Prayer as intercession and appeal is transformed into the feeling of "blessedness and love."[84] The individual demands no return from God, and Spinoza's intellectual love of God is simply part of the infinite love emanating from God, and asks nothing for itself.

A consequence of this complete merging of man and God in pantheism is "that the transition between God's divinity and human morality is made difficult for reflection."[85] Though the following chapter will indicate that deity and goodness are different conceptions for Alexander, they are nevertheless related, and in pantheism since all the finites are modes of existence of God, "good and evil are alike contained in him."[86] This old difficulty signifies that since evil and good are both contained in God, he cannot be worshipped. This is the great problem of pantheism. Both theism and pantheism are then religiously unsatisfactory, at least in some of their implications, and Alexander is of the opinion that persons convinced of these inadequacies "substitute enthusiastic devotion to goodness for religion proper."[87]

Pantheism, however, has the speculative advantage that it supplies the comprehensive and unlabored connection between man, nature, and God, which theism, as we have observed, fails to supply satisfactorily. But this very speculative advantage is at the same time a speculative defect in "merging individuality into the nebulous whole."[88] This speculative defect also signifies a religious insufficiency, for the Absolute of pantheism ultimately does not permit the finite creature the real independence which is required for a free being.

Both theism and pantheism are then philosophic views of religion which are partly satisfactory and partly unsatisfactory besides being impossible of reconciliation. It seems obvious that Alexander's own presentation of

GOD AND SPACE-TIME

Space-Time as the body of God whose divinity consists in his deity is different from either theism or pantheism:

> If the question is asked, whether the speculative conception of God or deity which has been advanced here as part of the empirical treatment of Space-Time and has appeared to be verified by religious experience belongs to theism or pantheism, the answer must be that it is not strictly referable to either of them, taken by itself; that in different respects it belongs to both; and that if a choice must be made it is theistic.[89]

In Alexander's metaphysics, then, objections are raised to the usual theistic and pantheistic conceptions of God as being irreconcilable one with the other. Nevertheless, when these conceptions are modified so as to be applied to certain aspects of Alexander's fundamental view of the universe as the body of God tending to deity, it seems that his view of God does justice to both theism and pantheism. For God is conceived as built on the same pattern as every finite, of which man is one, indeed on the same pattern as Space-Time itself. Every finite as well as the whole of Space-Time has a "body" part and a "soul" part. God's body is the whole of Space-Time and thus includes all finites as connected in the circumambient sea of spatio-temporal continuity in which they are not dissolved or absorbed. Thus God's body includes all finites as fragments, and the circumambient matrix of Space-Time in which these finites are sustained. At any moment of observation of Space-Time, whether it be primordial Space-Time or Space-Time developed up to our own moment of observation, God's body includes all that exists, and in respect of his body, God is then pantheistic, though the finites retain their individuality.[90]

DEITY AND THE RELIGIOUS CONSCIOUSNESS

God's soul is deity which does not permeate the whole world, as it does in the strict pantheistic conception,[91] but is an infinite part of Space-Time which carries the empirical quality of deity. God is in process towards this quality of deity, and the moment the quality is realized in "finite god or angel,"[92] deity is then present in a finite portion of space and time, but, according to the conception of multiple transcendence[93] a higher quality of deity looms ahead to be realized with the forward movement of the nisus of Space-Time, and with a still higher quality of deity ahead in the time series. God in respect of his quality of deity

> transcends all finites, because he is the whole world as tending to a higher order of finites. In this, which is the more important respect, the conception is theistic. [94]

Then follows a sentence which requires more explanation than Alexander has given to it:

> On the other hand, though he transcends all finites in quality, his deity remains within the world and he is in no sense outside it.[95]

Obviously, at any moment in the history of the finites in Space-Time, deity as the next empirical quality always transcends in quality the quality just added as the last addition to the hierarchical order of qualities. This is the meaning of Alexander's expression, "though he transcends all finites in quality." But to do justice to the view that God's deity "remains within the world and he is in no sense outside it" we must have recourse to the view of Space-Time as a total historicity of successive additions of qualities, all within Space-Time. The successive empirical qualities higher than mind and denoted as the various phases of deity are then obviously realized successively in the history of Space-Time in an infinite number of finite individuals, so that deity remains infinite but is within the world fragmented into an indeterminate number of empirical qualities manifested in an infinite number of individuals. But since Space-Time is an infinite succession the quality of deity remains in the future, and though fragmented into an increasing number of empirical qualities, Alexander can still state: "Yet his deity is not localized in any special class of finites."[96]

There is another sense, however, in Alexander's statement that God's deity is not localized in any special class of finites, and in this sense we may find ourselves in greater agreement. The higher qualities are dependent on those of a lower order, just as mind is dependent on the biological organism, and this organism dependent in turn on physico-chemical processes, and these are configurations of Space-Time. In this hierarchical order, deity is higher than mind—whether at one remove or at many removes—and is sustained by all the finites and ultimately by the whole universe:

> Since his deity depends on mind, and this in turn on finites of a lower order, until ultimately we reach the simple matrix of Space-Time; there is no part of the universe which is not used up to sustain the deity of God.[97]

Moreover, all human beings and finites "are comparable to organic sensa which God contemplates in enjoying his deity."[98] That is to say, the divine enjoyments of God consist of God's enjoyment of his deity, and his deity as supported by all the finites and by Space-Time is compresent with all of these finites as objects of his contemplation.[99]

All these objects of contemplation are the finites which are part of the body of God, and "He therefore possesses the totality which pantheism assigns to God."[100] These finites, as Alexander repeatedly insists, are not lost or absorbed in the body of God, but are the very substances which in their hierarchical order sustain the quality of deity. The connection which pantheism finds difficult to make between God and the finites is here given a significance which preserves the finites in their inherent individuality and quality and yet releases them from their isolation. They are no longer isolated, because God through his "body" of Space-Time includes and sustains these finites. And they are given a significance greater than their individuality and greater than their momentary connection in Space-Time by the fact that deity as a future emergent represents the goal of their efforts and is sustained by them.[101]

Alexander's conception of God and his deity thus represents immanent theism, though he prefers to avoid this term altogether due to its obscurity. Theism and pantheism represent the extremes of thought about the divine which, though difficult of reconciliation in traditional forms of thought, are reconciled in Alexander's novel type of metaphysics about God:

> They represent the two essential characters which God shares with all other things and with Space-Time itself, of being both body and soul. God is immanent in respect of his body, but transcendent in respect of his deity.[102]

Thus does Alexander claim to do justice to the two

conceptions of the divine which are present in the philosophy of religion, the theistic and the pantheistic. In fact he claims to do more than justice to them in that in his system they are reconciled and mutually enriched. These conceptions satisfy the religious consciousness informed by Alexander's system, and though he has been generous in interpreting his views so as to satisfy as much as possible traditional religious thought, he is aware that his notion of God

> seems to contain features incompatible with the philosophical or rather theological and traditional or conventional formulae which are inevitably mingled with the unreflective deliverances of religious feeling.[103]

There are, however, two questions which the "current reflective theism"[104] answers affirmatively but which Alexander's theism answers differently: Is God a Creator? and, Is God in Space and Time or does he exist independently of the process of Time?

Is God a Creator?—In approaching answers to these questions, Alexander counters by the suggestion that the immediate deliverances of religious emotion are data for science and for a system of metaphysics, but the semi-speculative conceptions which are traditionally constructed from these data "are not entitled to particular respect."[105] This is why Alexander interprets primitive notions of God as terrible monarch and more civilized ideas of God as benevolent father, as data for religious experience; but a speculative venture to transform the emotive meaning of these experiences through the statement "that God existed before the world and created it in so many days in a certain order"[106] is only an attempt to formulate in scientific terms the conception of the relation of God and the universe. Such attempts do vary from crude mythology to profound theology and are affected by tradition and custom. They are theories about God and not facts about what God is felt to be. Similarly the emotional overtones of the belief in immortality are "of the last importance"[107] but "it is of comparatively little importance to know that they think their soul must be immortal because it is immaterial."[108]

Alexander's purpose would appear to be the enhancement of the religious sentiment *qua* feeling with the depreciation of the current theological theories constructed to explain or justify this sentiment which may be difficult to validate through a rigorous metaphysical analysis. In this way, he prepares the ground for a more favorable reception of his own metaphysics to which he refers in the following passage:

> Thus a metaphysical theory, we may be prepared to find, may satisfy religious feeling and yet not altogether satisfy the current reflective conceptions about God; and at the same time we may find that in spite of this it may offer a better hope of solution of some of the practical difficulties to the religious mind.[109]

By "current reflective conceptions about God" Alexander means the theological conceptions of God in the Christian tradition. It is of the essence of Alexander's position that his own system, while not satisfying current theological conceptions of God, does satisfy religious feeling and may solve some of the practical difficulties of the religious spirit.

The sharpest contrast between theology and Alexander's metaphysics lies in the fact that theology regards God as creator, but Alexander regards him as creative in the sense that God's body is the whole of Space-Time including all the finites, and within this body the finites emerge through internal rearrangements of the matrix:

> because Time is the moving principle that brings out that constant redistribution in the matrix which is equivalent to the birth of finite forms.[110]

Even if we consider the nisus of Space-Time rather than Time as the moving principle, it still remains true that "Space-Time itself . . . is the creator and not God."[111] God is not creative of the finites but of the next empirical quality of deity, and yet there is a sense in which God is creator:

> It is only when we look back and identify God's body with its previous stages and ultimately with Space-Time itself that we can speak of him as a creator. God himself, that is the universe as tending to deity, is creative only of deity.[112]

There are two different conceptions involved here and it will be interesting to disentangle them and ascertain their relationship. If we "look back," that is to say, consider the vision of Space-Time at a moment and imagine this moment to be when no finites have as yet emerged from the matrix of Space-Time, then God is identical with primordial Space-Time, and God is indeed creator of all the finites and of the various phases of deity to which we have referred on several occasions. God is the creator, and creative precisely in the same sense that primordial Space-Time actually is. The other conception of God present in this passage is God as the universe as tending to deity and in this case God is creative only of "deity." Why this difference? It is due to Alexander's conception that the universe is in Space-Time, but

Space-Time itself is not in the universe, but is the stuff of which the universe is made. There is ambiguity here in Alexander's thought as to whether God shall be considered as the totality of primordial Space-Time (in which case he is creator), or whether he shall be considered as an infinite creature of the universe of Space-Time:

> God then, like all things in the universe—for Space-Time itself is not in the universe, whereas God, since his deity is a part of the universe, is in it—is in the strictest sense not a creator but a creature. I need hardly say I do not mean that he is a creature of our imagination or of our thought. He is an infinite creature of the universe of Space-Time.[113]

It may be that this ambiguity is due to a lack of precise distinction between the body of God and the "deity" of God. God considered as "deity" is the outcome of "the pre-existing finites with their empirical qualities"[114] and is indeed a creature, *but only qua deity*. But God considered as "body" cannot consistently be considered as being merely "in it,"[115] meaning in the universe, but is the whole universe of Space-Time. Alexander has clearly stated that when God's body is identified with Space-Time itself, "we can speak of him as a creator."[116] Is God's body less creative the moment we no longer "look back" at primordial Space-Time but consider his body as the universe as tending to deity, meaning the finites as tending to deity? It seems strange that before any qualitied existents have emerged from the matrix of Space-Time, God is identical with Space-Time and is then fully a creator, but the moment qualitied existents have arisen, God must be given a secondary position as a creature of Space-Time, and be regarded "in the strictest sense not a creator but a creature."[117] If this were so, we would have the incongruous conception of the maximum creativity of God effective when God is identical with primordial Space-Time, but a quick volte-face from God as creator to God as creature the moment material existents emerge. This confusion, we believe, is due to Alexander's lack of consistency in his conception of the meaning of the body of God. Had he maintained consistently that the body of God is Space-Time and not merely the finites in Space-Time, then at any moment of observation (or imagination), primordial Space-Time, or Space-Time at a moment, or Space-Time under the vision of its complete historicity, God is always creator. It remains true, however, that the deity of God as an infinite portion of total Space-Time is a creature.

Alexander believes that this very emergence of deity from lower stages of existence makes intelligible the mutual responsiveness of man and God which religion demands. The religious sentiment which culminates in worship implies co-operation and in Alexander's metaphysics this co-operation is interpreted in these terms:

> if our sentiment proceeds from a conation adapted to the universe in its forward tendency, God in his turn is adapted to that conation and satisfies it, and it is as satisfying it that we discover his deity. [118]

The doctrine of the fatherhood of God, however, is not quite appropriate until it is correlated more strictly into Alexander's metaphysics. God's deity is sustained by all the finites, and these in turn are sustained by Space-Time, so that the contribution which we make to deity *qua* finite is infinitesimal. But our dependence on God, which we recognize under the figure of fatherhood, signifies that God gathers up in his body the whole infinite world to which we belong. In trusting ourselves to the deity of God, we are aware of our continuity with the whole as permeated with a divine quality which emerges in deity. Alexander could have made use of his notion of the nisus of Space-Time which permeates every finite and makes us continuous both with the body of God and his deity. He also used the expression: "God gathers up for us in his person the whole infinite world to which we belong,"[119] but it is doubtful if Alexander really means that God is a person, since it is apparent that in his metaphysical scheme God as the totality of Space-Time is a structured creativity permeated by the nisus, and giving rise to persons, but this structured creativity is not itself a person. Alexander has not accentuated here as much as is desirable the difference between his conception and that of the personal God of traditional theology.

In any case, such symbolic phrases as "being lifted up in the arms of God," "lying in Abraham's bosom," "grace and redemption or forgiveness of sins,"[120] are interpreted as referring to "this mysterious largeness of sustainment,"[121] which means that we are sustained by the creativity of God which supports not only our little selves, but the totality of finites as tending to deity. But Alexander seems to be adamant that the notion of a creator God "is a hybrid blending of the creative Space-Time with the created deity."[122] We must not search for deity by a backward glance but through the forward view which is so characteristic of Alexander:

> In Meredith's 'Thrush in February' there occurs the line, 'the rapture of the forward view.' I here

commend in religion and theology the forward view . . . for the forward view man's life is preparatory to the outgrowth of the divine quality. Every man is in this notion prophetic of deity, and there are certain men of religious genius who, being prophetic in an eminent degree and with rarer insight, are distinguished by the name of prophets, of whom Jesus is one. God is not the already perfect being who for the benefit of imperfect man takes human shape, but is himself in the making, and his divine quality or deity a stage in time beyond the human quality.[123]

All finites, in this novel conception, have a part in sustaining deity, so that the remarkable reversal of the usual religious conception of duty as a command of God is suggested by Alexander in his statement that "it is religion to do our duty with the consciousness of helping to create his deity."[124] Whether this conception is satisfactory to the usual religious consciousness is a "question I would submit for consideration,"[125] he opines. However, he is convinced that love given and returned is as conceivable to a being greater than ourselves who draws us forward to himself for the strength of our aspirations, as to a being who draws us backward to himself in time because we are his creatures.[126]

Accentuation on "the forward view" has resulted in serious misunderstanding of Alexander's system—which he himself acknowledges:

A friend of mine jested to me of the God of Abraham, Isaac, and Jacob who is to exist a million of years hence. But the jest is a misconception. For the Universe as straining towards deity is a present reality. And the Universe so conceived is

DEITY AND THE RELIGIOUS CONSCIOUSNESS

God. It is only the actual existence of deity which belongs to the future.[127]

In concluding Alexander's discussion of God as creator or creative, we make the observation that such misconceptions of Alexander's system would have been avoided had Alexander placed greater emphasis on the universe as being the body of God, and had given greater prominence to the nisus of Space-Time as the manifestation of the creativity of God at any stage of the evolution of Space-Time. Not only is God creative of deity, but if our interpretation of the identity of the body of God and the Space-Time matrix inclusive of the finites is correct, then God is creator and not merely creature. God as identical with Space-Time and its emergents is a substantive concept of God, while deity as identified with a portion of Space-Time and as a quality would appear to be an adjectival conception of God.

God's supposed Timelessness.—Alexander gives an unambiguous answer to this question, and in doing so, we may add parenthetically, he substantiates the emphasis we have just made on the interpretation of God's body as Space-Time itself:

> God's body is not spaceless nor timeless, for it is Space-Time itself. His deity is located in an infinite portion of Space-Time, and it is in fact essentially in process and caught in the general movement of Time.[128]

As we have indicated on several occasions in the course of the development of Alexander's metaphysics, we have here two infinites of space and time, the infinity which is deity and occupying an infinite portion of Space-Time, but still a portion; and the total infinity

GOD AND SPACE-TIME

of Space-Time which includes deity and other infinites such as infinite numbers, infinite series, etc. God's body is not timeless but includes Time as both a continuum and succession. God's deity is not timeless but includes a part of infinite Time. But if we accentuate the successive character of Time and not its total continuity, deity is essentially a process in the general movement of Time. In calling deity a process, Alexander approaches his conception of the nisus.

For the criticism of the supposed timelessness of God, Alexander introduces moral considerations. A timeless God, upon reflective thought, suggests a being "not caught in the machinery of the world, but a spectator who directs from without."[129] Such a being appears as a spectator especially when the religious consciousness (and Alexander might have added the secular consciousness) finds inexplicable the presence of futile suffering endured by the just. If all things are determined by the will of God, the question arises as to why a benevolent being has not set matters in such a way that pain is spared his creatures. The believer may rest content with the contemplation of divine sovereignty: "He hath made man thus and he doeth right."[130] However, some will not be satisfied by such an answer, and apparently Alexander is of their number, for delivering his Gifford Lectures during the first World War the spectacle of "the cost of endless sacrifice of precious lives"[131] seemed to prey on his mind. He exclaims:

> how is it possible to rest content with the idea of a God who does not share these vicissitudes of his creatures but suffers them to exist?[132]

He reacts so strongly against this conception of an apparently spectator, indifferent God that he finds great advantages in his own view of deity as the outcome of this world's struggles and of the efforts of human beings insofar as these efforts have value. It is not God who allows the struggle, but the struggle which is to determine what future deity is to be. In this way God is not responsible for our miseries, but we are responsible for our acts, though Alexander does not meet the problem of miseries endured but not due to our acts. When men engaged in a global struggle pray to God symbolized as a person, the ideal so embodied is the call of the universe as a whole, but more exactly, the call of the tendency of the whole world to deity towards which the individual goes out in religion as he envisages the meaning of that tendency by means of his personal symbolism. In other words, though Alexander does not use this terminology at this point, it is the nisus of Space-Time which, acting on our minds and hearts as we are involved in conflicts, stimulates our being to appeal to a source of help which signifies the outcome of the nisus in terms of the elimination of evil and of greater social harmony. Alexander seems to consider the problem of evil from two alternatives: 1. The spectator, omnipotent, omniscient God of traditional theism who apparently does nothing to overcome the miseries of his children; 2. The rejection of the spectator view of theism for deity as a future empirical quality surpassing the highest that we find in human mind or spirit, but which our struggles help to construct. There may be other alternatives to the problem of evil, but they are not considered by Alexander. He seems satisfied with his summary of the situation:

> A created deity makes our human position more serious but frees it from the reproach of subjection to arbitrary providence.[133]

GOD AND SPACE-TIME

While the timelessness of God is a speculative problem for theism, that is to say, it leads to perplexities, pantheism is not in a more advantageous position. Spinoza's pantheism, for instance, includes Substance, Extension and Thought, but not Time, so that we do not understand how the finites issue from God. Alexander prefers the substitution of Time for mind:

> Whereas if in this scheme we substitute Time for mind, the world of finites arises out of the mere restlessness of Space-Time. Mind then becomes nothing but a finite of a particular empirical rank.[134]

It is worthy of note that in this instance, Alexander liberates his thought from the metaphorical views of Time as the mind of Space, but limits mind to a finite of a certain empirical rank.

Furthermore, a God of timeless Substance or Space-Time

> ceases also to be the object of worship—that is, ceases as such with mere attributes of Space and Time to be God. He needs the empirical quality of deity.[135]

But the empirical quality of deity is brought to birth through the activity of the nisus, so that in our interpretation of this phase of Alexander's philosophy, we would enhance the role of the nisus much more than he has done, so as to establish that the fundamental conception of the universe which evokes the religious sentiment is not merely Space-Time, but Space-Time as energized into hierarchical order by its nisus.

Summary.—Alexander's method in elaborating the relationship between his metaphysical conception of God as possessing deity and the religious sentiment is to take religious emotion as fundamental in man and elicited by the impact of the nisus of Space-Time which penetrates man and all finites. The advantage of this conception—and we agree with Alexander's emphasis at this point—is that religion is thus founded on Reality, and is not to be relegated to a mere subjective feeling, nor to a socially utilitarian system of ethics.

In describing the characteristics of the religious conception of God, however, Alexander seems deliberately to have chosen very general terms—God as greater than man, God different in quality from man, God as universal, God as responsive to man—so that there is a rough correspondence between these criteria and Alexander's own conception of God and deity. There is not a precise correspondence with the traditional view of God's omniscience, personality, creativity, and eternity. For instance, God's omniscience is transformed in Alexander's metaphysics—as we have attempted to indicate in detail—into the knowledge which is had by the finites, inclusive of man and higher than man. A close examination of this conception led inevitably to the view that deity through the ongoing process of Time becomes fragmented into empirical qualities of a higher order than mind and possessed by beings of a higher order than man. It is not correct, therefore, for Alexander to speak of God and deity in terms of "person"[136] and to refer to either in terms of personal pronouns such as "him," "he" or "his."[137] It is therefore incorrect for Alexander to speak of a loving mutuality between man and deity, except in the Spinozist sense in which man's love for God is an expression of God's love for himself.

This fragmentation of deity into an infinity of living existents, assuming that we carry through to its logical

GOD AND SPACE-TIME

conclusion Alexander's speculative venture, renders more precarious his conception of deity especially in its successive phases. What seems to remain is the conception of the nisus as creative process, and this is the reason why we tend to emphasize the nisus much more than does Alexander.

As a defensive strategy against the lack of correspondence between the religious criteria of the idea of God and his own conception, he then finds defects in two conceptions of the divine present in the philosophy of religion—theism and pantheism. The lack of reconciliation between these two conceptions of God, Alexander seizes upon as argumentation for their reconciliation within *his* framework of the body of God as the valid pantheistic element, and deity as the valid theistic element in his philosophy.

When considering in what sense God is a creator, we were not convinced of the conception of God as a creature of Space-Time, since Alexander equates Space-Time with the body of God, at least in some of his statements on the subject.

We are, then, making important modifications in Alexander's system insofar as it has been examined up to this point. These modifications involve:

1. An increasing doubt as to the utility of the successive phases of deity, though it seems that this conception is logically derived by an extension of his speculation as to finite gods and angels.

2. A heightened appreciation of the meaning of nisus as creative process active in Space-Time at all levels though not equally present in all the localities of Space-Time. This is the infra-pantheistic conception to which we shall recur in an attempt to compare it with modern

theologies of empirical theism, such as Henry Nelson Wieman's.

3. A rejection of God as a creature of Space-Time through emphasis on Alexander's statements in which he has clearly implied that the body of God is identical with the Space-Time matrix, plus finites.

Other modifications, especially in connection with value and emergence will be made in the critical part of the work.

CHAPTER IV

DEITY AND VALUE

The Uniqueness of the Religious Sentiment.—Alexander's contrast of deity with value may best be approached by giving due appreciation to his vindication of the unique quality of the religious sentiment. The religious sentiment is the sense of our outgoing to the whole universe in its process towards the as yet unrealized quality of deity.[1] Space is apprehended by intuition, sensible qualities by sensation, universals present in finites by thought, values by appreciation, and God as the universe straining to deity is apprehended by a sentiment "with a unique flavour of its own, corresponding to its specific object."[2] The religious sentiment may gather to itself other sentiments, such as our response to the phenomena of nature, especially if they excite the quality of awe, or our pursuit of truth, or our appreciation of artistic beauty, or our devotion to moral values. But though these other sentiments be interwoven with the religious sentiment, it suffuses them all with the flavor of its own quality, and is not merely any one of them or any combination of them. This is because

> The universe in its nisus towards deity acts on the mind in a manner more closely allied to the affections produced by purely physical conditions than to the feeling of goodness or beauty.[3]

DEITY AND VALUE

To be sure, aesthetic contemplation may first evoke the religious sentiment; or the pursuit of science may give the investigator the feeling of "the vast beyond which is unknown" and which presents a tantalizing sublimity which evokes the response to deity. Morality, however, in both primitive and advanced religions, is so closely connected with the religious sentiment that their separation involves closer examination. Morality and religion are not differentiated in primitive thought, any more than the separate branches of science are distinguished from one another. Moreover, religious sentiment is both "sanctuary of the heart"[4] and communal worship, and this binds the community together in divine observances which possess an institutional character. The strength of organized religion is due to a large degree to its communal and institutional character. "The interrelation therefore of religion and morality is of the closest,"[5] especially in their institutional character, but nevertheless the sentiment of religion and the sense of moral value are quite distinct, in a greater degree than physics and philosophy are themselves distinct from one another.

As additional proof of the distinctness of religion and morality, Alexander is of the opinion that the religious sense may be found in intense form in persons who have no special feeling for the good, or who may even be bad characters.[6] Fraud and hypocrisy may account for many of such persons, but Alexander thinks there is a residue whose sincerity of feeling towards God cannot or need not be doubted. Much more prevalent are the persons who are virtuous but blind to the sentiment evoked by deity. Religion may exist without virtue, and virtue without religion, and therefore, Alexander hastily concludes the two are distinct. He is therefore compelled to disagree with Höffding who stated:

> The religious relation is always characterised by the effort to hold fast to the conservation of whatever is valuable in existence, apart from any considerations as to what value man esteems most highly or what his conception of existence may be. But the existence of the religious feeling is only possible on the presupposition that men have experienced life, truth, beauty and goodness. The religious feeling comes into operation when these values are compared with actual reality.[7]

Alexander objects to Höffding's presupposition that religion is a secondary value based on a prior existence of goodness, and regards it as a defect. He also rejects Bradley's statement:

> Morality is led beyond itself into a higher form of goodness. It ends in what we may call religion.[8]

These rejections of the relationship between morality and religion are presented by Alexander for the purpose of further establishing his conviction that religion is a brute instinct or brute conation of human nature—brute not in its ordinary sense of baseness, but as given in the very structure of our constitution—and is not merely our constitution's response to morality or art. Enthusiasm for religion is distinguishable from the passion with which we approach nature, or beauty, or morality, or truth, and though a brute conation it is the highest which we possess since its object is the most perfect being. Alexander quotes exultantly from William James to make his emphasis more convincing:

> Like love, like wrath, like hope, ambition, jealousy, like every other instinctive eagerness and impulse, it adds to life an enchantment which is

not rationally or logically deducible from anything else. . . . If religion is to mean anything definite for us, it seems to me we ought to take it as meaning this added dimension of emotion, this enthusiastic temper of espousal, in regions where morality strictly called can only bow its head and acquiesce.[9]

Ethics, then, cannot be substituted for religion, though those possessed of an ethical passion may consider it as a religion, though it is not itself the religious passion. This is why Alexander criticizes the Ethical Culture movement: "Those admirable institutions, the Ethical Societies, do not for that reason seem to me to supply a really adequate solution of the problem."[10] Admittedly, the name "Ethical Culture" indicates an undue stress on ethics, but some pronouncements of Felix Adler seem to indicate that for him the all embracing cosmic sense was not lost:

> Religion in a broad sense may be taken to mean any cause in which we are supremely interested. But in its more special signification it means a cosmic faith—not only the desire to improve conditions among men in this little human colony that dwells upon one of the smallest planets of the universe, but an outreaching toward the vast scheme of things—a cosmic sense not only of mystery but of trust. An ethical religion means interpreting this immense Nature about us in terms of the highest that human nature can be or think of.[11]

Alexander would probably agree that in Adler's cosmic orientation there is an interpretation of religion which is more than regard for ethical values. Alexander, however, would still insist that religion is not merely a cosmic orientation, but an awareness

> of our failing, not in the eyes of men, but of the being in front of us, towards whom our brute instinct impels us.[12]

By "the being in front of us" Alexander means the quality of deity which is in front, or ahead, in a temporal sense.

Deity and Goodness.—In an attempt to indicate exactly where he differs from Höffding, Alexander explains his own conceptions of deity and goodness:

> In a striking formula Mr. Höffding has defined religion as the faith in the conservation of values. God is the principle of that conservation, and religious feeling is felt in the comparison of value with reality. My criticism of this conception is not that it is untrue, for it is true and of the highest importance, but that it is too reflective and describes rather something which is true of religion than what religion is. The faith of religion was, as we saw, a faith in the existence of deity, not in the conservation of value.[13]

The primary difference is this: "In the first place deity is not in itself a value, for values are human inventions and deity is ultra-human."[14] Deity belongs to the order of perfection as the highest quality, and not to that of value, which Alexander calls "a human invention." We shall return to the meaning of this peculiar description of value presently, but at the moment we wish to explain Alexander's position for what it may be worth. We recall that deity is the highest empirical quality, the next in the succession of the emergence of these empirical qualities, the next always higher than the preceding one. Deity, then, belongs to the order of perfection. Alexander, be it noted, assumes here that the order of succession in Time is likewise an order of perfection. The order of qualities are matter, life, mind, and the various phases of deity, and deity therefore belongs to this order of perfection among the emergent qualities, deity in fact being the highest quality. This highest quality is possessed by the highest being in the universe, God, but he cannot be called the highest value, for at the level of deity, there is no *unvalue* with which he can be contrasted. On the level of mind there is no quality as *unmind;* accordingly Alexander thinks on the level of deity there is no such quality as *undeity*. Values, however, belong to various levels of existence, and on the human level there is a distinction between goodness and evil, between beauty and ugliness, between truth and error.

Perhaps a clearer understanding of the difference between value and deity in Alexander's system may be had by having recourse to the treatment in which he brings out the distinction between value as relation, and deity as quality:

> The confusion comes when religion is numbered as value along with truth and beauty and goodness, and when we go on to think of God or his distinctive deity as a value. Now value is always, we have seen, a relation, a relation between the object valued and the valuer or the subject for which the object has value. Neither God and his deity, nor religious beliefs, nor religious institutions, are relations.[15]

But does Alexander mean that the highest values, truth, beauty, and goodness are relations between subject and object, and do not exist objectively? This is precisely what he means:

> Their pre-eminence as values is that they have no being apart from their value.... They are human inventions, made to satisfy certain impulses of men. It is quite true we discover the statue in the stone and the beautiful landscape in the natural show which is spread before our eyes. Still, to discover them we must invent. Their value lies in their being held together with the mind which values them, which they satisfy.[16]

Even the highest values are, for Alexander, not discovered in the objective world, but are invented! Apart from the activity of the mind which imputes values to objects, and thus makes of value a relation between mind and object, there is no objective value. *It is here that Alexander's epistemological and metaphysical realism breaks down for a view of value which contains large elements of subjectivism.* Values are then not discovered objectively as existing independently of the mind which values, but God is so discovered in his objectivity. It is for this reason that Alexander apparently wishes to maintain as great a gap as possible between value and God, for to him the former is a human invention, and the latter is most manifestly not an invention, being a discovery of the objective nature of reality:

> The object of religion is neither supreme value, nor merely good, nor a mere object of natural election. God is a thing either in the world or

DEITY AND VALUE

> transcending it; and his deity is not an instance of value, like beauty or goodness, but really *is* a quality in the sense of ordinary, secondary or primary qualities. He is not a human invention. . . . It remains that God is not a value, except in the sense of interesting us objectively, which he shares with anything that affects us.[17]

Alexander is here departing very markedly from the philosophical tradition which has connected most intimately reality and value. A passage from A. E. Taylor will indicate the sharp difference between the two views:

> The possibility of genuine worship and religion is absolutely bound up with a final coincidence of existence and value in an object which is at once the most *real* of beings and the good "so good that none better can be conceived," at once the Alpha, the primary and absolute source of being, and the Omega, the ultimate goal of desire and endeavour.[18]

For Alexander, the possibility of worship is bound up precisely with the *lack* of coincidence of existence and value, for worship is the emotion directed to the quality, deity, while values are human inventions, or imputations. In order the better to appreciate this disjunction of value from deity in Alexander's system, we shall discuss more fully the tertiary qualities as understood by Alexander.

Truth, Goodness, and Beauty as Human Inventions. —It may seem an introduction of a prejudice against Alexander to describe the tertiary qualities as human inventions, but since this is the very term used by Alexander, we shall see that in the final analysis his value system is subjective, even though at first blush, it may seem to be composite of subject and object:

> Values then are unlike the empirical qualities of external things, shape, or fragrance, or life; they imply the amalgamation of the object with the human appreciation of it. Truth does not consist of mere propositions but of propositions as believed; beauty is felt; and good is the satisfaction of persons. . . . We have values of tertiary qualities in respect of the whole situation consisting of knower and known in their compresence. Strictly speaking, it is this totality of knower and known, of subject and object, which is true or good or beautiful.[19]

The tertiary qualities are not objective like the secondary ones, for the secondary quality "yellow" is objective, but the beauty of the flower whose yellow quality is perceived is not objective, but is a subject-object determination. Yet it must not be understood that part of the beauty belongs to the flower, and part of the beauty belongs to the mind, as if the aesthetic appreciation of the flower were a composite of these two parts. While color is an objective character, beauty is superadded to the object:

> For the colour in being judged beautiful is still seen as colour; its beauty is a character superadded to it from its relation to the mind in virtue of which it satisfies, or pleases after a certain fashion, or aesthetically.[20]

Beauty as a character superadded to the object which

is then called beautiful applies even in cases where, uninformed by Alexander's theory, we would be inclined to call nature beautiful:

> We find nature beautiful not because she is beautiful herself but because we select from nature and combine, as the artist does more plainly when he works with pigments. . . . Nature does live for herself without us to share her life. But she is not beautiful without us to unpiece her and repiece.[21]

Even in cases where the mind need not select aspects of beauty, but where nature appears in the form of lovely scenery, even here nature is not beautiful in her own right:

> It is the mute Keats or Wordsworth or the numb Turner within us which makes these scenes lovely, though our lips shall never and could never speak a poem nor our minds direct our hands to use the brush.[22]

When we judge nature to be lovely, it is not because nature possesses this quality. On the contrary, it is due to the mute Keats or the numb Turner moving within us which calls forth our appreciation, an appreciation which blossoms out into full-blooded artistic response in the real Keats and the real Turner! It becomes increasingly clear that while Alexander speaks of beauty as an object-subject determination, without the subject as artist or as appreciator, the object is almost nothing. True, the object provides the material, but the object has artistic value, not in itself, but because the artist mixes his mind with the material (to use a vivid expression of Alexander, not to be taken literally), and thus imputes characters to the marble which, obviously, it did not have prior to the work of the artist:

> the work to be what it is, to convey its meaning, demands the presence of the artist's mind in its creation, or of his substitute the spectator in appreciation. Without them the marble has no appearance of life, and its form, however remarkable has no significance. If we found such strange shapes scattered among the shapeless blocks or masses of clay, they would be mere curiosities of nature.[23]

In Alexander's theory of beauty, therefore, the activity of the artist's mind is pre-eminent, and no work of art, and even no aspect of nature, has beauty in itself. Were a strange shape, similar to a work of art, found among the blocks of nature, it would not be called beautiful, but would be a mere curiosity of nature.

There is no need to develop further Alexander's theory of beauty, since we are primarily concerned with deity, not beauty as such, but we cannot leave the subject without taking due note that other theories have been proposed. A significant dissent from Alexander, with which we ourselves agree, is the following:

> The man who says of a landscape or a work of art that it is beautiful does not suppose himself to be in reality pronouncing upon his own feelings; he does not think that the beauty of the view is grounded in his admiration for it, but that his admiration for it is grounded in its actual beauty. The Value only fulfils its essential nature, only

achieves its essential excellence, in the moment when it is appreciated. It exists as value for Mind; Mind finds it and appreciates it; but Mind does not invent or create it in the act of appreciation.[24]

Now, turning to the value of truth, we find that Alexander distinguished between reality and truth, the former being Space-Time and its objects, and the latter arising when we sort out objects into their groups:

> To be real, then, is to belong to Space-Time, as our hypothesis implies and experience attests. The apprehension of truth, and of what corresponds to it on the perceptual level, arises when we proceed to sort out our spatio-temporal objects into their groups.[25]

Thus do we separate objects from their illusory appearances, for:

> In some judgments we apprehend reality truly; in others falsely or erroneously.[26]

But what is meant by apprehending reality truly? What is meant when we say we apprehend the truth of a judgment? The truth of a judgment is referred to the body of organized and systematized propositions about a science "in so far as they are in the possession of minds which think truly."[27]

But what is meant by thinking truly? In other words, what makes truth, true? Alexander dismisses the correspondence theory of truth, for the test of coherence:

> if truth is tested by reference to other propositions the test is not one of correspondence to real-

ity but of whether the proposition tested is consistent or not with other propositions. This is the test of 'coherence.'[28]

In a later treatment of the subject, however, Alexander was not so convinced that the correspondence test could be disregarded:

> Science exhibits two features one of which, coherence, it shares with art; the other is peculiar to science, its correspondence with fact. Each of these two features has been claimed by various writers to be the test of truth. The criterion of correspondence is the more obvious one, but rightly understood the two tests are identical. For coherence within the science involves correspondence with fact, and correspondence with fact involves coherence with the science.[29]

The truth of a science consists of the system of coherent propositions involving the subject matter of this science, this subject matter being those configurations of Space-Time which are investigated in this science, be it physics, chemistry, biology, or astronomy. But it is to be noted that the coherence of the propositions is a coherence as apprehended by minds:

> this truth is apprehended through intercourse of minds of which some confirm the true proposition and reject the false, and that truth is the proposition so tested as thus related to collective judging. Any reality is an occupation of Space-Time in a particular configuration. I call that its internal structure. Propositions made about this reality are asserted perspectives of it. The propositions belong to the reality; false ones introduce ele-

ments from elsewhere. True propositions are thus also real; but their truth is different from their reality. True propositions cohere; or rather false propositions are incoherent with true propositions and are rejected by us. . . . The rejection of error is performed at the guidance of reality through the clash of minds.[30]

It is important to realize that the rejection of error is not done by the individual investigator as such. Error is rejected through the clash of minds, for the coherence of a science is a coherence of this science as possessed by social minds. A proposition is found to be erroneous on its subjective, believing, side because it fails to cohere with social believings. The mind which has error is a heretical mind for it is an outcast from the intellectual community:

> The mind which has truth has it so far as various minds collectively contribute their part to the whole system of true belief; the mind which has error is so far an outcast from the intellectual community . . . in one way or another truth means the settling down of individual believings into a social whole and the condemnation of the heretical or unscientific believing.[31]

We wish to emphasize that in this treatment of truth, the value of truth is not correspondence with objective reality but coherence with social minds, so that error is not primarily lack of correspondence with objective reality, but rejection by the minds whose agreement is presumed to be a manifestation of the fact that they have the truth.

In considering the value of goodness, Alexander

reaches a similar conclusion. The good refers to the satisfaction of persons which is effected by right willing,[32] especially as this "right willing" is defined as the satisfactions of persons organized and made coherent in the relations of individuals with one another in the social group. Good does not exist apart from the wills which sustain it.

The regulative function of the social group plays a large part in defining whether individual conduct is good or bad:

> Goodness is the kind of conduct, or the kind of satisfaction secured by conduct, which can cohere with the claims of other persons. In so far as the individual is good he represents the collective wills of the society. His approbations whether of himself or others coincide with theirs. He is himself a microcosm which in his place mirrors the larger society. . . . So far as he is good he embodies the common judgment; he is the wise man of Aristotle, or the impartial spectator of Adam Smith, who judges that to be good which is attuned to the needs of all; or he is the standardised man.[33]

The good man is thus the standardized man who embodies the common judgment of what is expected of him by the collectivity. There seems to be little place for the moral or ethical innovator in such a theory of goodness, for the innovator by that very fact challenges the common judgment. Yet Alexander is adamant in his notion of conformity as the criterion of goodness:

> The judges of what is right or wrong, good or bad, are self-selected and impose their approba-

tions or disapprobations on the remainder. Those who do not conform are condemned as wrongdoers or immoral. . . . The objectivity of morals implies the relativity of morals to the conditions which call for a satisfactory distribution of services and satisfactions. There is no such thing as an absolute and eternal law of goodness. The absoluteness of a law lies in its being the satisfactory solution of the problem of distribution.[34]

The absoluteness of the good does not lie in its inherent or intrinsic character but in the satisfactory solution of the problem of distribution of goods and services and satisfactions in the community.

In summarizing this brief survey of Alexander's theory of the tertiary qualities, we may say that there are two trends of thought in the theory: 1. Value is a quality which belongs to the compound of subject and object, but the object does not have value intrinsically, for "the object has value as possessed by the subject."[35] 2. The judgment of the truth of the value experienced is checked against the judgments of others, so that "judging and sociality are convertible."[36]

For in judgment our objects or propositions come directly into relations of agreement or conflict with other persons. In judging a fact or willing one, our objects are patent to the observation of others as ours . . . a judgment of value is intrinsically social, and is related to a social type.[37]

The social emphasis on the judgment of value is indicative of the fact that Alexander differs from those who affirm that a judgment of worth is simply an individual emotive cry. In Alexander, the judgment of value, when verified through agreement or disagreement with other minds, possesses a social trans-subjectivity, not a radical individuality. But judgments of value are nevertheless "inventions" or "creations" of the human mind, the word "inventions" not of course referring to the elementary meaning of a mechanical invention:

> The values of beauty, goodness and truth are the highest creations of man, and the object of religion is still higher in the scale than man and his works.[38]

This elementary digression into Alexander's value theory enables us to perceive more clearly why he disagreed with Höffding's emphasis on religion's concern with the objectivity of value and reality. We may agree with Höffding against Alexander that religion is concerned with the objectivity and conservation of values, and that values as subjective creations of the human mind, or even compounds of mind and object, do not satisfy the religious consciouness. On the other hand, we may agree with Alexander against Höffding in the sense that Höffding did not appreciate as did Alexander that the value which pertains to religious emotion is *sui generis* and is more profound than our appreciation of truth, goodness, and beauty.

Deity on the Side of Goodness—To call God good is a wholly inadequate designation since deity is a type of perfection transcending human goodness, truth, or beauty, which in a sense are human creations, while deity is a quality fully as objective as the primary and secondary qualities which are not human creations. To be sure, the body of God as the whole world includes both good and evil, but the body of God is not the full reality of God. God is not the whole world conceived statically, but the whole world manifesting a tendency to deity, though actually this tendency is perceived as process, as nisus, rather than as accomplishment. The deity of God, however, is on the side of goodness, though transcending goodness.

In order to understand this conception it is necessary to recall the place which Alexander gives to value at levels lower than the tertiary qualities of truth, goodness, and beauty. On lower levels than human life, value is to be understood in terms of adaptation for the preservation of the type, so that the type which is adapted to its environment sustains its life and that of its descendants, while the type which is not adapted, or whose adaptations vary too widely, perishes:

> On the level of life value exists as the persistence of adapted forms of living being. To an adapted type that part of its environment on which it can react so as to sustain its life has value for the type, and the individual of the type is the corresponding subject of value, or it is a valuable form of life. The unvalues are those individuals or types which in their conjunction with the environment fail in competition with the values, and are eliminated. . . . The values of truth, goodness, and beauty, and their unvalues, arise by a process of competition amongst reals which has begun below the human level.[39]

The type which survives in the long run through the process of competition with types which are eliminated establishes its value, and is good. New types of finites

GOD AND SPACE-TIME

emerge in existence in a hierarchical order, and the survival values of each type are themselves in a hierarchical order, so that Alexander concludes;

> The universe works in experience so as to secure the survival of good, or rather that which survives in the long run in the contest establishes its value thereby and is good. To repeat a saying already quoted, "morality is of the nature of things."[40]

The victory of the higher type makes possible the rise and victory of its successor, and each victory in succession is in reality the rise of a higher type of good. Each type of good on its own level contributes to the emergence of the good which is the survival value of the next higher type. Reasoning by analogy, Alexander connects human good with deity in this manner:

> If we apply to the new quality of deity what we learn from the succession of empirical qualities, we conclude by analogy that the process by which good overcomes evil in the region of mind is one of the conditions of the emergence of deity; so far, that is, as human endeavour contributes to the emergence of this quality.[41]

That human endeavor contributes to the emergence of deity may seem a rather anthropomorphic notion for a philosopher as emancipated from orthodox opinions as is Alexander, but we must remember that he states that the process of the victory of good over evil in human minds is merely one of the conditions of the emergence of deity. What the other conditions are he does not state in detail, though one would presume that the human mind and its survival is merely one item in the long succession of hierarchical forms which eventually lead up to deity. Is not this succession of forms due to the creative force of the nisus of Space-Time rather than to the victory of good over evil in one of the forms of the ascending ladders?[42] Be that as it may, to Alexander goodness or good will is part of the material on which deity is built, "and deity is in the line of goodness not of evil."[43]

Equally so, deity is in the line of the other human values of truth and beauty. Valuable mental life is that which is concerned with truth, goodness, and beauty, and evil mental life is that type of human life which ignores these values and produces instead error, evil, and ugliness, which remain as finite realities, and may be considered as useless material, or even excrement discharged from healthy organisms into the outer Space. We shall return to the problem of evil in a moment, but at this time we wish to concentrate on the relation between human values and deity. Just as mind is some complex of life and grows out of valuable life, so is deity a complex of mind and grows out of valuable mental life, that life concerned with truth, goodness, and beauty. Such mental life is permanent and can give rise to higher existence, while that mental life which is evil does not contribute to the survival and existence of higher types. Deity is thus in the line of the highest human values, and not in the line of human evil.

Alexander now enlarges this conception of the connection of deity with value since human value is simply one instance of value, and value is

> the fitness of what is valuable to persist in the one reality of things, or, as it was put before, the return of the isolated finite into communion with reality. In this wider sense of value, deity remains

next to mental and even human values, but it is also in the line of all value, and our values are but its proximate material.[44]

Since value is the fitness of what is valuable to persist at any level of existence, all the levels which persist are therefore levels of persisting value, and the value at the human level is built upon the values which endure at the lower levels; more, the values at the human level conserve the values of the lower levels. In this wider sense, deity is an outgrowth from all values and represents the conservation of all values or valuable existence, for if one level of existents had died out in the course of the ascending evolutionary process, then higher existents would not have arisen in the line of development including the defective level, but from an alternate line. In this sense deity represents the conservation of all values or valuable types of existence. It does not represent the types of existence which have ceased to exist because they did not lead to a more evolved type of life, the dinosaurs for instance. It would appear that in Alexander's argument all values implicated in the persistence of types (not merely individuals) are conserved in the existence of higher types, up to deity. Hence, it is possible for Alexander to state: "All values are conserved in God's deity."[45]

But this assertion is not the same as Höffding's to the effect that religion is merely faith in the conservation of values. In other words, that values are conserved in deity is a fact about deity, as conceived by Alexander, but it is not the chief fact about deity. This primary fact is not value, as we have seen, but the distinctive quality which is deity—a quality above our own distinctive quality of mind or even of possible creatures higher than men. Religious sentiment is not essentially a matter of appreciation of value as such, but of appreciation of deity, which is "like the apprehension of colour or life, except that we cannot say what the new quality is like, for it is not revealed to sense or thought."[46] Alexander has remained consistent in his attempted vindication of the unique quality of deity in all his writings:

> Deity is a quality distinct from and superior to goodness or beauty or truth. I can be enthusiastic for beauty or truth, but I have no worship for them. They excite in me no religious feeling, though in many persons they may supply the place of religion, where no religion is felt. The mystics are right; we worship or love in God, not his goodness, but his godship or deity.[47]

Another way of clarifying the difference between deity and value is the following:

> Deity is the outcome of the onward sweep of all that is persistent and counts in the economy of the world. Human values are but the apex of that movement. Any facet of the advancing column of values may make the directer appeal to the mind, according to its capacity.[48]

Alexander could have added that human values are the apex of the onward sweep of all that is persistent at the present moment of Time in the history of the world, but that the emergence of existents higher than man in Time's succession will signify that the apex will rise above man in the direction of deity. There is, however, an advancing column of values which at the human level are our familiar tertiary qualities, truth, goodness, and beauty, and each of these makes a more direct appeal to the mind than values lower in the scale of evolution—the directness of the appeal being governed in part by the receptive capacity of the mind.

There would be value if the nisus stopped at any level, say at mind, But "the restlessness of Space-Time,"[49] to use a characteristic expression of Alexander, drives forms of existence in a hierarchical successive series of higher qualities, so that quality is different from value. But since value means the persistent type of existence, it is only in so far as value is established in that type "that the nisus forward becomes effective in the generation of a new quality."[50] A being on a particular level has the nisus to a higher level in so far as it contributes "to the general nisus of the world"[51] on that level. Alexander seems to reduce the creative force which the nisus possesses inherently when he writes:

> We help to the creation of deity in so far as through our goodness we are qualified to share in the universal bent towards a higher quality.[52]

It is worthy of note that this conception of deity being created partly by our efforts, by our goodness, is one quite foreign to religious thought, but it seems to be an unmistakable emphasis of Alexander. We had already met it in his previous chapter on "Deity and Religion":

> deity itself is the outcome of the world's movement and in particular, to the extent of their value, of the efforts of human beings. It is not God then who allows the struggle, but the struggle which is to determine, it may be not at once but in the end, what deity is to be; which ideal if either is on the side of the divine.[53]

It is difficult to determine just to what extent Alexander

believes that deity is the outcome of the inherent nisus in the world's movement, and to what extent it is the outcome of human values acting independently of the nisus as such. Since deity is held to be a quality immeasurably higher than mind, it would seem that even the most strenuous efforts of human beings on this little planet would have little to contribute to a future quality whose outcome is urged in Alexander's system as the work of the whole universe.

There is, however, an element of plausibility in Alexander's theories of value and deity and their relationship. Assuming for the sake of the argument that these theories are correct, then the highest quality, deity, rests on all the previous qualities, and since value to Alexander means primarily the persistence of existents with their qualities in the life struggle, deity in a sense rests on the lower qualities and the lower values which persist as types of organisms. More exactly, deity is in the line of value, precisely because deity implies the previous existence in Time of a hierarchical series of existents whose continued existence as a type (not necessarily as individuals) is simply their value. What we wish to point out is that deity depends for its appearance in Time upon the previous successive emergence of this hierarchy of types and their corresponding qualities in increasing order of complexity. That is to say, deity does not so much depend on value, as it is merely in line with value.

Good and Great Men.—Alexander is so concerned to connect value with the generation of types and the conservation of types of life under the process of Darwinian selection that he has difficulty in dealing with the value of the individual as such. Let us be clear about Alexander's orientation to Darwinism:

GOD AND SPACE-TIME

> The doctrine of natural selection explains not how types are generated, but how they come to have value. It is so far from being indifferent to value that it is wholly concerned with value; its very meaning is that values emerge through the trial of various types under certain external conditions, which trial determines whether in virtue of its gifts or constitution a type is worthy.[54]

Whether such a conception is entirely adequate we leave for more extensive criticism at the proper stage of this work. But Alexander has to break loose from his conception of value as the successful trial of various types to indicate just what is the nature of good and great men within the human type:

> Good and great men seem to us to have in them something divine, and the description is just if it is taken to mean that, being better and greater than the rest of us, they point the way to deity, and prepare the way as leaders in the human contribution to the world-endeavour.[55]

Their greatness is constituted by something other than their value as elements of a type that is preserved; it is constituted by the fact that they point the way to deity. This is another instance in which Alexander makes a sharp difference between value and deity. That great men, especially the founders of the historic religions, have in them "something divine"[56] is one of the most fundamental assumptions of religious believers. But Alexander, in being quite consistent with his metaphysical emphasis on the nisus, qualifies this assumption of religion by urging that these men do not possess the divine in its full totality of expression:

> Men of transcendent gifts of perfection are thus in their degree exemplars of this nisus. The description is false if it means that they in any sense possess the divine quality or even adumbrate it.[57]

Men of transcendent gifts, religious giants, do not possess deity attained, and in order to reinforce his point, Alexander makes an assertion which we have emphasized more than once in the course of this work:

> Even God himself does not as actual God possess deity attained, but only the nisus towards it.[58]

In actuality, therefore, Alexander admits that deity attained does not exist, however much he has used the conception of deity in most of his argumentations, but what does actually exist is the nisus to deity. This is another instance in which we feel that Alexander should have given a heightened recognition to the work of the nisus, and not so much to the presupposition of a distant deity which is never in actuality attained, since we have repeatedly shown that in the course of Time, it is fragmented into higher individuals of a higher hierarchical order than man, and recedes in the far distant future, so to speak.

Ordinary theism, however, is correct in conceiving of Jesus as an intermediary "to be more than man,"[59]—an intermediary between man and God. But this ordinary theism is inconsistent if it interposes "the conception of a miraculous person without parallel in the world."[60] That is to say, Alexander opposes the conception of the nature of the religious founder, or giant, whether it be in the Christian religion or in any other great world religion, as a miraculous intervention into the natural order. For him, as well as for all evolutionists, human greatness—whether it be in religion, art, social idealism—is a manifestation of the nisus which is a historical growth of qualities in Time, and this historical growth is of the very nature of Space-Time itself. Thus, to extrapolate Alexander's thought somewhat beyond its actual statement, in both his system of emergent evolution and in traditional religion, the supreme exemplar of religion is rooted in the nature of the Universe, but this rootage is interpreted quite differently in emergent evolutionism and in theism. This is, of course, an elementary consequence of the difference between the metaphysics of emergence and the metaphysics of traditional theism.

Nevertheless, it would seem that Alexander has been far too succinct in devoting only half a page of this two-volume work to the place of the personal exemplifier of greatness. The harmony, synthesis, intensity, and radiance which are closely allied with the nature of such individual greatness is what Alexander has omitted.[61]

The Problem of Evil.—Alexander's conception of evil indicates how far the pantheistic note is accentuated in his system. Since God's body is the totality of Space-Time up to the present actual moment, whatever is evil resides in God's body just as much as the good:

> the assertion we have made is not that evil does not exist in God—on the contrary it has been maintained to exist there, in God's body—but only that God's deity is on the side of good and not on the side of evil.[62]

But this conception merely tells us the locality of evil, within the universe, which is God's body; we must discover its nature. Here Alexander includes under evil all

DEITY AND VALUE

the processes of elimination which all living organisms manifest:

> Now life means also the continual death of parts of the body and the exclusion of material which is no longer utilisable in that form. All living involves partial death. But the life resides not in the disused elements but in the parts which remain and are active.[63]

The healthy organism puts away from itself disused or dead parts, useless material as in the excrement of food, as well as poisons which are generated by its own functions, and finally it destroys noxious germs. All these products of elimination, Alexander tends to consider under the general heading of "excrements,"[64] and one may inquire of their disposition. The answer, based as all his answers are, on the universe of Space-Time, is simple:

> There is a Space outside into which these excrements can be discharged and maintain an independent existence. But since God is infinite there is no extrusion possible beyond his limits; there is no Space outside him.[65]

Living organisms, then, discharge into the outer Space the diseased or noxious material which is no longer conducive to their life. But it is to be noted that Alexander remains consistent in his doctrine that the body of God is the whole of Space, so that the processes of elimination remain within the body of God since there is no Space outside of him.

Evil, obviously, does not merely exist in the form of rejected material from living organisms lower than man.

At the human level, "the individual mind suppresses or diverts unhealthy activities,"[66] such activities being "the human and wilful distortion of what is real."[67] At the level of human society, "unhealthy members"[68] are re-formed, or if need be, suppressed by society. The ruling concept of Alexander is that of health, whether it be of the individual organism below man, of man himself, of society, and even of deity, for

> Deity in the universe as a whole is like life in a healthy body.[69]

Since all life involves the utilization of food and the elimination of unusable or poisonous material, how shall we consider the processes of elimination as referred to deity? We shall discover better what deity eliminates if, on Alexander's system, we correctly interpret what deity conserves. Deity is on the side of that which it uses and is not on the side of that which it discards. Deity being a quality above the mental existence of human beings, even above the mental existence of beings higher than man,

> we shall think of it as equivalent to some form of goodness (that is of permanent mental, not necessarily human, life) and sustained by other kinds of mental process just as mind is equivalent to certain vital processes and is sustained by others.[70]

As deity is sustained by certain forms of mental life, which in some way Alexander assumes to be "permanent,"[71] so deity rejects other forms of mental life which, because evil, are impermanent:

> Thus the maintenance of the life of deity means also the death or discarding of certain parts of its

basis, that is, certain forms of mental life.[72]

This rejection from deity is discarded into the Space outside deity which is the body of God, just as the rejection of evil or diseased products from organisms is dispersed into the surrounding Space. There is this difference: material such as carbonic acid when excreted from a finite living organism remains as carbonic acid; but the impermanent and evil mental life which is discarded from the mental life of deity, does not continue to exist in its mental form but is reduced to lower forms, possibly material elements. This material cannot be good mental life or it would be used by deity, so that in Alexander's system, our yearning for that aspect of Reality which is absolutely good is satisfied to some degree through his conception of deity as containing only good mental life. Of course, it is to be remembered that when Alexander speaks of the mental processes or the mental life of deity, he is using his familiar principle of the constitution of every finite organism, even the universe itself, in terms of "body" and "mind." The mental life of deity is immeasurably higher than our own mental life, though our mental life is closer to it than lower levels of existence.

The mental life discarded by deity suffers dissolution and may be used again only when it has been broken down to be reconstructed by deity:

> It suffers therefore dissolution in its character of mental existence, and can be used again only when it has been "unmade to be remade," and may again be taken up and utilised for the purposes of deity.[73]

A not too elevating illustration for the work or redemption of the highest quality of the universe is given by Alexander in terms of the corruption of a battlefield which may serve the growth of crops, and thus this corruption is ultimately serviceable for good human life.

Waste products are therefore discarded from all living finites, and from the living infinite, deity. In this theory of evil, all unvalues, not merely badness, ugliness and error, but all impermanent forms of finite existence, are contained, not in deity, but in the body of God. Deity, in which there is no evil, is based on hierarchical substructures of existents, down to Space-Time, and these substructures contain evil as well as good. But what is evil from the point of view of the human level undergoes change so as to become good, or acquire value, and support the divine, since deity is in the line of value:

> Error and ugliness and wickedness are finite realities and remain as such unvalues, in the body of God. But perishing in that form they are used in a changed form for the purposes of deity.[74]

This is Alexander's philosophical foundation for such religious conceptions as the ultimate redemption of evil in all its forms by processes in which God "unmakes but to remake the soul."[75] Just what these processes are Alexander does not make clear.

While deity is constructed out of good mental life, Alexander wishes to reassert that it is neither good nor evil, nor a value but a new perfection in which there is no distinction of values.[76] He returns here to his essential dichotomy between value and deity. God's body, as we have observed, contains both good and evil, but these terms apply only to finites, for God "as a whole . . . is neither."[77] Alexander, however, does not make clear whether in the advance of Time all forms of evil will be "remade" by deity so that in the flow of infinite Time, evil would become infinitesimal and good itself infinite. On the contrary he seems to emphasize the acceptance of evil as real, and he quotes with approval Socrates' remark: "Evil, O Gloucon, will not vanish from the earth."[78] It cannot vanish since it is the imperfection through whose defeat the finite existents acquire their value. Value in terms of persistence of type is reflected in this assertion of Alexander.

We are, of course, in revolt against the existence of evil, but this revolt springs from two sources: 1. a theoretic fault; 2. a defect of temper.

1. The theoretic error is that of emancipating God from Time, for we may ask, If God allows the existence of evil, why did he not make the world otherwise?[79] In Alexander's metaphysical system, such a question implies a reversal of the course of evolution in Time, for deity is sustained by the good of all lower levels, and the evil of these lower levels is discarded by deity:

> God is helpless to prevent evil, for his deity is the outgrowth of good, and God does not foresee the evil or the good, but so far as he is equivalent to the whole world is himself the theatre of the content between value and unvalue.[80]

This remarkable agnosticism on the part of God in Alexander's system reminds us of a sentence we examined at length in a previous chapter:

> Deity does not know, but only the minds know which are included in the body of God.[81]

Such a conception, Alexander admits, rejects the traditional belief "in a God who precedes his universe."[82] Nor does he allow for "a pre-existing overruling purpose"[83] for such evidence of providence in the sense that men's purposes are turned to an issue which they have not imagined, merely shows that the whole is greater than its parts, and may exhibit features beyond the knowledge of man.[84]

A conception of God which is other than Alexander's, especially pantheism or theism, renders the problem of evil insoluble. In the purely pantheistic conception, deity is held to animate all parts of the world alike, while in Alexander's system, deity animates only that part which in due time is fitted to carry deity.[85] Deity for Alexander contains only what is good for poisonous mental life has been ejected into the infinite Space outside of deity. Hence, Alexander overcomes the problem of the presence of good and evil in God, which is the problem of pantheism, by postulating that in deity evil is rejected. But he does not overcome this problem in so far as God's body is concerned, for, as we have seen, this body which is the whole of Space-Time up to the present moment contains both good and evil. The theistic conception of God existing in perfection independently of the world is also rejected though Alexander does not make clear his ground of criticism at this point. But he had indicated his objection in a previous chapter:

> If God precedes the world (to use a useful but inexact phrase) and all things are determined by his will, why should a benevolent being not take a course which spares his creatures pain?[86]

Without investigating answers which have been given by exponents of traditional theism, Alexander prefers to present his own view of the resolution of evil as obviating the difficulties of both pantheism and theism. But the resolution of evil as discord does not occur on the level on which good and evil both exist. The resolution, so far as it is effected, is effected on the higher level. The evil remains done, but by perishing in its evil form it may subserve deity.[87]

On the level on which evil exists, it remains a discord, but there is no discord in the higher quality for the discord has been resolved into harmony much as a musical discord is so resolved. However, if the evil is harmoniously resolved by subserving a higher quality, this resolution can only take place during the later birth in Time which attends the existence of this higher quality. Nay, if the evil is ultimately resolved only by deity, then its amalgamation will be infinitely delayed, since Alexander has told us repeatedly that deity is a nisus and not an accomplishment.

The problem of evil presents an insoluble character when attended by theoretical error—that is, by attempts at solution under the philosophical views of theism or pantheism, and these attempts, in Alexander's judgment, cannot succeed. Success is achieved when theoretical error is replaced by the theoretical correction of Alexander's own system, but we have seen that evil, as portrayed in his system, can only be removed through the hope that deity in the far distant future will resolve it into a greater harmony.

2. The defect of temper which renders the problem of evil insoluble lies in our "disinclination to accept the facts of experience which do not accord with our wishes."[88]

This temper, however, may be compounded of many ingredients, some worthy of praise, and some worthy of condemnation. This temper is indeed the manifestation "of the virile resolution to overcome evil."[89] It is also an expression of our shame at our own weakness and of our pity for the weakness and distress of others. The fairer side of our impatience with evil is thus acknowledged by Alexander, for had he not written elsewhere of sacrifices endured for justice's sake: "The spirit of revolt is so precious that these sacrifices may be worth while."[90]

Our impatient temper, however, is not so praiseworthy when it issues in "mere indignation at disagreeableness, and imputation of the wrong to God,"[91] or when it believes there must be something amiss in the world.

Such defect of temper is overcome when we face the facts of experience in their stark reality. We are the children of the same nature which sometimes overwhelms us; the permanent forms of life secure their adaptation to their environment through a process of experimentation which involves prodigal loss; goodness itself is the issue of such experimentation to discover which form of social adjustment satisfies our wants in the face of an environment which may be partly friendly and partly unfriendly. It is not for us to state whether such conditions of existence are good or bad; we can merely acquiesce, but this intellectual acquiescence is far from passive submission. It is

> the incentive to the practical effort for amelioration, in accordance with our impulse to mould things to the heart's desire.[92]

Such an attitude is not to be confused with submission to an inscrutable will; neither does it mean the acceptance of evil as created to brace our spirits.[93] Such an attitude is quite different from the traditional religious

DEITY AND VALUE

belief in a pre-existing purpose in the world, for Alexander frankly states:

> There is no overruling and pre-existing purpose in the world upon which we should throw the blame for what we cannot help, or which we need thank for its subtle device of helping us by pain.[94]

Nevertheless, the temper of acquiescence is also that which impels to amelioration, and this same attempt at betterment is recognized as implanted in us

> by the same Space-Time out of which we are precipitated, and secures the deity to which the world is tending.[95]

In other words, there is no pre-ordained or pre-determined purpose imposed on the world, but since Space-Time manifests a historical growth of finites, the pattern of amelioration which comes to consciousness in human beings is an immanent pattern ultimately securing "the deity to which the world is tending."[96]

It is to be noted, once again, that since deity is a nisus and not an accomplishment, Alexander cannot consistently speak of deity being secured, but of the tendency of the world to deity. It is the nisus of Space-Time which implants in us the moral indignation which makes us active in causes involving individual and social betterment. In this criticism of Alexander, we are heightening the role played by the nisus, a role which Alexander does not always recognize since he appears to be so occupied in developing the character of "deity" in relation to the finites, to the whole of Space-Time, to value, and to good and evil.

The Question of Immortality.—We have already observed how much Alexander's position differs from that of traditional theism. We shall observe this difference even more in his discussion of immortality. The subject is not easy to handle

> for no one would care to wound the sentiment of longing to rejoin in a future life our companions in this life.[97]

There are, however, prejudices of theory and temper which operate in our approach to the question of immortality, and when these are removed we shall see that the desire to continue our work in a future life

> cannot overrule the facts of our apparent limitation to the time and place of our bodily life.[98]

The data of our knowledge, in Alexander's opinion, do not permit us to assume that the mind can continue without its instrument, the body. To be sure his opinion is based on a "metaphysics of mind"[99] in which the mind is constituted of a certain complexity of living processes which have the mental quality. But Alexander is so convinced of the truth of this metaphysical position with respect to the human mind that "we are certainly not entitled . . . to support a thesis which would lend itself"[100] to the wish that our minds should continue to exist apart from our bodies. Our wish for continued existence should rather be replaced by the resignation of our work to others.

Alexander has indeed given us a drastic position with respect to the religious hope for a future life, but he mitigates the impact of his view by stating that the wish for a future life is not on the same footing as the sentiment of religion. As he has repeatedly told us, the religious sentiment is a fundamental attribute of our nature called forth by the objective existence of the nisus rising to deity. The religious sentiment is an experience realized in various degrees to be sure in different individuals, but its inherent basis in the structure of our nature cannot be doubted. But the future life may well be doubted since it cannot be known from direct experience except through the continued existence of our minds after death:

> Failing such demonstration, we do no injustice to this desire if we suppose it to be, like so much of our more definite religious beliefs, an attempt to convey something else in a form more obvious to our minds.[101]

This something else which we mistakenly convey by the vivid imagery of life after death is the continuance of our work by others through the continued devotion of many generations.

Should someone suggest some evidence as to the continuation of human life after death, Alexander believes we should "scrutinise the evidence presented to us with more than ordinary rigour"[102] and we should not permit our personal wishes to accept it with more than ordinary welcome. In spite of such evidence as has been claimed by some investigators of psychical research, Alexander declares,

> The personal continuance of our lives beyond the life of our bodies is fully accredited by none.[103]

He admits, however, that a large part of his present speculative system would have to be seriously modified were such evidence to be verified:

> should the extension of mind beyond the limits

of the bodily life be verified, so that a mind can either act without a body or may shift its place to some other body and yet retain its memory, the larger part of the present speculation will have to be seriously modified or abandoned.[104]

There is, however, another argument, which is brought forward to support the continuation of personality after death. It is the principle of the conservation of value which

might be understood to mean the persistence of myself because my life is valuable or a value.[105]

But this is based on an error, for in Alexander's value theory, values arise in the contest of types and are established among types. They may be exhibited in individuals, for these are the embodiments of types, but it is the type or the species which is the embodiment of value, and not the individual as such. "We must content ourselves with the continuance of species rather than of persons."[106] The continuance of our human ideals should satisfy us, for nature may involve "the physical destruction of mind,"[107] to quote a forthright expression of Alexander! Should the continuation of human values through the persistence of the human race as a type prove unsatisfactory, there is available the higher satisfaction which consists in our awareness that the persistence of human efforts in tradition is doing the work of preparing deity, since, as was explained previously, deity is in the line of human value, as well as the values of lower levels. But this preparation of deity will take place *"in God's good time* and, it must be added, *place."*[108] Alexander's favorite emphasis on deity as a quality occupying a portion of Space and Time, though an infinite portion, recurs in this last quotation. As we have indicated in previous discussion, the thought that our efforts prepare the emergence of deity seems to overlook the inherent creative work of the nisus which drives existents to higher syntheses, so that our efforts are ultimately part and parcel of the nisus rather than the reverse.

Deity and Feeling.—An old metaphysical question to which Alexander wishes to make his contribution is whether God suffers pain or is perfectly happy. He gives his own solution to this problem in terms of his fundamental metaphysical assumption:

> God, regarded as the infinite ideal, is of the same structure, body and mind, as we and all existents and Space-Time itself.[109]

In other words, God has a "body" and God has a "mind" which is deity, an infinite portion of the infinite Space-Time. Pain exists in the body of God since finite creatures which endure pain are located within this all-inclusive body. But God's deity has no pain; neither has it pleasure if by pleasure we mean the feeling of agreeableness in successful, unobstructed work. But what about the existents on a higher level than man, the cumbrous phrase we suggested to render more explicit Alexander's postulation of finite gods and angels? Do these have pain and pleasure? Alexander answers in the affirmative:

> Finite deities would be aware of pleasures and pains in their bodies, like the rebel angels in *Paradise Lost,* but also their deity would be aware of the defects and smoothness of the working of their mental substructure, and this would be felt

by them as something analogous to our pains and pleasures.[110]

Just as pain and pleasure are vital conditions of our bodily substructure which we contemplate and of which we are conscious, so a finite deity would feel pain and pleasure as a condition of its substructure, but this substructure in a finite deity includes not merely a material body, but also a mental substructure, since the "mind" of the finite deity is a complexity of this mental structure which emerges as a quality beyond human mind. Thus does Alexander utilize his speculative scheme to indicate not only the hierarchical nature of finite deities, but the location of their pains and pleasures. As to just what they would experience as pain or pleasure, he admits that we do not know since "deity and deising are on a level above consciousness."[111]

Just as Alexander in previous treatments of deity considered the possibility of finite gods, and then made a sharp separation between these beings higher than man and deity as such, so does he in his discussion of finite deities and their feelings of pleasure and pain, and deity as such, which he finds devoid of either pleasure or pain. The reason for this sharp difference between deity and ourselves is that we are finite creatures, and that our pains and pleasures arise from our finitude, either body or mind. Pain is the result of a threat to the destruction of our pattern of existence, and the threat may come from without or from within, such as a serious disease. But deity being infinite is not limited to a finite pattern of existence. The threat to deity's existence cannot exist:

> To an infinite being there can be no such menace. There is no form which it has to maintain in the

face of other beings. The conditions do not here exist upon which painfulness and pleasantness depend.[112]

Alexander does, however, hold out the possibility:

> We may therefore adopt the Aristotelian saying that God enjoys continuous pleasure.[113]

He does not develop this point further.

So long as we are dealing with the infinite deity of God, and not the finite deities or angels, deity is not subject to distinction of evil or good, or of any other value, such as truth, goodness, and beauty. This judgment is in keeping with Alexander's view that deity is not subject to the categories.[114] Deity is in the line of values, and depends on values, but is itself a perfection not to be contrasted with any imperfection.[115]

The persistent emphasis which Alexander places upon his notion of deity makes him disagree with Matthew Arnold who stated that God is the eternal not-ourselves which makes for righteousness. Alexander's dissent is unequivocal:

> If the power which makes for righteousness is not ourselves, there is no other power which makes for righteousness. God is, if we may use such language, the power which makes for deity.[116]

It is because of our efforts for righteousness that we have faith in the nisus of the universe, and derive from this faith assurance in continuing the work of righteousness. Our minds and our values of truth, goodness, and beauty, as well as values lower down the scale, such as economic value, do not end the series of emerging empirical qualities. Our virtue is "only part of the presupposition on which depends the emergence of the next higher quality to mind which we call deity."[117] The phrase, "part of the presupposition" would seem to indicate that only to a very partial degree do we assist in the emergence of deity. The presupposition whose part is not mentioned by Alexander we assume to be the inherent character of the nisus of Space-Time itself which drives the finites to ever higher hierarchical structures and qualities.

Summary.—The development of Alexander's conception of God and deity has now been terminated. We have considered this development under three aspects: God and deity in their metaphysical relationship; God and deity and the religious sentiment; and finally deity and value. We have endeavored to follow Alexander step by step so as not to omit any important factors in the progressive exposition of his views, but our explication has not been in all cases a slavish one. We have indicated certain obscurities in his treatment of God, and particularly of deity, and where a major disagreement with Alexander's views was implied, we have intimated that we would return to it in the critical part of this work.

A number of problems arise from our exposition. Are Space and Time physical realities as Alexander intimates? Are they as closely united as he imagines? What about the challenge of absolutists and idealistic philosophers to his evolutionary views? Where does he stand in relation to other philosophers of "becoming"? Has he stressed sufficiently the creative role of the nisus? Are his approaches and his rapprochments to traditional conceptions of God really convincing? Is there a break in his realistic system between his emphasis on qualities as objective and values as subject-object determinations? Is the definition of value in terms of survival of the type, of Darwinian "adaptation" sufficiently cogent for his assertion that deity stands in the line of value? Moreover, and this is perhaps the most important question, just what validity is there to the typical Alexandrian conception of deity as occupying an infinite portion of Infinite Time and Space in the ever receding future? If deity is a nisus and not an accomplishment, does not a rigorous application of the reality of the nisus necessarily invalidate the whole notion of "deity" in any terms other than an impulse of creativity? To these questions and problems we now address ourselves.

PART II

EVALUATION AND CRITICISM

CHAPTER I

THE SYSTEM AS A WHOLE

Space-Time as Mathematical Abstraction or Physically real?—There is no doubt that in Alexander's system, Space and Time are physical realities independent of the human mind, and in their intimate relation or combination as Space-Time, comprehend the whole of reality as an everlasting Becoming generating qualitied existents from the simplest form to the most complex, especially as there seems to be no ground for imagining the emergent process stopping with man. The creative impulse, or nisus of Space-Time, is held to be active and to give birth in future Time to a number of existents higher than man, called by Alexander finite gods or angels (a rather unfortunate appellation), and to give birth to deity, the highest empirical quality in the order of qualities emerging successively in the time order. In Alexander's view, God is not a personal, creative being apart from Space-Time, but is the universe of Space-Time straining to achieve the quality of deity.

In other words, the chief characters of this vast cosmic drama are primordial Space-Time, at the stage during which no qualitied existents have as yet emerged from the vast panorama of point-instants of infinite dimensions; the hierarchical order of existents appearing in Time and occupying an ascending order of levels of reality; and finally, deity, an infinite portion of Space-Time, but smaller in size than total Space-Time, this deity being such that no categorial characters may be applied to it, neither any characterization of good or evil, nor of the feeling of pain or pleasure. It is not itself a value though it stands in the line of the values of all the lower levels. It is a quality, the highest in the order of qualities, and if we imagine it as realized in the universe, it would appear as the "color" of the universe. The vast cosmic drama, as developed by Alexander, is constituted by the existence of all finites, including deity itself, as configurations or complexities of Space-Time, specific qualities being correlated with each type of complexity of the portions of Space-Time which are the finites. There is no configuration in existence without its corresponding quality, though primordial Space-Time did exist without any quality beyond the most primitive motion, the change of time-coefficients of point-instants derived from the flow of Time.

The whole system depends upon Space and Time considered as metaphysical realities animated by a certain restlessness manifested in the nisus driving existents to the incorporation of higher qualities. A first objection to the system by J. E. Boodin may be considered:

> No doubt exists in Alexander's mind that the abstract concepts of mathematics are attributes of the real world. They are not for him, as for Henri Poincaré, pragmatic conventions contributed by the human mind and relative to the needs of description. . . . For Alexander everything emerges from the complexities of space-time. The abstractions of space and time are invested with metaphysical properties which have nothing to

do with the mathematical origin of these concepts. Space becomes a metaphysical continuum and not just a mathematical continuum, and thus space furnishes continuity to the instants of time.[1]

Boodin apparently regards space and time as fundamentally mathematical concepts, and denies them the objective, metaphysical reality which Alexander gives them. Had Alexander constructed his vast cosmic scheme from mathematical abstractions, then Boodin's criticism would be justified:

> Can we make our concepts anything we want them to mean in order to do the work we want them to do? It would seem as though, if we want such abstract names to do so much work, we should at least pay them extra. . . . But such work is magic, not logic. And a magnificent magician Alexander is. His book makes the Arabian Nights' Tales tame to one who can follow. But we always feel that there is more in the mind of the manipulator, to account for such wonderful appearances, than the abstractions he exhibits to us.[2]

There is indeed more in the mind of the manipulator precisely because Alexander has repeatedly stated that space and time are abstractions from the reality of Space-Time, and that Space-Time is a plenum. Leaving aside for the moment the question whether Space and Time are indissolubly connected as they are in Alexander's theory, it may be said that philosophers who do not regard Space and Time in such intimate union nevertheless regard Space as not empty but a plenum. For instance J. E. Turner asserts:

> The recent developments of the Theory of Rela-

tivity have an important bearing upon the meaning of "space." For the physicist no longer regards "pure" space as being absolutely empty; it is a plenum rather than a vacuum.[3]

And, of course, Alexander was aware that the Theory of Relativity connected time with Reality as a fourth dimension of space, and drew encouragement from the theory, but added his own modification:

> Time does with its one-dimensional order cover and embrace the three dimensions of Space, and is not additional to them.[4]

Let us return, however, to Boodin's charge that Alexander has been working with merely mathematical abstractions of Space and Time. Alexander had already dealt with mathematical space and time, and in his view the mathematician's Space is not abstract but based on real Space:

> The mathematician's Space is that which we have identified as the framework of real motions. It is within this Space, whose reality has been already maintained as essentially involved in Space-Time, that the mathematician draws his lines and circles and parabolas by an ideal selection.[5]

Even the constructions of higher geometries or arithmetic are not divorced from experienced Space-Time, but are built upon it:

> In higher geometry or arithmetic we have ... works of art whose materials are derived from experienced Space-Time, however intricately combined by thought.[6]

THE SYSTEM AS A WHOLE

In attempting to refute Boodin's charge in connection with mathematical time, we shall bring the testimony of Bergson to bear on the ground that both Bergson and Alexander take Time seriously. Alexander speaks of Time as a continuity and Bergson of Time as a flux. Bergson emphasizes the fact that the mathematical treatment of Time as so many divisions, T_1, T_2, T_3, overlooks the real flux of Time. To make this point clearer and his rejection of mathematical abstractions of Time more persuasive, he gives the following supposition:

> Suppose that the rapidity of the flux becomes infinite. Imagine, as we said in the first pages of this book, that the trajectory of the mobile T is given at once, and that the whole history, past, present and future, of the material universe is spread out instantaneously in space. The same mathematical correspondence will subsist between the moments of the history of the world unfolded like a fan, so to speak, and the divisions T_1, T_2, T_3, ... of the line which will be called, by definition, "the course of time." In the eyes of science nothing will have changed. But if, time thus spreading itself out of space and succession becoming juxtaposition, science has nothing to change in what it tells us, we must conclude that, in what it tells us, it takes account neither of *succession* in what of it is specific nor of *time* in what there is in it that is fluent. It has no sign to express what strikes our consciousness in succession and duration.... Yet succession exists; I am conscious of it; it is a fact.[7]

Here Bergson accentuates the succession and duration

191

of Time, precisely the characteristics of Time which Alexander stresses. Both Alexander and Bergson agree in regarding mathematical time as an abstraction from the real succession of Time which is a fundamental datum of our experience.

Are Space and Time intimately united in Space-Time?—This is a question on which Bergson would differ from Alexander, for Bergson emphasizes real duration (durée réelle) as a continuous flow of Time, and space for him does not occupy the importance which it does in Alexander's system. Philosophers have usually disagreed with Alexander on this question, and in reply to their criticisms, Alexander could only reiterate his conviction with more aplomb:

> In other words, I wanted to deepen our sense of the obligations of S and T to one another, that each was a part of the other's being. It is probable enough that I have not succeeded. A very competent correspondent told me that he would give his boots for the proposition to be true, but that he did not think I had proved it. I feel in my bones that the proposition is true. If I have not succeeded in the proof some one else may; and I am not afraid to be wrong in a good cause.[8]

Such forceful repetition, obviously, does not constitute proof. That space, time, and matter are closely allied is, however, acknowledged by J. E. Turner:

> In concrete experience, of course, it is impossible to dissociate these three entities—matter, time and space—from one another. Their union is so indissoluble that they constitute a triune continuum, from which the space-time continuum becomes,

THE SYSTEM AS A WHOLE

at a later stage, distinguished as a separate aspect.[9]

The distinction of the space-time continuum at a later stage must be taken to signify a later time in our conceptual experience. Actually, in Alexander's system, the Space-Time continuum is held to exist in a primordial stage before matter is evolved out of it. While it may be difficult to prove that Space and Time are abstractions from the one reality of Space-Time, there is a piece of evidence which we wish to introduce as tending in the direction of the intimate union of matter (which occupies space) and time. This evidence is the discovery of radioactive isotopes whose atoms disintegrate in the course of time into simpler atoms, and these continue the process until a stable atom is finally reached. Physicists have discovered families of such isotopes, for instance, "the uranium-radium family," "the uranium-actinium family," and "the neptunium family,"[10] and the members of such disintegrating families of atoms are specified not only by their atomic weight but by the time element during which they endure, the half-life period being defined as follows:[11]

> By assuming an initial number N_0 at $t = O$, then on integration . . . it follows that the number N of particles remaining after the lapse of time t is
> $$N = N_0 \, e^{-\lambda t}$$

When N/N_0 is set equal to $\frac{1}{2}$, the number of particles remaining is half the number of original particles, and the half-life is the time taken for this disintegration to take place. Depending on the isotope considered, the half-life may be many thousands of years, or it may be just a few seconds. The point we wish to make is that the atom of such a radioactive element will retain its nature only for a definite length of time after which this atom will disintegrate into a simpler atom, radiation being given off. It would seem that time is a constitutive element of radioactive atoms, so much so that they cannot be defined without specifying their "half-life" period. This is an instance which indicates that time is closely allied to radioactive atoms, that time is a specifiable dimension of such atoms. This is not a proof, we repeat, that Space and Time are intimately unified, but it is an important piece of evidence pointing in that direction.

Alexander's emphasis on Space-Time itself, even in its primordial form as a system of point-instants before any qualitied existents have arisen, as a plenum, may seem strange, and G. Dawes Hicks expresses a very plausible incredulity:

> I suppose that the nearest approach which we know, on a large scale, to the "skeleton universe of Space-Time" would be those vast fields of inter-stellar space which have been thought to be filled by an ether, but which our author would say are full of Time. Has there, however, in the history of human science, been a single instance recorded of what could conceivably be regarded as a new empirical existent, endowed with a specific quality, emerging from this huge realm of Space-Time?[12]

And yet, it would appear that here again we may bring forward recent theories of astronomy which, while not proving Alexander's system, nevertheless tend in the direction of giving some weight to this view of Space-Time as a creative plenum in which materiality is the first emerging quality. Fred Hoyle, one of the younger

British astronomers, has introduced a new theory of the universe in the sense that the galaxies are condensations of hydrogen gas thinly distributed in the vast fields of inter-stellar space which seemed so empty to G. Dawes Hicks. This gas he calls "background material" which corresponds to Alexander's first emergent, materiality, and is not to be dismissed as inconsequential since its total mass is much greater than the mass of the galaxies combined. We shall allow Fred Hoyle to clarify this new insight into a cosmology:

> What is the present density of the background material? The average density is so low that a pint measure would contain only about one atom. But small as this is, the total amount of the background material exceeds about a thousandfold the combined quantity of material in all the galaxies put together. This may seem surprising but it is a consequence of the fact that the galaxies occupy only a very small fraction of the whole of space. You see here the characteristic signature of the New Cosmology. We have seen that inside our Galaxy the inter-stellar gas outweighs the material in all the stars put together. Now we see that the background material outweighs the material in all the stars put together. Now we see that the background material outweighs by a large margin all the galaxies put together. And just as it is the inter-stellar gas that controls the situation inside our Galaxy, so it is the background material that controls the Universe as a whole.[13]

Again, we do not say that this new cosmological theory of Hoyle proves Alexander's doctrine of Space-Time as a plenum; we merely state that new investigations in cosmology tend in the direction of a rejection of Hicks' remarks about the vast, empty, inter-stellar spaces, for the supposition that these vast spaces and times contain mysterious background material which does emerge into hydrogen. Galaxies, suns, planets, forms of life rising to consciousness in man, are then, on the theory of the New Cosmology, condensations of the simplest element, hydrogen gas distributed throughout the whole of Space. This is roughly in agreement with Alexander's theory of levels of emergents, except that for Alexander a configuration of Space-Time with emergent qualities of life and mind is obviously something much more delicately involved than merely a condensation of hydrogen gas!

But a more difficult question is: Are atoms condensations of Space-Time? Alexander believes that at the level of primordial Space-Time spatio-temporal relatedness exists apart from physical events, since these physical events are a later birth in Time. But this is not accepted by all emergent evolutionists, for instance, C. Lloyd Morgan:

> I seek in vain for evidence that spatio-temporal relatedness does exist apart from physical events. I can pierce no deeper than events which, in their primordial form are not only spatio-temporal, but physical also.[14]

In other words, Morgan accepts a physical world in Space and Time, but not the emergence of this physical world from Space-Time. But, once more, recent theories in astronomy while not proving Alexander's *doctrines,* are highly suggestive that matter emerges from Space-Time. Highly pertinent is the idea of the continuous creation of matter as expressed by Fred Hoyle:

THE SYSTEM AS A WHOLE

The idea that matter is created continuously represents our ultimate goal in this book. . . . Material simply appears—it is created. At one time various atoms composing the material do not exist, and at a later time they do. . . . Continuous creation . . . can be represented by precise mathematical equations whose consequences can be worked out and compared with observation. . . . The new material does not appear in a concentrated form in small localized regions but is spread throughout the whole of space. . . . Without continous creation the Universe must evolve towards a dead state in which all the matter is condensed into a vast number of dead stars. . . . With continuous creation, on the other hand, the Universe has an infinite future in which all its present very large-scale features will be preserved.[15]

Fred Hoyle is not too clear about this process of continuous creation. If it means creation from previous non-existent material, then his theory is similar to traditional doctrines of creation *ex nihilo*. If it means creation from a primordial stage of diffused materiality throughout the universe, then creation is not the correct term, and he should use some other term, such as transformation. To be sure, we do not have here a strict emergence of particles of matter from Space-Time, but we do have emergence from a more fundamental diffused entity spread throughout all space. By analogy, the doctrine of Space-Time as a physical plenum and not merely emptiness, seems plausible though not actually proved. Just what is the matrix from which particles of matter are created, or more precisely, transformed? A conjecture is offered by Viscount Samuel in a recent article which bears the influence of Hoyle:

> If, as some hold, the theory of the continuous creation of particles is well-founded, must there not be a matrix out of which the particles may appear and into which, if they prove unstable, they may disappear again? What is that matrix?[16]

Relativity theory replied to this question by offering the suggestion that it is Space-Time with its curvatures, but Viscount Samuel prefers a continuous state of quiescent energy:

> Why, then, may we not infer that the manifestations of active energy do not come spontaneously from nowhere, but emerge from a universal continuum of energy, already present in a state of quiescence?[17]

We do not have here the Space-Time matrix of Alexander, but we do have a universal continuum, a plenum of potentiality from which all the phenomena of nature emerge. A plenum of potentiality, of quiescent energy, which erupts into active energy in the forms of finite material emergents is what Viscount Samuel has in mind as the fundamental form of the universe. But this is not very different from what Alexander has meant by Space-Time. Is there a profound difference between the views of Viscount Samuel and those of Alexander, or is the difference merely a matter of a different terminology? We leave the question open, and merely indicate that investigations of Hoyle and Viscount Samuel render plausible the conception of a plenum of potentiality which fills all Space and from which processes of nature emerge. Viscount Samuel criticizes present-day physics which is all too content to ignore questions of ontology for the play of mathematical symbols without reference to metaphysical reality. Alexander would have sympathized with Viscount Samuel's rejection of bodiless mathematical symbolism in his search for an all-pervasive creative reality in the universe.

Another question to be brought before Alexander is this: The ascent from Space-Time to matter to life to mind may take place in isolated parts of the universe, but is there any reason to suppose that these isolated ascents will be contemporaneous or simultaneous, except by sheer accident? That is to say, Alexander's evolutionary theory should be modified so as to permit a very large number of historical emergences in various parts of infinite Space-Time, and these processes may begin at any time and anywhere in Space-Time. It may well be that a solar system similar to ours with higher forms of life existed ten billion years ago, and it may well be that another solar system with higher forms of life will exist ten billion years from now. We do not necessarily think of Space-Time producing at one moment throughout the infinite expanse of Space the emergent of materiality, and then at a definite moment but later in Time producing the lowest forms of life evolving simultaneously in parallel lines of development in various galaxies, and then forms of reflective life at the same stage of civilization whether these appear on the earth, or on some planet within, say, the Andromeda galaxy. The point is perhaps elementary, but it signifies an important modification of Alexander's system to the effect that Space-Time is characterized by lines of development in various stages or levels rather than by parallel lines all at the same stage of evolution.

Is Space-Time a Changeless Whole or Historical Through and Through?—This question has already been considered briefly in an earlier part of this work.[18] We have shown, on page 14, that Alexander sometimes uses such expressions as "Space-Time as a spatial whole,"[19] and "the whole of Space-Time"[20] and this might lead readers to assume that he refers to the Whole of idealistic philosophy in which Time is unreal, and change non-existent.[21] Alexander, on the contrary, makes clear that Space-Time is historical as a totality. Let us recall his assertion to this effect:

> It has become a commonplace to say that the world and everything in it is historical, that the world is a world of events. Instead of space and time, a world laid out in space and moving forwards in time, we have space-time, time entering into the very constitution of things; a four-dimensional and no longer a three-dimensional world.[22]

For Alexander therefore, Time enters into the very constitution of things. He takes Time seriously, as he reminds us on occasion, and this means that he considers Time in its irreversibility, its continuity, and its succession. The successiveness of Time does not mean that the world is being recreated at every instant. We have seen how Alexander rejects such a view:

> For the moment which is now would be a now which perished utterly and was replaced by another now. Time would cease to be duration and would be nothing but a now, for the different nows would have no continuity. We should vanish utterly at each moment and be replaced by something like ourselves but new; to the greater glory perhaps of a Creator who would be com-

pletely unintelligible, but to the confounding of science in his creatures.[23]

Bergson is in agreement with Alexander here, for the latter pays Bergson the following compliment:

> Perhaps it is Mr. Bergson in our day who has been the first philosopher to take Time seriously.[24]

Bergson is in agreement with Alexander in stressing the continuity of Time and objecting to mathematical time, an objection which bears on the interpretation of mathematical time given by Boodin and to which we have already replied:

> When the mathematician calculates the future state of a system at the end of a time t, there is nothing to prevent him from supposing that the universe vanishes from this moment till that, and suddenly reappears.... But he is always speaking of a given moment—a static moment, that is—and not of flowing time. In short, *the world the mathematician deals with is a world that dies and is reborn at every instant—the world which Descartes was thinking of when he spoke of continued creation.* But, in time thus conceived, how could evolution, which is the very essence of life, ever take place? Evolution implies a real persistence of the past in the present, a duration which, is, as it were, a hyphen, a connecting link.[25]

We have sufficiently indicated that for philosophers who take Time seriously, progression of the world in Time is real and not a mere recreation of the world at every moment. Moreover, Time and change are equally real, and not merely deceitful appearances of some unchanging Absolute. Some idealistic philosophers, however, have taken issue with Alexander on this point as well as on the general tendency of evolutionary and emergent philosophies to take time and change seriously, a tendency which they regard as one of the main characteristics of "modernist philosophy." We shall consider briefly a few of these objections, and attempt to reply to them. For instance, Wilbur Urban is quite confident the universe as a whole does not change:

> Of the universe . . . it is meaningless to say that it evolves. It is even meaningless to say that it changes. The universe cannot change, because any change introduces something that is, and this by hypothesis falls within the whole. The whole, if it changes is not the whole, but something less. All that is includes all that can be. There can be nothing more than it.[26]

But one may object that if all that is includes all that can be, then all that can exist in the future is actually existing now, and the future as a real future disappears. At times Urban seems to accept evolution as valid for parts of the universe, never for the whole:

> Yet it remains true that evolution can be applied —with any really intelligible meaning—only to the part, and never to the whole.[27]

But Urban quickly argues from the hypothesis that the universe as a whole does not change, to the hypothesis that the temporal view of things is not ultimate, and thereby implies that time is unreal:

> From an ultimate metaphysical standpoint, pro-

gress is unintelligible as applied to the universe, and the temporal view of things with which progress is bound up is not ultimate.[28]

Not only is a temporal view unreal, space and time are themselves not ultimate, and from the standpoint of a philosophy of value merely phenomenal:

> The ultimate meaninglessness of absolute space and absolute time, and the ultimate unintelligibility of a world without limits and without beginning and end, are among those insights of traditional thought which no amount of sophistication can really darken. If there is to be direction in space and time, if space and time themselves are to have meaning, they must get it from something other than themselves.[29]

It is one thing to assert that space and time need to be supplemented by an additional principle, be it nisus, emergence, or value, or the apparently non-temporal character of logical relations. But it is quite a different thing to assert that the introduction of such a principle renders space and time ultimately unreal. Yet this is what Urban seems to do:

> The substitution of logical relations for the sensuous intuitions of space and time means that the intelligible world is non-spatial and non-temporal.[30]

To such arguments, it would seem that the retort of Bergson is applicable:

> This amounts to saying that physics is but logic spoiled.[31]

Over against Urban who urges that

> the traditional conception of space and time . . . presupposes a super-sensible intuition of a non-temporal and non-spatial order.[32]

one may reply in the words of Bergson that, on the contrary, intuition itself is based on duration, and that the essence of things is not non-temporal but temporal:

> He who installs himself in becoming sees in duration the very life of things, the fundamental reality.[33]

And Bergson, as Alexander, asserts real duration and real becoming and contrasts these fundamental notions with the changeless Being of idealist philosophy:

> Real duration is that in which each form flows out of previous forms, while adding to them something new, and is explained by them as much as it explains them, but to deduce this form directly from one complete Being which it is supposed to manifest, is to return to Spinozism. It is, like Leibniz and Spinoza, to deny to duration all efficient action.[34]

We are aware, of course, that there are differences of detail between Alexander and Bergson, but we wish at this juncture to emphasize their broad agreement in asserting the reality of Time against such philosophers of idealism as Urban and Bosanquet who deny the ultimate reality of Time. Turning to Bosanquet's arguments, we find that they parallel in a general way those of Urban:

> The universe is all that exists, and the question, strictly stated, is whether we can attach any signi-

ficance to saying that this totality goes fundamentally—I do not say in every detail—from its character and assumes another. Its nature reveals itself in changes, partial and correlated; but there is nothing to justify a suggestion that the whole changes its nature.[35]

It is becoming increasingly clear that these two views of the Universe, the one based on changeless Being, and the other on ultimate Becoming, are two fundamental views implying different intellectual, emotional and religious responses. To Bosanquet this difference

> would lie in our absolute assurance that this succession in existence was only a succession because, so to speak, its finite character admitted, as essentially imperfect, of no other form in general and as a rule; but that behind it, as many of its features and our responses to them betray, there lies a total perfection, which to approach and apprehend through the finite and its essential nexus with the infinite is the very gordian knot and touchstone for a man, for life, and for philosophy.[36]

This conception denies the view of Alexander which is the total historicity of things, and that of Bergson which is that of Becoming in real Time. If a choice is forced upon us between these two fundamentally different apprehensions of the universe, then we decide for the view of the creativeness of reality, a view which is broadly similar to that of Alexander and Bergson, and expressed by John Laird:

> The theory of the creativeness of all reality denies the legitimacy of trying to find an explanation of becoming itself, that is to say, it refuses

to peer behind the scenes in order to find something that makes going go. It declares that process, transition or becoming is wholly ultimate.[37]

To be sure, some idealists such as Bosanquet and Urban find a legitimate though subordinate place in the universe for histories of fragments of the universe, for creative or evolutionary processes in the course of life on earth, but they rapidly pass from such grudging concessions to evolutionary realities to a vindication of a greater reality which does not change. The temptation lies then in denying change altogether, not merely for the whole, but also for the parts. W. T. Stace is an eminent idealist who unblushingly abandons himself to this temptation in his otherwise very perceptive work, *Religion and the Modern Mind,* and after very valuable attacks on positivism concludes that religion essentially consists in the vision of an eternal order as experienced by the great mystics of both East and West:

> The eternal order is revealed in the mystic experience of the saint. The natural order is the space-time world which is revealed to the intellect and to science. . . . God and the eternal order is the sole reality, and the world and the natural order are illusion. . . . That the world is an illusion is the standpoint of the eternal. This latter view finds actual expression in the Hindu doctrine of *maya,* and, in a less fully developed form, in all those philosophies, such as those of Plato, Spinoza, the German idealists, and Bradley, who hold that the space-time world is "appearance," or is not "the true reality," or is "half real," or has a low "degree of reality."[38]

THE SYSTEM AS A WHOLE

While we value the significant insights which W. T. Stace has brought to a study of religion as challenged in modern times by positivistic naturalism and Humean skepticism, we do not agree that his solution is the only remedy against these evils of modern philosophy. As John Wild has stated in criticism of those who take this solution:

> They may agree with the ancient Greek philosopher, Parmenides, and the modern idealist, Bradley, that change, being contradictory, never really occurs, and is only an illusion. This means dismissing the whole world of nature and human life itself as an illusion, for everything with which we are in any direct contact is changing.[39]

Alexander's philosophy, to be sure, is more than a philosophy of change; it is a philosophy of emergence, of levels of complexity which arise in Time through the activity of the nisus which drives existence to higher and higher levels of complexity and quality. The universe manifests this active tendency, though the rates of change may be vastly different for a galaxy which endures through billions of years and for the flower which blooms for one summer. In any case the reality of Time as both succession and continuity, and not eternity which denies time as illusion, must be acknowledged as a central feature of Alexander's system. There is thus an important distinction between Hinduism, Buddhism, Western absolute idealism and Process philosophy of which Alexander's is an instance. Also, there is an important distinction between Alexander's temporal Process philosophy and reductive materialism, though critics tend to ignore it.

GOD AND SPACE-TIME

One further point must be raised before we leave this section. John Laird's assertion to the effect that "becoming is wholly ultimate" must not be taken to mean that the universe is recreated at every moment, each moment involving an absolute discontinuity. This is the well-known doctrine of Descartes according to which the universe is recreated by God at every moment. We have observed that this conception is particularly distasteful to Alexander who stressed the infinity of Time, the reality of process, and the continuity of existents in Space-Time. The pre-existing parts of a whole are not lost in the whole any more than finite existents are submerged in the Whole of Space-Time. Hence there is no radical discontinuity but continuity within the process of Becoming. There are even changeless elements in Alexander's system, and they are:

1. The system of points which is motionless.

2. The categories which circulate through Space-Time and may appear at any time and place as patterns of existents. Successive categories may originate in Time, but once existing as patterns of existents, they may exist without change at any time future to their first appearance.

3. The qualities which, once they have appeared, may be repeated anywhere at any time, whether isolated or within an emergent complex.

4. The nisus as supreme category, operating at all levels, in the infinity of Time.

The extreme temporalism of Alexander does not deny changeless elements, especially that creativity which Alexander calls the nisus. It is not creative evolution which makes change ultimate, but contextualism, as H. N. Wieman indicates:

In contextualism, change is ultimate. . . . In contrast to this view, the present writing asserts that there is something which retains its identity and its unity through all change in itself and through all change in other things. It is creativity. Creativity characterizes one kind of event. Every event is continuously changing, and so also is the kind of event characterized by creativity. But this kind of event has a certain identity and unity throughout all its manifestations, namely, the character of being creative of all the changing orders of the world so far as they are accessible to human life at all.[40]

Is Alexander's Metaphysics Materialism?—This possibility requires consideration since the accusation has been brought forward by J. A. Leighton:

> Dr. Alexander denies that his system is a materialism since, in the cardinal instances of life and mind, these qualities are not *caused* by their primary and secondary substrata but *emerge* by "complication." Life, in his terminology, is the "enjoyment," in a new simplification, of a complex of secondary qualities; mind is the enjoyment of that specific complex of vital qualities which constitutes innervation, the basis of consciousness. . . . If life emerges from a physical order in which there was no life, and mind from that particular complication of the physical order which is vitality, then we have a new materialism. . . . Dr. Alexander's imposing and ingenious attempt to deduce all the empirical qualities in existence from pure space-time is materialism.

. . . Space-time is too abstract, too thin, too mechanical in the geometrical sense to constitute the stuff of reality, a primal motion-stuff in which emerge, by its thickening-up, all the higher orders of existence. . . . Alexander's space-time is a materialistic absolute stated in terms of modern kinematics.[41]

The fundamental objection which we would bring against Leighton's attack is that he has interpreted Alexander's system in terms of a "complication" or a "thickening-up" process which is purely mechanical, so that on this basis life is simply a highly complex mechanical process, or a complication of spatio-temporal geometry in fundamental Space-Time. It seems that Leighton omits the emphasis placed upon the emergence of new and higher qualities as correlated with these complexities. The complexity is really qualified with a new quality, and is not merely a thickening up of the old qualities of the lower levels. To be sure, the physico-chemical processes persist in living forms, but life is *also* vital. Again life is not *merely* physico-chemical, but its vital character is dependent on an integration which must be regarded as new metaphysical entity:

Given merely physical and chemical processes, we can only generate life when we have hit upon the requisite form of integration. Thus life is *also* physico-chemical, because in its separable activities it is comparable with other physico-chemical processes. But it is not *merely* physico-chemical, because merely physico-chemical processes are not alive, and they do not give us life until the requisite complexity of integration is attained. So important is it to remember that besides elements there is the form of their combination, and that the form is as much a reality as the elements and gives them their significance.[42]

Furthermore, utilizing John Laird's argument for the creativeness of all reality, and Alexander's serious attention to Time as real, there is no reason why the assumption of a primordial Space-Time without matter, or life, or mind, should cast undue reflection on the existence of higher organisms and human beings with intellectual, artistic, and spiritual qualities *now* in existence. The passage of Time is not merely a mechanical complication of Space-Time; it implies much more, the emergence of levels and of qualities correlated with these levels as metaphysically real. We are personally much more disposed to agree with Alexander's own defense than with Leighton's accusations:

> As for materialism, that is a word of abuse. . . . If materialism means, as it is taken to mean, that there is nothing but matter and its forms, and that mind as something with a distinctive character of its own does not count in the system of things, which would be the same as it is without mind, it is neither naturalism nor a possible philosophy. For at least minds are not stones, and the world of physical matter has at any rate ended by producing minds. Materialism can only become reasonable by allowing an element to exist in matter which has affinity with the latest outgrowth from matter which is mind. But then matter ceases to be sheer matter and acquires life.[43]

Minds as emergent products of the evolutionary process make a vital difference to the rest of nature, which would have to be assumed under an entirely different character had it not produced minds. Nature, whether considered as Space-Time in motion or as the evolution of forms of life not necessarily from Space-Time but from some substantial principle, has the capacity of producing minds possessed of the spiritual qualities with which we are made familiar through the achievements of the human spirit in art, literature, science, religion. The emergence of this capacity from a Universe which is not, in its primordial form, apparently mental, is the general problem of Process philosophies[44] of which Alexandrian Space-Time-ism is a significant contribution. Attempted solutions may be made in terms of Bergson's creative evolution, or C. L. Morgan's emergent evolution, or R. W. Sellars' evolutionary naturalism, or J. C. Smuts's holism and evolution, or Conger's system of epitomization,[45] or philosophies of natural law which stress active tendency,[46] or finally Alexander's Space-Time system in which the creativity is attributed either to Time as the mind of Space, or to the nisus of Space-Time.

Alexander's system belongs to the general class of metaphysical theories which are subsumed under Process philosophy. But it is very tempting for the idealist critic or the traditional religious critic to challenge Process philosophy, as is done by Leighton, as sheer materialism. The direct reply to such abuse is given by J. C. Smuts who emphasizes the all-important difference between matter as understood by evolutionary philosophy and the old dead matter of mechanical materialism:

> If we believe that life and mind come from matter, if they are evolved from matter, if matter holds the promise, the dread potencies of life and

mind, it can for us no longer be the old matter of the materialists or the physicists. The acceptance of the view for which the materialists fought so hard means in effect a complete transformation of the simple situation which they envisaged. Matter discloses a great secret; in the act of giving birth to life or mind if shows itself in an entirely unsuspected character, and it can never be the old matter again. The matter which holds the secret of life and mind is no longer the old matter which was merely the vehicle of motion and energy. . . . If Evolution is accepted, and life and mind are developments in and from the physical order, they are in that order, and it becomes impossible to continue to envisage the physical order as purely mechanical, as one in which they have no part or lot, in which they are no real factors, and from which they should be logically excluded.[47]

Some types of idealism, such as Leighton's, ultimately deny matter and are all too ready to throw the accusation of "materialism"—what Alexander calls a term of abuse—to Process philosophies which include the reality of matter as merely the lowest level in an ascending order of dynamic tendencies. Yet it is significant that other types of idealism ally themselves with evolutionary philosophy and reject the narrow-minded view of matter still embraced by idealists of the former type:

> The idealism of Holism does not deny matter, but affirms and welcomes and affectionately embraces it. If Holism begins as realism and ends as idealism, it does not spurn or deny its own past; in Holism both realism and idealism have their proper place and function and indeed find their justi-

fication and reconciliation. It breaks with Naturalism only at the point where Naturalism becomes purely materialistic, and in effect denies the creative plasticity of Nature, presents Nature as an anatomical museum, as a collection of dead and dried *disjecta membra*, instead of the interwoven body of living, creative progressive unities and syntheses which she essentially is.[48]

It is also interesting to note that the theory of levels implied in Process philosophy, and which fully accepts matter as one of the levels, is the metaphysics adopted by an American empirical theologian:

> The metaphysics here defended is different from all the foregoing. It is not materialism in the traditional sense, which asserted that pellets of matter accidentally fall into combinations to form all the objects of the world as we behold them, or at any rate to produce such illusions. On the other hand, if matter is identical with energy and if energy in the form of the creative event, working against the resistance of other forms of energy, produces all the good in the world, the evil being precisely this resistance to the creative event, then the metaphysics here upheld could be called a kind of materialism. But this kind of materialism must be sharply distinguished from everything bearing that name in the past. Since it must be so distinguished, it is misleading to call it materialism. Inanimate matter as known to common sense is *not* what creates all else, according to this philosophy. Rather, matter as known to common sense is merely one level

in that progressive creation which generates all the levels of order.[49]

The conception of a static materialistic nature is also rejected by philosophers who, while not precisely emergentists, indicate a profound appreciation of the active tendency in nature to form "new determinations" what J. C. Smuts calls "progressive unities and syntheses":

> Every being we know not only preserves its own being but constantly tends towards further new determinations not in existence before. Inorganic things move to new positions; plants grow; desire moves animals to new satisfactions; and men pass on to further decisions and acts. . . . The world of nature is existential and historical. To be is to be in act, and this is to be active.[50]

It is one of the triumphs of modern biology, however, to demonstrate that the active tendency of the world of nature, at the level of life, is manifested in the *organizing* capacity of protoplasm:

> Through all the complexity which it is the task of the biologist to analyze thus runs one fundamental fact common to every living thing: protoplasm *builds organisms*. It does not grow into indeterminate, formless masses of living stuff. The growth and activity shown by plants and animals are not random processes but are so controlled that they form integrated, coordinated, organized systems. The word *organism* is one of the happiest in biology, for it emphasizes what is now generally regarded as the most characteristic trait of a living thing, its *organization*. Here is the ulti-

mate battleground of biology, the citadel which must be stormed if the secrets of life are to be understood.[51]

In Process philosophy, therefore, nature is characterized by:

1. An active tendency in Space and Time, Alexander's nisus.

2. This active tendency is manifested at all levels, from the lowest to the highest; from the inorganic to the organic to the mental to the spiritual.

3. This dynamism of nature implies a forcible rejection of the dead matter of the mechanical materialists for a new concept of matter as flexible, plastic, capable of being integrated in systems of organization sustaining qualities and activities immeasurably higher than physico-chemical activity. Organization, found on every level of existence, is thus a metaphysical principle intimately associated with the active tendency of the nisus.

4. The new organization is not merely an intricate complexity, but has the character of an organic unity, a "whole" to use a term expressing the philosophy of J. C. Smuts:

> The goal of the organizing process seems always to be a *single, whole individual*.[52]

5. The whole individual is itself a system of systems, lesser wholes, cellular organizations, right down to the atom which is itself a pattern of organization:

> The ordinary division of a living organism into parts composed of cells, cells themselves, parts of cells, colloidal aggregates, molecules, and atoms, has been brought by Woodger under the notion of "hierarchical order."[53]

THE SYSTEM AS A WHOLE

6. This hierarchical order of systems of systems, of wholes composed of an organization of lesser wholes, often appears as simple, but this simplicity is "an *aesthetic* simplicity" which J. E. Turner defines as:

> It is invariably the result, that is to say, of the harmonious co-operation of a number of diverse elements—and usually of an extremely large number whose limits of differences are very wide. . . . the "simplicity" in question is not in itself deceptive, but on the contrary essentially real and highly valuable.[54]

Such are the characteristics of Process philosophy which we offer not as exhaustive explanation but merely as suggestions to indicate that the whole weight of such philosophy—of which Alexander's system is an example —is to deny reductive materialism and accentuate patterns of organization, novelties, wholes on an ascending hierarchical order of levels of reality. It is to be acknowledged, however, that Alexander has at times used language which seems to deny the reality of new patterns of organization which cannot be reduced to lower levels:

> Each new type of existence when it emerges is expressible completely or without residue in terms of the lower stage, and therefore indirectly in terms of all lower stages; mind in terms of living process, life in terms of physico-chemical process, sense quality like colour in terms of matter with its movements, matter itself in terms of motion.[55]

It would seem that Roy Wood Sellars, who could stand the accusation of materialism far more than Alexander, is nevertheless on surer ground when he asserts:

> The higher levels cannot be led to the lower without a remainder. We must take time and novelty seriously.[56]

Alexander should take time and novelty much more seriously than he has done in the quotation we have just given. The new type of existence can indeed be reduced in terms of the lower stages, but only at the cost of ignoring, even destroying, the organization which the creative process of the nisus has produced in *time*.

While it must be admitted that creative evolution is quite different from traditional theism, some philosophers of religion have perceived in it something much more amenable to the requirements of a religious view of life than the mechanism and materialism which Leighton seems to find in Alexander. An important distinction is made by A. S. Pringle-Pattison on this very issue between a lower Naturalism and a higher Naturalism. Leighton interprets Alexander in terms of a lower Naturalism, while we prefer to interpret him in terms of a higher Naturalism. We shall let A. S. Pringle-Pattison define these terms:

> It is important, I suggested, to distinguish between the lower and the higher Naturalism. The lower Naturalism is that which seeks to merge man in the infra-human nature from which he draws his origin—which consistently identifies the cause of any fact with its temporal antecedents, and ultimately equates the outcome of a process with its starting-point. A higher Naturalism will not hesitate to recognize the emergence of real differences where it sees them, without feeling that it is hereby establishing an absolute chasm between

THE SYSTEM AS A WHOLE

one stage of nature's processes and another. What we have to deal with is the continuous manifestation of a single Power, whose full nature cannot be identified with the initial stage of the evolutionary process, but can only be learned from the course of the process as a whole, and most fully from its final stages. . . . The philosophical point is that in each case we do pass to a new plane or level of existence, qualitatively different from the preceding and opening up, through that difference, a new range of possibilities to the beings which it includes.[57]

An emergent metaphysical system, such as Alexander's therefore, is not to be read merely in terms of its lowest degree of integration, such as primordial Space-Time, for Time and higher levels up to man, and the possibility of a higher level of "deity," are just as metaphysically real as the lower levels. Reality is then to be read in terms of its highest emergents, not in terms of its lowest phase. In other words, man is organic to nature, a culmination of nature, and not a mere spectator of a nature which in the words of Leighton, consists of "the product of material motions."[58] To quote once more from A. S. Pringle-Pattison:

> The idea of nature as a completed system and of man as a spectator *ab extra* is essentially false. The intelligent being is rather to be regarded as the organ through which the universe beholds and enjoys itself. From the side of the higher Naturalism, I sought to emphasize man's rootedness in nature, so that the rational intelligence which characterizes him appears as the culmination of a

continuous process of immanent development.[59]

Incidentally, this conception of nature beholding and enjoying itself through intelligent beings regarded as organs of the universe, is somewhat like that of Alexander when he states that

> we and all finites are, in the phrase we have used, comparable to organic sensa which God contemplates in enjoying his deity.[60]

The only difference is that Pringle-Pattison, distinguished theist, wrote about the universe, and Alexander, accused of being a materialist by Leighton, wrote about God. But since for Alexander, God is the whole universe in travail to produce deity, the conception of the universe as beholding itself through its highest products—so far as we know, men—regarded as organs of the universe, is very much the conception envisaged by Pringle-Pattison.

In reply to J. A. Leighton, we state that although Alexander has not given the emphasis required to the creative process of the nisus, his emergent metaphysics is not to be interpreted as sheer unrelieved materialism. The view that mind is based on living processes, and these include physico-chemical changes, is not necessarily a materialistic view, as Archbishop William Temple well knew:

> *My consciousness is not something else within the entire organism which is myself, taking note of the relations of that organism to its environment; my consciousness is itself that organism, being not only physical but psycho-physical, as related to its environment, namely to the universe of which it*

THE SYSTEM AS A WHOLE

is a part, though as the spiritual elements in the organism become predominant, the concomitant physical relations become relatively less important and may finally drop away.[61]

To be sure, Archbishop Temple is quite aware that such a view of consciousness is quite different from that which asserts the existence of "mind-stuff," but he is not unduly disturbed, nor should we be:

> the essential difference between mind and matter remains. It may be a difference of mode in the activity of one entity; indeed that view seems more probable than one which asserts either the existence of a "mind-stuff" or the activity of thought apart from anything which thinks. But the difference remains—the difference between action in response to stimuli without any contribution except inertia, and action initiated by appetitive appreciation of presented or imagined good.[62]

Action in response to stimuli in the form of inertia is simply the action of matter devoid of life, while action initiated by appreciation of the good is the response of the organism which is physico-chemical, *and also* vital, *and also* mental and spiritual.

Prediction in Alexander's System.—Among philosophers whose metaphysic is somewhat similar to that of Alexander is W. P. Montague, who has expressed admiration for *Space, Time, and Deity*, with, however, some qualification:

> although the present essay is a protest against one aspect of that work and a plea that when con-

fronted with the emergence of new levels of being we should put search for a rational etiology in place of the attitude of "natural piety."[63]

By "natural piety" Montague has reference to an essay of that title by Alexander in which the conception of the famous calculator of Laplace is discussed, and of the predictions of the future of the universe which might be made by such a calculator. The predictions which such a calculator might compute are severely limited by Alexander:

> Laplace's calculator might foresee that at a certain point a certain complexity might arise, whose actions were capable of measurement and would be those of living things. He could never affirm that this form of action would have the quality of life, unless he lived to see. He might predict ethereal waves but could not predict them to be light; still less that a material body would be material or when touched by light would be red, or even merely look red to a living body with eyes. All known forms of action could be predicted in their measurable characters, but never in their emergent ones.[64]

Emergent qualities are then accepted with "natural piety" because of the limitations of the predictive power, in view of the higher levels which cannot possibly be known ahead of the time at which they emerge in Time:

> A being who knew only life could not predict mind, though he might predict that combination of vital actions which has mind. But the limits of prediction are still narrower. In general, let A be a lower level and B the next higher level. A

being on the level A could not predict B. A being on the level B could possibly predict the whole future in terms of A and lower levels, but not in terms of B, *e. g.,* if he lived at the beginning of life, he could not predict the forms of life, except possibly in terms of physico-chemical action.[65]

In fact, Alexander further limited the predictive power of the calculator by suggesting that each level, such as the level of life, contained a great variety of forms of life "which may approximate to differences of quality"[66] so that predictions by a mathematician who knew the formulas pertaining to a lower quality on a certain level could not be made for the higher qualities of this particular level. The emergence of qualities which cannot be predicted is, then, acknowledged with natural piety, but it is just this natural piety which W. P. Montague attacks as "scientific treason" as we shall see:

> Whenever we are confronted with the emergence of a novel form, we never rest content with an attitude of "natural piety." "Natural piety" is scientific treason, a betrayal of the faith that has generated progress and enabled us to replace the helpless acceptance of novelties as brute facts with an increasingly satisfactory understanding and mastery of their genesis.[67]

As examples of emergent products which W. P. Montague no longer looks upon with helpless "natural piety" are the very simple ones of the emergence of ice into water, or the emergence of the new qualities of a chemical compound from the structure of the atoms:

> Ice emerges into water, and motion emerges into heat, but it is the molecular theory that gives us

an understanding of how in each case the transition is possible. When we pass from the intramolar to the intra-molecular or interatomic, we find in the minds of all chemists the methodological ideal of explaining the emergence of the new qualities of chemical compounds in terms of the quantitative relations of the atoms composing the molecule.[68]

But Montague apparently forgets that the chemist, to use an expression of Alexander, has "looked to see" the new compound, and then, has carried on experiments to decompose it and to build it up again so that he knows from what combination of atoms and under what conditions a compound with certain specified qualities will be formed. Had the chemist considered the atoms separately prior to their combination he would have been unable to predict the compound they would form or its qualities. This predicament of the chemist is examined at great length by C. D. Broad, and we cannot repeat all his arguments here, but shall rest content with a few quotations to indicate that W. P. Montague has not examined the situation at sufficiently close range, and that Alexander emerges victorious from the argument:

> Oxygen has certain properties and Hydrogen has certain other properties. They combine to form water, and the proportions in which they do this are fixed. Nothing that we know about Oxygen by itself or in its combinations with anything but Hydrogen would give us the least reason to suppose that it would combine with Hydrogen at all. Nothing that we know about Hydrogen by itself or in its combinations with anything but Oxygen would give us the least reason to expect that it

would combine with Oxygen at all. And most of the chemical and physical properties of water have no known connection, either quantitative or qualitative, with those of Oxygen and Hydrogen. Here we have a clear instance of a case where, so far as we can tell, the properties of a whole composed of two constituents could not have been predicted from a knowledge of the properties of these constituents taken separately, or from this combined with a knowledge of the properties, or other wholes which contain these constituents.[69]

Whenever we presume such a prediction it is because we are utilizing a suppressed premise that

> we have examined other complexes in the past and have noted their behaviour; that we have found a general law connecting the behaviour of these wholes with that which their constituents would show in isolation.[70]

In other words, the chemist has studied the complex water and already discovered the behavior of the complex and how and under what conditions it is made up of its constituents hydrogen and oxygen. Then, after he "has looked to see," he can predict the formation of water. Again, C. D. Broad makes the impossibility of prediction under other conditions very clear:

> The example of chemical compounds shows us ... if we want to know the chemical (and many of the physical) properties of a chemical compound, such as silver-chloride, it is absolutely necessary to study samples of *that particular compound*. It would of course (on any view) be useless merely to study silver in isolation and chlo-

rine in isolation; for that would tell us nothing about the law of their conjoint action.[71]

Hence, the investigator, in the words of Alexander, must "look to see" both the compounds and the elements, and after proper scientific investigation, he may be able to formulate the law connecting the chemical properties of silver-chloride with those of chlorine and silver, and this law is, in the words of C. D. Broad, "an *unique* and *ultimate* law."[72]

There is a point, however, in Montague's objection. That "scientific treason" with which he belabors Alexander would be justified if Alexander were so naive as to imagine that organic chemists will stand paralyzed with "natural piety" when facing the organic synthesis they have just completed. On the contrary, every organic synthesis first laboriously produced is further investigated for more efficient methods of production so that in the chemical laboratory natural piety soon changes into profitable industry. Alexander would not deny the importance of subjecting synthetic chemical compounds of the greatest complexity to the most drastic chemical tests in an endeavor to discover their constitution, but he would be right in insisting that when the compound is first synthesized, its properties are entirely novel and express a unique law connecting *that* compound with *its* elements under specific circumstances. But even if we did know all there is to know in that organic synthesis of a new individual studied in one of the most intractable of all sciences—embryology—there would still be natural piety in the consideration of how the highest level, mind, has emerged from a single cell, just as there may very well be natural piety in our enjoyment of a

THE SYSTEM AS A WHOLE

great symphony even when we know the sound which is made by every instrument in the symphony and precisely how it is made.

It would appear that C. D. Broad sustains Alexander and Bergson in their assertions that the typical calculating mind of Laplace is unable to predict the structure and properties of emergent existents from a knowledge of the structure and properties of their constituents. An attitude of "natural piety" is therefore more consonant with the standpoint of the reverent emergent evolutionist than the attitude of Montague who is an evolutionist of a different character. To be sure, "natural piety" is a much more modest metaphysical point of view than traditional theism, but it is in agreement with certain types of evolutionary theism is rejecting the mechanical and deterministic universe which the assumption of complete prediction presupposes. If such is the case, then, in the words of Alexander and Bergson, all is given, *tout est donné*:

> Either, then, the infinitely calculating mind of the hypothesis is unable to predict, or it is supposed by a *petitio principii* to know more than it really knows, and prediction is unnecessary. In the end it assumes Time to be unreal, or what is the same thing, that the universe is completed: that, in Mr. Bergson's phrase, *tout est donné*.[73]

If everything is given at once, there is no real birth of the future in Time, and we are simply advancing in mechanical patterns of existence which have been determined for us. The protests of both Alexander and Bergson against sheer mechanism bear on this very point, and we need not repeat them at this stage. There

227

are, however, certain obscurities in Alexander's doctrine of the future and the meaning of deity which we shall consider in the following chapter.

Summary.—We have endeavored to cast a rapid glance at Alexander's system as a whole and have summarized the major objections brought against it. When challenged as to his doctrine of Space and Time being abstractions of the reality of Space-Time, Alexander can reply very little but what is emphatic reiteration. As to the doctrine that emergents have arisen from complications of circumambient Space-Time, it is manifestly impossible to prove this doctrine and very few philosophers are in agreement with Alexander with respect to it. We have merely given some aspects of the New Cosmology—new in the sense that it introduces novel elements to the theories of Jeans and Eddington—and indicated that this cosmology tends in the direction of Alexander's system. We have questioned whether the ascent from materiality to forms of life, to mind, and eventually to deity, can be assumed as simultaneous for the whole universe, and have indicated that cosmic histories of galactic systems into stars, into solar systems, and possible forms of life, need not be contemporaneous and may appear at different periods in the flow of Time. We have attempted to defend Alexander against the criticism of philosophical idealists, such as Wilbur Urban and Bernard Bosanquet. We have denied that Alexander's system involves a mere mechanical complication of Space and Time, as if it were a materialism, but have emphasized Alexander's doctrine that life and mind are more than mechanisms though including mechanical systems and physico-chemical systems. We have sought the assistance of such distinguished theists as A. S. Pringle-Pattison and William Temple, Archbishop of

THE SYSTEM AS A WHOLE

Canterbury, to support Alexander's theory of mind. We have examined the criticisms brought by W. P. Montague against Alexander's doctrine of "natural piety" with respect to the problem of predictability, and have found this criticism unfounded through an argumentation based on C. D. Broad.

Obviously, all these problems are too briefly examined for a full philosophical study of Alexander's system, but we are not examining in this work Alexander's complete philosophy but primarily his doctrines of God and deity to which we turn in the following chapters.

CHAPTER II

GOD, DEITY, NISUS

The Four Conceptions of the Divine in Alexander's System.—A simplified idea of Alexander's system as bearing on his view of God and deity is given in these terms:

> God is the whole world as possessing the quality of deity. Of such a being the whole world is the 'body' and the deity is the 'mind.'[1]

Upon closer examination, however, we indicated towards the end of Chapter II of the "Exposition" section of this work that this elementary summary of Alexander's system may be more precisely divided into the following views of the divine:

1. The body of God as the whole of Space-Time, which means primordial Space-Time plus the existents it contains up to the moment of our observation. This is the pantheistic conception of God since it is all-inclusive. There is no Space outside God since the Space of the universe is all the Space there is, and at any time the universe does not grow into a previously unoccupied region, nor does it create more Space. It is also the substantive idea of God, not in Spinoza's sense of God as Substance, but rather to contrast this conception of God with the conception of "deity" which, in Alexander's system, is a quality beyond mind. A quality performs

an adjectival function to the existent or existents which possess it, and deity is thus an adjectival conception.

2. The "deity" of God is then the next empirical quality to be realized in the universe, and held to occupy an infinite portion of infinite Space-Time, but nevertheless a portion. It is not an individual and the categories and other characteristics, such as good and evil, or beauty and ugliness, or truth and error, cannot be applied to it. The contrasting qualities of good and evil, beauty and ugliness, truth and error do indeed characterize existents in Space-Time, and do exist within the universe as the body of God, but do not characterize "deity" as such. While God as the whole of Space-Time, including good and evil, is thus an unsatisfactory pantheistic conception of God, Alexander gives a heightened conception of deity in which the imperfections of his conception of God seem to be purged and replaced by characteristics of the traditional conception of a timeless God. Well does John W. McCarthy state:

> To his credit it should be observed that Alexander has also tried to adjust the values associated with a timeless God to his emerging deity.[2]

This is the theistic, even apparently transcendental, conception of God in Alexander, and he claims that the conceptions of pantheism and theism, while contradictory in other systems of religious philosophy, are reconciled in his fundamental metaphysic of Space-Time straining to achieve deity. It would seem that Alexander writes on occasion as if deity were substantive and not adjectival, but on closer examination, deity dissolves into what we have called the multiple phases of deity.

3. The multiple transcendence of deity, and not the mere transcendence of deity, is the name we have given

to Alexander's conception reiterated many times, that once deity is realized by becoming the highest quality in an emergent higher than man in a future birth of Time, there is a higher deity ahead of this emergent, and a realized deity ceases to be deity as such. But since Time is real both in its succession and in its infinite continuity into the future, we have indicated by means of our diagram on page 69 that the multiple phases of deity are a continuous process through the development of finites of higher complexity than man. Deity as such recedes into the future, but in the process of Time appears to be fragmented into finites. There is thus, if we follow through Alexander's metaphysical assumption concerning deity as the *next* higher quality, a progressive fragmentation of the quality deity into the highest quality, the "mind" of any number of levels of finite existents. These fragmentations of deity are no longer called "deity" by Alexander, but deity remains irrevocably ahead in the temporal sequence. We feel we are justified in stressing the conception of the multiple transcendence of deity, even when it has not been mentioned by other commentators, for it plays an important part in Alexander's speculative thought:

> For, again following the lines of experience, we can see that if the quality of deity were actually attained in the empirical development of the world in Time, we should have not one infinite being possessing deity but many (at least potentially many) finite ones. Beyond these finite gods or angels there would be in turn a new empirical quality looming into view, which for them would be deity—that is, would be for them what deity is for us. . . . If the possessor of deity were an exist-

GOD, DEITY, NISUS

ent individual he must be finite and not infinite.[3]

The forward movement of Time implies, then, nothing less than the fragmentation of the quality of deity into an increasing polytheism of finite existents higher than man. The conception of the multiple phases of deity, or of the multiple transcendence of deity is thus seen to imply a polytheistic system of numerous angels and finite gods emerging on the levels higher than man. This is, obviously, a conception unsatisfactory for religious purposes. However, on examining Alexander's system more closely, we find that these multiple phases of deity, while logically implied in the development of the world in the future, do not exist in the world of the present moment. Nevertheless the inevitable fragmentation of deity in the future birth of Time will provide us with an important criticism of deity in Alexander's system.

4. Deity is a nisus and not an accomplishment in the fourth conception of the divine in Alexander's system, for after he has developed speculatively the constitution of finite gods and angels in the future and of the deity which would still exist ahead of them in Time, Alexander makes a very important qualification:

> We are now led to a qualification of the greatest importance. The picture which has been drawn of the infinite God is a concession to our figurative or mythological tendency and to the habit of the religious consciousness to embody its conception of God in an individual shape. . . . But the infinite God is purely ideal or conceptual. The individual so sketched is not asserted to exist; the sketch merely gives body and shape, by a sort of anticipation, to the actual infinite God whom, on the basis of experience, speculation declares

to exist. As actual, God does not possess the quality of deity but is the universe as tending to that quality.[4]

The sketch of the infinite God, by which Alexander means the universe and the infinite deity with its successive phases, is not asserted to exist actually, that is, at the present moment in Time. What is actual is the universe as tending to deity, the universe as possessing the nisus or impulse to deity. What is not actual is deity as a future quality, or more precisely the fragmentation of deity in successive classes of existents higher than man and emerging at certain periods in future Time. Deity as infinite, and lending itself to the fragmentation process here mentioned, is held to exist in the future. In precisely what sense we shall examine below, but actually at the present moment it does not exist as realized quality but only as process, for we can never eliminate Time from the nature of the universe or any of its existents:

> To suppose that the infinitely great must be completed is to eliminate Time from its nature.[5]

Again,

> God as an actual existent is always becoming deity but never attains it.[6]

It would appear, therefore, that when Alexander is confronted with the question of what exists actually of a divine nature in the world, he is obliged to give a much more modest answer than his speculation as to an infinite deity in the distant future consisting of an infinite portion of Space-Time characterized by that ineffability of quality which, if realized, would suggest that poetic transport associated with Meredith's *Hymn to Colour*.[7] This more modest answer, which involves in Alexander's thought a radical transition from future deity to present nisus, is given in his words which we shall emphasize later when bringing forward a radical criticism of the whole conception of a futuristic deity:

> The actual reality which has deity is the world of empiricals filling up all Space-Time and tending towards a higher quality. Deity is a nisus and not an accomplishment. This, as we shall see, is what prevents the conception from being wholly theistical.[8]

In fact, we shall develop the view that the nisus of Space-Time is an infra-pantheistic conception.

These are, then, the four main conceptions of Alexander as to the divine: the body of God; the deity of God; the multiple phases of deity; and the nisus. We shall examine each of these more thoroughly.

The "body" and the "mind" of God.—That God has a body and that God has a mind is a fundamental aspect of Alexander's metaphysics. And the body of God is not to be understood in a metaphorical or figurative sense. Let us repeat once more Alexander's own words:

> God is the whole world as possessing the quality of deity. Of such a being the whole world is the 'body' and the deity is the 'mind.'[9]

It is well to admit at the outset that the conception of God having a body is one which theology has not favored, and that it is not the mark of emancipation and enlightened metaphysics but of anthropomorphism:

> One is amazed at the number of people who

aver that God is a Spirit and yet picture him with a physical body. (Still no serious theologian has asserted that a personal God has a physical body, except perhaps Swedenborg.) Here we see a good example of the *kind* of anthropomorphism to be avoided. To say that a human person could not exist without his nervous system, muscles, bone, and skin is in no way proof that God too has a body. Indeed, the historic contention is that absence of bodily form constitutes a major difference between the divine Person and the human.[10]

Here, as in many other respects, Alexander's views on theology differ markedly from those of traditional theism. Why is he so emphatic about this division of God into "body" and "mind"? Because with him such a division is a fundamental principle of the construction of Space-Time. Or better expressed, the union of body and mind is a basic conception holding for all finites as well as for Space-Time. It is Alexander's well-known formula for Space-Time:

> It is that Time as a whole and in its parts bears to Space as a whole and its corresponding parts a relation analogous to the relation of mind to its equivalent bodily or nervous basis; or to put the matter shortly that Time is the mind of Space and Space the body of Time. According to this formula the world as a whole and each of its parts is built on the model with which we are familiar in ourselves as persons, that is as union of mind and body, and in particular as a union of mind and brain.[11]

It is interesting to note that Alexander seems to take our

familiar pattern as union of mind and body to be repeated in the world as a whole and in each of its parts. It would be true to say that for Alexander man is the pattern of all things, rather than the famous statement of Protagoras:

> Man . . . is the measure of all things, of the existence of things that are, and of the non-existence of things that are not.[12]

Again, for Alexander, it might be said that man is the contemplator of all things, or the enjoyer of all things, or the discoverer of all things; but he is the *pattern* of all things rather than the *measure* of all things. One may well inquire, Is Alexander justified in making such a vast extrapolation to include the universe and the parts it embraces from the constitution of our persons? Alexander has here a quick *volte face* to the effect that the universe's pattern is not based on us, but rather that we exemplify the pattern of the universe:

> But as this may lead to the misapprehension that we are the standard and exemplar of things, the statement is better made in the reverse and truer form that we are examples of a pattern which is universal and is followed not only by things but by Space-Time itself. . . . Qualities will be seen to be the special form which on each successive level of existence the mind element assumes.[13]

The formula that each successive quality of existence is the "mind" of lower levels has its difficulties when applied to the course of evolutionary forms, for it is not clear in what sense life is the "mind" of material existence, nor in what sense secondary qualities of matter are the "mind" of primary qualities of **matter**, and even more difficult to perceive in what precise sense matter is the "mind" of primordial Space-Time. Can we be so certain that Space-Time itself and its parts are constituted on a union of body and mind? Can we assume that this general pattern pervades the universe and all its existents? If so, how shall we interpret the following questions? What is the mind of the earth? What is the mind of the solar system, of our galaxy of some tens of billions of stars? Is the color of a star the mind of its atomic constituents? If a star has no color, such as the dark companion of Sirius, then just where is its "mind"? The danger of applying "mind" to inorganic objects leads to such fantastic speculation as investing individual molecules with psychic qualities—a strange view apparently held by the distinguished philosophical theologian Charles Hartshorne:

> What is the perspective that belongs individually to a molecule as a man's perceptions belong to the man? Does the molecule's perspective possess quality, and if so how can it lack feeling or sensation? Does it possess the past as real in the present, and then how can it lack memory?[14]

The view that the highest quality of an existent higher than man is its "mind" seems to be on a sounder foundation analogically than the view that qualities lower than human mind, such as life, or materiality, are themselves "mind" of the level immediately below them. It seems that the term "mind" may be taken only in a metaphorical or analogical sense, as is indicated by Dorothy Emmet:

> The general principle is that the distinctive quality of the structure at its own level is the "mind"

of that structure. "Mind" here does not mean consciousness or thought, which is the quality characteristic of the level we call "mind" proper. It is "mind" in an analogical sense, the characteristic of a new qualitative synthesis.[15]

The postulation that all existents as well as Space-Time itself, and God, are therefore unions of "body" and "mind" seems to rest on shaky ground, that is, on a very wide extrapolation of the constitution of human beings as body and mind. We have already observed that to consider God as having a body in the whole universe is an anthropomorphism which very few theologians accept. Let us continue our inquiry to investigate in what sense, if any, deity can be the "mind" of God.

Assuming for the sake of the argument the existence of an infinite quality, deity, at some future time in the history of the universe, in what way can we call this quality the mind of God? Obviously, it is postulated to be immeasurably higher than man, higher than man's highest mental and spiritual capacities, and has thus some affinity with the conception of a divine being which is generally held to be higher than man. But we must remember that for Alexander deity is not a substantive being, but a qualitative conception, an adjectival property of the universe. Has deity self-consciousness, awareness, goodness, on a scale infinitely superior to such qualities in man? The answer is decidedly in the negative, and the passage in Alexander which is crucial for this issue is the following:

> Deity does not know but only the minds know which are included in the body of God. Deity knows only in the extended sense of knowing which is not human knowing nor any extension

of it. God's 'knowing' is his contemplation of things, his 'knowledge' the objects of his acts of enjoying his deity. Moreover, infinitely as his deity is extended in space and time, and though he contemplates the whole of Space-Time, even deity contemplates only those qualities which have been hitherto developed within Space-Time, and he cannot foretell the quality which shall in good time supersede his deity, any more than we humans can foretell what qualities shall supersede mind. There is always impending over him the menace which Prometheus levels against Zeus of supersession by a higher God.[16]

Our familiar conception of the successive phases of deity is clearly indicated in this passage, though we would modify the expression "supersession by a higher God" to mean "supersession by a higher phase of deity." As we have indicated previously, Alexander sometimes uses "God" to mean a higher phase of deity, but were he consistent he would use "God" for the whole universe as straining toward any of the phases of deity. It therefore never is a higher God, as such, which is ahead in Time, but a higher phase of deity. However, this correction is a secondary matter besides the essential point in this quotation which is this: "Deity does not know but only the minds know which are included in the body of God."

We have already discussed the meaning of this conception.[17] The conclusion to which we arrived as a result of that discussion was that the quality of deity is, in the course of time, fragmented into the highest quality of beings of a hierarchical order higher than man. This highest quality is what corresponds to "mind" in these higher beings. Therefore, mind can be postulated in a strict sense only of the highest quality of these beings, and not of the infinite deity which lies further ahead in Time. Also, knowledge can be postulated only of man and of beings higher than man, and not of the quality of deity, assumed to exist in its ineffable singularity ahead in time of any complex living forms higher than man. For we must hold Alexander strictly to his statement:

> Deity does not know, but only the minds know which are included in the body of God.[18]

And if deity does not know, how can Alexander claim that deity knows in an extended sense which is not human knowing, as he does in the statement just following the one we have given:

> Deity knows only in the extended sense of knowing which is not human knowing nor any extension of it.[19]

Why does Alexander introduce this affirmation of deity's knowledge in an extended sense of knowing, when he has just made a statement to the effect that deity as such does not know but only the minds know which have evolved in the course of time, and which are, like all finites of whatever order, within the body of God? It would seem that Alexander was aware that a strict interpretation of his phrase about deity's lack of knowledge would result in a disparagement of his conception of deity. To obviate this conclusion, he hastened to add that deity knows in an extended sense of knowing, and that deity though infinite in Space and Time, contemplates the qualities developed up to its own level. But is this the infinite deity, the final pervasive ineffable quality poised ahead of any existents in Time? It would appear it is so since Alexander writes: "infinitely as his deity is extended in space and time."[20] But a further difficulty develops as it appears that he switches from this meaning into that of the existents who have incorporated in Time the quality of deity, so that a further deity exists in the future. The successive phases of deity seem to dog our steps at every point in our exposition! The clarification of Alexander's meaning is difficult precisely because he shifts from his conception of deity as some infinite, ineffable, portion of Space-Time, always ahead of any existents, that is to say always higher than any existents we may imagine as emerging in future Time, to the conception of deity as realized (and therefore ceasing to be deity) in the highest quality of these existents higher than man. When Alexander concentrates his attention on these higher existents, he is inclined to the view that his conception of God and deity is merely mythological:

> The picture which has been drawn of the infinite God is a concession to our figurative or mythological tendency.[21]

It is correct, therefore, for commentators sympathetic to Alexander's peculiar theism to assert:

> A luminous possibility is advanced which, we are then told, is not really possible. In this form the view satisfies only partially, and perhaps does not satisfy at all, man's religious propensities.[22]

But to return to our problem of the knowledge or the lack of knowledge of deity! It is our contention that it is these finite existents, the finite gods or angels of Alexander, as well as man, that know in the real sense of knowledge as contemplation of objects and enjoyment of the mind. These are the only minds that exist in the succession of Time, the minds that are intimately associated with bodies, and thus belong to spatio-temporal finite existents. We are not convinced that deity as that infinite portion of Space-Time held by Alexander to exist at some distant future time beyond any emerging existents really knows anything at all! Nor are we convinced of a recent classification of Alexander's God as:

> Extreme Temporalistic Theism . . . God as Purely Temporal Consciousness, Knowing or Partially Knowing the World.[23]

We agree with the characterization of "extreme temporalistic theism" but we disagree with God's knowledge of the world in Alexander's theism, since we have just shown that deity as the mind of God does not know anything, but knowledge applies only to men and finite beings higher than men through their "mental" quality. Far from deity actively knowing anything, it must be remembered that it is a receptive rather than an active power, for has not Alexander asserted that our moral struggles and efforts are actually constructing deity?

> It is not God then who allows the struggle, but the struggle which is to determine, it may be not at once but in the end, what deity is to be; which ideal if either is on the side of the divine.[24]

Hartshorne and Reese, we believe, should have classified Alexander's theism with Wieman's theism as

> Extreme Temporalistic Theism . . . God as Purely Temporal but Not Conscious and Not Knowing the World.[25]

The theological rapprochement of Alexander and Wieman we shall consider presently.

Our conclusion of the whole question of the "body" and the "mind" of God, is first, that the expression "body of God" is too anthropomorphic for any system of metaphysics, such as Alexander's, which claims to be enlightened, and, secondly, that the "mind of God" as deity is not sufficiently clarified. When clarified we find that knowledge is not possessed by deity, but by the minds which are assumed to emerge in Time. Only these minds know and deity does not know. These minds are not overruling or overarching the whole universe, but are strictly possessed by finite existents within the whole universe. Therefore, the universe does not have a mind, but minds exist within the universe whose knowledge is limited to the investigation of qualities up to their minds, up to the level of their "minds." We find increasingly dubious two of Alexander's conceptions of the divine: the whole as the "body" of God; and "deity" as the mind of God.

Theism and Pantheism in Alexander's System.—Part of Alexander's strategy is to affirm that theism and pantheism are two conceptions of God in the philosophy of religion which are irreconcilable, and that therefore the philosophy of religion labors under insuperable difficulties.[26] Referring to theism and pantheism, he states that

> these conceptions . . . belong to the philosophy of religion; they are a blending of data derived both from philosophy and religious experience.[27]

An easy reply is that the philosophy of religion, and especially theology, have discussed theism only as relevant to their purposes, and have rejected forms of pantheism, such as Spinoza's for instance. When Alexander

GOD, DEITY, NISUS

points to a contradiction between theism and pantheism, the traditional philosophy of religion is not at all perturbed, since it has already rejected one of the terms of the contradiction, the pantheistic term.

A more serious criticism of Alexander is that the immanence of traditional theism is not clearly distinguished from pantheism, so that the contradiction between theism and pantheism exists within the theistic conception:

> Thus the so-called immanent theism has never, so far as I know, been clearly distinguished from pantheism; there is always lingering about the conception a suspicion that without much regard for consistency it seeks to combine the religious attraction of theism with the speculative attraction of pantheism.[28]

The doctrine of immanence, however, signifies not that God is to be identified with the world and the finites, but that he sustains them. Alexander's strategy in indicating weaknesses in both theism and pantheism is not as thoroughgoing as he imagines, for he apparently was not quite precise as to just what it is orthodox doctrines assert about theism. What he can claim is that there are many different doctrines of God within the general category of theism, and that their existence in this varied form cannot be the ground for claiming any of them final.[29]

While Alexander is insistent that theism and pantheism are irreconcilable, he makes a plea for his own conception of God and deity as affording the only possible reconciliation:

> The union of transcendence and immanence is

> effected, but not in the way of either theism or pantheism. Pure transcendence and pure immanence are, as we saw, irreconcilable. But in different respects God transcends and indwells. His deity, though a part of the world, within it and not without it, transcends the inferior order of developed creations, including man; but being the whole world as it tends to deity or is engaged in the production of deity, God takes in within himself the whole world and is therefore immanent in it. He is transcendent, as it were, in respect of his mind (to use a human analogy) and immanent in respect of his body. His transcendence and his immanence are united through their different functions in God's total being.[30]

Furthermore, Alexander claims that in the more important aspect, his conception is theistic:

> he is not a being on the level of man, with personality and mental powers like man's, raised only to a higher pitch, but transcends all finites, because he is the whole world as tending to a higher order of finites. In this, which is the more important respect, the conception is theistic.[31]

We have already called attention to the difficulties of God's body as the whole world, and God's mind as deity, but quite apart from these objections, it may be said that Alexander is emphatic that deity is within the world, in no sense does it transcend the world. God's deity transcends all the finites but is this sufficient to make of Alexander's conception, in the last resort, transcendent theism? Our answer must be in the negative, for a conception of deity as being contained within the world,

GOD, DEITY, NISUS

and occupying only a part of the infinite world of Space-Time has not the character of transcendence usually associated with theism, for transcendence has meant transcendence beyond the world, not merely beyond the finites of the world. As William Temple states,

> God is active in the world, and its process is His activity. Yet he is more than this; He is creator and therefore transcendent.[32]

Alexander's conception is therefore not transcendent theism, but is rather influenced by pantheism. Certainly, a God who in his character of deity occupies a portion of the infinite world, is not the transcendent God of theism, but savors of an immanent conception. Even what we have called the transcendent phases of deity are not really transcendent but ultimately immanent. Alexander's view of God—quite apart from the difficulties of deity—is not theistic, especially so when he states that

> as being the whole universe God is creative, but his distinctive character of deity is not creative but created.[33]

Alexander's insistence, however, that his conception of God is both immanent and transcendent has led to a variety of opinions as to his system. We agree with Rudolf Metz's conclusion that Alexander has not been successful in claiming theism for his view.

> God is immanent in the world in relation to His body, but transcendent in relation to His mind or deity. Yet this argument does not seem to be in harmony with Alexander's doctrine elsewhere, but looks like a mere play of ideas. His theology

is thoroughly pantheistic and his concept of God is so completely involved in the texture of the world that all his efforts to save the transcendence of God and to justify theism against pantheism are in vain.[34]

Rudolf Metz's judgment is one with which we are profoundly in agreement. We are, therefore, bound to qualify some statements in Cornelia Geer Le Boutillier's study of Alexander in which the essential immanence of Alexander's deity is not appreciated. For instance,

> Alexander's God is not discoverable in nature. He is, as it were, potentially transcendent. But He is not existent as a knowable Being. For Bergson, God is, as I have shown, entirely immanent.[35]

Whatever may be the differences between Alexander and Bergson, they cannot be reduced to the immanence of God for Bergson, and the transcendence of deity for Alexander. Mrs. Le Boutillier's inadequate statement is due to the fact that Alexander did not always make clear when he was writing of God as the whole universe tending to deity, and when he was writing of deity as a future existent possessed by God. Hence, God, as the whole universe tending to deity, is discoverable in nature. Furthermore, even deity is wholly within nature, in no sense beyond the universe of Space-Time, so that the transcendence of Alexander's deity is a transcendence only from the point of view of our own existence at this moment of Time. It is in no sense a transcendence beyond the universe. Again another hasty comparison between Alexander and Bergson is:

> In contrast to Alexander, Bergson emphasizes the

GOD, DEITY, NISUS

unification of the divine powers, and brings them into the very stuff of nature.[36]

Are not the divine powers unified in Alexander as the whole universe tending to deity? Is not deity just as much within the universe as is Bergson's *élan vital*? Alexander has so accentuated the transcendence of deity as an existent quality at some far distant future time that his doctrine is easily misinterpreted as the transcendence of traditional theism. It is odd to perceive this error in an otherwise scholarly anthology:

> Examining in full his statements about God and deity, for example, one finds that he asserts the universe to be contained in God, while deity (eternally) transcends that universe.[37]

In the first place, the universe is not contained in God, but God *is* the universe of Space-Time as tending to deity. God as "body" and the whole universe of Space-Time absolutely coincide and it cannot be said that one is within the other. Secondly, deity does not transcend the universe, since it is an infinite portion within infinite Space-Time, but in the future. Thirdly, deity does not eternally transcend the universe, for such a formulation would imply that deity lies in an eternal realm completely divorced from that infinite temporality which is what Alexander means by Time. Our discussion of Alexander's meaning of eternity as infinite Time and not as the traditional notion of a quality distinct from time, negates, unfortunately, the assertion just made by Hartshorne and Reese.

We insist with Metz that Alexander's deity is still immanent within the universe of Space-Time, and is nowhere transcendent from that universe, since in Alexander's system, Space-Time is all there is. To be sure, there are difficulties in the conception of deity as a future quality forever receding with the advance of Time, this very advance of Time which apparently fragments this deity into higher existents, so that a deity in the future beyond this advance in Time is postulated to exist.

We need not labor the point that a pantheistic conception of the universe as the body of God is unsatisfactory. The apparently transcendent, but really immanent and pantheistic, conception of deity is also unsatisfactory, and here we may give due weight to Mrs. Le Boutillier's criticism:

> How can we, as he asks us to, have faith that a new and higher order of being will unpredictably and unintelligibly arise and survive in the future? If Alexander would sacrifice temporal futurity and show us in the here and now potency in an intelligible sense known and discerned to be higher than human actuality, how quick we would be to bow the knee to it.[38]

When we take Time seriously, as does Alexander, there seems to be an insuperable difficulty in relating the religious sentiment to a futuristic deity existing in a future time when we ourselves will no longer be in existence. When pressed with such an objection, Alexander introduces his conception of the nisus, but as we have indicated many times, he has neglected the nisus as a creative power for much metaphysical elaboration of the meaning of deity as the "mind" of God, which elaboration proves to be unsatisfactory under close examination.

John Laird's Criticisms.—Although we have criticized a number of Alexander's views, it is relevant at this point to introduce the examination of Alexander's peculiar theism by John Laird, a friend of his who asserted:

> Alexander was, quite certainly, a theist in his own Alexandrian way, a way that was never insincere.[39]

Nevertheless, Laird found many expressions of difficulty in Alexander's exposition of God and deity:

> In Alexander's exposition, "deity," "the quality of deity," "actual deity" (or "God"), "the *nisus* towards deity" and other such phrases are used in a way that often strains the attention if it is not downright misleading. Sentences like "Even God himself does not as actual God possess deity attained but only the *nisus* towards it" (S.T.D., ii, 418) or "God is, if we may use such language, the power which makes for deity" (ii, 428) are instances. I shall therefore allow myself, quite frequently, to use other words.[40]

The way out of the difficulty seems to be the division of the various views of the divine into the four conceptions we have introduced at the beginning of this chapter, and the investigation of their status and validity. But Laird is right in pointing out the lack of precision with which Alexander has used these terms. Laird accepts the central conception of Alexander that the universe is in *process*, but is doubtful that *process* inevitably signifies *progress* along the emergent ladder of the *nisus* for the whole universe:

> If we accept the premiss (which I personally am unable to reject) that *process* belongs to the mar-

row of all existence, including God's, we might boggle at the further premiss that the *process* must be *progress*, and again at the gloss that such progress is quite clearly and specifically along the emergent ladder of the *nisus*. If Space-Time in its early career was a fluid submaterial magma the emergence of materiality would seem to be a universal cosmic step.[41]

But can such a universal ladder be asserted for the whole universe, or shall we postulate, as in fact we did in the previous chapter, a number of historical planetary emergences in various parts of the universe? Laird seems to support this latter view:

> A critic might be disposed to say that even if the ladder had been exemplified in the existence of this planet, it was only a planetary and not a cosmic ladder, and, for that matter, probably episodic even in a planetary way. The emergent ladder of the *nisus* might be quite a little ladder, and something of a cosmic curiosity instead of being that with which the entire universe was and had always been in travail.[42]

Turning now to Alexander's conception of deity as the "rung in the ladder immediately above mind,"[43] Laird seems to be impressed, as was Le Boutillier, with the transcendence of this deity, and is inclined to believe that such theologians as Maritain and Karl Barth might give it approval:

> Such a conception, in very many ways, may seem to be a most generous type of theism. It might extort a certain reluctant approval from M. Mari-

tain and even from Herr Barth, for these authors, in very different ways, agree in insisting that the divine is altogether above the human, in kind as well as in degree, and is falsified if it is philosophised into an objective ideal of "perfect" knowledge like unto (although magnifying) all human knowledge.[44]

But Laird has not made clear that the reason for the "reluctant approval" would probably be that Maritain and Barth would readily perceive—perhaps more readily than Laird himself—that this generous theism is fundamentally a type of pantheism, and furthermore, that this deity—except in the sense of the nisus—does not actually exist.

Having acknowledged the sincerity of Alexander, the possibility of planetary rather than cosmic emergence, and the objective theism of the system which is above human knowledge and human values, Laird, however, proceeds to a more minute examination in which puzzling features seem to accumulate:

> Alexander's doctrine seems to be crammed, if not even to be choked, with several serious difficulties.[45]

1. The first difficulty is that theologians would claim that God is ultimate, while in Alexander's system,

> the progressive historicity of things *would* be ultimate, the last word in any metaphysics, but God or deity, that is, the achievement of the next stage above "mind" in the ladder of emergence would not be ultimate at all.[46]

Laird acknowledges this radical difference between theism and Alexander's emergent God, but seeks to justify the latter on the ground that

> the *nisus* was more worshipful in the long run than the particular emergent stage that we call deity, but, no doubt, there may be a certain ingratitude in complaining of a "deity" that *ex hypothesi* is incommensurably higher than the best that is human.[47]

This is all that Laird states on this particular problem of Alexander's theism, the futuristic deity to which we shall return presently.

2. Even though Alexander elaborated on the possible existence and construction of finite gods and angels, he stated that the question of their actual emergence in the universe was "trivial and scholastic."[48] But Laird pursues the subject. If it be assumed that minds have emerged late in the cosmic process, and not merely late in the history of the earth, and if it be further assumed that finite deities have emerged above the stage of mind, but through the stage of mind, then "we should necessarily encounter them unawares."[49] Should we meet them, we should never know it, according to Laird's conjecture, on the principle of Alexander that our knowledge is enjoyment of the mind, but contemplation of lower levels than mind. We could not contemplate beings whose "mind" is higher than our own mind—at least on Alexander's theory of knowledge—but is Laird right in assuming that we would encounter them unawares? Since these higher beings are constructed on the basis of mind, and mind on the basis of life, and life on the basis of materiality, and materiality on the basis of Space-Time, these beings would possess a living body built of

GOD, DEITY, NISUS

physico-chemical processes subserving the organs of this body, so that their highest quality, what is "mind" for them, and "super-mind" for us, would necessarily be intrinsically connected with a material body, and be a union of body and mind just as we are. We certainly would encounter them with some awareness of their material contours and biological structures and functions, though the precise nature of their "super-mind" would remain unknown to us. But would this bar communication with them? We may agree, however, with Laird:

> *Such* speculation is indeed "trivial and scholastic," but there is a more serious point.[50]

This more serious point is the supposition of Alexander's view of the historicity of things according to which "we *do* know" that Space-Time existed prior to the level of materiality, that at a certain time in past history, materiality "supervened upon it universally,"[51] then forms of life once more supervened universally at a certain time throughout the whole cosmos, and finally mental life supervened in circumscribed forms but universally at a certain historical period throughout the universe. On this rigid emergent view holding for the whole universe,

> the cosmos would have no room for "angels" or for "gods" until it has evolved through these stages. . . . But there is nothing to forbid the belief that there may be plenty of angels *now*, and plenty of Jovian gods above angels, and plenty of Promethean gods above Jovian gods.[52]

Laird's rejoinder to this process of rigid emergence for the whole universe proceeding from Space-Time to materiality, to life, to mind, to deity, is very similar to the objection we raised in the previous chapter. It is that we do not know "anything of the kind"[53] with respect to the whole universe, though we do have some evidence of the origin of human minds on this planet through the evolutionary process of life on this earth. The limited evidence of life on this planet is too weak to infer a similar evolutionary series for the universe with its millions of galaxies:

> What right have we to infer that superhuman levels may not have been established aeons before life appeared on this planet? Since Alexander's conception of the historicity of things implies progress as well as process, we should have to say, I suppose, that deity could not be co-eternal with the world, or at any rate that some high level of existence (perhaps a level much higher than mere deity) could not come *first*.[54]

Laird here means that if the ascent to deity means a progress of perfection to deity, and not mere process of change, then deity cannot be co-eternal, that is, cannot occupy the same infinite Time as the world,[55] though it may occupy an infinite portion of this Time, but in any case it did not come first since it presupposed lower levels in Time. By "a level much higher than mere deity" Laird here means a phase of deity higher than the first phase above the human mind, according to our development of the phases of deity. If, however, Alexander's metaphysics means process and not progress, deity is no longer regarded as emerging in the distant future and is replaced by divine process "co-eternal with the universe" as Laird states, or as Alexander would prefer to put it, divine process co-existing with the universe throughout the universe's infinite Time. But Laird's own words are as follows:

> But if process and not progress is all that Alexander has proved (and I do not think he proved more), then divine process, or a process still higher, might very well be co-eternal with the universe. That is what many people believe who believe in God's "eternity" and also in the "redemption" of the human race. Credible or not the conception implies no inconsistency.[56]

That is to say, if Alexander's grandiose cosmic scheme of emergence as progress is limited to the emergence of life, mind, and possibly forms of life higher than mind in planetary systems at any periods in the infinite Time of the cosmos and not at specified periods late in its history, then we may postulate a divine process co-eternal with the universe. This, to be sure, is quite different from Alexander's conception of deity as a future emergent, but it is not necessarily in contradiction with his notion of the nisus of Space-Time as an activity throughout the whole history of Space-Time. When the function of the nisus is emphasized as active throughout all Time, then the nisus becomes co-eternal with the universe. But it is worthy of note that we are here using the terms "eternal" and "co-eternal" in Alexander's sense of infinite Time, or everlasting Time, and we believe that Laird is using them in that sense also. Having agreed with Laird up to this point, however, we question his claim:

> That is what many people believe who believe in God's "eternity" and also in the "redemption" of the human race.[57]

On the contrary, that is not what many people believe with respect to God's "eternity" for in traditional theism, as we indicated in Chapter I of our Exposition, eternity is of an entirely different quality from everlasting or infinite Time. While we tend to agree with Alexander's view of eternity as infinite Time, we must confess that this is not the usual religious conception, so that Alexander's view of process, shared by John Laird, is not "eternity" in the usual traditional sense. And religious people who believe in God's eternity also believe in many specific doctrines about God which go far beyond his character of being merely "co-eternal with the universe." We are not at this time discussing the pros and cons of traditional doctrines of God, we are merely making distinctions. As to "redemption of the human race," John Laird does not make clear what he means except that possibly he indicates that redemption is a continuous process in time. But what theory of redemption he has in mind and how he relates it to Alexander's system he does not state beyond this vague temporal expression.

3. The third problem raised by Laird is to the effect that in Alexander's metaphysics, actual deity is held to be finite. Is this so?

> Here, however, one may wonder whether, as so often, the system may not have manufactured difficulties which, without it, would not exist.[58]

John Laird refers to the famous seaweed illustration which we had better give in full:

> The mental structure of which a portion more complex and subtle is the bearer of deity, must not be thought necessarily to be a human mind or aggregation of such, but only to be of the mental

order. To assume it to be of the nature of human mind would be as if a race of seaweeds were to hold that mind when it comes (the quality of deity for seaweeds) must be founded on the life of seaweeds, and minds the offsprings of seaweeds.[59]

Alexander did not wish to portray the emergence of deity as a complexity of the human mind though it would be of a mental order. Just as life in man and life in seaweeds are greatly different in quality, Alexander supposes that deity as the next emergent after human mind must be higher than if deity were directly constructed on a portion of the human mind as such. It is built on a mental order, but where will Alexander find in his system the mental order of sufficient elevation and delicacy to carry the deity next to mind, since it is said to be next to human mind? In John Laird's opinion the system has manufactured difficulties for itself which could be avoided on the supposition that deity is constructed on other *rapports* than a *rapport* with mental order:

> Such a *rapport* might be between our minds (or the minds of the elect among us) and the minds of Martians and Saturnians. It might be a *rapport* between our minds and their stars, or more generally, a cosmic *rapport* that had nothing to do with the finite boundaries of living bodies and of living body-minds. So far as I can see the proof of the finitude of (actual) "deity" rests upon the finitude of the theatre (*i.e.* of the human body) in which the mental rung of the ladder of historicity invariably emerges from the merely vital rung. If bodily contours be held to be irrelevant, anything in the world may be supposed.[60]

While these questions are highly speculative, one wonders whether John Laird's emendations of Alexander's conception of deity are as satisfactory as he thinks for the support of a doctrine of infinite deity. He is unsatisfied with the finite deities which Alexander postulates as the order of existents on the level immediately superior to that of man, and finds the assumption of finite bodily contours for these deities to be the stumbling block. If a finite deity is postulated as carried by finite body, then Laird assumes that infinite deity had rather be assumed as carried by a relation between our minds and the minds of the Saturnians and Martians, but this would not give an infinite base for deity unless the Martians and Saturnians were infinite in number! Similarly to postulate a relation between our minds, and "their stars" (the sun?), would afford little metaphysical comfort to Laird since the infinity he requires would demand that our minds be infinite, or that the sun be infinite! It seems that with the speculation of bodily contours as irrelevant, "anything in the world may be supposed," but then infinite deity would be merely one possibility of a large number of possibilities, and we do not see what Laird gains through these extravagant suppositions of the nature of finite gods and angels, which suppositions become increasingly grotesque rather than philosophically enlightening.

As a matter of fact, the speculation of Alexander as to the existence of finite gods or angels in no way detracts from the infinite deity, since this deity always exists in its infinitude beyond any realized and fragmented deity into existents of a higher order than man. But whether this infinite deity actually exists in the future is another question, with respect to which we have already raised many objections.

4. An objection of John Laird more cogent than the one we have just mentioned is to the effect that Alexander writes repeatedly of deity as "a new quality above man to which *the whole world* tends."[61] Why should the whole world be occupied in straining after deity? Why should the world be thought of as possessing deity? This objection had already been raised by G. Dawes Hicks:

> Why should God be conceived as the *whole* world possessing deity? If deity be an empirical quality, as is mind or life or colour, is there more reason why the whole world should be the body of God than that it should be the body of any one of these qualities? Are we, indeed, to suppose that the whole world is the body (say) of mind prior to mind's emergence, but that when it does emerge its body shrinks into a very insignificant portion of that world.[62]

This may well be called "the shrinkage theory" of the body of God, and Alexander is involved in these difficulties simply because of his peculiar notion of applying deity to any level of existence, high or low:

> For any level of existence, deity is the next higher empirical quality.... For creatures who possessed only the primary qualities,—mere empirical configurations of space-time,—deity was what afterwards appeared as materiality, and their God was matter.[63]

The "shrinkage theory" applies in this way. Since deity is any quality higher than the level immediately preceding, the universe in its totality may just as well be said to strain after the quality of materiality, or the quality of life, or the quality of mind, as of the quality of deity. On the same argumentation, if the whole world is the "body" of deity, why is not the whole world equally the body of the qualities of materiality, of life, or of mind? The difficulty for the case of mind is crucial, for according to the general principle just enunciated, the whole world can justifiably be called the body of mind, immediately prior to mind's emergence, but once finite minds have emerged, then their body is no longer the whole world, but their actual finite bodies. There is, then, a shrinkage from the whole universe as straining to produce the quality of mind to the very insignificant parts of the whole world which are the biological bodies which carry individual minds. If the "shrinkage theory" holds, then G. Dawes Hicks is perfectly justified in making this observation:

> So far from being infinite, the argument would rather lead to the conclusion that God's body, could it ever be formed, would be the most infinitesimal complex of movements possible—a portion (say) of a mental existent that had become complex enough to have the quality of deity, just as our mind is a portion of the organic processes complex enough to have the quality of consciousness.[64]

Returning to John Laird, we find that he has the same difficulty in accepting Alexander's view that the whole world tends to produce deity. He does not use the "shrinkage theory" of G. Dawes Hicks, but simply acknowledges that to make sense Alexander's theory must mean "the whole world" in a remote not a proximate, sense:

Plainly, however, there can be no difference between the sense in which "the whole world" is straining towards deity, and the sense in which there has been straining towards mentality, that is, towards the emergence of my mind or of yours. ... In terms of Alexandrian canons "the whole world" with its universal *nisus* is only the *Urleib* and not the *Leib* of any mind, its remote and not its proximate body. Similarly, "the whole world" could only be the remote and not the proximate body of emergent deity, unless, as we saw under (2), deity, while presupposing minds as the rung in the ladder from which it ascends, is regarded as a pervasive and not as a limited actuality.[65]

These are, then, the chief criticisms of John Laird with respect to the conception of God and deity in Alexander's system. It is becoming increasingly clear that Alexander has involved himself in almost insuperable difficulties with his conception of a futuristic deity as the "mind" of God, whose "body" is the whole universe, a futuristic deity which in the course of Time becomes fragmented into any number of polytheistic gods and angels of a higher hierarchical order than man. Pursued consistently pantheism becomes fragmented into polytheism in this peculiar system due to the rigid adherence of its author to deity as merely a future empirical quality, and not to a pervasive activity within the universe which ought *not* to be conceived after the pattern of persons as unions of body and mind. While a full comparison of the evolutionary views of Boodin and Alexander lies beyond the scope of this work, it would appear that Boodin avoids the difficulties of Alexander in this respect:

> If we think of the material world as the body of God, we must not conceive the relation on the analogy of the emergent human soul and its body. The world is rather the body of God as sound is the body of music or as the instrumentation gives body to the harmony. But the ultimate harmony is in the medium of God. We cannot conceive God as dependent upon the material world as we, who emerge from the biological past, are dependent upon our bodies.[66]

Increasingly, we find Alexander's deity difficult to validate in its original formulation, and the conception of a pervasive activity at all levels, such as that of the creative impulse of the nisus, becomes worthy of examination.

Dean Inge's Criticism.—One of the most forthright attacks on Alexander's conception of deity is found in *God and the Astronomers* in which the distinguished liberal Episcopal theologian, strongly impressed with the second law of thermodynamics, vindicates this law against the optimistic ascent implied in Alexander's conception of deity. We can well expect that the "gloomy Dean's" criticism will not be given *d'une main morte,* for referring to "the God of Professor Alexander" he states:

> His fortunes are entangled with those of the Cosmos, which is merely the externalisation of Himself. This notion of God is common to most of our philosophers, including even the late Professor Pringle-Pattison, who, great and inspiring teacher as he was, was never quite a theist in the Christian sense. And all the time it was certain, known to the very men who preached this opti-

mistic and pantheistic creed, that the ultimate fate of such a God was just to die—to lose consciousness, to be for ever extinct. Why was it that neither men of science nor philosophers faced this crushing refutation of their hopes?. . . . And yet, if Jeans and Eddington are right, this emerging, evolving, improving God is no God at all, for surely a God under sentence of death is no God . . . . the Second Law of Thermodynamics is *irreversible*. It has a unilinear direction. All the ponderable matter in the universe is moving in one direction, towards ultimate dissolution.[67]

We have, however, already touched upon this problem when discussing the cosmological theories of Fred Hoyle to the effect that the continuous creation of matter provides an ever-recurring opportunity for the formation of solar systems with evolutionary ladders of life presented by Alexander's metaphysics. True, a solar system might die in the sense indicated by Dean Inge, but another would be formed in which beings organized on a hierarchical level such as are found on this earth might in the course of Time emerge. Hoyle's theories are speculation and are not to be taken as refutations of the second law of thermodynamics. R. G. Collingwood, however, is not as impressed with the second law as is Dean Inge, on the ground that this law is derived from our habitual observation of short-term processes, and may eventually be dismissed as illusory when long-range processes of a constructive nature are investigated:

> May it not be the case that the modern picture of a running-down universe, in which energy is by degrees exchanging a non-uniform and arbitrary distribution (that is, a distribution not accounted

for by any laws yet known to us, and therefore in effect a given, ready-made, miraculously established distribution, a physicist's Golden Age) for a uniform distribution, according to the second law of thermodynamics, is a picture based on habitual observation of relatively short-phase processes, and one destined to be dismissed as illusory at some future date, when closer attention has been paid to processes whose time-span is longer?[68]

It would seem that Dean Inge's case against "the God of Professor Alexander" is not conclusive. Assuming attention given to the long-range processes of nature, the very processes Alexander envisages in the development of primordial Space-Time into materiality, life, mind, and qualities higher than mind, through infinite Time, there is no reason to suppose that the universe as a whole is running down. It may be running down in some portions, and being built up in others. Even were we to restrict Alexander's evolutionary ladder from a grandiose cosmic ascent to the emergence of life in planetary systems—and only a small proportion of stars are assumed to have such systems—such emergence is not nullified by the second law. The separate emergent processes at different times in various parts of the universe, though not necessarily simultaneous, might yet be manifestations of a more comprehensive law of hierarchical order, the law of the nisus, for instance. Hence, though the conception of Alexander's deity may be seriously criticized, it is not as drastically nullified as Dean Inge imagines through his invocation of the second law of thermodynamics.

A Radical Criticism of Alexander's Deity.—We now

GOD, DEITY, NISUS

wish to bring forth a criticism of Alexander's conception of infinite deity existing at some future Time in which we shall attempt to dispose of this notion. It has to do with Alexander's conception of the future and in what sense the future may be real. Discussing the memory of past events and the expectation of future events, he states:

> In like manner the expected future event, *e.g.* that I shall be seeing a friend, is enjoyed not as present but as future. It has the mark of the future on it. The act of expecting it on the other hand is present.[69]

The event has the mark of the future on it. Does it exist in the future, all ready-made in some future portion of Space-Time before we actually make it ourselves? It is difficult to secure from Alexander a precise answer to this question. Taking Time seriously means for him two things: the successiveness of Time, and its infinite continuity in past, present, and future. But are future events already in existence in the future, events into which we shall naturally glide as we come to them through the flow of Time? Alexander in one sentence seems to deny such a conception for the present contains the seed of the future:

> The world which works upon our religious suggestibility is the actual world, but that actual world contains the seed of its future, though what future forms it will assume is hidden from us, except so far as we can forecast them in spatiotemporal terms.[70]

This assertion is consistent with Alexander's treatment of the problem of prediction. We (or rather a **Laplace** calculator) can predict future events in spatio-temporal terms (such as an eclipse of the sun) but not their qualities. However, Alexander seems to give due weight to the predictions of clairvoyant people, perhaps more than their due weight:

> The future will be what it will. But since it will be the causal outcome of what is present actually, there may be minds so sensitive to the influences at work in the world that they may divine certain future events.[71]

The question at issue is: Do the events exist ready-made in the future, and are we coming upon them gradually through our experience of the succession of Time? If the events exist throughout all Time, past, present, and future, then Alexander has taken Time so seriously that the present is obliterated, and there is no real future for us since it lies ready-made. His conception would be that of an Absolute Whole with which he has repeatedly indicated his disagreement in his conviction that the whole of things is historical through and through. Nevertheless, he is ambiguous in some of his statements. For instance, it is not clear whether he means that the future quality of deity actually exists in the future, though, of course, it is not known now because: a) we cannot now know the future, unless we are clairvoyants free from fraud; b) in any case, our cognitive powers could not know qualities higher than mind. Nevertheless, he asserts that in religious experience the quality of deity may be felt as giving a flavor to our awareness of the whole world:

> we may suppose that in religious experience the vague future quality of deity is felt, not in its

quality, for that cannot be known, but as giving a flavour to the experience of the whole world which it does not possess as merely an object of sense or thought.[72]

Just as Alexander contends for the reality of events in the past as past, he seems in some expressions to contend for the reality of future events as future:

> The past event, it is true, does not exist now, and if existence is taken to be present existence, the past clearly does not exist. But if we avoid this error and take Time seriously, the past possesses such reality as belongs to the past, that is, to what is earlier than the point of reference. . . . As to the later or future, there is at bottom no greater difficulty in speaking of the future as being real and existing really than there is in respect of the real existence of the past. A future or later point does not occur now, and therefore it is now not-yet, just as the past is now no longer. It has what reality belongs to it in the real Time.[73]

Here Alexander seems to indicate that existence does not mean merely present existence but past and future existence. Furthermore, to take Time seriously does not mean merely the flow of Time, but the reality of Time stretching into the infinite past and the infinite future. The events apparently are located both in the past and in the future. Of course, they cannot be predicted even by the Laplacean calculator, but the question of their determinate existence in the future is a different question. Another quotation in which the succession of Time is given a secondary place with respect to the continuity of Time is the following:

When therefore we consider Space-Time with reference to an instant of time, that is to a point-instant in respect to its time, we shall have the whole of Space, not occurring at one instant, but filled with times of various dates. There is a continuum of events filling Space but divided by the point of reference into earlier and later.[74]

If by events Alexander means the elementary point-instants, then a meaning might be given to the view that the Space-Time matrix stretches out in the future, but in the future only in the form of the elementary motions of point-instants, these elementary motions being organized into qualitied events only through the advance of the nisus in Time. But if by events Alexander means qualitied events connected with their appropriate qualities of matter, life, mind, and perhaps phases of deity, then how could these exist in the future? If they do the universe is a block universe, and our inner sensation of the flow of Time is an illusion. And yet, there are times when Alexander seems to lend himself to such an interpretation:

> we realise that in thinking of the history of the past or divining the future, the events are located not in one place and still less in no place at all, in the places where they occurred or will occur, but however inaccurately we may apprehend their positions.[75]

It seems to be clear from this quotation that for Alexander, Space-Time may be considered as stretched out in its infinite continuity in Time, and events in the past are located in the places in the past where they occurred, and events in the future are located in the places in the future where they will occur! And yet there are passages where Alexander again vindicates the real flow of Time against the continuity which smothers this flow:

> Since the instants of abstract Time are homogeneous, the conclusion is drawn that in an infinite Time everything which can happen has happened. But this overlooks what is essential to Time, that it is creative: that something comes into being which before was not.[76]

This is the key phrase, "something comes into being which before was not," and if this is Alexander's real meaning for taking Time seriously, then the events cannot be located in the places where they will occur, for they have not yet been formed. Our sense of a real future is substantiated not by the strange conception that future events already exist and are divined by clairvoyants, but rather by the conviction that future events have not yet been formed, and that we shall have a part in forming them in due time.

But if future events do not yet exist in any sense of the term, does this imply that Space is generated by the flow of Time? Some commentators have claimed that this was Alexander's meaning, for instance Liddell:

> But we must remember that Alexander describes Space as generated by Time, and Time carries quality.[77]

But this is clearly false, as indicated by Alexander:

> We have to think of lines of advance as displacements of the present in relation to past and future over positions in Space. . . . There is no new Space to be generated as Time goes on, but within the

GOD AND SPACE-TIME

whole of Space or the part of it the instances of Time are differently arranged, so that points become different point-instants and instants become also different point-instants.[78]

If there is no new Space to be generated by the advance of Time into the future, then Space exists in the future, but only in the form of these immovable points which, with their time-coefficients, are the structure of Space-Time in its most elementary form:

> Points do not of course move in the system of points, but they change their time-coefficient.[79]

We seem to be very far from the consideration of the existence of the infinite, ineffable deity in the distant future when we are considering merely point-instants, but the relationship and the argument we wish to derive will be clear from the following diagram:

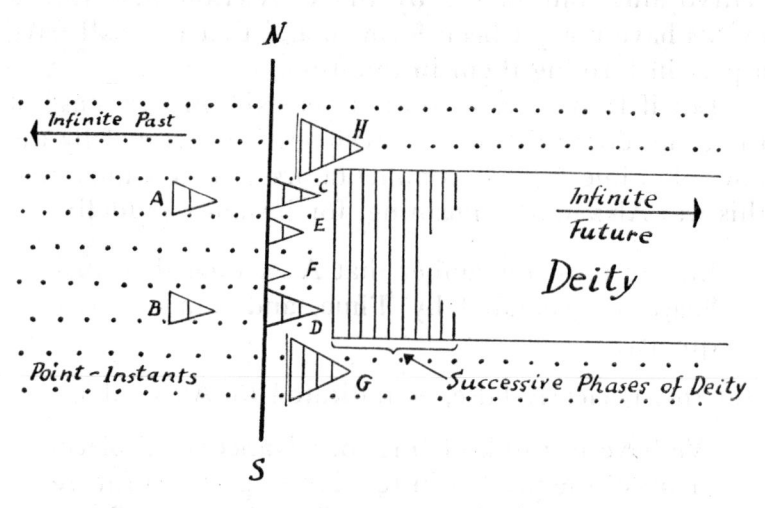

It is obviously difficult to represent Alexander's system, the finites, the flow of Time, the elementary point-instants, and future deity, but the diagram may be considered as a rough approximation sufficient for our present purposes. The points are the point-instants arranged as a two-dimensional plane extending to the infinite past and the infinite future, but it should be remembered that they signify three-dimensional infinitesimal points associated with the fourth dimension of Time. These point-instants represent the most elementary aspect of the matrix of Space-Time, this matrix being a circumambient sea surrounding the islands—the emergents of various hierarchical order—which have arisen in it, which rise in it at this time, and will rise in it in future Time. NS is the present, and A and B represent existents of two striations or levels, matter and life, which exist in past Time, and are real as past. On the line of the present NS, we find C and D, existents of three striations or levels, each striation representing a quality which has been brought into existence through the driving power of the nisus. C and D have three striations and represent human beings, since they have the qualities matter, life, and mind. The existent E has two striations and represents any form of life devoid of human mind. F has only one striation, and represents a non-living existent, say, a stone. As Time flows on through the movements of the present NS to occupy positions which are now future, we may speculate that existents of a higher order than man will emerge, the famous "finite gods" and "angels" of Alexander. The triangle G represents an existent with four striations, matter, life, mind, and the first phase of deity. The triangle H represents an existent with five striations, matter, life, mind, and the first two phases of deity. We may suppose, as we have mentioned *ad nauseam* in this work, the emergence of beings of a higher order than man in future Time.

The finites which exist to the left of line NS are in the past, and they exist as past, for if we adopt Alexander's view that Time is laid out in Space, then Time is laid out in past Space, either in the form of instants for points in the past, or in the form of the time-coefficients for a finite in the past, whether this finite be a stone, an animal, or man. We must assume—on Alexander's system—that these finites are not obliterated, but are conserved as past, and it is an elementary assumption in theology that not even God can change the past. Hence neither the onward movement of the nisus nor deity itself can make the slightest change to the events which are diagrammatically represented by A and B in the past to the left of the present, line NS.

The finites which exist at the present time, at the present moment of the development of Space-Time, are represented on the line NS which is the flow of Time in the present moment. These finites may be lifeless or living things. In so far as they endure, they will be carried from present to future with the flow of Time along NS. In so far as they do not endure, they will remain fixed in their proper places and times in the region of the past to the left of NS.

Now the crucial question is this: Do the finites which will exist in the future already exist in their appropriate places and times in the region of the future? Alexander has given ambiguous answers to this problem. If they do exist, then "there is nothing new under the sun" and all events of the future are fixed in their rigid positions just as unalterably as events in the past. Furthermore, the movement of the present, NS, would be the most illusory motion imaginable, for it would not make the slightest difference to the organization and emergence of finites and events in the future. We would be reduced to the vision of Space-Time as a changeless Whole with the necessary consequence of the illusion of Time, the total unreality of Time. Since Alexander takes Time seriously as succession, that "something comes into being which before was not,"[80] we must reject the view that future events exist in the future in the same fixed character as they exist in the past—however much Alexander may have been ambiguous on this question, as we have observed in some of his quotations. Future events G and H cannot possibly exist when our point of reference is the present time, NS. The future events and finites, of whatever order of emergence, do not exist at all for the creative advance which drives the finites onward to the future and adds successive qualities to them above human mind is the advance of NS, the present, from past to future. But this advance is more than the flow of Time. It cannot be anything less than the creative advance of the nisus,

> that restless movement of Time, which is not the mere turning of a squirrel in its cage, but the nisus towards a higher birth.[81]

The creative role of the nisus is greatly clarified by a simple inspection of this diagram. To the left of the nisus, NS, empiricals are fixed in their position in the past. The nisus cannot touch them. The events to the right of the nisus, NS, do not yet exist, for they have not yet been organized by the creative, sustaining, driving, force of the nisus. If we wish to be true to Alexander's view that there is no growth of Space in Time, for Space in its totality already exists, then we must postulate that what exists in the future is not events, but the matrix of point-instants. This matrix contains merely redistributions of instants among points free from the emergence of even the most rudimentary atom or electron—unless and until the creative action of the nisus animates these instants into the emerging finites. As the nisus moves forward, then, the point-instants to its right, in the future, merely change their instants, for they are less distant in time from the advance of the nisus. To the right of the nisus—to be true to Alexander's conception —merely point-instants exist, the most elementary forms of existence which have not yet been energized and galvanized into finite empiricals of various orders and levels through the action of the nisus. As a commentator has stated:

> Past history has been and is real, present history is just now real, future history is not real at all until time brings it forth. The future is Alexander's negative; it holds all possibilities, limited only by the engendering facility of the continuum itself. The future is the simple part of that continuum where emergence has not yet taken place.[82]

There can be no future events, such as G and H, while the nisus, NS, occupies its present position in Time as shown in the diagram. It is clear, however, that the creative action of Space-Time is present preeminently in the generative flow of the nisus, that very

> nisus in Space-Time, which, as it has borne its creatures forward through matter and life to mind, will bear them forward to some higher level of existence.[83]

Our emphasis on the nisus has consequences of the

GOD, DEITY, NISUS

greatest importance for the conception of deity. In the diagram, deity is represented by the uncompleted rectangle, uncompleted because deity occupies an infinite portion of infinite Space-Time. The successive phases of deity are represented roughly by striations, and it can be observed that these striations correspond in time with the striations of existents H and G higher than man. As higher qualities than mind are fragmented from deity, these qualities cease to be "deity" but belong to finite empiricals, and deity remains a reservoir of yet higher phases in the future, as may be readily observed from our diagram. We have, however, in Alexander's system an irreconcilable dualism of creative agencies. On the one hand, he has asserted that the nisus drives the finites forward to higher levels of existence, a role we have constantly emphasized. On the other hand, these higher levels are higher qualities which are presumably fragmented or detached from deity! This dualism gives rise to embarrassing questions which Alexander has nowhere clarified in his exposition. Is deity to be envisaged as a being which gives fragments of itself for the elevation of existents into higher "mental" qualities? But deity is not a being, it is merely a quality. Does a quality divide itself into successive phases, and how are the phases distinguished when deity is held by Alexander to be resistant to the application of the categories, and is not an individual which can be repeated, but a singular quality? How shall we imagine this infinite lake of the quality deity somehow poised on, or even constituted of, the most elementary building blocks of Space-Time, the point-instants? How can deity be built of point-instants without any intermediate hierarchical orders within its structure, when finites have such a hierarchical structure? It is becoming increasingly clear that this infinite lake of deity is a useless metaphysical postulate in Alexander's system. Are the finites formed by the unending advance of the nisus or are they formed by the fragmentation of deity? Do these two metaphysical factors vie with each other in the travail of the world's creative advance into novelty? The advance of the nisus as creative force from past to future is portrayed so graphically by Bergson with his conception of duration that another factor seems superfluous:

> Duration is the continuous progress of the past which gnaws into the future and which swells as it advances.[84]

Again:

> Real duration is that duration which gnaws on things, and leaves on them the mark of its tooth.[85]

Applying this vivid imagery to Alexander's nisus, does the nisus gnaw into the future, and since deity is in the future, does the nisus gnaw into deity to break up the fragments which make up our familiar finite gods? Does the nisus gnaw on deity and leave on it the mark of its tooth, in the sense that a fragment of deity is cut off from the rest of infinite deity to become the highest "mind" of an existent higher than man? It would appear that these speculations leave but a passive role to deity, and that it has no creative function of its own. There cannot be two creative principles in Alexander's system, the nisus of Space-Time, and the deity of Space-Time, or else we have indeed a very strange pantheism with two divine principles with their respective functions not clearly determined.

The whole logic of the situation as we have attempted to define it with our diagram lies in the conclusion that the creative role is that of the nisus and not of deity as such. Finite future existents do not yet exist and can have no part to play in the creative advance of the nisus in Time. Similarly, a future infinite existent, even when pictured as an infinite quality of deity, can have no part to play in the creative advance of the nisus.

The Vindication of the Nisus.—The defense of the nisus which we have just made, and the depreciation and final rejection of the function of deity, may be criticized on the ground that we have ignored Alexander's statement, which we have ourselves quoted many times to the effect that

> The actual reality which has deity is the world of empiricals filling up all Space-Time and tending towards a higher quality. Deity is a nisus and not an accomplishment.[86]

Deity, in this quotation, is a continuous process in the advance of Time, and it is not an accomplishment, for it is never actually realized. Unfortunately, Alexander has depressed this creative quality of the nisus for elaborate speculations about the relation of deity as an infinite quality in the future, an infinite portion of Space-Time, to the world of empiricals, the world of value, and traditional conceptions of God. Alexander has not been satisfied to present deity as a creative process, but to discuss deity as a locality in future Space and Time. A few quotations will make clear the fact that for Alexander deity has definite location in future Space-Time:

> Deity is an empirical quality, but though it is

> located in a portion only of the universe . . . yet that portion is itself infinite in extent and duration.[87]

Again,

> his deity . . . is lodged in an infinite portion only of this whole infinitude.[88]

Again,

> Deity is located only in a portion of the infinite whole of Space-Time.[89]

This insistence on the spatialization and temporalization of deity in future Space-Time is in contradiction with deity as a present impulse actually active in energizing the finites to higher qualities.

The purely passive role of deity is indicated in the many assertions of Alexander that our present struggles help to create deity:

> It is not God then who allows the struggle, but the struggle which is to determine . . . what deity is to be.[90]

The vindication of the reality of the flow of Time into a future which cannot be constituted of any existents, of any infinite localization of Space-Time as deity, signifies that we have discarded entirely the conception of deity as future—on which Alexander places so much stress—and have replaced it by the conception of deity as nisus, as creative impulse—on which he places so little stress. When he does refer to it, he does so in the general character of an impulse to creativeness:

> This impulse of creativeness I call the nisus of the universe, borrowing an idea from Spinoza and

GOD, DEITY, NISUS

agreeing, as I think, with the spirit though not all the details of Mr. Bergson's *élan vital*.[91]

To be sure, Bergson has elaborated his doctrine of the *élan vital* with respect to the various directions of the evolutionary process, vegetable and animal, as well as with a discussion of the important differences between intelligence and instinct, and his peculiar theory of the genesis of matter. Alexander has been very brief in associating his theory of the nisus with the details of biological sciences and the theories which modify Darwin's original conception of natural selection. While Bergson is acquainted with the modifications of Darwinism, Alexander is not,[92] for the nisus as creative process means quite simply the formation of things in the present, their sustainment through the duration of their existence, and the creation of new things:

> This nisus not only leads to the formation of things and to the sustainment of them, but impels the world forward towards new creations, bringing forth the new out of the bosom of the old. It creates chemical bodies and keeps up their form by the stability of their functions; but also, and this is perhaps more striking, drives on 'the chemic lump,' in Emerson's words, to 'ascend to man.'[93]

This is an exceedingly brief formulation of the work of the nisus, but it implies complex processes at present studied by philosophy and the various sciences:

1. "The formation of things" refers not only to the formation of physical things out of Space-Time—a point on which we do not commit ourselves—but the formation of simple forms of life from an organization of com-

plex molecular structures not previously possessing life. This is a difficult problem still taxing the ingenuity of organic chemists and biologists, let alone philosophers.

2. "The sustainment of them" refers to the continued existence of things and organisms as organized wholes so that the function of the organism is to maintain its inherent structure and wholeness in spite of change in external conditions. This is a function of that mysterious "organization" which is the central citadel still resisting the efforts of distinguished biologists.[94]

3. The world is impelled "forward towards new creations" refers to the whole problem of the emergence of the new as a synthesis possessing new qualities and resting on syntheses of lower order—the whole problem of emergent evolution and creative evolution is involved here.

This impelling of the world to new creations must not be thought in terms of the extension of the world's bounds, for "such a notion is unthinkable, for the universe is boundless."[95] It is a ceaseless impulse to produce finites "and alter the grouping of events into things."[96]

> Things, we have seen, are clusters of events; and the world's nisus sustains some of these clusters and produces others new by fresh combinations which it strikes out in the heat of its desire.[97]

The expression, "strikes out in the heat of its desire" is the only one we have been able to find in Alexander which suggests more than impersonal creativity. The nisus, however, is not to be considered in personal terms, or in terms of a personal God creating the universe. The notion is pantheistic, in so far as it implies that the nisus is a creative force pervading the whole universe, but forming new groupings of events out of pre-existing materials in a favorable environment. That is to say, a flower does not grow in inter-stellar space, but from the soil of the earth, and presupposes conditions of heredity and environment. In the sense that the nisus seems to operate along well-defined lines of creative evolution, the conception might be called infra-pantheistic, that is, less than pantheistic.

Can the nisus, however, be reduced to the element of time? This is Alexander's opinion:

> Now this nisus is the element of time in the primordial world, its principle of mobility and restlessness.[98]

But can mere Time in its succession and irreversibility be saddled with the responsibility of the whole evolutionary process? Professor Dorothy Emmet does not think so:

> The mere notions of temporal succession and irreversibility do not tell us why there should be complexes of motions so organized as to make possible unified syntheses, still less syntheses with new emergent qualities. I believe that Alexander's notion of the qualitative synthesis is a valuable one, but it surely takes more than Time to produce these syntheses. We must be able to say that there is a general tendency for complexes of one order to combine with each other under suitable conditions to form complexes of the next order. Hence we must allow some fundamental property or properties in the world besides S-T, something which makes possible these complexes or organizations which are the bearers of qualities at

their several levels. Alexander in fact admits this, when he speaks of a *nisus,* or creative tendency in S-T. But can you really get this out of his notion of S-T as an infinite four-dimensional continuum? I do not think so, unless you implicitly assume that the mere fact of succession necessarily means creative advance.[99]

Dorothy Emmet points out further that much of the difficulty of understanding Alexander is due to his oscillations between two views. In one view, Space-Time is an infinite whole characterized by point-instants, and the redistribution of instants among points.

In the other view T stands for what Whitehead calls "the advance into novelty."[100]

And in Dorothy Emmet's view, which we share, this advance into novelty is *not* merely the succession of time:

This is not just because it comes latest in time, but because it expresses a new form of organization, characterized by new qualities. . . . There must be some other fundamental property or properties to the process besides S-T. We should have to emend Alexander as has been suggested—starting from the "continuum of events," define S-T as certain properties of its structure, but say that events must have properties over and above their S-T structure in virtue of which they can interact and be related in qualitative syntheses. If we could say this, it would be more plausible to say that the *nisus* which makes for "advance into novelty," which is not Time but is measured in terms of Time, is the "mind" factor in the events whose extended patterns (measured in terms of Space) are the "body" factor.[101]

Our criticisms of Alexander's conceptions of Time as the mind factor of Space, and of the nisus as equivalent to Time, are thus substantiated in the sense that the nisus must be postulated as a creative force operating within the Space-Time world and its creative syntheses. Whether the nisus can be given the full quality of mind, even of cosmic mind, is a moot question. We prefer to consider it in Bergson's sense as a wave of creativity which he associates with life, considered in the broadest terms:

> From our point of view, life appears in its entirety as an immense wave which, starting from a center, spreads outwards.[102]

Again,

> The impetus of life, of which we are speaking, consists in a need of creation.[103]

These are obviously very general descriptions of the creative work of the nisus. More precision is possible when we attempt to relate the nisus to the Creator of traditional theism, and to the idea of process in Alexander and Whitehead. We believe that Alexander would agree with Whitehead in the characterization of the nisus as immanent process of creativity rather than as the instrument of a Creator existing externally to the universe:

> There are two current doctrines as to this process. One is that of the external Creator, eliciting this final togetherness out of nothing. The other doc-

trine is that it is a metaphysical principle belonging to the nature of things; that there is nothing in the Universe other than instances of this passage and component of these instances. Let this latter doctrine be adopted. Then the word Creativity expresses the notion that each event is a process issuing in novelty. Also if guarded in the phrases Immanent Creativity, or Self-Creativity it avoids the implication of a transcendent Creator.[104]

Of course, in his very innocent phrase, "Let this latter doctrine be adopted," Whitehead has made a distinction of tremendous significance. Yet it is one which we believe Alexander would favor, and which we ourselves favor. The nisus can be considered as the expression of an immanent Creativity "belonging to the nature of things" and not necessarily due to the activity of an external Creator. Even when Whitehead dignifies this immanent Creativity by the traditional name of God, he still insists that God cannot be considered apart from temporal creatures and apart from creativity:

It is the function of actuality to characterize the creativity, and God is the eternal primordial character. But of course, there is no meaning to 'creativity' apart from its 'creatures,' and no meaning to 'God' apart from the creativity and the 'temporal creatures,' and no meaning to the temporal creatures apart from 'creativity' and 'God.'[105]

Such a view of the nisus of Space-Time as immanent creativity within Space and Time avoids the troublesome difficulties into which Alexander was led in his doctrines of God and deity. Modifications and rejections of some of those concepts in the light of the foregoing discussion would seem to be as follows:

1. Space-Time as the body of God, and futuristic deity as the mind of God are rejected because they are precarious generalizations from the organization of man as a body-mind structure.

2. Attempted reconciliations suggested by Alexander in which the problems and contradictions of theism and pantheism are overcome through Alexander's God-deity concept which apparently is enriched by the best of both theism and pantheism, are rejected for the simple reason that Alexander's various views of God, whether as Space-Time, nisus, or ever-receding deity, are all immanent. Alexander should have admitted that his views were immanental and should have defended them as such without invoking dubious correspondences to more traditional forms of theism.

3. The immanental character of the nisus as a metaphysical principle imbedded in the nature of things is frankly accepted, and compared with Whitehead's doctrine of cosmic Creativity involved in the temporal flow of existence. We do not at this time raise the whole contentious issue of Whitehead's elaboration of "eternal objects" which is dismissed by philosophers who nevertheless find value in the philosophy of organism.[106]

4. More extensive discussion should have been given by Alexander relating the nisus to the difficult problems of the organization and emergence of living forms. Both Bergson and Smuts indicate a much greater knowledge of biological research than does Alexander.

That the doctrine of the nisus as cosmic creativity has found acceptance among emergentists is evidenced by C. Lloyd Morgan's adoption of it—with certain differences from Alexander's view to be examined later:

For better or worse, while I hold that the proper attitude of naturalism is strictly agnostic, therewith I, for one, cannot rest content. For better or worse, I acknowledge God as the Nisus through whose Activity emergents emerge, and the whole course of emergent evolution is directed.[107]

Further consideration of the nisus in its relation to value is the task we shall attempt in the following chapter.

Summary—We have criticized the views of Alexander chiefly with respect to his doctrines that the whole universe is "the body" of God, and "deity," a future portion of Space-Time, is "the mind" of God. Criticism of G. Dawes Hicks and John Laird have revealed many obscurities in the thought of Alexander on this point, for if deity is held to be a future empirical quality emerging in the Time process in the succession of other empirical qualities such as color, life, and mind, why should not the whole universe be the "body" of color, or that of life, or that of mind? We have continued our own criticism of "deity" by reiterating that in Alexander's system, deity becomes fragmented into the "mind" portions of existents higher than man, Alexander's well-known "finite gods." In such a conception, Alexander's system appears to be a pantheism of the universe on which (or rather within which) is superimposed a polytheism of finite deities—a bizarre conception to say the least. We have considered Dean William R. Inge's objection to deity on the ground of the second law of thermodynamics, but have replied that this law is insufficient evidence with which to deny a creative process in the universe. Deity, in other words, can be challenged on other grounds than those brought by the learned Dean.

Our own chief objection to Alexander's futuristic conception of deity is to ascertain whether it has any possible or intelligible relation to Time as a flow and to the activity of the nisus within the flow of Time. Created emergents can only be due to one creative factor, for if nisus and deity are both creative, then Alexander's system becomes a ditheism. On the argument that finite existents do not yet exist in the future but are formed by the activity of the nisus, we have concluded that neither does futuristic deity exist, poised mysteriously on an infinity of future point-instants. The conceptions of the universe as the body of God, and deity as the mind of God, are thus eliminated, and the nisus as the Immanent Creativity of the universe is vindicated.

CHAPTER III

DEITY, VALUE, PERSONS

A Criticism of Alexander's Theory of Value.—There seems to be a definite break in Alexander's system at the very point where he discusses the tertiary qualities, for with him they are not objective like the secondary and primary qualities of matter, but are human creations or human inventions, as we set forth in Chapter IV, "Deity and Value," in the first part of this work. There is a break in realism for a subject-object determination theory of value which has strong affinities with a subjectivistic point of view. There seem to be three main characteristics in Alexander's theory of value:

1. Value as the subject-object determination or compound in which the subjective pole has prominence:

> The object has value as possessed by the subject, and the subject has value as possessing the object. The combination of the subject and the thing which is valued is a fresh reality which is implied in the attribution of value to either member. Value as a 'quality' belongs to this compound, and valuable things, truths, moral goods, works of beauty, are valuable derivatively from it.[1]

But the attribution of value to the object is done by the

valuing subject, for the object does not possess value intrinsically. It is here that Alexander's theory, which at first sight appears to be a combination of subjective and objective theories, really shows its inherent subjectivity. This is particularly true of his theory of beauty and goodness. Without going into an extensive discussion of artistic beauty, the following expression of what is beautiful is characteristic of Alexander's whole treatment of this field:

> Thus what is beautiful in a work of art is its form or design, and this is the significance given to the material of the art by the artist and recognised by the appreciative spectator. . . . We are thus prepared to hear that beauty does not belong to the material alone, but is distinguishable from it as depending on the contemplation of its form by a mind which is fused with the work of art in the manner explained; that is, which has supplied the significance to the material, and must be there to sustain that significance.[2]

The mind must be there to sustain that significance, so that on this theory aesthetic value does not exist apart from the appreciative or creative mind. With respect to questions of right and wrong, the appreciative mind of the artist or spectator is replaced by the approving or the disapproving mind:

> I can judge you to be doing right or wrong only so far as I see you willing an object which I approve or condemn.[3]

2. Value in Alexander's system is not merely a subject-object compound but is constituted by agreement

among the various subjects, an agreement which rejects the opinion which differs as heretical or as in error. The collective will regulates the individual will:

> Goodness is the kind of conduct, or the kind of satisfaction secured by conduct, which can cohere with the claims of other persons. In so far as the individual is good he represents the collective wills of the society.[4]

Good is not then an objective quality but is determined by the coherence of wills among one another:

> Badness is more plainly a reality, just as much as goodness; but it is not good, and it is incoherent with what is good.... The problem of morality is to secure a coherent distribution of satisfactions among persons.[5]

The coherence theory of goodness is matched in Alexander's system by a coherence theory of truth as a coherence of various minds acting collectively:

> The mind which has truth has it so far as various minds collectively contribute their part to the whole system of true beliefs; the mind which has error is so far an outcast from the intellectual community.[6]

In order to present Alexander's position as forthrightly as we can, we shall add one more quotation which seems to be required as it summarizes what is fundamental for him:

> The judges of what is right or wrong, good or bad, are self-selected and impose their approbations on the remainder. Those who do not conform are condemned as wrongdoers or immoral.[7]

We shall see that such an assertion has elicited serious repercussions from Alexander's critics, but at present we shall pass on to the third characteristic of Alexander's value theory.

3. Value is value primarily for a type and only secondarily for an individual. The types of life which survive do so through a process of natural selection and competition. Even though Alexander claims that his theory, as applied to species of animal life, is not sheer Darwinism, it is difficult to see a marked difference between Darwin's natural selection and Alexander's own theory of the inherent value of types merely because of their survival in competitive conflict:

> It is not natural selection which is the cause of success, but the gifts of the types engaged in competition, and competition is but the process through which their gifts receive expression.... Competition is the means to the supremacy of the adapted over the unadapted types, and brings value into being by the rejection of unvalue.[8]

The forms of life present on the planet are therefore successful types whose survival is due to the fact that less successful types were rejected in the struggle for existence. Alexander even applies his favorite conception of the successful type to man in pursuit of the values of truth, beauty and goodness:

> The minds which judge truly, or behave rightly, or produce or recognise beauty, are the successful types developed on the level of mind, when to consciousness are added reflection or judgment and with it intrinsic sociality.[9]

Even though these are condensed expressions of Alexander's theory of value, they are sufficient to indicate how much they differ from objective theories of truth, goodness, and beauty. A host of problems arise which we do not believe are adequately discussed or solved by Alexander, and to these we shall turn in an endeavor to indicate that he need not have abandoned his epistemological and metaphysical realism when elaborating his value theory, and that his system would be immeasurably strengthened had he retained some form of value realism. Also, if it can be shown that the tertiary qualities are as objective as the secondary qualities, then the disjunction between value and deity which Alexander emphasizes will require reconsideration. Even though the preceding chapter brought forth many objections to the conception of deity, it is still necessary to evaluate and criticize the relation between deity and value, and if fresh arguments can be adduced against the doctrine of a futuristic deity, then the cumulative evidence against deity will increase immeasurably in persuasive power.

Let us begin with a rival theory to that of Alexander with respect to beauty. It is that of Theodore Meyer Greene whose interpretation of aesthetic quality is objective. To be sure, Greene is aware of subjective theories of beauty in which

> Aesthetic quality is . . . asserted to be merely a function of aesthetic evaluation, and evaluation, in turn, is not conceived to be the discovery of an objective quality in things.[10]

But this is a view which Greene rejects and in adopting an objective theory, he pays his respects to G. E. Moore, though without developing Moore's views:

> Aesthetic quality is, I believe, *as objective* as the

secondary qualities of color and sound, and may (following G. E. Moore) be entitled a tertiary quality. It is "objective" in the sense of actually characterizing certain objects of awareness and not others, and therefore as awaiting discovery by the aesthetically sensitive observer. It is correctly described as "objective" because it satisfies the generic criterion of objectivity, namely, coercive order.[11]

It is significant that the realistic analysis of Greene directly implies that aesthetic quality is as objective as the secondary and primary qualities. This is one of the corner stones of modern Realistic philosophy, and it is no secret that it marks the great division separating subjective from objective theories of value. Subjectivists in value theory quickly assert that since Galileo it is simply the mark of ignorance *not* to regard all qualities but the primary qualities of matter as subjective. This subjective philosophical tendency extends from Galileo to the British empiricists, the modern positivists and language philosophers.[12] Nevertheless, Realistic philosophy challenges this whole trend by examining the position of Galileo:

The reasons given by Galileo for asserting the subjectivity of all but what came soon after to be called primary qualities was that he dogmatically declared the objects of physics to be exhaustive of the reality of the physical world.... When the realistic axiologist reaches this point in his speculations, he finds that there can be no reason for denying to the common-sense physical world in which we live the reality which much of modern philosophy has attempted to deny to it. It is this world in which we live, the physical world and not the world of physics, that is for our purposes, if not for those of the physicist, real. But as real, it has among its basic discoverable features many which cannot be dealt with cognitively unless we employ the categories of end, purpose, and value, in order to grasp it as it is.[13]

If, however, Galileo's distinction is maintained along with the whole modern subjectivist trend in epistemology, value theory, and metaphysics (if anything of it is allowed by empiricists!), then the fantastic situation arises in which this infinitesimal creature, man, lost in cosmic immensities devoid of value, nevertheless seems to have the capacity to exude his own subjective, emotive evaluations and, in Alexander's value philosophy, to project these into the universe! But the incredible nature of such subjectivism has been aptly characterized by Paul Weiss:

> Value is a natural phenomenon. Excellence of any kind, beauty, power, purity, comprehensiveness, and their negates are facts as hard as smell and shape, number and size. With thinkers of a century or so ago, it could of course be said that there were no values in nature. But since the world we daily confront is permeated with values, we should then have to say that the nature we daily know is an illusion, a man-infected, man-distorted nature. We should have to maintain that man had the fatal and unique gift of endowing what was in fact valueless with the appearance of value, and thus, alone of all beings, of self-deceptively hiding nature from himself.[14]

Greene's conviction that the tertiary qualities are as objective as the secondary qualities, such as color, sound, etc., and the primary qualities, can be philosophically sustained. Greene further indicates his indebtedness to Moore in his view that aesthetic quality is indefinable:

> This quality, like other ultimates, is unique and therefore indefinable. It can be apprehended only by "direct acquaintance."[15]

Moore had stated, " 'good' does denote a simple and indefinable notion,"[16] and it is axiomatic that his discussion of the naturalistic fallacy was directed to pointing out the profound error in the definition of good in terms of something else, such as pleasure, satisfaction, interest. Furthermore, contrary to the view of some subjective ethicists, Moore's naturalistic fallacy is not his sole doctrine but is merely preliminary to his central position which is that of the intrinsic goodness and beauty of an "organic whole"—a conception to which we shall refer more extensively in our criticism of Alexander and our attempt at a reconstruction of his system.

Without elaborating the ethical theories of Moore and the aesthetic doctrines of Greene,[17] it may be added that Alexander could have interpreted the content of a work of art not merely in terms of the meaning which the artist imputes to it, but in terms of universals existing objectively in this work of art. As Greene indicates:

> The chief content of a work of art consists of the artist's interpretation of certain universals.[18]

Greene divides universals into "perceptual universals"[19] which may be phenomenal objects of all sorts, or typical qualities or relations manifested by such objects, and "spiritual universals"[20] which may be further classified into religious, social, and introspective. The religious spiritual universals include religious emotions and attitudes as awe, reverence, contrition, conversion, a sense of forgiveness, and are further related to man's various interpretations of deity; and it is significant to note that Greene makes very broad this theocentric orientation:

> whether the deity to whom the finite agent seeks to relate himself be an idol, a human being endowed with divine attributes, the world of nature, the mystic One, or the God of theism.[21]

A painting of a religious subject, furthermore, represents the crucial meaning of the religious experience as expressed in persons. The religious experience of that which has divine meaning and quality in the world is expressed so intensely and harmoniously "in its richest flowering"[22] that nothing less than the concept of incarnation will do:

> since all truly religious art is incarnational, making visible the invisible and figuring forth the spiritual to sense, the more profound this incarnational revelation, the more significant the work of art becomes for all who are at once artistically sensitive and religiously minded.[23]

There is no need to pursue further Greene's profound work on aesthetic appreciation in order to clarify the very real contrast between an objective theory of value—so objective, in fact, as to require the very incarnation of profound universal meanings in sensible material—and Alexander's theory where any aesthetic meaning expressed or incarnated would simply be the transference or imputation of this meaning and quality to the material from the mind of the artist, whatever that mind might contain.

Whether we are dealing with aesthetic value or with ethical value, our own criticism of Alexander will be based on objective theories of value, and this will eventually require from us a suggestion as to what Alexander's system *might be* if it were reconstructed to include an objective theory of value. The meaning of such an objective theory of value, in contradistinction to Alexander's subjective-objective theory where the subject predominates, is not far to seek, nor difficult to state. For instance Konvitz makes it clear:

> From the experient's viewpoint, however, value is where he finds it, and that is always in the object. Good is not in me but in my conduct, the object at the performance of which I strain. To you, I may be a good man; but to you I am an object. Beauty is in the music and not in the state which it induces in me; for I can, conceivably, take an opiate which will induce the same emotional state, and yet I will call neither the drug nor the effect beautiful.[24]

To be sure, we may postulate a subject-object whole, or an organic whole in G. E. Moore's sense[25] in which the whole is composed of an objective quality, our cognition of this quality, and our appreciation of this quality by an appropriate emotion. But be it noted that Moore's whole emphasis is that this whole might be valueless or positively evil unless the emotion was appropriate to the objective quality of beauty or of goodness in the object perceived:

> All of these emotions are essential elements in great positive goods; they are *parts* of organic wholes, which have great intrinsic value. But it is important to observe that these wholes are organic, and that, hence, it does not follow that the emotion, *by itself*, would have any value whatsoever, nor yet that, if it were directed to a different object, the whole thus formed might not be positively bad.[26]

Whether we agree or not with G. E. Moore's theory of good as indefinable, the crucial point of his doctrine is that emotion by itself is valueless or may indeed be very bad unless it is directed upon the object of value which elicits this emotion in the first place. That is to say—to choose an extreme case—the emotion of ecstasy would be intrinsically bad if present in the mind of a Nazi torturer and if elicited by the sight of the person he injures or tortures.

Let us leave the question of aesthetic value to discuss Alexander's theory of goodness. The critical aspect of this theory is the great reliance it places upon collective opinion as the determinant of what is good. For instance,

> In so far as the individual is good he represents the collective wills of the society.[27]

To be sure, Alexander can point to examples where collective opinion and agreement on the part of a committee yield a situation of value because it prevents further conflict. The settlement of a strike is a case in point:

> Or take a more serious conflict such as a strike which is settled by agreement. Before that agreement is made, what is economically right is not known. There are the employers desiring one

thing and the workers another. The peaceful settlement of the strike means that employers and workers have entered into each other's wishes. When the adjustment of wishes fails, the issue is left to force, to poverty, and starvation, which means that the way of economic justice has not been found.[28]

Alexander could have added that this adjustment contains relative value if both employers and workers are free to express their wishes without coercion one from the other. Still, the resulting adjustment is only relative to a particular stage of economic advance, and may not be an absolute good. For instance, we may well imagine that a committee of slave-owners and slaves met in the South prior to Lincoln's emancipation of the slaves, and it is not difficult to suppose such a committee coming to a very agreeable adjustment as to conditions of slavery in which both slave-owners and slaves agree. But this collective adjustment would leave untouched the whole issue of slavery itself.

Alexander introduces as a correction upon agreement of a committee or a conference the examination of the consequences which result from this agreement:

> besides considering the desires of persons in the committee or the conference, the parties may at any moment and throughout be considering the actual consequences which may follow in the way of good, that is, happiness or unhappiness, from the adoption of any proposed course. That may modify action . . . but the primary determinant is the claims of the parties, their desires and wills.[29]

Quite apart from the question whether good can be

equated with happiness is the problem of consequences which does not meet the situation at least in the following modern example. No doubt we may assume that committees or representatives of the German government and of the Gestapo agreed that it would redound to the happiness of the German nation if the Jews were deported and liquidated. We can imagine the same committee meeting months or years after this decision was taken and rejoicing that the consequences have been as intended—the deportation and liquidation of the Jews! We are not saying that Alexander acquiesced with the policies of the Nazi government. Alexander's support of unpopular causes, and sympathy with the Zionist movement, are too well-known for anyone to level at him such an unwarranted accusation. We merely wish to point out that his ethical theory is such that it can be used to justify glaring evils which he himself would condemn. The coherence theory of good, the theory of social agreement, is insufficient, for as Konvitz states:

> From whatever point we view the matter, we are driven to the same conclusion: the coherence theory supplies no moral guide, nor even defines the limits of political activity. For its norms are as easily satisfied by the Kingdom of Hitler as by the Kingdom of Heaven.[30]

A serious charge against Alexander, then, is that he has not given due recognition to the role of the prophet in visualizing and proclaiming larger vistas of good than are acknowledged by the collective will of the coherence theory :

> For the good . . . may, like the prophet's voice, exist to condemn the organization of which it is

a part, but if it is *good* character or conduct, it is good in some larger or other systematic whole of which it is a functioning part, a system projected in contemplation, an "ideal," some Promised Land.[31]

An even better characterization of the creative work of the prophet is found in Raphael Demos's defense of the prophet's insight into the evils sanctioned by people who consider themselves good:

> Prophecy is the most important channel through which novel moral valuations flow into the reservoir of human experience. The prophet is the enemy not so much of the bad as he is of the good people in the community—the good who are satisfied with evil. While they mean well, while, in fact, they are permeated with good will, they are wrong in their moral opinions; thus, they are more to be feared than the recognizably wicked members of the community, because their sincerity makes them a stronger bulwark of evil. It is when good people have wrong values that society is organically sick. Hence it is the good people who crucify or otherwise destroy the prophet. . . . The prophet has claimed to speak *sub specie aeternitatis,* to declare eternal verities, to see the truth from a perspective beyond the limitations of common humanity. We will construe this to mean that the prophet is endowed with an acuteness of moral vision transcending the inertia of tradition.[32]

Alexander, however, might claim his theory makes room for the "prophets of wise change" in that the prophet may eventually win the approval, or work upon the sympathies of the group:

> there may be some who refuse to accept the collective decision, and are excluded from its benefits as recalcitrants. On the other hand, there may be a few (or even one) who, advancing at the beginning a claim which is contrary to the general views of the rest, so work upon their sympathies that they impose their desires upon the whole. These are the successful reformers, the prophets of wise change.[33]

It is difficult, however, to reconcile this doctrine of the affable collective so readily agreeable to a consideration of the views of someone it holds to be recalcitrant with that other rigid doctrine of Alexander in which the collective will, by definition, is good while the will of the recalcitrant or heretic is excluded and automatically regarded as bad. Furthermore, is the unsuccessful prophet who dies by crucifixion among those "excluded . . . as recalcitrants"? Alexander seems to be insufficiently acquainted with the great tragedies and martyrdoms of history, in which prophets and social reformers were not able to persuade the collectivity, but were rather destroyed by it. Yet, the contrast between the intrinsic moral ideals of the prophet and the sanctimonious lethargy of the community, which is at times roused to destroy the prophet, is the very contrast between priest and prophet which penetrates into our consciences and illumines our moral insight. It is not simply a case of the long wait over extended periods of history until future generations of men acclaim the spiritual insight of the prophet. The prophet will no doubt have his society in the future, but his intrinsic worth is not due to the recognition of this society, but in fact precedes it. It is difficult to avoid an intuitionist view of ethics in which the very clash of the prophet with supposedly good people energizes our moral insight and makes us declare that values reside intrinsically with the prophet rather than with his Pharisaic detractors. We know intuitively that society based on ideals of love and good will for the least of men is superior ethically to any society which has as yet existed. We need not wait for long processes of history to validate this judgment, for we verify it in small areas of social life, such as the family and voluntary societies. Indeed, the distinction between actual human achievement and social idealism has been magnified by the Neo-Orthodox school of theology to such a degree that human fulfilment is pictured in some mysterious realm known to God alone. This pessimistic strain is rejected by J. B. Pratt:

> Nor can one significantly assert that the Christian ethic is an impossible ethic for man because the demands it makes are so lofty that human nature can never completely fulfil them.[34]

Alexander, to be sure, recognizes the value of gifted teachers, at least in one part of his works, and acknowledges the criticism of Bergson:

> A different and weighty doubt is raised by Mr. Bergson's recent contention that there are two sources of morality, one social and the other the teaching of specially gifted individuals, who may be prophets or even mystics, men who propose new ideals of life founded not upon social experience but upon deeper insight into man's nature. It has been implicitly answered already. Such

teachers reveal to man new passions which had not been suspected before, or not in this simplicity and fulness. They enlarge the contents of human nature or alter the spirit of man's actions. Still, like other reformers, they propose an ideal which is fitted for use among men, and their ideal is a social one—"that you love one another." They do not supersede society but propose a new form of it. When their teaching has been accepted society has been transformed.[35]

But the situation is not as simple as Alexander makes it, for some questions arise from his statement. Before the teaching has been accepted by society, is the teaching worthless or heretical? This has often happened in history. Does the society which Alexander portrays as being transformed by this teaching accept it as easily as he assumes? His own statements would appear to deny this facile transformation of society:

> The judges of what is right or wrong, good or bad, are self-selected and impose their approbations or disapprobations on the remainder. Those who do not conform are condemned as wrongdoers or immoral.[36]

This is no agreeable discussion and adjustment between a social group, or a committee, and a wise reformer, in which various views are compared with dispassionate objectivity. This is an imposition by a self-selected group, and are not the pages of history full of such impositions upon reformers, prophets, and heretics? A much more enlightened view of the ethical function of a group is given by John Wild:

> If we ask what brings the group into existence

and what permanently sustains it in being, we must answer *love of the common good* on the part of its potential members and that obligation to pursue this good which arises from an understanding of the natural sanctions called forth by lethargy and neglect.[37]

A group activated by love of the common good and by the obligation to pursue this good even when presented by a prophet, reformer, or heretic, will be less inclined to exclude the higher reality of the good so introduced than the group which declares that there can be no higher ethical reality than that which has already been achieved by agreement. Disagreement in Alexander's theory automatically means exclusion.

The same problem with respect to the rejection of "error" arises in connection with the theory of truth according to which the mind which has truth

> has it so far as various minds collectively contribute their part to the whole system of true beliefs; the mind which has error is so far an outcast from the intellectual community.[38]

Commentators are not slow to bring forth denials of this theory of truth:

> The objection occurs readily to mind that mayhap the mind which has *truth* is an outcast from the intellectual community, e. g., Bruno, Galileo. "One is ten thousand to me if he be the best," says Heraclitus, and so it must be to everyone. The memorial statue to Bruno was put up by the generation that he foresaw and not by the generation into which he was born.[39]

It is difficult to reconcile this coherence theory of truth, as coherence between social believings, and the correspondence which Alexander elsewhere implies between the facts of nature and sensible experience:

> It is illegitimate to suppose a chasm between the brute facts of physical nature as presented in sensible experience of particulars and the most abstract principles; and data of sense are a part of the body of physical science, just as they are in the historical sciences. Facts and principles make up a single system, the facts being massed together for the most part in the form of empirical laws.[40]

It is because the human mind does not contemplate with favor such a chasm between reality and sense experience and the interpretations of sense experience, that it is not quite correct to say with Alexander that "Truth is the satisfaction of disinterested curiosity."[41] Rather we would say with Whitehead that

> Our purposes seek their main justification in sheer matter-of-fact. All the rest is addition, however important, to this foundation. Apart from blunt truth, our lives sink decadently amid the perfume of hints and suggestions.[42]

It is not merely curiosity which leads us to truth, but a deep need of our nature which is not satisfied until it is assured that its sense data, its mental apprehensions are more than just subjective data or mentalism but correspond to objective reality. Of course, the quest of truth is inexhaustible, and all theories stand in need of greater precision, but this precision is achieved at the bidding of reality in its impact upon the mind and is not merely the impulse of curiosity or the conventionality of mathematical symbolism which all too often denies a reference to objective reality. The value of truth in a non-utilitarian sense is best appreciated in the researches into cosmic and galactic phenomena engaged in by astronomers. What possible pragmatic value can there be whether the universe is finite or infinite, expanding or contracting, whether in this or that region of space the galaxies are more concentrated than in another region, whether the red shift in spectral analysis of star light is correctly interpreted by the theory that the distant galaxies "run away from us"? There is no pragmatic value to these investigations whatever but there is profound intrinsic value, the value of Truth for its own sake.

Our discussion up to this point has been concerned with the contrast between Alexander's subjectivist theory of truth, goodness, and beauty, and an objective value theory, without stating too precisely just what is this objective theory. Some formulations of it may be given:

> This thesis is an assertion of ethical realism, the existence of a real good and evil embedded in the nature of things and subject to human choice, altogether independent of any human opinion or tyrannical decree.[43]

Or, again, it may be expressed in the following manner:

> Values are somehow entangled in physical objects, and the proposition holds for *all* values, whether moral, aesthetic, or any other kind you choose to mention. On the face of it, they are objective because they reside *in* the object which they qualify or characterize and *in* which we perceive them.[44]

We are thus in disagreement with Alexander's value

theory which holds that values are human inventions, and on the contrary hold that they are objective determinations of things and persons. But this is not the complete meaning of value as we shall now attempt to explain.

Among the objective theories of value to which we have referred, that of G. E. Moore seemed to have a special attraction. Nevertheless, it must be admitted that it has a defect which it is important to note. It is too static. It is quite consistent with the position of a static observer placed within the universe and being aware of various atomistic entities or "organic unities" of indefinable values existing at an instantaneous moment of observation. We have here that instantaneous section of Space-Time which Alexander rightly rejected for the full historicity of the universe. Furthermore, Moore's apparently analytical, atomistic, mind prevented him from giving due weight to a metaphysical theory of value, for he interpreted such theories as sheer dictation by some supernatural agency. Moore's interpretation overlooks one aspect of Alexander's system which we have continued to emphasize and it is the stress on the reality of time. Objects and persons do not exist in repeated moments, but have real duration, and manifest changes such as growth and evolution. Each existent is a synthesis of qualities of matter, life, mind, organized into a "whole" according to the hierarchical order to which it belongs. But each existent also performs functions of maintaining itself and realizing its potentiality. Static essentialist thought is to be contrasted with thought which gives due weight to causal efficacy, dynamic tendency, potentiality:

Essentialist thought is pluralistic. Every object is

analyzed into separate structural elements. The static order (the world at a moment) is viewed as a set of fixed, simple units, ideas, impressions, or atoms incidentally ordered by external relations which do not affect their inner core of determination. The dynamic order is similarly analyzed into a discontinuous succession of essences, each of which first appears and then disappears without trace. Essences do not act or tend to anything beyond. Hence, potency and causal efficacy are minimized, in spite of the evident facts of experience.[45]

John Wild corrects this static essentialism by presenting "active tendency as an ontological principle,"[46] and "necessarily constitutive of any finite being."[47]

This thesis is confirmed by all the data to which we have access at the macroscopic level of everyday experience, where we never find abstract properties but always dispositional properties tending to act in certain ways. It is now also confirmed by recent evidence concerning the nature of microscopic and submicroscopic entities. The Cartesian idea of an inert matter incapable of action unless externally pushed or pulled has now passed into eclipse. Physical reality is no longer statistically conceived as tiny billiard balls, but rather dynamically as fields of force or energy.[48]

This dynamic tendency applies not only to inanimate matter, but especially to living organisms, be they amoeba, oak tree, or man, and this dynamic tendency consists in realizing the capacities of such organisms according to their nature. Whenever plant, animal, or man is injured, deprived of development, functions, natural potentialities, something intrinsically good is being frustrated, is being destroyed. This dynamism, however, is not some vague, discontinuous process of change but determined by the structure of the entity concerned:

> The essential structure of the entity, determining its tendencies to proceed in a certain direction, is a natural norm, not constructed by man but embedded in the very being of a changing thing and discovered by ontological analysis.[49]

This doctrine of natural norms is the characteristic note of natural law as an ethic of moral realism diametrically opposed to Alexander's theory of value as a human invention, or as sanctioned and defined by the agreement and approval of the group. It is also important to note that in John Wild's formulation natural law is an ontological issue much broader than the question of theism and nontheism, and is not the preserve of any particular historic Church. It is the grounding of moral norms in nature which is its characteristic mark, these norms being embedded in the particular ontological nature or structure of things and determining their dynamic tendency to realize their potentialities:

> The basic issue between the defenders of natural law and its opponents has never been that of theism versus nontheism. This is a peripheral metaphysical issue. The basic issue concerns the nature of moral norms. Are they grounded in something which exists independently of human interest and opinion, or are they man-made? The philosophers of natural law are moral realists. They hold that certain moral norms are grounded on

nature, not merely on human decree. It is this thesis that binds together the various strands into a single tradition and which radically separates all of them from the subjectivist schools of modern thought.[50]

These norms embedded in the nature of any finite entity determine the dynamism of the entity in a direction suitable to the fulfilment of its nature. If the entity is an "organic whole," such as a living organism, natural law is definitely embedded in the structure of this organism so as to maintain its wholeness and restore it whenever it is injured. Immanent normative structure is definitely implied in the active tendency of any organism, from the lowest to man himself, to maintain its "organic unity," its wholeness. For man, the moral law is founded on his specific nature, and the essential tendencies which bring that nature to completion, to fulfilment:

> Value is tendentially rooted in fact. The justifiable moral imperatives are not arbitrarily laid down by the human mind, but rather discovered in the tendential structure of human nature.[51]

The theory of natural law, with its emphasis on active tendency of entities, and the fulfilment of these entities according to their nature, is a correction to the static theory propounded by G. E. Moore in which the good is an indefinable, irreducible though fully objective quality. Such a theory may be valid for unchangeable inanimate objects or works of art, but it seems to have little to say about the good of living organisms including man. Moore's theory must then be supplemented by a theory of self-realization, such as natural law, and this is what we have just indicated all too briefly. When, however, a contest between a lower form of life and a higher form takes place, it seems that natural law theory implies a choice as to which "organic unity," germ or man, is of the greater value. The self-realization of man according to natural law does imply the destruction of the self-realization of the germs which otherwise would destroy man. Man is therefore an organic unity of still greater goods. When that fulfilment is challenged by the fulfilment of lower organisms an instantaneous direct intuition must be assumed of the comparative value of the two normative structures of fulfilment, Direct intuition of value at a moment may be invoked to decide which "organic unity" shall remain alive and this is perhaps an instance where Moore's intuition, quite apart from the temporal evaluation of a tendency, may be invoked. However, even in this contest between two organisms, one more highly structured and valuable than the other, nature sometimes does provide an immanent norm in the destruction of that micro-organism injurious for man's self-realization.

As to Alexander's theory of the survival of the fittest and his facile assumption that such survival implies the survival of values, it is not easy to differentiate his theory from sheer Darwinism. We are not, of course, challenging the theory of Darwinian evolution, though Alexander seemed to be ignorant of modifications introduced by later investigators which rendered less tenable the theory of survival in the strict sense of elimination of the unfit. Gaylord Simpson's studies provide a fertile source of such modifications of Darwinism.[52]

Also, it is to be noted that theories of adaptation and natural selection do not explain the arrival of new forms of life. As Woodger states:

Natural selection will not help us at all because it only deals with the survival of immanent changes, not with their origin. It helps us to see how some attempts towards new modes of organization would not be successful after they had been reached, but not how they were reached.[53]

And in higher organisms adaptation to the environment is not the key to survival, but rather independence from the environment:

Where organisms are said to 'possess minds' rendering prevision possible it is not difficult to see that an enormous possibility of independence of contingent circumstances will thereby be achieved. . . . Progressive evolution thus appears to be a process of evolution towards freedom from environmental contingency. Accordingly the notion of 'adaptation' does not express adequately what seems to have occurred in progressive evolution.[54]

But whatever may be the debates of modern evolutionists as to just in what sense Darwinism shall be taken or modified, it is becoming increasingly clear that it has nothing to contribute to our understanding of modern society. In the words of Hofstadter:

Whatever the course of social philosophy in the future, however, a few conclusions are now accepted by most humanists: that such biological ideas as "the survival of the fittest," whatever their doubtful value in natural science, are utterly useless in attempting to understand society; that the life of man in society, while it is incidentally a biological fact, has characteristics which are not reducible to biology and must be explained in the distinctive terms of a cultural analysis . . . that there is nothing in nature or a naturalistic philosophy of life which makes impossible the acceptance of moral sanctions which can be employed for the common good.[55]

Such a forthright conclusion by an investigator of social Darwinism, that complex of ideas which derived from the notion of survival of the fittest some rather dubious justification for certain economic and political practices in the nineteenth and twentieth centuries, restores to us moral evaluation as to the meaning of survival, and not sheer survival as the meaning of moral evaluation:

> The survival of the fittest does *not* mean, as one might suppose, the survival of what is fittest to fulfil a good purpose—best adapted to a good end: at the last, it means merely the survival of the fittest to survive; and the value of the scientific theory, and it is a theory of great value, just consists in shewing what are the causes which produce certain biological effects. Whether these effects are good or bad, it cannot pretend to judge.[56]

Deity and Value—The sharp separation which Alexander has made between deity and value must now be examined. Though we have seriously questioned the reality of futuristic deity, and brought strong arguments against it in the last chapter, it seems desirable to consider the dichotomy presented by Alexander as to deity and value. Deity is held by him as a future quality of the universe, the "color" of the universe if it could be realized. Deity is not value, however, for values are human inventions. Value on levels lower than man is simply the survival of the type of finite existences through adaptation to environment:

> The establishment of value and the extirpation of unvalue is the sign of adaptation. Value means in its simplest term that the individual or type, any function of which is valuable, is not self-dependent entirely but in its independence belongs to the whole Space-Time of which it is a complex. Unvalues are indeed realities but in their unvaluable form do not fit in with the world of empirical things generated within the whole Space-Time and cannot therefore persist in the measure assigned empirically to their kind.[57]

It is clear that Alexander assigns value to those finites which survive as a type, and unvalue to those which disappear as a type. When Alexander, then, writes that deity is "in the line of all value"[58] does he mean anything more than that deity is the highest emergent in a long line of emergents of lower complexity whose chief value is their persistence, or adaptation? Each type of existent has specific qualities correlated with its complexion of Space-Time, and the persistence of any existent is merely the persistence of its qualities, and this persistence is nothing more or less than its value. Deity as conceived to be in the line of value though not itself value, is merely the statement that deity is in the line of empirical qualities, of which it is held to be the highest quality. We fail to see that Alexander adds anything new by connecting value and deity, in this particular fashion, for his meaning is already implied in the view that deity is an empirical quality. As to the conservation of values in deity, let us be clear as to just what is implied in Alexander's principles:

> In this wider sense of value, deity remains next to mental and even human values, but it is also in the line of all value, and our values are but its proximate material. In this sense deity represents the conservation of all values or valuable existence whatever, and is an outgrowth from them. All values are conserved in God's deity.[59]

Are they really? Value as adaptation of type so that the type survives merely means the presence of some structural factor or organization within the type. When a higher type evolves from this lower type, an additional structural factor is probably developed from the organization of the lower type, but the lower type may no longer exist. For instance, the development of the modern horse from the primitive horse signifies a certain elaboration of structure, but the primitive horse no longer exists. The value of the primitive horse, in so far as Alexander equates value with adaptation of type to environment, simply resides in the spatial-temporal configurations of primitive horses in Space-Time which is past, and is not present in Space-Time of the actual moment which includes living horses! Values are conserved only in the sense that organizational or structural patterns are conserved in a higher type, but the types of a lower order may no longer exist. Hence their value is not conserved. If we recall our fragmentation of deity into beings of a higher order than man, then value is conserved in them only in so far as they utilize in their minds or bodies some structural pattern descending from an existent of a lower order. Do existents of a lower order, such as men, persist side by side with these finite deities? We do not know. All types of life which no longer exist when the stage of finite gods is reached, have obviously perished in the past, and their value is not conserved. But they had value while they existed. How long must a type exist in order that its value be conserved in deity? Obviously when a type ceases to exist through competition with other types, its value is not conserved, though it did have value while it lasted. Hence, on Alexandrian principles, it is not true that "all values are conserved in God's deity."[60] This statement could be true only in the following strange view, namely, that all types of existence from the lowest amoeba to the finite gods will be conserved in their actual existence as an innumerable menagerie of animals, plants, men, beings of a higher order than men—all conserved within the qualitative atmosphere of deity at some far distant future time. It takes no special mental effort to realize that many of these types have now become extinct, others will probably become extinct when they fail to survive in the struggle against superior types in the future. All types of existence which do not survive up to the ultimate moment of future time in which the infinite deity is held to reside, inevitably have perished in previous time, and are not conserved.

We fail to see that Alexander has justified his assertion that all values are conserved in God's deity. All values, in so far as they are conservation of type, might be held to be conserved in the localities of time and space in which they occurred in past Space-Time. But these values, in so far as they became extinct types, are certainly not conserved in the present actuality of time, much less in futuristic deity. And if futuristic deity is rejected, as we indicated in the preceding chapter, Alexander's own formulation of the conservation of value is unjustified. The principle of the conservation of value may be justified metaphysically if we postulate that Space-Time is pervaded, not merely by Space and Time and finite existents with their correlated qualities, but by a principle of Value, so that finites may become embodiments of values in various degrees of realization. Since we believe existents to possess objective tertiary qualities as well as secondary qualities, the nisus of Space-Time drives existents forward not merely to a succession of higher syntheses of qualities, but also to higher embodiments of truth, goodness, and beauty. We may hold with Alexander that there are no degrees of beauty, but degrees of approximation of beauty, and hold, as he does not, to an objective theory of beauty:

> At any one time there are no degrees of beauty, and what are called degrees of beauty are degrees of approximation to beauty; there is a scale of less or greater defect of beauty. Beauty is beauty and is itself perfect. There is, however, a scale, which I called the scale of greatness, in beautiful works according to the subject matter of the work.[61]

In the reconstruction of Alexander's system so as to include the objectivity of value, the nisus becomes a principle of creative advance generating and sustaining finite existents of a hierarchical character of qualities, but also of a hierarchical character of values. The finites are incomplete but in the process of Time display a tendency towards an increasing richness in the embodiment of value. To this conception and the relation it bears to such empirical theism as that of Henry Nelson Wieman, we shall return presently.

Alexander's Theory of Evil—When we consider how

much Alexander stresses persistence of type as the essential value of a type of life, it is not difficult to realize that his conception of evil is directly related to processes of life. The healthy organism excretes "its disused or dead parts"[62] as well as noxious elements, and "poison which its own functions generate."[63] These poisons are discharged into outer Space, which, be it noted, is the body of God in Alexander's system. God contains in his body good and evil, so that an unsavory pantheistic conception remains in Alexander's system. It remains unresolved *a fortiori* if the conception of futuristic deity is abandoned.

The elimination of unhealthy activities is applied by Alexander to the mental life and to the life of society:

> So too the individual mind suppresses or diverts unhealthy activities and the society reforms or at need suppresses its unhealthy members.[64]

This is indeed a very simple conception in which unhealthy activities are left undefined. Strangely enough, the same idea is applied to deity which is supported by mental life, and the evil mental life is ejected from deity into the body of God, and this mental life is further broken down into lower forms. These lower forms, which have presumably lost their character of mental life, consist of material which

> can be used only when it has been "unmade to be remade," and may again be taken up and utilised for the purposes of deity; as the corruption of a battlefield may serve the growth of crops and ultimately be made serviceable for good human life.[65]

Is it not clear that Alexander is obsessed with biological imagery in declaring that evil consists of "waste products"[66] of both the finites and the infinite being of deity! These waste products are evil, but "perishing in that form they are used up in a changed form for the purposes of deity."[67] The image of the corruption of a battlefield being used to fertilize crops may be valid when we have crops in mind, but it seems grotesque to expand this illustration so that we assume that the evil mental life below deity is broken down into waste products, and that ultimately these waste products will be utilized by a futuristic deity for its own purposes!

The whole discussion of evil in Alexander seems a strange reduction to biological process. How much more relevant to infractions of the dignity of man are the types of moral evil enumerated by Raphael Demos:

(a) Some errors are due purely to wrong assessment of matters of fact . . .
(b) the failure to recognize the moral value of knowledge and wisdom, or the moral evil of sacrifice, are strictly moral errors . . .
(c) the exaltation of tyrannical power . . .
(d) errors in moral feeling which come from propaganda and indoctrination . . .
(e) erroneous moral feeling by the leader or the teacher.[68]

The man who recognizes these evils in himself and resolves to eliminate them as much as possible has a much higher view of the ethical life than if he considered himself merely as a healthy organism eliminating waste products. Furthermore, a futuristic deity unmaking these waste products to remake them into instruments fit for its purposes implies an infinitely long period for this creative work of reclamation or redemption to be achieved!

We may agree with Alexander, however, in bearing evil with more humility and acquiescence where our efforts can avail nothing, but with a temper of resolution where they do avail. We may well admit with A. S. Pringle-Pattison the great difficulty of reconciling certain aspects of existence with a theistic or rational religious position:

> There are features of the world-process, I have admitted, so horrible that we often feel them to be frankly intolerable. The agonies of helpless suffering from age to age and the depths of infamy and cruelty which the human record discloses—how are facts like these to be reconciled with the controlling presence of a principle of reason and goodness?[69]

We may agree with Pringle-Pattison as to the great difficulty of reconciliation of cruelty with a divine principle, but it would seem that on Alexander's speculative system, the reconciliation would be equally difficult if not more so. The facts of undeserved suffering are regarded by him as "waste products" which would have to wait until a futuristic deity could be presumed to unmake these products to remake them for its own mysterious purposes. Alexander seems to overlook the agony of waiting for the action of a futuristic deity, while more traditional theistic systems may be troubled and perplexed about the ultimate origin of evil, yet they state that in this moment of actuality, "God is our refuge and strength, a very present help in trouble."[70]

A notion of Alexander which is particularly unpalatable is his expression of revolt "at the cost of endless sacrifice of precious lives"[71] in World War I, and his strange satisfaction that this loss of lives is perfectly acceptable when we consider that this is "the struggle which is to determine . . . what deity is to be."[72] If he holds a struggle to be empty sacrifice from a human standpoint, how could it be anything else from a divine standpoint since in Alexander's view the struggle is not a method through which deity is educating the human race, but is rather the useless fight by means of which deity is built! Bergson has a much more elevating apprehension of the ethical contrast between war and a God of brotherhood:

> The contrast is striking in many cases, as for instance when nations at war each declare that they have God on their side, the deity in question thus becoming the national god of paganism, whereas the God they imagine they are evoking is a God common to all mankind, the mere vision of Whom, could all men but attain it, would mean the immediate abolition of war.[73]

While evil in man and in Nature may be difficult of complete resolution with a principle of absolute Goodness, Pringle-Pattison offers a view of Nature which calls forth man's utmost courage and dignity:

> Nature is more than a training-school of the moral virtues in the specific sense; it is an element, savage and dangerous, into which the human being is thrown to show what stuff he is made of—an element testing with merciless severity his powers of courage and endurance, but drawing from him thereby the utmost of which he is capable. Life for the individual in such a medium is a series of opportunities, but the use he makes of them depends upon himself.[74]

The Uniqueness of the Religious Sentiment—After having given so much caustic criticism of Alexander's theory of value, we shall pay him our respects by agreeing heartily with his vindication of the religious sentiment as *sui generis* not to be reduced to any other categories:

> However many other elements gather around it and swell the full tide of the religious sentiment, its essential constituent is something with a unique flavour of its own, corresponding to its specific object, and is distinct from other emotions, and its apprehension of its object distinct from other kinds of apprehension.[75]

While the religious sentiment may gather to itself the quest for truth, the appreciation of artistic beauty, the commitment to moral ideals, in its unique quality it transcends all of these and is never without a sense of the mystery of the universe—the mystery of the universe as it tends ultimately to deity. Alexander at times interprets religion as a "passion for deity,"[76] but since we have thrown clouds of suspicion on the conception of a futuristic deity, we prefer to adopt another formulation of his in terms of nisus:

> the religious appetite or emotion depends upon the whole make-up or constitution of the mind, and body, and is the response of it to the whole of reality in its nisus towards a new quality.[77]

We may translate the expression "nisus towards a new quality" into "nisus towards greater enrichment of quality and value" without doing grave injustice to Alexander's thought. Our response to the creativity of the nisus is "a brute or crude instinct,"[78] but if the expression is regarded as not suitable because of its reference to brute instinct, Alexander explains that "it is the highest we possess in so far as it aims at the most perfect object" and "it is given in our constitution."[79] Religious passion is of a different character from the passion for truth, beauty, or goodness, and in an address subsequent to the writing of *Space, Time, and Deity,* Alexander considered the religious emotion in terms of Rudolf Otto's *mysterium tremendum:*[80]

> One of the elements of religious feeling is the sense of mystery, of something which may terrify us or may support us in our helplessness, but at any rate which is other than anything we know by our senses or our reflection. And it is natural to believe that there is something real, some feature of actual existence, which calls forth this sentiment in us. Mr. Otto calls this the 'numinous' element in the world, inventing a happy word from the Latin word *numen* which means divinity . . . in recognising the existence in real fact of this numinous element in the world, I follow him, and though in no way concerned with Turkey or the Moslem religion profess myself in this respect an Otto-man.[81]

This pun on the name of Rudolf Otto signified, however, a very serious appreciation of the numinous element in the universe. We may well suppose that Alexander accepted Otto's explanation of the meaning of numinous in terms of the awe, the majesty, the mystery, the fascination, the graciousness, of the divine element in the world without subscribing to Otto's doctrine of this divine element as completely Other. The sense of the mystery of the universe is not to be understood, then, as a sense of perplexity and defeat but as a profound feeling of wonder, fascination, cosmic support, a sense which is more deep-seated than the particular theological or philosophical formulations we may associate with the divine. It is because of Alexander's genuine appreciation of this sense of the "numinous" character of certain aspects of the universe that he felt impelled to make the sharp distinction between deity and value by a derogation of the objectivity of value.

An important question, however, arises from Alexander's vindication of the religious sentiment. Is it mere psychologism, or the uninstructed enthusiasm manifested all too often by religious people? No, it is not, for it can be substantiated by studies of the nature of religious experience on a sufficiently broad basis. For instance, a recent work by Joachim Wach propounds certain criteria of this experience in terms which are remarkably similar to those Alexander uses:

1. Religious experience is a response to what is experienced as ultimate reality; that is, in religious experiences we react not to any single or finite phenomenon, material or otherwise, but to what we realize as undergirding and conditioning all that constitutes our world of experiences. . . .
2. Religious experience is a total response of the total being to what is apprehended as ultimate reality. That is, we are involved not exclusively with our mind, our affections, or our will, but as integral persons. . . .
3. Religious experience is the most intense experience of which man is capable. . . . Religious loyalty, if it is religious loyalty, wins over all loyalties. . . .

4. Religious experience is practical, that is to say, it involves an imperative, a commitment which impels man to act. This activistic note distinguishes it from aesthetic experience, of which it shares the intensity, and joins it with moral experience. Moral judgment, however, does not necessarily represent a reaction to ultimate reality.[82]

While religious experience is distinct from morality, it would seem that Joachim Wach places a closer connection between ethics and religion than did Alexander who imagined too easily that the religious man could be "a downright bad character."[83] The religious sense, it would be more correct to say, transcends the ethical sense, but is far from being indifferent to it. Such an assertion is in agreement with our modification of Alexander's system in which the creative nisus does elicit the religious consciousness, but is also the principle of the conservation of value.

Another judgment in which Alexander may be justified lies in his separation of the religious sentiment and the intellectual or speculative system which may be constructed to account for it:

> while the immediate deliverances of the religious emotion as to what it feels are data for science, the same value cannot be set on its semi-speculative conception about these data.[84]

Joachim Wach would probably agree with this statement of Alexander especially if by speculative conception we understand a kind of inferior science or philosophy in terms of which religion is erroneously thought of in certain quarters:

> That is to say, religion is emphatically not a kind

of underdeveloped 'science' or 'philosophy.' This misinterpretation, still widely current, is an unfortunate legacy from the rationalistically-minded era of the Enlightenment. The experience which we call religion is rather an awareness of apprehension, not lacking a cognitive aspect but not defined by it, a recreation to something that is sensed or apprehended as powerful. Rudolf Otto has spoken of a *sensus numinis* (sense of awe), and this term seems to me a very apt designation.[85]

The religious sentiment, then, cannot be equated with merely primitive science, or primitive philosophy. Tillich makes the point that it can neither be equated with a description of reality in theological or philosophical terms, for it is deeper than these:

> the value-producing processes (Whitehead) or the uniting processes, (Wieman) or the character of wholeness (Hocking) can be called the especially religious experience. But if this is done, one must have a concept of what a religious experience is. Otherwise one would not recognize it within the whole of experience. This means that there must be another kind of experience, an immediate participation in religious reality, preceding any theological analysis of reality as a whole.[86]

There is no need to multiply authorities to indicate that Alexander is much more persuasive in his awareness of the distinct and unique character of the religious sentiment than he is with respect to his value theory. And his very assertion of the character of religious experience as more profound than the metaphysical terms which attempt to interpret it enables us to make modifications in his system without calling in question the genuine character of his apprehension of religion as an emotion. A word of caution may be stated at this point. While religion is more than intellect, more than ethics, more than aesthetics, this quality of transcendence is not to be interpreted as the assertion that religion can be irrational, unethical, or unlovely. It has been these things all too often. Religion, while being a unique response of our total selves to the mystery, awe, and grandeur of the universe in its creative aspects, should complete its effect on us in our renewed devotion to the search for truth, in our commitment to moral values, and in our heightened sense of beauty. When this practical aspect of religion is ignored, it tends to deal with the irrational and "the wholly other."

The Problem of Immortality in Alexander's System.— We recall that Alexander was insistent that positive proof of individual human survival after death was not forthcoming, and he felt that immortality was not an essential value of religion. His conviction was also based on his view of the human spirit as being indissolubly connected with the human organism, so that he doubted whether the mind of man could survive the death of the body. He admitted, however, that could survival be proved,

> the larger part of the present speculation will have to be seriously modified or abandoned.[87]

Without going into an extensive consideration of the various theories of the mind-body problem, it may be suggested that the conception of individual survival is not the only conception of immortality offered by the more reflective thinkers. Dean Inge, for instance, pours scorn on the cruder aspects of human survival:

> The revival of so-called spiritualism, and the cult of necromancy, among masses of the half-educated, show how very crude are the notions of a "future life" among many who do not reject the idea altogether. Priestcraft of the baser sort, and sheer charlatanism, have been quick to exploit the pathetic cravings of the bereaved, the number of whom was so sadly augmented by the destructive war of 1914-1918.[88]

And even more downright is the learned Dean's assertion:

> Belief in survival has no necessary connection with religion. There is an irreligious belief in it, and there is a religious disbelief in it.[89]

The religious disbelief in it, as meant by Dean Inge, is prompted by the materialistic imagery of enjoyment in heaven, or compensation in terms of enjoyment for misery endured on earth. Immortality is understood by Inge not primarily in terms of duration but of eternity, that eternity which is a quality of the divine different from endless time. In fact Dean Inge goes further and agrees with Schleiermacher that the immortality of religion is communion with the infinite:

> "In the midst of finitude to be one with the infinite, and in every moment to be eternal, this," says Schleiermacher, "is the immortality of religion." It is the old counsel of Aristotle, that we should "be immortal as far as may be."[90]

Can immortality be interpreted in this sense in Alexander's system? To be sure, Alexander uses the word "eternal" to mean "infinite time" so that we could not be aware of infinite time in every moment, but we could adopt for his system the other meaning of immortality as communion with the infinite not communion with an eternal quality or being which is the more traditional sense of eternity. Space-Time and its existents are infinite, and since the universe is characterized by an increasing richness of qualities arising out of the potentiality of primordial Space-Time, it is not too much to suppose that a heightened awareness of the infinite world of emergent qualities is in reality a communion with the infinite. And if we modify Alexander's system to include the objectivity of value as a creative principle within it, then to be one with the universe of Space-Time is also to be one with the universe of Space-Time-Value.

A. S. Pringle-Pattison is also inclined to think of immortality in terms of communion with spiritual values rather than in terms of personal continuation of life after death, though he does not judge uneducated views of the latter possibility with as much condemnation as does Dean Inge:

> we do well to remember that the 'hope of immortality' is not to be regarded like the scientific prediction of an eclipse, or any other event in the temporal series. It is the supreme assertion of spiritual values, above all an assertion of the infinite value of the human spirit that has realized its vocation and entered into its heritage. And just for that reason the life beyond remains something which we cannot translate into concrete detail.[91]

In our reconstruction of Alexander's system to include the tertiary qualities of truth, goodness and beauty as objective in the same degree as the secondary qualities, it is possible to interpret immortality in Pringle-Pattison's sense of the supreme assertion of the objectivity of value in things and persons as ultimately based on a ground of Value in the universe. Can not death be interpreted as absorption into this world of value, so that the individual is not perishing into an alien world but is being absorbed in the same universe of Value which has produced all qualitied existents and supreme persons whose lives cast a glow of reality over all future Time? The idea of absorption is not foreign to the thought of eminent theologians, such as Troeltsch, for instance:

> he yet holds that the final end of the whole ethical process must be 'the union of the creature with God' (Gotteiningung der Creatur), his 'submergence' (Wiederuntergehen) in the divine life.[92]

Immortality we then interpret as meaning, in this life, communion with the value-creative aspects of the universe (obviously rejecting communion with un-values), and as meaning, in death, absorption within these same value-creative aspects of reality. We do not claim, however, by this little digression to have solved the problem of immortality. We are merely trying to reduce the gap between Alexander's denial of survival and religious sentiment by calling attention to recent pronouncements on the idea of immortality which, while not denying outright individual survival, certainly do not give it the prominence which popular religion gives to it. All we wish to suggest is that Alexander could have been more sophisticated in his approach to immortality had he taken advantage of modern conceptions of immortality as communion with the infinite which contains spiritual values. His subjectivist theory of value may be partly responsible for his literal approach.

A Reconstruction of Alexander's System to Include the Objectivity of Value—We have already hinted at such a reconstruction in this chapter, and we now wish to indicate at greater length just how a theory of value in an objective sense might be included in Alexander's metaphysics.

Theories of value vary from those which give a supreme ontological status of Truth, Goodness, and Beauty to such an eminent degree that the universe of Space and Time and its existents tends to disappear ultimately, to those which deny an ontological reference altogether and limit value to the expression of an emotive cry at a particular moment. The range in value theories from objectivism to subjectivism may be summarized in the following list though we do not claim that this enumeration is complete:

1. An extreme objective value theory, such as that of Urban, in which Space and Time are merely "phenomenal":

> This idea—that space and time are somehow "phenomenal" of value in its ultimate sense, that they are the necessary forms in which values are realized, and yet the values themselves transcend these forms—is an imperishable element in traditional philosophy. . . . Space and time may be "phenomenal," but they are phenomena *bene fundata*. By themselves they may be meaningless and unintelligible, but as expressions of "symbols" of non-spatial and non-temporal meanings and values they are highly significant.[93]

However, we do not feel the necessity of affirming the reality of Space and Time in merely symbolic form, or in "phenomenal" terms for the sake of emphasizing the supposedly greater reality of value. There is no need of denying the ultimate reality of a universe of Space-Time and its existents in order to give due recognition to the objectivity of value among these existents. Under no condition whatever do we feel obligated to depreciate the universe of Space, Time, existents, and their qualities.

2. The second objective theory is that in which existence and goodness are brought into closer relationship. Well does Raphael Demos criticize certain modern philosophers, and Alexander is among them:

> There is a curious inconsistency in the attitude of certain realistic philosophers, in that while they are realists as to physical fact, they are idealists or subjectivists as to value. Yet it is not easy to see why the arguments which make for objectivity in the realm of physical fact fail to yield objectivity in the other realm of value.[94]

While Professor Demos holds that value and physical fact are equally real, he admits it is a difficult problem to show their relation:

> There must be some internal relatedness of the two when there is so much sharing and interplay. One can only suggest the vague hope, or guess, or even insight that ultimately the two—value and fact—are not wholly independent of each other. What, precisely, the relatedness is, the writer cannot say. But if there be interpenetration, it is one in which value has its innings as well as fact; it is

not a one-sided reduction to existence; if value goes down the bottomless well of the ultimate being, fact goes down too. And as long as we stay above the well, so does the mutual irreducibility as between value and existence remain.[95]

Later on in his article, however, Professor Demos has a somewhat different formulation:

> The position defended in this article has a maximum and a minimum phase; the former is that values are independently real; the latter is that values have as much reality as sensory objects, no more and no less.[96]

In the reconstruction of Alexander's realistic system which we suggest, objects and their primary and secondary qualities are real, and the values inherent in these objects and apparent as tertiary qualities are equally real. The affirmation of the reality of tertiary qualities does not involve the derogation of secondary qualities, nor vice versa.

Other value theories are subjectivist in the sense that they do not assert the reality of values existing independently of the human mind. All of these varieties of value theory differ among themselves as to the degree of subjectivism they assume, but we generally find them unconvincing. They are:

3. The ethical theory that values are objective but only in so far as they are experienced by minds:

> We can . . . rule out at once the sense of "objective" as referring to what exists independently of being experienced.[97]

We believe that this view, while it is to be praised for

criticizing the more extreme subjective theories, is not itself a radical axiological objectivism but merely an objectivism within a larger mental inter-subjective theory.

4. Alexander's theory in which value is a subject-object determination, but the part played by the subject is pre-eminent. We have already discussed this view at length and indicated its inadequacies.

5. The theory that value is what is approved, desired, or of interest is a subjective theory since no objective criterion is offered but merely the individual approval, desire, or interest.

6. The most subjectivist theory is that emotive theory so well represented by Professor Stevenson in which

> "ethical judgments" are partly judgements about the speaker's psychology claiming to be true and partly the expression of emotive attitudes.[98]

As we proceed in this enumeration of value theories from the most objective to the most subjective, we pass through a marked lessening of interest in metaphysics until we reach the strange theory that ethics is simply an emotive cry, in which metaphysics is simply regarded as a vestigial remnant of outmoded ways of thinking. Obviously a metaphysical theory of the universe requires a theory of value which is objective in the full sense and is not merely an objectivism within a larger subjectivism. We cannot bring ourselves to accept a theory of the Good regarded as ontologically prior to the existence of the universe in Time and Space. In agreement with T. M. Greene's view that tertiary qualities are just as objective as secondary qualities, and in agreement with Raphael Demos' position that values have as much reality as sensory objects, we believe that the universe of Space, Time, matter, primary, secondary qualities, life, mind, and possible qualities and values above mind, is a fully objective system, and the assertion of values need not imply the derogation of the spatial and temporal aspects of the existents of the cosmos. Whether existents are ultimately determinations of Space and Time or whether they require a substantial principle is a question we have left open. In a reconstructed Alexandrian system, either is possible.

An attempt to relate the objectivity of value to the objectivity of existents within the Alexandrian system may be made under the assumption that the fundamental units are point-instant-values, so that ultimately the universe is not merely Space-Time, but Space-Time-Value. The driving force of the nisus organizes, then, not merely point-instants into matter with primary and secondary qualities, but into matter with these, plus in addition, tertiary qualities. Qualities of goodness and beauty thus inhere in objects with the same degree of objectivity as qualities of color, scent, hardness, chemical and physical properties, precisely because the nisus has synthesized the elementary point-instant-values into objects in which both qualities and values inhere with the same degree of objectivity. It is possible to consider objects as "organic wholes" in which the elementary values of the point-instants are organized in such a way that the whole object presents the objective goodness, beauty, or harmony which it actually does possess. A painting is an organic unity which possesses an intrinsic beauty, but this is because the material paint has been arranged by the artist in a particular pattern so that the immanent beauty is brought out. There is obviously an infinite number of ways of arranging the same amount of paint in patterns which do not possess this beauty. This reflection seems to indicate that the principle of "organization" is a metaphysical principle applying not merely to the synthesis of qualities in objects, but to the synthesis of values in objects.

Furthermore, in Alexander's system, the Space-Time matrix is traversed by universals which are the plans of construction of the finites and may appear at any time and at any place in the matrix where they are required to give embodiment to objects. Similarly, we may postulate that the Space-Time-Value matrix is traversed by universals of value which are the plans of construction of the finites as value-centers, and may appear at any time and at any place in the matrix to give embodiment of value to these same objects. There is no reason to imagine that every object manifests the universal "beauty," any more than we imagine that every object manifests the universal, "circle," or "cube," or "ellipse." Not all objects manifest the same degree of beauty, and not all objects manifest the same degree of goodness. Indeed, the organization of beauty and goodness in an object may be so distorted that the object actually appears as ugly and evil. We must further suppose that the work of the nisus is to synthesize the organization of values in objects in such a way that the object will manifest the most inclusive and harmonious system of values. This arrangement, however takes Time, so that we may consider objects as incomplete manifestations of value, and striving, through the activity of the nisus, to become richer embodiments of value than they actually are. An Aristotelian principle of self-realization may be invoked to complete our reconstructed theory of value to give due weight to the tendency, to the potency in things to realize their inner being, their inner potentiality.

Such a reconstructed Alexandrian system gives us an enriched conception of primordial Space-Time. It is not merely physical Space-Time devoid of any quality except the most primary motion, but it is Space-Time-Value traversed by innumerable universals of quality and value which may manifest themselves at any time and place to give to objects and persons the required patterns under the direction of the nisus. In such a system Space-Time-Value becomes the richest Reality imaginable, animated by a dynamism ever striving to realize greater manifestations of value in Space and Time.

The objectivity of value in existents in the world of nature[99] provides an interesting distinction between value in natural objects and value in persons. Shall we say that value in persons is merely the awareness of general ideas such as brotherhood, amity, good will, peace, social harmony, dwelling as vague aspirations in some unsubstantial, rarefied, other-worldly region? When ideals are so regarded, they are easily assimilated to an idealistic doctrine of Platonism,[100] but we find that there is an important Aristotelian criticism of this interpretation:

> one might say that the principal thrust of Aristotle's criticism of the so-called Platonic theory of Ideas is that the latter errs in the direction of being too "metaphysical," in the modern sense: it dislocates the proper and primary objects of philosophy, transporting them from the real world of change with which our senses acquaint us, and placing them in a supposedly other-world of Ideas.[101]

A different doctrine from that of other-worldly ideas

seems to be necessary for a full objectivism of value relevant to the human situation. What Gregory Vlastos has to say is pertinent at this point:

> Instead of beginning with beautiful dreams, and then casting about to see how we can coax the world to make them true, let us begin the other way round: Let us look at reality itself and discern its own structure, its own historic direction, its possibilities, its opportunities, its commands.[102]

This apprehension of reality itself and its own structure is given by the doctrine of natural law to which reference has already been made:

> It is based, not on any human opinion or desire or construction, but on the very nature of man and the universe he inhabits. Hence of all our faculties reason alone, which apprehends things exactly as they really are, is able to apprehend its prescriptions.[103]

This law is not merely an *a priori* characteristic, as distinguished from an empirical character, after the distinction usually made by positivists. It is not made of vague aspirations for a divine realm of peace and rest assumed to exist "above" this world. It

> is rather discovered by reason as embedded in the very nature of things and caused by whatever causes have produced human nature itself and the natural world of which man is a part.[104]

Natural law enables us to gain some understanding of the nature of man, of the pattern of activities which characterize this nature, as well as the norms of ethical conduct toward which human nature approximates by its actions.[105] Value is not then merely the sentiment of approval, or the agreement of some committee, or the interest of any individual or any special group for any object whatever. Ethical value is embedded in persons as natural law, and this law is just as natural as the more physical laws which are manifested in the law of gravitation, the acceleration of falling bodies, etc. We see no insuperable reason why this conception of natural law could not be incorporated in Alexander's system.[106] In fact, Alexander's emphasis on taking Time seriously further implies agreement with the conception of human nature being perfected through activity in the temporal order.

A further consideration is this, Are laws immanent within the universe, or are they imposed from without? In Alexander's system, it is clear that there is nothing outside the universe of Space-Time, and that the whole emergent process takes place in Time as a manifestation of "restlessness," which is not mere circular motion but the driving force of the nisus or *élan vital*. It seems consonant with Alexander to interpret laws of nature as immanent, embedded in the nature of things, and this is precisely what the doctrine of natural law means.[107]

A further modification to be applied to Alexander's Space-Time system beyond the addition of Value as an intrinsic characteristic of the emergent patterns may be sesured from a study of J. C. Smuts's *Holism and Evolution*. Alexander's philosophy in which an increase in complexity in the collocations of movements of a finite locality of Space-Time brings forth a further complexity of motions intimately associated with a new quality on a higher level than previous qualities of this finite locality, is inadequate from the point of view of Smuts's system. Alexander overlooks—or does not sufficiently account for

—the remarkable principle of "organization" which unifies into an organic unity, or an organic whole, the finite living existents, whether they be simple forms of life or man himself. We have pointed out that this factor of organization which sustains the life of the whole organism is the central citadel of biological inquiry and must rank as a metaphysical principle. Complex existents do not emerge merely by the accumulation of complexities of motion, nor the gradation of higher qualities resting on rows of lesser qualities, after the manner of a layer cake or a skyscraper. The new quality suffuses the whole organism and the whole and the parts are in most intimate union. As G. E. Moore stated:

> To say that a thing is an 'organic whole' is generally understood to imply that its parts are related to one another and to itself as means to end; it is also understood to imply that they have a property described in some such phrase as that they have 'no meaning or significance apart from the whole.'[108]

The creative, evolutionary process does not simply accumulate complexities of motions associated with layers of qualities, but rather produces wholes with the capacity to maintain themselves by commerce with the environment and with other wholes. This is, of course, the dominant conception of Jan Christian Smuts which we shall give in his own words:

> Wholes are dynamic, organic, evolutionary, creative. The mere idea of creativeness should be enough to negative the purely mechanical conception of the universe.... There is a creative activity, progress and development of wholes, and the

> successive phases of this creative Evolution are marked by the development of ever more complex and significant wholes. Thus there arises a progressive scale of wholes, rising from the material bodies of inorganic nature through the plant and animal kingdoms to man and the great ideal and artistic creations of the spiritual world. However much the wholes may increase in complexity and fruitful significance as we go upward, the fundamental activity which produces these results retains its specific holistic character all through.[109]

Mechanical interpretations are rejected for the creative activity which produces wholes which sustain themselves, and may we not suggest that this self-maintenance of the whole, whether relatively simple or complex, implies a norm imbedded in the whole, and are we not justified in invoking natural law as immanent in the formation and sustenance of wholes? And in the fundamental activity which has the same "holistic character all through" do we not have the very character of the nisus of Space-Time which sustains organic unities, and transforms simple unities into more complex ones—more complex wholes? And Smuts's system has the virtue that it considers value as implied throughout the various gradations of wholes, and not merely, as in Alexander's philosophy, value as persistence of type or value as projection from the mind to object inherently devoid of value.

> The efficiency, utility and beauty, in short the values of matter, arise from the structures which are the outcome and the expression of its own inherent activities. In every real sense the idea of value applies as truly and effectively in the do-

> main of the physical as in that of the biological or the psychical. In both cases value is a quality of the forms and combinations which are brought about. Whether they are structures resulting from the activities of matter, or works of art or genius resulting from the activities of the mind, makes no real difference to the application of the ideas of creativeness and value in either case.[110]

Value is just as much a structural characteristic of a whole as its spatio-temporal extension, its pattern of organization, its degree of wholeness, its range of qualities. It follows that in our application of Holism to Alexander's Space-Time system to include Value as a fundamental characteristic, it is necessary to postulate point-instant-values which exist in primordial Space-Time-Value before any wholes have been formed. Even of this primordial system, the great assertion of perennial philosophy could be made: *Ens est unum, verum, bonum*.[111] But the primordial Space-Time-Value matrix does not remain quiescent but gives birth to atoms, cells, organisms, man himself, according to a principle of Creativity which may be variously designated as the nisus of Alexander and C. Lloyd Morgan, the *élan vital* of Bergson, the Creativity of Whitehead, or the principle of Holism of Smuts:

> This creative Holism is, of course, responsible for the whole course of Evolution, inorganic as well as organic. All the great main types of existence are therefore due to it, such as the atom, molecule, cell, organism, the great groups of plant types, the great groups of animal types, and finally the human type. . . . But more; as we proceed upward in the course of Evolution we find Hol-

ism the source of all values. Love, Beauty, Goodness, Truth: they are all of the whole; the whole is their source, and in the whole alone they find their last satisfying explanation.[112]

The creative Holism as the source of values as well as of complexity of structure, wholeness, and qualities, is clearly indicated in contradistinction with Alexander's nisus which is concerned with the production of ever higher complexities and qualities, but not values. In our reconstructed Alexandrian system, however, the nisus is given the character of the holistic principle of Smuts.

Let us attempt to focus our attention on this reconstructed nisus. It is interpreted in immanent terms. It is related to Bergson's *élan vital,* and is not to be thought of as characterized by either mechanism or finalism, for Bergson's argument that finalism is a type of mechanism appears convincing:

> Radical finalism is very near radical mechanism on many points. Both doctrines are reluctant to see in the course of things generally, or even simply in the development of life, an unforeseeable creation of form.[113]

Mechanism simply means the compounding of physical motions associated with one quality and with no principle of emergence, wholeness, creativity. Finalism, on the other hand, implies that all emergent wholes exist ready-made in some eternal realm and are automatically transferred to the temporal world according to some preestablished plan. The rejection of finalism by Bergson is likewise a rejection of the finalist philosophy of du Nouy, whose popular works on evolution have evoked such widespread but perhaps undeserved response. An element of tentativeness, spontaneity, as well as creativity must be postulated for the nisus.

It is also related to Whitehead's doctrine of creativity, so that the nisus may be regarded as the most comprehensive of all the categories in the universe of Space-Time-Value and its emergents. It permeates all other categories, and operates at any time and at any place where the organization of material has reached such a state of complexity that a new quality emerges along with a new pattern of organization and a new degree of wholeness. In the words of Whitehead:

> 'Creativity' is the universal of universals characterizing ultimate matter of fact.... 'Creativity' is the principle of *novelty*. An actual occasion is a novel entity diverse from any entity in the 'many' which it unifies.... The 'creative advance' is the application of this ultimate principle of creativity to each novel situation which it originates.[114]

Transforming the Whiteheadian language into Alexandrian terminology, it is not difficult to see that an actual occasion characterized by novelty is the synthesis of parts into one whole whose organization of parts is such that the whole has a new quality.

Summarizing our reconstruction of the Alexandrian system to include the objectivity of value, certain essential steps seem necessary:

1. The primordial matrix is not of point-instant, but of point-instant-values, and the whole matrix is then a Space-Time-Value world.

2. The new qualities which emerge in time are characteristics of a new pattern of togetherness, uniting parts and whole in intimate relations, so that the doctrine of

emergence is perceived to be part of a more fundamental law, the emergence of wholes according to Smuts's philosophy.

3. The new whole is not merely made up of a complexity of lesser wholes unified in a new synthesis, but has value qualities embedded in its very structure, since all wholes are emergents from the Space-Time-Value matrix.

4. Each whole manifests a directed activity for self-maintenance and independence from the environment according to immanent natural norms within the whole. The contribution of natural law philosophy at this point has been given due prominence.

5. The activity of the primordial matrix which pervades the whole of reality but produces wholes in certain finite localities has been interpreted in terms of the nisus of Alexander and Morgan but with modifications derived from the philosophies of Bergson, Smuts, and Whitehead.[115] Bergson's élan vital introduces the important consideration that the nisus is neither mechanism nor finalism; it is not a cosmic Mind in which all reality in its infinite temporal flow is already present. The nisus is the fundamental principle of Holism of Smuts, or of the Creativity of Whitehead, "the universal of universals," more comprehensive than all other universals and categories which are the patterns of construction of wholes.

6. The modification of Alexander's system to include personality and especially the personality of the religious genius will be suggested presently.

Alexander and Hylomorphism—It is comparatively easy to find similarities among the systems of Alexander, Morgan, Whitehead, Bergson, Smuts, with the important differences which we have suggested but not exhaustively examined. Alexander's system is so rich that it is possible to find relations not merely with emergent philosophies but with Hylomorphism.

If the finites are not complications of Space-Time, then we may assume a principle of substance or prime matter in the Aristotelian sense to account for them. If Alexander's system is modified in an Aristotelian direction, then Space-Time is replaced by prime matter, space and time become adjectival to material existents as intimate combinations of form and matter, and the potentiality of primordial Space-Time from which all existents emerge is replaced by the potentiality of prime matter:

> The *first* matter . . . is not nothing. Yet it is not fully actual. It is incomplete, or *potential,* being not yet fully formed but able to be formed in an indefinite variety of ways. Only such a purely potential or dynamic being could underlie all the radical, evolutionary changes of nature and give them continuity.[116]

Alexander himself must have been aware of the broad similarity between his concept of Space-Time and the Aristotelian prime matter, for he regarded Space-Time as stuff and not as some unsubstantial mental fluidity pervading the whole universe:

> In truth, infinite Space-Time is not the substance of substances, but it is the stuff of substances. No word is more appropriate to it than the ancient one of *hyle* (υλη).[117]

The indeterminate, potential character of prime matter is replaced in Alexander's system by the indeterminate, potential character of Space-Time itself, so that at any point in the course of Time any qualitied emergent may arise from simpler levels. Space-Time, however, is not as indeterminate as is prime matter in the Aristotelian system, for Alexander assumes that it is ultimately constituted of motionless points intimately associated with instants as time-coefficients. These time-coefficients are rigidly redistributed among the points since the advance of Time in its succession and irreversibility is an ultimate fact of nature.

Furthermore, Aristotelianism stresses Being, and in Alexander's system, Being is Space-Time, and all configurations and complexities of Space-Time are in reality complexities of Being:

> The only question, then, that is left for the metaphysician is of what nature is this primordial world which literally underlies the universe we know . . . which is being itself . . . It has been suggested that the stuff of the world is space-time itself.[118]

In one mode of comparison between Aristotelianism and Alexander's Space-Time system, it would seem that prime matter and its infinite potentiality and appetition is replaced by Space-Time. In another mode of comparison, it is Being and not prime matter which is Space-Time. In this case, this total Space-Time, inclusive of its emergents, qualities, wholes with their values, is Being, while Space-Time in its primordial form may be held to correspond to prime matter. The forms which are assumed by prime matter may be considered as the various complexities of Space-Time which characterize emergents. The qualities of the finites are called in the Aristotelian system "accidents." But we must not carry these broad analogies too far, for we must admit that

Alexander's system does not use such categories as "essense," "existence," "potency," "act," the four causes of Aristotle, nor the First Cause.

To be noted, also, is the fact that the principle of Substance and the principle of individuation are lacking in the Alexandrian system, and Alexander in fact proclaims his ignorance of why Space-Time should break up into these finites emerging in Time and bearing the richness of quality with which we are acquainted. His only answer is that we must accept these emergents and their qualities with natural piety.

It would seem that Alexander's system—in its original form or in its reconstructed form—is more amenable to the categories of creative evolution and Holism than it is to the categories of Aristotle. Were Alexander's system to be radically modified so that it would no longer be Space-Time-ism, but a system describing the potentialities of evolving prime matter in time, then the similarities would be more pronounced. It would be correct to state that such an eminent Aristotelian as John Wild is naturally more sympathetic to Hylomorphism than to philosophies of emergence. Yet he acknowledges that there is some truth in such recent philosophies:

> It is understandable therefore that recent philosophy should be characterized by a marked emphasis on the active dynamism of nature and on such key concepts as creative evolution, emergent evolution, the creativity of Whitehead. . . . I believe that this view is close to the truth.[119]

Alexander and Wieman—Having indicated some relationships of Alexander's system with other emergent systems as well as with Hylomorphism, the question arises as to whether a fruitful comparison may be made with a philosophy of religion. The answer is affirmative for the creative nisus as creative event has been utilized by empirical theists to define their conception of God. Henry Nelson Wieman has developed such a conception, deriving it partly from Whitehead, but objecting to Whitehead's insistence on a "primordial order in the sense of an order distinguishable from the creative event."[120] The meaning of creativity for Wieman may be given from a long quotation:

> The form of the creative event working at the higher levels of value is created by its working at the lower levels. Whether or not it ever did begin at some lowest level, mounting upward ever since; whether or not there are, even now, levels far higher than the human; whether there are a rise and fall of levels throughout the cosmic whole of things or an upward march forever—these and many other such matters we do not know and consider it futile to speculate about. All we know is what has happened upon this planet, and even that we know but slightly. But we do know enough to live in absolute commitment of faith to the creative event and to serve it above all else by striving to provide whatever conditions it may demand, whether these be physical, biological, personal, or social.[121]

Applying this conception to the nisus, it would appear that we do not know whether the nisus began its activity at some lowest level, nor whether it has created the famous finite gods and angels of Alexander, or whether it will make an endless ascent to ever higher and higher qualities. And yet, in spite of the modesty of this conception of the divine, Wieman claims that it provides sufficient meaning and value for his commitment to it. No doubt this conception of God as a structured creativity active in certain regions of the universe, or as a category of categories, is very meager as compared to the transcendent conceptions of God presented by traditional theism. Yet, they have not found universal assent and have not been free from unethical overtones. John Wild is of the opinion that when reason is rejected for "irrational, fideistic grounds" in religion, an autocratic conception of God tends to result:

> This ejection of reason from religion has helped to produce those anthropomorphic conceptions of God, more characteristic of the West than of the East in which He is conceived as an arbitrary tyrant or cosmic pantocrat, ruling the world like an imperial dictator, and fitting everything, good as well as evil, heroic sacrifice as well as brutal torture, into the inflexible pattern of a providential plan.[122]

It may be that revulsion against this autocratic conception of God has led, in part, to the speculative interpretation of the divine element in reality in terms of an immanent creativity rather than in terms of an autocratic predetermination of all events from all eternity.

While Wieman very seldom mentions Alexander, it is possible to list a number of important characteristics which belong to both their systems:

1. Both accept a universe of levels for the pattern of emergence.

2. Both accept the principle of a creative activity pervading these levels, Alexander calling it nisus, and Wieman calling it growth. In Wieman's description, we recognize our familiar evolutionary ladder from electron

to organism to culture by relations of mutual support. It would seem that Wieman is inclined to stress relations of mutual support of the parts so that they form a whole, while Smuts emphasizes the "holistic" character of the whole which conditions the role which the parts play:

> Growth is the formation of bonds of mutual support and mutual control and mutual facilitation between diverse activities. . . . Growth extends from the lowest to the highest cosmic levels. We do not know that growth began with electrons, but for purposes of exposition we can so represent it. Electrons formed connections of mutual support and mutual control and thus gave rise to a new kind of unity called an atom. Atoms did the same and formed molecules. Molecules grew by creative synthesis, forming ever more complex molecules, until we had the colloid and at last the cell. Cells grew by creative synthesis giving rise to the multicellular organism. Similarly, we can trace the process through the growth of culture and the interpenetration of cultures.[123]

3. Both refuse to call God "Mind," for in Alexander's system, God as body is the whole universe as tending to deity, and God as "mind" is not strictly mind, but a quality immeasurably above mind. If we reject both these conceptions of "body" and "mind" of God and retain the one of nisus, then the nisus is active at all levels of existence, mental and sub-mental, and possibly super-mental. Wieman's objection to the concept of God as Mind is this:

> Mind is only one of the levels that God brings forth as he forever works to make the world more

organic and more rich with value. To identify God with any one of these levels, whether it be matter or life or mind, seems to me to be a mistake.[124]

To be sure, in the case of Wieman the nisus or principle of Growth generates levels of values and not merely levels of qualities, as is the case with Alexander's original system. The reconstructed Alexandrian system which we briefly suggested would agree much more with Wieman's own metaphysics:

> God is the creative order which works through all levels to sustain and actualize the most inclusive and perfect system of all value.[125]

Since both Growth and nisus are regarded as creative activities within the universe—and it is not known just to what degree the nisus is active in distant galactic systems—both Alexander and Wieman are infra-pantheistic rather than pantheistic. "Infra-pantheism" is the word we have coined to express an activity immanent within the universe, but leaving open the question of its range of operations.

4. Both regard the question of the ultimate origin of the universe as futile. Note Alexander:

> The world which is Space-Time never and nowhere came into existence, for the infinite becoming cannot begin to become.[126]

Note Wieman:

> How everything got started no one knows and no one can ever know, because a pure beginning out of nothing is unthinkable. It is utter guesswork to speculate about it. Furthermore, it is very

doubtful that things ever had a pure beginning out of nothing. It is quite as probable as any other guess that existence of some sort has always been.[127]

5. Both regard the principle of Creativity as worthy of supreme commitment. Note Wieman:

> Faith is wholehearted and utter readiness for the fullest and freest spontaneity of responsiveness to the unforeseeable riches of each emergent situation.[128]

Note Alexander:

> The whole world with its real tendency to deity stirs in us from the depths of our nature a vague endeavour or desire which shadows forth its object.[129]

Perhaps one might be hypercritical and suggest that a better formulation would replace "shadows forth" by "illumines" for the typical religious awareness at its peak is announced in terms of brilliant illumination rather than the shadowing forth of an Unknown God!

6. Both regard this principle of creativity as objective in reality rather than as subjective. For instance, Wieman indicates his difference from John Dewey when he declares:

> According to him, the creative mind of man gives to the world the structures discovered there by inquiry. The very process of inquiry creates the structure, which is the product of its search.... But the basic structure found by philosophical inquiry and much that is vaguely known to common sense are produced not by human inquiry

DEITY, VALUE, PERSONS

and not by human experience but by creative energy. . . . Furthermore, the creativity which he upholds is that of the human mind, not a creativity working antecedently to the mind, creating it along with the world.[130]

We wish to emphasize this profound philosophic difference between Wieman and Dewey even more than Wieman himself might be inclined to do. Dewey's view that the process of inquiry creates the structures of the universe is sheer subjectivism while Wieman's view that human inquiry discovers antecedent structures is nothing less than the profound contrast between subjectivism and Realism.

7. Both require observational evidence of survival after death before they will accept belief in personal immortality. Wieman declares quite frankly:

> Theistic naturalism limits its position to findings that can be verified. It finds no empirical evidence concerning what happens after death save what is known concerning the decomposition of the body. If there is some kind of immaterial entity which continues to exist after the body passes away, we have no observational data to that effect.[131]

It would be erroneous to conclude from this blunt statement that Wieman leaves the problem in this negative position. He contracts unending existence with eternal life much as we did in discussing Alexander's views on immortality:

> *Immortality* means unending existence of the individual after death; it is quantitative. *Eternal life* is qualitative. . . . Eternal life is life that par-

ticipates in what is eternal. . . . But what is the eternal? The eternal is that order of value which is God. Its status in existence is always changing. As a form of existence in this world it may grow. But as order, structure, principle, whether in existence or not, it is eternal and changeless.[132]

We must be careful here to make clear that since Wieman's theology is usually associated with a wholly temporal view of existence his view of eternity is the same as that of Alexander—unending time. Eternal life is communion with the structure of reality and value which is God and which is a changeless creative principle though its manifestations are always changing as they appear at the levels of our evolutionary ladder.

In spite of these many points of similarity, Wieman is not as successful as is Alexander in giving to religious experience its due recognition as the total response of our being to the *mysterium tremendum* of the universe, "as something uniquely attractive and *fascinating*"[133] and which is the very nisus of creativity. The element of fascination, of wonder, of mystery, which is *sui generis* and, as Alexander has rightly insisted, distinct from our appreciation of the values of Truth, Goodness, and Beauty, is not given its proper recognition in liberal and naturalistic theologies. In traditional theism—whatever objections may be raised to its supernatural elements—this characteristic is elicited by the conception of the divine as incarnated in a supreme person of surpassing qualities of love, mercy, compassion, righteousness. This supreme person is the religious founder or the religious giant which piety and speculation usually equate with the God of the universe. Traditional theism, in spite of its difficulties, has won support by its imaginative presentation of the divine in human symbolism through the incarnation of spiritual qualities in a historic person.[134] Religion as the fulfilment of personality through communion with the divine rather than as the clarification of intellectual problems raised by science and philosophy has obviously been the strength of the historic faiths of both East and West. Such a discussion leads us to the examination of the relevance of personality for Alexander's system.

Has Alexander overlooked Personality?—The only reference to men of supreme gifts is as follows:

> Men of transcendent gifts of perfection are thus in their degree exemplars of this nisus.[135]

He adds that they cannot be equated with his futuristic deity, and he adds little else. There was a great opportunity here for Alexander to bring his evolutionary system to a fitting conclusion through a presentation of the creative genius as the culmination of the emergent pattern of the nisus, but Alexander failed to do this. In our present effort to modify Alexander's system, we shall attempt to do just this.

So far as we know the highest existents are persons, incarnating in themselves tertiary qualities in various degrees, the significant person being the one who incarnates these qualities with such an intensity that his life is fully integrated with the quality which forms his particular spirituality. Why not regard the spiritual as that peculiar quality of life which is so intensely exemplified by a person that the person and the quality are completely suffused and shine as one glorious, harmonious, universal, artistic reality. This is indeed suggested by the distinguished philosopher of education, Robert Ulich:

The *summum verum,* as expressed in thought, meets in the kingdom of the Spirit not only the *summum pulchrum,* as expressed in art, but also the *summum bonum* as expressed in great deeds. For ethical action, in the deepest sense of the word, springs from man's capacity to harmonize his life with the constructive order inherent in existence. . . . So, in our way, we have now arrived at the old sacred trinity of intellectual, esthetic, and ethical truth or value within one parent source, namely the mysterious contact of the human mind with the forces of growth inherent in the universe.[136]

The real greatness of spiritual giants may be appreciated as emergents from the universe itself; as culminations, summit characters, the highest organizations of the nisus of Space-Time itself. Having discarded the futuristic quality of deity, the value of such great persons is not primarily connected with their pointing to deity, as Alexander supposes, but rather with the fact that they represent the highest potentialities of Nature. In this view Nature is not some mechanistic, materialistic, concatenation of dead matter, but is a creativity to be interpreted by the character of its highest emergent, the supremely great religious person. We cannot be moved by a significant personality without being moved at the same time by the universe which has produced this personality. Any type of greatness whether it be in truth, beauty, or goodness, cannot be enjoyed without implying the universe in which it is present. Alexander referred approvingly to

Lotze's saying that music in its movement of tones is the reflection of the great movements that go through the universe. . . . No one who listens to great music and abstains from surrendering himself merely to the emotion which it is apt to excite, who tries to listen to it as music, can help feeling its affinities in obscure ways to the great goings on of nature and of human affairs.[137]

How much more shall we feel the affinity of the supremely great religious personality "in obscure ways to the great goings on of nature and of human affairs," especially to the creative advance which is the nisus! The intensity of the religious giant, an intensity harmonized into an artistic effortlessness, evokes its own mystical response. Since the supreme exemplar of religion is a manifestation of the creativity of the universe, this mystical response is not merely a sense of oneness with the universe, but a sense of communion with the universe as producing the significant religious personality whose misson is to incarnate some universal value with a peculiar radiance and power. The mystical emotion evoked by this fascinating and tremendous mystery seems to be an experience of the universe, the supreme person, and the value incarnated, all realized with a flash of insight. It is this impact of religious genius which evolutionary theologies and philosophies seem to overlook while we contend the attempt should be made to interpret the supreme synthesis which is the great exemplar of religion in terms of a culmination of the creative forces of the universe, "the personality-producing activities of the universe."[138] Historic religions have had the wisdom to do this task in terms of "christologies" and theories of the "incarnation." The need to perform this task in an interpretation of the incarnation as cosmic culmination is pressing. Well does Tsanoff terminate a recent work on this very subject with an affirmation of this interpretation:

> In the masterpieces of genius nature is seen in a new and revealing light. As this is the highest expression of being that we know, we are inclined to esteem it as the heart of reality. That indeed has been man's religious worship of the infinitely perfect Creator. The conviction that in its creative activity the mind somehow reaches the summit of reality has marked poet and sage and saint. Genius is creative in aspiration and achievement, and it contemplates the vision of Creative Reality.[139]

That personality is the highest level of universal evolution is again attested by J. E. Turner:

> the final results—the highest levels and types—of universal evolution are conscious personalities that are essentially free in the sense of being self-determined; and this attribute of freedom, still further, is capable of illimitably wider expansion. It indicates the fundamental tendency of all future development of personality, in the direction of the fuller rational and aesthetic apprehension of the Universe inseparably allied with an ever profounder emotional responsiveness, which together culminate in the free choice of universal purposes and the conservation of universal values.[140]

There is one further fact to be emphasized in our attempt to delineate further this theory of the religious genius as an incarnation of the personality-producing forces of the universe committed to the conservation of universal human values. Such commitment may involve tragedy for the religious giant, but the strange paradox lies in the fact that in the encounter of the religious genius with the forces of evil, tragedy is transmuted into victory. Without adopting in toto the theological presuppositions of A. A. Bowman, we feel that the flame of the human spirit shines with a peculiar brilliancy at the very time when it seems that all is lost—and yet all is won:

> But what are the marks by which we should *know* a saviour of mankind? Who is he? Surely the answer is, He, wherever he may be found, in whom the light of the spirit breaks most unmistakably through the meshes of the flesh. And the supreme test is that the spirit should flame forth more and more radiantly as the body goes down before the embattled forces of nature, that the ideal forms of spirituality should emerge with ever-growing clarity and splendour as the powers of evil close in; that the unseen energies of a hidden life should transmute disaster into triumph. Where these symptoms appear we may with safety assume incarnation of the divine, the presence of God's delegate on earth.[141]

In such a vision of the flame of the human spirit as the culmination of the creative aspects of the universe —creative aspects which shine even more brilliantly through the self-sacrifice of the saviour, "wherever he may be found,"—Alexander's natural piety becomes full religious piety.

CHAPTER IV

CONCLUSION: WHAT IS LEFT OF ALEXANDER'S SYSTEM?

What Elements are Rejected?—It is fitting to bring to a close this study of Alexander's conception of deity with an enumeration of the elements we have found unconvincing:

1. The cosmic extrapolation of the nature of man as a union of body and mind. In this extrapolation, a mental aspect and a body aspect are ascribed to every finite existent from the smallest to the greatest, even to Space-Time itself, and to God. The instant is the mind of its point, materiality is the mind of Space-Time before the emergence of matter, Time is the mind of Space, a quality is the mind of the level immediately below it, the whole universe of Space-Time up to the present moment is the body of God, and the mind of God is the futuristic quality of deity. We have found this extrapolation unconvincing for arguments already discussed, and we have suggested that the usage of Alexander as to "body" and "mind" is metaphorical rather than strictly metaphysical.

2. The whole conception of an infinite deity existing in the distant future has been shown to be untenable for two main reasons:

a. When closely examined it appears to imply a fragmentation of phases of deity so that these become the highest quality of existents higher than man, the finite gods and angels of Alexander. The bizarre conception of a number of polytheistic gods existing within the "body" of God results, and it is obvious that this conception is highly unsatisfactory.

b. Even though these finite gods were realized, the quality of deity, since infinite, is presupposed by Alexander to recede into the future. But a quality cannot exist in the future, since existents in Space-Time, whether finite or infinite, are actually formed through the movement of Time. If Alexander really means to take Time seriously, he must abide by his conviction that Time is a flux, be consistent with his approval of Bergson's famous phrase, *tout est donné,* in which Bergson rejects the view of all the events of Time, past, present, future, as totally given; he must, furthermore, maintain that the finites are formed and endure within the flux of Time, and that they cannot possibly exist ahead of the advance of this flux in the future.

3. Alexander's subject-object theory of value has been discussed at sufficient length to indicate that it involves a radical departure from the general trend of his Realism. As Konvitz states:

> At nearly every point of his theory of truth Alexander' comes pretty close to giving up the ghost of realism.[1]

Alexander's basic conviction that values are human inventions is challenged by F. E. England, and it is a challenge which we share:

> Alexander's belief that truth, beauty and goodness are human inventions must surely rest on

grounds other than those just stated. The fact that the constructive impulse may be satisfied in the creation of the objects of fine art is no warrant for declaring that beauty is a mere human invention. If the instinct of curiosity reaches its highest degree of satisfaction in the possession of truth, that is no reason for thinking that truth is man-made. The gregarious or social instinct may have had a good deal to do with the regulation of social morality, but it in no wise follows therefrom that goodness is a mere human invention.[2]

We have suggested that Alexander's system could be improved by introducing a realistic theory of value in which are inherent qualities of things and persons existing independently of our apprehension, approval, and desire. We have utilized the objective theories of the tertiary qualities of G. E. Moore and T. M. Greene and others to substantiate such a realistic theory, the objectivity being based on its coercive order. Interestingly enough, Wieman supports Greene on this issue, quite irrespective of other peripheral issues on which these two religious thinkers may differ:

> truth is antecedent, coercive, and determinant for all inquiry. It is ineluctably imposed upon the mind and its world . . . forms of beauty are created but are, like forms of truth, antecedent, determinant, and coercive for the individual who seeks and achieves beauty. They are there to be discovered and brought into the actual world of events.[3]

We have further suggested that a doctrine of natural law, as interpreted by John Wild, does justice to the dynamism of nature, the tendencies towards self-realization and maintenance of natural entities including man according to a norm embedded in such entities. The Space-Time matrix is replaced in this reconstruction by a Space-Time-Value system existing spatially, temporally, and historically, and characterized by "holistic" tendencies in which ever greater accumulations of value are concentrated in the "wholes" whose self-perfection is their natural law. An objective Value system existing independently of our desires and approvals in qualitied creative structures is again the position of Wieman:

> The fathomless deeps of qualitied structure have been built through countless ages of noncognitive interaction between cells, complex organism, and nonliving things. Our existence is rooted inextricably in these depths of value. We cannot really live for and by and with anything else.[4]

4. Alexander's peculiar theory according to which all finites in the world are complications of Space-Time with the appropriate correlated qualities we have not found entirely convincing, but we have left the question open for further investigation. We have suggested that recent cosmological speculations of Fred Hoyle and Viscount Herbert Samuel tend in the direction of assuming the existence of a continuous medium or ether of energy throughout the whole universe and filling interstellar and inter-galactic space. While not confirming Alexander's concept of physical Space-Time as the source of existents, these speculations tend to make us regard with sympathy Alexander's postulation of a real, objective, physical Space-Time as a *plenum,* and his protests against the reduction of his basic conception in terms of mathematical abstractions of Space and Time.

5. Alexander's conception of an emergence in Time for the whole universe so that the levels of pure Space-Time, materiality, life, mind, and possible qualities higher than mind, are held to emerge at certain periods simultaneously for the whole universe may be too comprehensive to be warranted by the facts. We would rather postulate histories of emergence in various parts of the universe, in galactic systems and especially in the development of life upon planetary systems. There may also be devolution as well as evolution, though whether devolution ultimately nullifies evolution is a question on which there is little evidence if any. It is worthy of note, however, that eminent biologists postulate a cosmic principle of greater application than the evolution of living forms on this planet:

> All reality, in fact, *is* evolution, in the perfectly proper sense that it is a one-way process in time; unitary; continuous; irreversible; self-transforming; and generating variety and novelty during its transformations.[5]

And there is a suggestion in Huxley—just a suggestion to be sure—that the interests and values of man are not mere human inventions projected onto reality:

> It is not true that the nature of things is irrelevant to the interests of man, for the interests of man turn out to be part of the nature of things.[6]

6. Alexander's rejection of immortality in its literal form seems to indicate lack of knowledge of more elevated and more philosophical forms of the theory which we have briefly suggested.

7. Alexander's theory of evil as "waste product" seems too unimaginative in an age which has suffered

WHAT IS LEFT OF ALEXANDER'S SYSTEM?

from manifestations of cunningly designed and perpetrated evils masquerading as spiritual virtues and not merely as waste products! Such pretended virtues as the superiority of a master race, the autocracy of state and religion, the distatorship of a class, are not merely poisons rejected by healthy organisms, they form the very life of diseased organisms all the more dangerous since they disguise their purposes under the appearance of devotion to the most elevated values. To unmask these forms of evil, a concept of "ideology" is required, and this concept has been utilized by socially-minded theologians and sociologists. By ideology, we mean, "a system of beliefs, held in common by the members of a collectivity."[7] But Parsons indicates that distortions are always present in ideologies:

> The cognitive distortions which are always present in ideologies, often compulsively motivated, will tend to be uncovered and challenged by the social scientist. Some of the results may be accepted, but only painfully and with allowance for a process of assimilation and adjustment over time. Because of this situation there will, more or less inevitably, be a tendency for the guardians of ideological purity in a social system to be highly suspicious of what social scientists are doing.[8]

Heroic religious figures, past and present, have challenged these ideologies. It is unfortunate that Alexander did not make room in his discussion of ethics for these more insidious evils and their ideological manifestations.

8. The extremely brief treatment of supreme exemplars of religion as manifestations of the nisus of Space-Time is much too inadequate. Alexander, on the basis

of his emergent system, could very easily have developed a theory of the "incarnation" as a culmination of the cosmic process, as a summit character synthesizing harmoniously dimensions of the human spirit. John Laird, in fact, after rejecting such theories of the incarnation as involving "a cosmic Adam, or a cosmic Mohammed, or a cosmic Christ" for "to argue so would be to confuse between the solar system and the solar plexus,"[9] nevertheless admits that "incarnationists" have something of value to contribute, which is consonant with the rejection of a mechanical universe:

> Often they say something like this: The universe cannot be wholly "mechanical" although there is mechanics in it. The pervasive co-adaptations in its pattern are of a super-mechanical order, and biology gives a better indication of that order than mechanics does. We may therefore infer that vital processes gather up and exemplify, with an unintended emphasis, a general inter-cosmic category. Mental and spiritual processes are still better exemplifications of the same category. Man the microcosm (as it were) collects and expresses the cosmic ethos, and does so quite humanly, that is, as a human body-mind. There is no accident in this. There is just metaphysics. Therefore the fact of "incarnation" is among the great realities.[10]

Laird, however, has merely given us the beginnings of a new theory of the incarnation, for he ends his article by stating: "I shall leave this suggestion without comment."[11] As culmination and exemplification of cosmic processes which have a "holistic" character, such a new conception of the incarnation might well engage the attention of emergent evolutionists and naturalistic theists.

Elements of Lasting Value in Alexander's System. —After having rejected so many characteristic features of the Alexandrian system, it might well be asked why he was chosen as the basis of this study. In order to answer this question, we must bring some of our own philosophical predilections to the fore.[12]

a. We were influenced increasingly by a direct realism in philosophy and epistemology. As a result of studies of realistic epistemology, we became aware of the gulf which separates certain modern trends, such as pragmatism, positivism, semanticism, and a realistic conception of epistemology and metaphysics.[13]

b. We had been impressed for some time with evolutionary and emergent philosophies, such as those of Samuel Alexander, Roy Wood Sellars, Henri Bergson, A. N. Whitehead, J. C. Smuts, and felt the need to do further investigation of at least one of these systems.

c. We felt that the religious sentiment is *sui generis*, and not to be reduced to merely "the religion of democracy," or "the religion of science," or any of the equivalences which are so easily made in an age of increasing industrialism.

d. We had felt for some time a strong opposition to subjective idealism, which tends to mentalize the whole universe, which tends to volatilize matter, and which gives rise to fantastic notions of spirituality.

The study of Alexander's philosophical system, and particularly of his conception of deity, was an attempt to secure metaphysical grounding in a total view which would unify the four trends of thought just mentioned; realism in epistemology, emergent evolutionism in metaphysics, the conception of the religious sentiment as unique and irreducible; and a refusal to interpret this sentiment in terms of mentalism and subjectivism. To some degree, Alexander's whole metaphysical system provides the unification of these four directions, but only to a degree since we have indicated several serious objections to his philosophy. Nevertheless, some important elements remain valid:

1. In order to focus on the element of value, we must cast our net very wide for the fundamental point of view which is emphasized by Alexander is metaphysics. Alexander was not content to reduce philosophical enquiry to subjective epistemology, or the abstract and abstruse formulations of symbolic logic, or the construction of "ethical sentences," or the psychological study of pleasures and pains. For him, philosophy primarily meant metaphysics, and he was quite ready to use Aristotle's definition of this discipline:

> If we may neglect too nice particulars of interpretation we may use the definition of Aristotle, the science of being as such and its essential attributes.[14]

Metaphysics is the most comprehensive of all studies, the investigation of being *qua* being, of existence in its most pervasive aspects, of ultimate questions of structure, matter, change, life, mind, and value, to name but a few of these. When referring to Whitehead and Alexander, R. G. Collingwood praised such investigations as the grand manner of philosophical writing:

> Each of these is a philosophical genius of very high order, and their works mark a return to the grand manner of philosophical writing . . . This

grand manner is not the mark of a period; it is the mark of a mind which has its philosophical material properly controlled and digested . . . it is marked by calmness of temper and candour of statement, no difficulties being concealed and nothing set down in malice or passion. All great philosophers have this calmness of mind, all passion spent by the time their vision is clear, and they write as if they saw things from a mountain-top.[15]

It must be admitted, however, that this grand manner, this calmness of temper, this all-comprehensive and fascinating study of the aspects of Being as such, is becoming lost in no small part due to the passing fashion of studies of "minute philosophers" into symbolic logic and ethical subjectivism. These studies ignore metaphysics, in fact pour scorn upon such an outmoded study, and imply that it is "meaningless." However, the main schools of metaphysics regard the trend towards logical positivism which characterizes so much of modern philosophy with no little displeasure. It is not difficult to find expressions of this dissatisfaction. For instance, a Platonist in a courageous review of a recent book on science takes issue with the view of science as a study of mere sensations:

> Mr. Conant may be described as a phenomenalist and a relativist as to science. Science proceeds from the past and present phenomena to a prediction of the unending procession of sensations in the future—a procession in which no fixed unitary pattern is to be found. Rather the endless procession is a phantasmagoria.[15a]

And Professor Demos vindicates metaphysics when he continues:

> I would go further and defend the view that a scientific theory, too, purports to state what is the case, that science is an attempt to provide a map or portrait of the real constitution of the real universe.[16]

Here is the justified objection of an Aristotelian against the reduction of philosophy to sensations:

> Any concept, like substance, self, or causation, which does not refer to such a sensory item, is dismissed as either meaningless or a pure subjective construction. This view is the source of a widespread movement which is now known as positivism.[17]

Here is the timely protest of a distinguished idealist against the trivial studies of some present-day philosophical inquiries:

> while strident alien ideologies have been winning much of the civilized world, the philosophers have been preoccupied with—well, what? With such things as the status of sense data, the meaning of meaning, the reduction of the number of primitive propositions required for deductive logic, the question whether a priori statements are all of them, or only some of them, tautologous. Philosophy was not always thus. At the turn of the century it was still generously conceived, and was devoting itself to questions of large significance for understanding the world and for living in it.[18]

WHAT IS LEFT OF ALEXANDER'S SYSTEM?

Nor is a materialist satisfied with the present situation for he finds that a majority of vocal and contemporary naturalists all too often side with positivists:

> That strictly they comprise a wing of the same phenomenalistic party with the franker positivists, however, is witnessed not merely by their common genealogy and their exchange of compliments, but also by their common resentment of Anglo-American realism and the boast that by their doctrine each of the persistent problems of philosophy is either exposed as not a genuine problem at all, or bequeathed to a special science. If the leanest kine of philosophy are not to eat up the fat, the materialist must league with whatever other unbashed philosophers may still aspire to knowledge in the grand style.[19]

This league between different metaphysical systems is precisely what we have in mind when we make the present enumeration. Roy Wood Sellars as an evolutionary naturalist affirms ontology:

> I am an unashamed ontologist and a convinced believer in the ontological reach of science. And this in spite of pragmatist, Viennese positivist, or religious personalist. If empirical knowledge is not knowledge of what exists, then it is not knowledge.[20]

A vindication of the great visions of philosophy against the inroads of semantics is voiced by W. P. Montague, whom we shall classify as an emergent realist:

> Whether old fashioned or not, I simply cannot

bear to see philosophy smother under a mountain of piffle, and especially at a moment in history when the problems of man's world and of man himself are crying so stridently for solution, or at least for consideration. I am on the one hand too frightened and on the other hand too stirred and thrilled to play the nice new game of semantic analysis.[21]

It seems apparent that there is increasing criticism of subjective studies in epistemology, logical analysis, semantics, positivism, sensationalism, by the major metaphysical schools: Platonism, Aristotelianism, Idealism, Materialism, and Evolutionary Naturalism, at least the type represented by Montague. All these schools stress the ancient role of philosophy as the investigation of Being, of the ramifications of this all-comprehensive study with such divisions of philosophy as epistemology, ethics, philosophy of art, philosophy of religion. And when we speak of metaphysics as the study of Being, we do not necessarily mean timeless Being, but Being as a systematic total historicity as is found in Alexander's system. Nor do we mean a Being apprehended by supersensible faculties existing "behind" spatio-temporal-qualitative existence. At this point in our inquiry we do not wish to engage in controversy with various metaphysical positions, whether Being is mental, material, timeless or temporal, for we are convinced metaphysicians have something much more important to do—the defense of their common territory against the inroads of those who deny any "real" world whatever. That the need for this common defense is being increasingly perceived is evidenced by a remark which Donald Williams of Har-

WHAT IS LEFT OF ALEXANDER'S SYSTEM?

vard made: "The materialist and the religionist are both agreed that something objective is the case." This something objective can provide the greatest fascination for metaphysical inquiry and for the support of an adequate religious view of the world. Otherwise we shall be left with a subjectivism of sensations condemned by W. T. Stace in words which may seem harsh but which nevertheless are justified:

> The "real" world is no more than what one may suppose some low-grade organism, a crocodile perhaps, to perceive; merely sensations of hot, cold, color, light, sound, hard, soft, pleasant or unpleasant smells and tastes, succeeding one another forever. In these sensations there are no doubt "regular sequences," that is, repetitions of the same following the same, which we dignify by the name "laws of nature." But how does that make the sensations any more sensible? Any suggestion that there is in all this any plan or purpose, or that the world so conceived is a moral order, must plainly be . . . no more than a fiction.[22]

Of course, the objection may be raised that these questions of metaphysics are so remote from the daily and urgent concerns of men and women that they should be disregarded. Or it may be said that religion is concerned with the transforming power which changes men from their worst to their best. But if the world is merely "a senseless drift of sensations which follow each other with endless and meaningless iteration,"[23] then individuals are shorn of their structured beings, and disappear into two-dimensional inter-subjective sensations of one another, very much like the disappearance of the Cheshire cat in *Alice in Wonderland*.[24] Paul Weiss's criticism of the phenomenalist applies here:

> That position disintegrates before one's eyes. Firstly, the sense organs themselves vanish into sensory content, and since, for the phenomenalist, the sensory is impotent and isolate, the organs must be incapable of conveying sensory content to us. An epistemology which can acknowledge only sensory content has an unmediated world afloat in the nowhere, possessed by nothing, given to no one, unknown and unknowable.[25]

Before we are able to consider the important issue of the transforming power which enriches men's lives, we must then consider the all-important question whether the *being* of these men is given due recognition, and we would like to utter this word *being* with the sense of philosophical victory and exultation which only Paul Weiss can give to it.

We are inevitably led to questions of ontology as the grand manner of philosophical inquiry, and it is precisely because Alexander occupies an important place in this *philosophia perennis* that we believe his defense of metaphysics will find a permanent place in the history of philosophical systems.

2. A second element of abiding value lies in Alexander's Realism. While all the metaphysical schools have—or should have—an intrinsic and implicit kinship in their common understanding of the essential task of philosophy against those who misunderstand or ridicule this task, within the area of metaphysics we choose a realistic metaphysics of levels of existence as a type of

perennial interest. One very difficult question which may be raised about such a philosophy of levels is this:

> *Why* should space-time generate matter; *why* should matter generate life; *why* should life generate mind?[26]

However, such a question is one which no system of metaphysics can ultimately resolve satisfactorily. An ultimate point seems to be reached in all metaphysical investigation at which we must accept Reality as it is in itself, with all its varieties, riches, emergent patterns, as well as its more intractable, cruel, aspects. Two unanswerable questions are: 1. Why should anything exist? 2. Why this particular emergent with these particular qualities should exist at this particular time and place. For, as Etienne Gilson stated:

> A metaphysics of existence . . . will never exhaust experience. . . . For even though, as is impossible, all that which exists were known to us, existence itself would still remain a mystery. Why, asked Leibniz, is there something rather than nothing?[27]

Similarly Tillich writes:

> The ontological question . . . "Why is there something; why not nothing?" But in this form the question is meaningless, for every possible answer would be subject to the same question in an infinite regression. Thought must start with being; it cannot be behind it, as the form of the question itself shows.[28]

Nor must we postulate another Being behind the being we encounter in our world:

Ontology is not a speculative-fantastic attempt to establish a world behind the world; it is an analysis of those structures of being which we encounter in every meeting with reality.[29]

Epistemological realism no less than metaphysical realism we believe to be an abiding element in Alexander's system, for it gives us the assurance that the mind can know the objective world and is not barricaded by the deceptive game of appearance and reality. To be sure, the mind does not know the object in all its inexhaustible features, and the value of experimentation lies not merely in making predictive statements about the future state of our sensations, but in determining additional characteristics of the object in question. And when we reflect on the qualitative nature of natural objects, and especially of persons, the philosophy of direct realism gives us a direct approach to this world of quality. The secondary qualities of color, scent, sound, are not merely subjective as the critical realist implies, but give us an apprehension of the qualitative character of the universe. If nature is not qualitied, then Whitehead's irony applies:

> The poets are entirely mistaken. They should address their lyrics to themselves, and should turn them into odes of self-congratulation on the excellency of the human mind. Nature is a dull affair, soundless, scentless, colourless; merely the hurrying of material, endlessly, meaninglessly.[30]

In our reconstructed Alexandrian system, we held to the view that the tertiary qualities were as objective as the secondary. We find such a view supported by A. S. Pringle-Pattison:

And what is thus asserted of the secondary qualities will hold also of what Professor Bosanquet in one place calls the tertiary qualities, the aspects of beauty and sublimity which we recognize in nature, and the finer spirit of sense revealed by the insight of the poet and artist. These things are not subjective imaginings; they give us a deeper truth than ordinary vision, just as the more developed eye or ear carries us farther into nature's refinements and beauties.[31]

Metaphysical realism allied to epistemological realism will then remain an abiding interest in the Alexandrian metaphysics. If reconstructed with a value realism, which it does not at present possess, Alexander's system would, in our opinion, rest on a much sounder foundation.

3. A third permanent element in Alexander's system is his emphasis on the reality of Time as a succession, on the process of reality as historical change, on reality as process or becoming. Metaphysical systems which ultimately deny the reality of time, change, and evolution would appear to have little appeal in a world which is full of critical situations which can only be considered in time and, if possible, solved in time. That present struggles are somehow already resolved in a changeless Whole or in the vision of an eternal present in the mind of God seems to nullify the reality of our moral efforts. The future is one which we build in the reality of Time. It is not already mapped out for us to accept passively as we come upon it. The reality of time as stressed by Alexander, Bergson, Smuts, and Process philosophers generally, gives due recognition to the common man's experience of temporal existence and its contingencies

and possibilities while the philosophy which stresses the unreality of Time obviously does not. Such a philosophy seems to scorn the experience of the common man, and a philosophy worthy of the name must be one which justifies common experience and gives intimations of insights into the depths of Reality tinged with meanings of surpassing beauty for humanity.

4. A fourth abiding element in Alexander's system is his recognition of religious experience as a distinctive response of the whole human personality irreducible to our appreciations of truth, goodness, and beauty. The sense of the tremendous mystery of the universe in its upsurge to richer realization of its potentialities which include supreme exemplars of human greatness, will appeal to philosophers of religion of many varying persuasions.

5. Alexander's conception of God as nisus, which is the one conception of the divine we felt had more justification than the others already discussed in detail in the body of this work, may be compared with Bergson's *élan vital*, and the principle of Holism in Smuts's philosophy, as well as Whitehead's doctrine of the creative advance of Nature. It seems to be a permanent element for the philosophy of religion oriented to a metaphysics of levels of existence and of emergence of higher levels from lower levels.

The Justification of Alexander.—It would appear from the whole discussion involved in this work that Alexander's system, especially as it bears on his conception of deity, is fraught with a multitude of problems, questions, issues, to which various answers have been given so that the system dissolves into confusing fragments with the central question of the primary concern of religion forgotten in a welter of subsidiary problems.

WHAT IS LEFT OF ALEXANDER'S SYSTEM?

The challenging Foreword of Dr. Henry Nelson Wieman has led us to give a more affirmative answer than would appear from the preceding pages. Two questions remain to be answered: the philosophical justification of Alexander's system as bearing on deity, and the religious justification of such elements in his system as carry unmistakably a religious reference.

We have already indicated grounds for giving great value to Alexander's metaphysics and to his Realism in view of the philosophic currents which are bent on a subjectivism of sensations and a rejection of ontology. Alexander's system is—as we have repeatedly stated—a system of emergent levels of existence and qualities which has close affinity with Smuts's *Holism and Evolution*. In fact, Alexander's metaphysics is closer to that of Smuts than to that of Bergson and Whitehead. What is the general problem which enervates the mind and which is solved by such Process systems? It is the existence of gaps in our knowledge of the world—gaps which appear to be deep chasms in reality itself—and yet which a most insistent demand of the philosophic consciousness refuses to accept as ultimate.

> Among the great gaps in knowledge those which separate the phenomena of matter, life and mind still remain unbridged. Matter, life and mind remain utterly unlike each other. Apparently indeed their differences are ultimate, and nowhere does there appear a bridge for thought from one to the other. And their utter differences and disparateness produce the great breaks in knowledge, and separate knowledge into three different kingdoms or rather worlds. And yet they are all three in experience, and cannot therefore be so

> utterly unlike and alien to each other. What is
> more, they actually intermingle and co-exist in
> the human, which is compounded of matter, life
> and mind.[32]

Smuts argues that this co-existence of matter, life, and mind in the human organism is a strong indication that the three levels do not belong to three separate metaphysical realms. Some are content with two metaphysical realms and this seems to be the position of such defenders of a religious view of the world as W. T. Stace in *Religion and the Modern Mind,* and A. A. Bowman in *A Sacramental Universe.* These works are of the highest value in defending the religious enterprise from the subjectivism and positivism which we have already castigated. And yet some philosophers cannot accept two or three metaphysical realms, and Smuts in particular, Smuts argues that this co-existence of matter, life, and mind, acknowledges

> the still greater mystery of their actual union in
> the threefold incarnation which continues human
> personality.[33]

A fundamental characteristic of the human mind is its drive for a unitary conception of reality, a drive so insistent in philosophers that even the positivist Moritz Schlick acknowledges it:

> Our craving for knowledge . . . urgently demands
> a continuously increasing unification of nature.[34]

It is this unification of nature which Alexander's system provides, doing justice to the levels of materiality, but not reducing levels of life and mind to matter, as we have explained abundantly. Alexander does not go to the extreme of unification by denying the level of matter or the level of mind. It is not unification by obliteration, by the attempt of the elusive reductive materialist to reduce mind to matter, or the attempt of the subjectivist to reduce matter to mind, even to eliminate matter entirely. Each realm is affirmed as part of Reality. The astronomer may discover millions of galaxies containing billions of suns—with masses beyond the power of human imagination—and Alexander as a Process philosopher would not feel the slightest need to deny the totality of this matter. The biologist and anthropologist do discover innumerable species of the almost infinite variety of abundant life on this earth, and no future generation of men can ever deny this richness. It is an essential part of the whole emergent Process. And the testimony of religion is that Value is integral to the universe and brought to a focus in dedicated personalities who incarnate universal values. A religious view of the universe under an emergent philosophy is one which apprehends the vast, creative Process as culminating in the religious giants of the race. And that apprehension is a distinctive quality, the "numinous" element in the world, acknowledged with profound insight by Alexander. But of this more later.

Let us make a digression and inquire why we have not succumbed to a very popular tendency in current discussions of science and religion, and solved the problem by either denying matter or mentalizing matter. Much has been made in the last twenty years of discoveries of intra-atomic phenomena as linked to the universe of numberless galaxies and interpreted by Einstein's theory of Relativity. The general conclusion appears to be a denial of objective reality—that very denial which Viscount Samuel protests. But this is precisely what Lincoln Barnett does in *The Universe and Dr. Einstein,* a work which has misled tens of thousands:

> Thus gradually philosophers and scientists arrived at the startling conclusion that since every object is simply the sum of its qualities, and since qualities exist only in the mind, the whole objective universe of matter and energy, atoms and stars, does not exist except as a construction of the consciousness, an edifice of conventional symbols shaped by the senses of man. As Berkeley, the archenemy of materialism, phrases it: "All the choir of heaven and furniture of earth, in a word all those bodies which compose the mighty frame of the world, have not any substance without the mind."[35]

It would seem that Berkeley is fast becoming a "controversial person" in modern philosophy, for while Stace eulogizes him in his study of religion, A. A. Bowman seems to be much closer to the truth of the matter when he links Berkeley with positivistic and subjectivistic tendencies represented by Ernst Mach, Richard Avenarius, Karl Pearson, C. Lloyd Morgan and Bertrand Russell.[36]

Serious theologians are not persuaded by such popular arguments which either deny matter, or reduce it to a mental construction. For instance, the very expressive Dean of St. Paul's finds the operations of Berkeleyan philosophers rather bewildering:

> Matter has certainly been defeated to a transparency; there is next to nothing left of it.[37]

And the vigorous Dean argues for an ontological posi-

WHAT IS LEFT OF ALEXANDER'S SYSTEM?

tion in science supporting Realism:

> I maintain, with Meyerson, that science is fundamentally ontological. Its starting-point is naive realism or common-sense philosophy. It assumes, I mean, that the objects which it studies are real.[38]

Nor is he impressed with the popular but uninstructed "back to Berkeley" trends of scientific and philosophic thought so well represented by Lincoln Barnett:

> I have not been able to follow those who hold that the decomposition of material particles, which were formerly supposed to be solid and indestructible, is a valid argument in favour of a spiritual as opposed to a materialistic view of ultimate reality. Although I hold that ultimate reality is "spiritual," not material, I cannot admit that matter dissolved into radiation is more "spiritual" than matter in a solid or liquid state. We may refuse to call it any longer matter, but this is not a refutation of materialism. This argument, which is used by some Christian apologists, seems to me frivolous. . . . I have crossed swords with those physicists who take refuge, in a rather confused manner, in Berkeleyan idealism as an escape from certain apparently insoluble problems in their own subjects. Science, I hold, can never be independent of the realism with which it starts, and therefore can never become purely mathematical.[39]

Process philosophy, and that instance of it in Alexander's system, does not fall prey to the popularizations so well punctured by Dean Inge. It accepts the material level, but denies that it is the only level and accentuates

387

the higher levels of life and mind. In fact, Alexander went further and postulated finite deities! But, more important than any level, Process philosophy emphasizes that the key to its inner meaning is a universal dynamism combining parts into wholes, from electron to molecule to cell to living organism to man himself. The unitary tendency which is the metaphysical impulse of positivist as well as Realist, finds its fulfilment in this universal dynamism, whether it be called principle of emergence, principle of Holism, nisus of Space-Time. It is here that the justification of Alexander as a philosopher of religion must be sought. And the philosophical and religious justification of Alexander will enable us to answer that primary question raised by Henry Nelson Wieman in the Foreword as to what is the essential concern of religion.[40]

Just as the philosopher regardless of his metaphysical position is fascinated by the search for a principle of unity in the universe, so the religionist is fascinated by the search for the soul's unity as dependent on the world's unity:

> In the sense of completeness, totality, wholeness, both philosophy and religion require a quest of the world's unity as a basis for the soul's unity.[41]

In Process philosophy this principle has received various names: nisus of Space-Time, the *élan vital*, the Holism of Smuts, the creative advance of Whitehead. In fact, a nisus principle is postulated by both Alexander and Morgan, and in view of Morgan's phenomenalism, criticized by Woodger, we much prefer the intimate combination of Realism and Evolutionism as found in Alexander. Woodger's criticism is quite pronounced:

WHAT IS LEFT OF ALEXANDER'S SYSTEM?

> He does not seem to be in *any doubt about evolution*, but he is, apparently, in some *considerable doubt* about the existence of an independently real physical world or about what our sense-experience tells us about it (assuming that it exists).[42]

We do not need to repeat our arguments for Realism in order to reject this peculiar system of Morgan in which there is evolution of a highly dubious reality.

A further justification of Alexander lies in the fact that liberal theologians have reacted favorably, if not to all, at least to some aspects of Alexander's system. We found a large number of similarities between Alexander and Wieman, the proponent of empirical theism most oriented to a metaphysics of levels of existence.[43]

D. C. Macintosh, another liberal theologian, finds persuasive force in both Alexander's and Morgan's emergent, creative process, though he frankly declares that the idea of a nisus towards deity is fantastical. This may seem a harsh rejection of Alexander's conception of the nisus, but it is really not the case for it is the nisus towards a futuristic deity which Macintosh finds unsubstantiated, not the nisus towards present forms of existence, consciousness and mind. This vindication of the nisus is precisely what we have emphasized throughout this work:

> Professor S. Alexander and Lloyd Morgan are on fully scientific ground . . . when they describe the progressive emergence, in the course of evolution, of consciousness, intelligence, and personality; and one may even go further and claim essentially scientific knowledge of God as the principle of emergent evolution, if we mean by that term sim-

ply whatever creative principle is necessary to explain this progressive emergence of new and higher forms of existence which differ in kind from all that was explicitly contained in the earlier stages of this process. . . . But when Alexander speaks of this principle of emergent evolution not only as a *"nisus* toward deity," he becomes not only unscientific but fantastical.[44]

The nisus of the world as the principle of progressive emergence is thus regarded as scientifically justified, but not the futuristic deity. It is to be noted, however, that Alexander's philosophy of religion is not entirely based on the conception of a futuristic deity which exercises mysteriously a flavor of its character from the future to persons in the present. This would be an impossible relationship, and it is corrected by Alexander's emphasis on the nisus as the divine factor in the world which at the present moment grips us into communion with its creative energy:

> It is the world in its nisus forward that grips the finite conative complex which is fitted to it. It excites religion in us, and we in turn feel the need of it.[45]

Furthermore, Alexander is on sound religious grounds when he asserts that the religious emotion or appetite is not conditioned by a specific organ. Let us recall once more his central position:

> But the religious appetite or emotion depends upon the whole make-up or constitution of the mind and body, and is the response of it to the whole of reality in its nisus towards a new quality. In that forward movement due to the onward

WHAT IS LEFT OF ALEXANDER'S SYSTEM?

> sweep of Time our minds with their substructure of body are caught and our religious response is at once the mark that we are involved in that nisus, and that our minds contribute in their part towards it. . . . For the world is not merely what it is for intellect alone; its nisus towards what is higher enters into its constitution, and as impregnated with this tendency it affects the mind by ways other than cognition, though interpretable in the ways of cognition. The whole world with its real tendency to deity stirs in us from the depths of our nature a vague endeavour or desire which shadows forth its object. Then intellect comes into play, and discovers in detail the characters of this object, and finds at last what it truly is, the tendency of the world forwards towards a new quality.[46]

Let us admit at once that this new quality does not exist as a vague ineffable lake resting on an infinity of point-instants in the future, as we have repeatedly asserted. Yet this major correction in no way nullifies Alexander's conception of religion as something much more profound than intellectual understanding, and as the response of our inmost selves to the mysterious nisus of the world.

Again, Alexander is right in insisting that the object of religion is not an imaginary being, nor is the religious sentiment merely a psychological state:

> the object of religious sentiment is no mere imagination which corresponds to a subjective and possibly illusory movement of mind. We are in perpetual presence of this object, which stimulates us, some of us more, some less.[47]

Alexander is also justified in raising the object of religion higher than the values of beauty, goodness and truth:

> The values of beauty, goodness and truth are the highest creations of man, and the object of religion is still higher in the scale than man and his works.[48]

Even if we make the important addition that the values of truth, goodness and beauty are not merely human inventions, but are constitutive of the Universe and are in fact qualitative aspects of the nisus as a Value-creative principle throughout the levels of reality, still it remains true that the nisus as the divine, creative, "holistic" principle of the world does call forth the response of our total personalities in a way which is not reducible to either of the tertiary qualities. The nisus is thus more than the principle of the conservation of values since the response we make to it is more than the appreciation of values, no matter how highly they may be regarded. Alexander is right against Höffding at this point.

Just what is this response? It is our response to a sense of the "numinous" element in the world. Alexander here declares himself to be an "Otto-man," that is to say, he finds the delineation of this vital element by Rudolf Otto the key to at least one important element of religious apprehension:

> One of the elements of religious feeling is the sense of mystery, of something which may terrify us or may support us in our helplessness, but at any rate which is other than anything we know by our senses or our reflection. And it is natural to believe that there is something real, some fea-

ture of actual existence, which calls forth this sentiment in us. Mr. Otto calls this the 'numinous' element in the world . . . in recognising the existence in real fact of this numinous element in the world, I follow him, and . . . profess myself in this respect an Otto-man.[49]

Alexander did not further explicate his acknowledgement of the "numinous" in terms of the meanings given to it by Otto and as they may be related to his system. He certainly implied that our response is other than cognitive, ethical, or aesthetic, and is of an entirely different quality. On at least one occasion he suggested that it comes to full fruition in mysticism:

> There is a sound and a dangerous mysticism. The sound variety is an essential ingredient in all religion; it is not too much to say that it is the vital ingredient of religion, without which religion is a thing of form.[50]

There is need, then, to examine more fully than did Alexander the meanings attached to this sense of the "numinous" by Otto, and in this way we may be able to justify Alexander's philosophy of religion in directions which he did not specifically express but which are in no way contradictory of his basic philosophic position. The various elements in the meaning of the "numinous" are then to be correlated, as far as is possible, with Alexander's philosophy:

1. Otto is dissatisfied with the usual meaning of "holy" as perfect goodness, and presents the overplus of meaning involved here by coining a new word:

> I shall speak then of a unique 'numinous' category of value and of a definitely 'numinous' state

of mind, which is always found wherever the category is applied. This mental state is perfectly *sui generis* and irreducible to any other; and therefore, like every absolutely primary and elementary datum, while it admits of being discussed, it cannot be strictly defined.[51]

This is obviously the distinctive quality of the religious sense which Alexander affirms.

2. Otto implies that this peculiar category is not necessarily the province of the Christian religion:

> There is no religion in which it does not live as the real innermost core, and without it no religion would be worthy of the name.[52]

Alexander's religion, in spite of the many unusual and problematic features which it presents in its intellectual formulation and which we found unconvincing, may therefore be included in Otto's apprehension of the essence of religion.

3. Again, the numinous

> is the emotion of a creature, abased and overwhelmed by its own nothingness in contrast to that which is supreme above all creatures.[53]

Alexander might demur at this declaration of the nothingness of the creature, since he believes that the individual can contribute to the nisus. Yet, strictly speaking, the creature appears to be overwhelmed only in contrast to that which is supreme above all finite existents. Is this so very different from Alexander's philosophy? That which is above all creatures is indeed the whole universe of Space-Time containing numberless galaxies animated by the nisus towards higher and higher levels of reality and value.

4. The characteristic note of Otto in developing the meaning of the "numinous" is the *mysterium tremendum,* the sense of the tremendous mystery of the universe, a sense which admittedly has had "barbaric antecedents" but which

> may become the hushed, trembling, and speechless humility of the creature in the presence of—whom or what? In the presence of that which is a *Mystery* inexpressible and above all creatures.[54]

It is not difficult to orient this feeling of humility to the apprehension of the universe of emergent forms and patterns of Alexander, of holistic tendencies in Smuts,[55] and other philosophers of creative evolution. The various attempts to explain this vast process in terms of emergent qualities on higher levels, of patterns of organization which unify "wholes" from cell to man himself, of values which are embedded in these wholes, is very suggestive of the overpowering dynamism of the Universe. Yet when all is said and done, there remains a feeling of the extreme poverty of our intellectual concepts in the presence of this tremendous mystery of the Cosmos in its ascent from lowest to highest levels. This tremendous mystery of the man-nature synthesis, of this synthesis in which man appears to be organic to nature, remains, in the words of Keats, to "tease us out of thought as doth Eternity."

5. Also, the "aweful majesty" with which Otto further characterizes the *mysterium tremendum* can be ascribed to the awe-inspiring majesty of the universe which in its infinitude generates in us the sense of the

sublime, as Kant so well expressed.

    6. Another element of the *mysterious tremendum* is the *urgency* or *energy* of the numinous object. . . . The element of 'energy' reappears in Fichte's speculations of the Absolute as the gigantic, never-resting, active world-stress.[56]

It also reappears in Alexander's meaning of the nisus as the restlessness of Space-Time. Obviously, this is a symbolic expression which but meagerly expresses the energies of the Universe which defy imagination and organize all forms of existence and of life. Otto emphasizes that all our expressions of this urgency are symbols for what is ultimately non-rational. Alexander would grant that the sense of the "numinous" grips us more directly than through the rational consciousness, but is amenable to rational inquiry. In Otto's insistence on a non-rational element there may be a dangerous opening for regarding the irrational as the mark of the divine. This possibility has brought objections from Henry Nelson Wieman and Dean Willard L. Sperry to the effect that if religion is regarded as ultimately irrational, then there can be no rational criterion with which to evaluate violence and disruption.[57]

Alexander and Wieman would also disagree with Otto's description of the *mysterium tremendum* as "wholly other" for in a philosophy of creative immanence, the tremendous energy of the nisus is, to be sure, not a subjective affair; it is "other" than we are, but not completely other since it has produced us, and since our souls respond to its "numinous" quality. If the religious object were "wholly other," there could be no possible relationship, whether described in rational or affective terms, and Otto simply could not write his book so full of perceptive suggestions as to the meaning of the "numinous" element in the universe.

7. Another aspect of the numinous experience is "something uniquely attractive and *fascinating*."[58] The mystery is not something which bewilders us and makes us turn to what is less problematic. On the contrary it is something which attracts and allures:

> The 'mystery' is for him not merely something to be wondered at but something that entrances him; and beside that in it which bewilders and confounds, he feels a something that captivates and transports him with a strange ravishment.[59]

This fascination produces its own peculiar graciousness, wonderfulness and rapture in the mysterious beatific experience of the divine element in the world. It rises to the "noblest Mysticism,"[60] that in which the *mysterium tremendum* is experienced not in its sense of mystery but "as something that bestows upon man a beatitude beyond compare."[61]

This element of fascination may certainly be appropriated within the world system of Alexander, for what is more fascinating than this whole evolutionary process of Space-Time, matter, life, and mind, with unsearchable energies and riches tantalizing for both philosopher and layman alike? The wonder is that it has happened at all, and yet how it has taken place, just how the unending variety of forms of life, of incarnations of beauty, truth, and goodness, and more personal values, have emerged from a universal matrix, is still an unsolved problem. Yet it is not an issue which we may merely thrust aside for more practical concerns. It excites in us that positive aspect of the sense of mystery, the feelings of wonder, rapture, beatitude, as our intense straining to comprehend the incomprehensible activities of the creative nisus produces in us the mystical emotion which draws us ever nearer to this tremendous Mystery. That mysticism need not be thought solely in terms of identification with a timeless Absolute but also as union with a temporal creative impetus has been pointed out by Bergson:

> an experience closely resembling ecstasy . . . an effort at oneness with the creative impetus.[62]

Mysticism as oneness with the creativity of the universe is, of course, capable of interpretation in terms of Alexander's nisus. In fact one might suggest that the familiar expressions suggestive of the ineffable mystical experience, such as "vital heat," "fierce glow," "flame," "luminous," "light," "enlightenment," "illumination," "irradiation," "consummation," etc., seem to apply much more to the mysterious and fascinating energy of the nisus than to the immutability of a timeless Being.

8. A further aspect of Otto's thought as to the "numinous" which may be adapted to Alexander's religious philosophy is the sense of "numinous unworthiness and disvalue" which the creatures experience when confronted with the awful majesty of the universe. The contemplation of the creative richness of the universe, not merely in its sublime cosmic depths and energies but in its aspects of transcendent beauty and value produces its inevitable reaction in the feeling of being surrounded by a surpassing richness and of not being worthy of it, a feeling deeper than the sense of wrongdoing. But this spiritual depression is not the last word. The last word is the restoration of the individual soul to this encompassing richness so that it feels the mystery,

fascination, and sustaining power of the Universe enveloping it and transforming it from its self-alienation to an experience, if not of mystical union, then of communion with that emergent Order of reality which is the source of all our values and of that response which is nothing else than adoration.

Such are the extensions of Alexander's philosophy of emergence interpreted in terms of the categories of Otto —extensions which we trust are not against the spirit and substance of Alexander's system.

There is an additional element which seems to be overlooked by both Otto and Alexander and which we have pointed out before in this study. This is the doctrine of the "incarnation" as cosmic culmination, as integration of the creative forces of the Universe at the human level in great cosmic personalities who live intensively and yet harmoniously a quality of life with which their whole personality is suffused in indissoluble union. This is the quality of utter righteousness as found in the Hebrew prophets, of love and compassion in Jesus, of self-mastery in Buddha, of devotion to scientific truth in Einstein. It is the essential mystery of the universe rising to a peak of achievement in an "incarnation" of surpassing beauty which is one of the ever-fascinating and enchanting aspects of the "numinous."

Our suggested doctrine of the "incarnation" is one which has affinity with the conception of the late Professor Robert James Hutcheon of the Meadville Theological School, Chicago, in which he wrote in glowing terms of man bringing reality to a focus:

> In the infinite depths of the universe it may be that other creatures bring reality to a richer focus than man; but for us, at least, on our present level

of experience and knowledge, the divinest thing known is our humanity at its best. To the cry of the bewildered Job: "Oh that I knew where I might find him, that I might come even to his seat," the best answer is the celebrated saying of St. Chrysostom: "The true Shekinah of God is man." Our humanist friends are only repeating the truth of this great saying when they declare that the great world-spirit finds its highest expression in humanity, and that in humanity we must look for the deepest manifestations of the divine.[63]

And this sense of the divine as expressed in man is not lessened but intensified when the tragic element enters, as it so often does, in the lives of the giants of the race:

> For the mature religious mind, religious experience has in it an element of the heroic and sometimes the tragic.[64]

It is in this peak of tragedy that the greatest contrast in the Universe pierces our souls—on the one hand the religious hero enduring his sufferings with his faith unabated, on the other hand the destructive forces of the universe or of his religious contemporaries. But it is this contrast symbolically expressed as the unending contest between light and darkness which vivifies our souls.

What is, then, the essential element and concern of religion? It cannot be given in a single sentence or in a single process such as the transformation of human lives from the worst to the best that is possible in human destiny. Religion asks a further question, What is the nature of this transformation? This is a transformation which is the peculiar result of a distinctive religious apprehension of the Universe *not* to be equated with such current terms as "the religion of science," or "the religion of democracy," but which is *sui generis*. That is not to say that the religious person should not devote himself to scientific truth or the advance of democracy, but the religious apprehension of the world is irreducible to these worthy causes just as the appreciation of great art cannot be reduced to terms of science and democracy. The religious apprehension of the world involves, then:

1. The sense of the tremendous mystery, majesty, and over-powering quality of the Universe.

2. This sense is to be recognized not as a static contemplation of pure Being, but as imbued with the dynamic quality of the Universe which energizes forms of existence into greater and greater "wholes."

3. The culmination of this emergent "holistic" Process in persons dedicated to universal human values to such a degree of intensity that the value and the person are suffused in indissoluble unity.

4. The sense that this "incarnation" of the religious giant with the quality he exemplifies is a culmination of the creative forces of the Universe, symbolized as God.

Neither the apprehension of the immensity of the Universe, nor of its dynamic quality, nor of the religious giant, nor of the quality he incarnates, is sufficient by itself to give us a fully matured religious feeling. The immensity of the universe may evoke Kant's idea of the sublime, or the intellectual ecstasy of Camille Flammarion, but it is not as such religion. The sense of the over-powering dynamism of the Cosmos culminating in the myriads of plant life and animal types would only give us a zoological and botanical religion. To be sure, some "naturalists" have found this experience delightful. Again, the attitude of devotion to historic persons talented in religion, the arts, sciences, social reform, is not sufficient. Nor is the pragmatic exploration of human values as such in a local community by means of a humanism divorced from the richness and depths of the cosmic grounding of values, and also divorced from vast areas of human history and culture, sufficient to be dignified by the name of religion.[65]

The religious sense is nothing else than the vivid apprehension of all these elements: the immensity and majesty of the Universe apparent in the energy and dynamism of its evolutionary processes and culminating in the emergence of the religious genius who unites in himself a universal value with such intensity that his life and the value are completely suffused in an "incarnation" of human excellence and cosmic creativity. It is this cumbersome but necessary intellectual formula which very weakly expresses the "numinous" experience which justifies Alexander's philosophy of religion. It is this experience which is the transforming power which enables one to reject evil for the best that may be obtained, which expands our vision, enlarges our sympathies, enables us to work for ideal ends, and gives us an inner glow which maintains our sense of victory even in tragedy—in Tillich's words, "the courage to be."

This sense of the numinous is what the experience of worship attempts to re-create, and "religion's glory is the glory of worship."[66]

Perhaps the most fitting conclusion of this study of Alexander's conception of the divine element in the Universe is that given by George P. Conger:

In spite of all . . . criticisms, the work of Alexan-

WHAT IS LEFT OF ALEXANDER'S SYSTEM?

der stands out like a mountain upon the horizon, and for our time serves to mark out a new land in philosophy of religion. Until it appeared, with supernaturalism for many thinkers dissolving like a cloud and the idealistic systems evaporating like a mist, there seemed little besides a barren naturalism available as the philosophical home of man. But if Alexander is right even in a few of the main outlines of his work, there are other possibilities, and realists and naturalists may find God in their own ways. These possibilities need to be studied eagerly and in detail. It begins to look as if the majesty of the universe as understood in modern times and the power of religion as experienced in the past could be combined.[67]

NOTES PART I

Chapter I

1. Rudolf Metz, *A Hundred Years of British Philosophy* (New York, The Macmillan Company, 1938), 622-623. One might challenge Metz's statement to the effect that "The influence of Alexander's doctrine . . . has been so far confined to the Anglo-Saxon world" for one may call attention to the lucid French study by Philippe Devaux, *Le Système d'Alexander* (Paris, Librarie Vrin, 1929). Devaux has also introduced Russell and Whitehead to French and Belgian readers though he deplores the isolation of British from Continental philosophy.

2. Samuel Alexander, *Philosophical and Literary Pieces*, edited with a Memoir by his Literary Executor, John Laird (London, Macmillan and Company Ltd., 1939), 65. Hereafter designated as PLP.

3. Samuel Alexander, *Space, Time, and Deity* (New York, The Humanities Press, 1950); Copyright first edition, 1920; reprinted 1927; reprinted 1950 by special arrangement with the Macmillan Company, Vol. I, 1-2.

4. An epistemological rather than a metaphysical distinction between realism and idealism is found in W. P. Montague, "The Story of American Realism," *The Ways of Things* (New York, Prentice-Hall, 1940), 230-261.

5. *STD.*, Vol. I, 8.

6. For a cogent criticism of Bradley's philosophy of Appearance and Reality to which we indirectly refer here, see A. Seth Pringle-Pattison, *The Idea of God in the Light of Recent Philosophy*. (Oxford, at the Clarendon Press 1917), 225-242.

7. Samuel Alexander, "The Basis of Realism," *Proceedings of the British Academy* 1913-1914 (London, Humphrey Milford, Oxford University Press), 279-280.

8. *Ibid.*, 284.

9. *Ibid.*, 284-285.

10. *STD.*, Vol. I, 23.

11. *Ibid.*, 24.

12. *STD.*, Vol. II, 55.

13. *Ibid.*, 56.

14. *Ibid.*, 138.

15. *Ibid.*, 139.

16. *Ibid.*, 140.

17. *Ibid.*, 142.

18. John Wild, *Introduction to Realistic Philosophy* (New York, Harper

NOTES PART I

and Brothers Publishers, 1948), 422.

19. J. E. Turner, *A Theory of Direct Realism* (New York, The Macmillan Company, 1925), 7. For Turner's criticism of critical realism, similar to that of Alexander, see "The Inadequacy of Critical Realism," 124-137.

20. Roy Wood Sellars, *The Philosophy of Physical Realism* (New York, The Macmillan Company, 1932), 106.

21. *STD.*, Vol. II, 97.
22. *Ibid.*, 98.
23. J. E. Turner, *op. cit.*, 129.
24. A. Seth Pringle-Pattison, *The Idea of God in the Light of Recent Philosophy* (Oxford, at the Clarendon Press, 1917), 121-122.

25. I have in mind such a definition as: "We obtain the most adequate and at the same time most comprehensive definition of religion . . . by regarding it as the response or attitude of humanity, when this response is taken as being an *explicit* unity or real whole, to the Universe, likewise taken as a whole."—J. E. Turner, *Essentials in the Development of Religion* (New York, The Macmillan Company, 1934), 32. The bearing of this definition on Alexander's system will be more fully explored later.

26. S. Alexander, "Some Explanations," *Mind*, N.S. Vol. XXX (October, 1921), 411.

27. *STD.*, Vol. I, 40.
28. *Ibid.*, 59.
29. *Ibid.*, 40.
30. *Ibid.*, 41.
31. *Ibid.*, 41.
32. *Ibid.*, 42.
33. *Ibid.*, 43.
34. *Ibid.*, 74.
35. *Ibid.*, 67.

36. *Ibid.*, 61. An illustration of the meaning of motion in Space-Time through the change in time-coefficients may be found in the movable sentences which express the latest news in Times Square, New York. A system of electric light bulbs is so controlled that a sentence will move along through light-bulbs being successively lit and shut off through this control. The word "the," for instance, moves along because the light bulbs corresponding to the pattern for "the" are lit for a fraction of a second, then extinguished, immediately after which the next pattern of bulbs making "the" is lit. In this way, the bulbs correspond to the immovable points of Alexander, and the successive lighting and shutting off of their light corresponds to the change of time-coefficients which is motion.

37. *Ibid.*, 61.
38. *Ibid.*, 62.
39. *Ibid.*, 45.
40. *Ibid.*, 71.
41. *Ibid.*, 63.
42. *Ibid.*, 63.
43. *Ibid.*, 63.
44. *Ibid.*, 143.
45. *Ibid.*, 150.

NOTES PART I

46. Full discussion of sections and perspectives is outside the scope of this work. For a cogent abbreviation, see Devaux, *op. cit.*, 64-76.
47. *STD.*, Vol. I, 67.
48. *Ibid.*, 67.
49. *Ibid.*, 75.
50. *Ibid.*, 69.
51. *Ibid.*, 71.
52. *Ibid.*, 80.
53. *Ibid.*, 80-81.
54. *Ibid.*, 65.
55. *Ibid.*, 82-83.
56. In what way Alexander uses the term "eternity" we shall discuss in due course.
57. *STD.*, Vol. I, 65.
58. *Ibid.*, 341.
59. Rudolf Metz, *op. cit.*, 634.
60. Bernard Bosanquet, *The Meeting of Extremes in Contemporary Philosophy* (London, Macmillan & Company Ltd., 1921), 166.
61. *STD.*, Vol. I, 183.
62. *Ibid.*, 185.
63. *Ibid.*, 189.
64. Devaux, *op. cit.*, 79.
65. *STD.*, Vol. I, 191.
66. *Ibid.*, 197.
67. *Ibid.*, 199.
68. *Ibid.*, 199.
69. *Ibid.*, 206.
70. *Ibid.*, 217.
71. *Ibid.*, 222.
72. *Ibid.*, 270.
73. The interesting discussion of "Mental Space and Time," chapters III and IV of Book I of *Space, Time, and Deity*, we omit as extraneous to our purpose, which is to lay the foundation for a discussion of deity.
74. The term is not Alexander's but one which we have coined.
75. *STD.*, Vol. II, 38.
76. *Ibid.*, 39.
77. *Ibid.*, 43.
78. *Ibid.*, 44.
79. *Ibid.*, 44.
80. *STD.*, Vol. II, 45.
81. *Ibid.*, 46.
82. *Ibid.*, 68.
83. Samuel Alexander, "Natural Piety," *PLP*, 304-305. Sellars and Alexander are both emergent evolutionists, the chief differences between them being: 1. Alexander is a direct realist; Sellars a critical realist; 2. Alexander finds room in his philosophy for deity; Sellars does not.
84. *Ibid.*, 308.
85. *STD.*, Vol. II, 8. It is remarkable how often evolutionary philosophers quote these lines from Browning. The quotation is also found in

NOTES PART I

C. Lloyd Morgan, *Emergent Evolution* (New York, Henry Holt, 1923), 4; S. Alexander, *Beauty and Other Forms of Value* (London, Macmillan and Company, 1933), 95; A. S. Pringle-Pattison, *op. cit.*, 95.
    86. *Ibid.*, 49.
    87. *Ibid.*, 52-54.
    88. *Ibid.*, 55.
    89. *Ibid.*, 57.
    90. John Wild, *op. cit.*, 420. For a discussion of modern realism, see *The Return to Reason*, ed. John Wild (Chicago, Henry Regnery Company, 1953).
    91. John Elof Boodin, *Cosmic Evolution* (New York, The Macmillan Company, 1925), 38.
    92. *STD.*, Vol. II, 61.
    93. *Ibid.*, 65.
    94. *Ibid.*, 65.
    95. *Ibid.*, 69
    96. *STD.*, Vol. I, 342.
    97. Devaux, *op. cit.*, 87.
    98. *STD.*, Vol. I, 337.
    99. *Ibid.*, 342.
    100. *Ibid.*, 337-338.
    101. *Ibid.*, 339.
    102. *STD.*, Vol. II, 336.
    103. *Ibid.*, 337.
    104. *Ibid.*, 338.
    105. William R. Inge, *Mysticism in Religion* (Chicago, The University of Chicago Press, 1948), 64.
    106. Mary Whiton Calkins, *The Persistent Problems of Philosophy* (New York, The Macmillan Company, 1925), 440.
    107. *STD.*, Vol. I, 340.
    108. *STD.*, Vol. II, 366.
    109. *Ibid.*, 366.
    110. S. Alexander, "The Historicity of Things," *Philosophy and History* (eds., Raymond Klibanski and H. J. Paton; Oxford, Clarendon Press, 1936), 11.
    111. S. Alexander, "Ptolemaic and Copernican Views of the Place of Mind in the Universe," *The Hibbert Journal*, Vol. VIII, No. 1 (October, 1909), 61.
    112. *STD.*, Vol. I, 338.
    113. *Ibid.*, 343.
    114. *Ibid.*, 343.
    115. S. Alexander, "The Historicity of Things," *op. cit.*, 15.
    116. Roger Hazelton, "Time, Eternity, and History," *The Journal of Religion*, Vol. XXX, No. 1 (January, 1950), 7.
    117. Raphael Demos, ed., *The Dialogues of Plato* (Jowett Translation; New York, Random House, 1937) Vol. II, "Timaeus," par. 38, p. 19.
    118. W. R. Inge, *op. cit.*, 54.
    119. Roger Hazelton, *op. cit.*, 8.
    120. S. Alexander, "The Historicity of Things," *op. cit.*, 15.

NOTES PART I

121. Alfred N. Whitehead, *Process and Reality* (New York, The Macmillan Company, 1929), 70.
122. *STD.,* Vol. I, 343.
123. *STD.,* Vol. II, 338. We are omitting in this introductory chapter the treatment of value, which, in Alexander's exposition, precedes his development of deity. We prefer to consider value and deity together in a subsequent chapter of this study.

Chapter II

1. *STD.,* Vol. II, 341.
2. *Ibid.,* 342.
3. "Spinoza and Time," *PLP,* 376.
4. *STD.,* Vol. II, 342-3.
5. *Ibid.,* 343.
6. *Ibid.,* 344n.
7. *Ibid.,* 344-345.
8. *Ibid.,* 345.
9. *Ibid.,* 346.
10. *Ibid.,* 346.
11. *Ibid.,* 347.
12. *Ibid.,* 347. This analogy was suggested to Alexander by Meredith's *Hymn to Colour,* which on page 60 of Volume II of *STD* he quotes in part:
> But love remembers how the sky was green,
> And how the grasses glimmered lightest blue;
> How saintlike grey took fervour; how the screen
> Of cloud grew violet; how thy moment came
> Between a blush and flame.

13. *Ibid.,* 348.
14. This seems to be a modification of Alexander's position on p. 53: "It is by no means clear that matter is the next level to quality-less motion. . . . On the contrary it is most probable that there are intervening levels." Which supposition is correct is, of course, a matter for scientific investigation, in particular, atomic and electronic.
15. *STD.,* Vol. II, 349.
16. *Ibid.,* 349.
17. *Ibid.,* 350.
18. *Ibid.,* 353.
19. *Ibid.,* 345.
20. *Ibid.,* 347.
21. *Ibid.,* 353.
22. *Ibid.,* 353.
23. *Ibid.,* 354.
24. S. Alexander, "Ptolemaic and Copernican Views of the Place of Mind in the Universe," *The Hibbert Journal,* Vol. VIII, No. 1 (October, 1909), 65.
25. *STD.,* Vol. II, 354.
26. *Ibid.,* 356.

NOTES PART I

27. *Ibid.*, 356.
28. *Ibid.*, 365.
29. *Ibid.*, 356.
30. *Ibid.*, 366.
31. *Ibid.*, 358.
32. *Ibid.*, 358.
33. *Ibid.*, 358.

34. The difficulty in the comprehension of infinites of various sizes may be assisted through awareness of the fact that mathematicians have discovered transfinite numbers of greatly varying sizes. See Edward Kasner and James Newman, *Mathematics and the Imagination* (New York, Simon and Schuster, 1940), 54. Also note *STD*, Vol. I, 43: "An infinite class is defined by mathematicians as one to which a class can be found corresponding, one to one, to the original class and yet a part only of the original class." Also note Bertrand Russell. *The Principles of Mathematics* (New York, W. W. Norton & Co., 1939), 122: "Of two infinite classes, one may have a greater or a smaller number of terms than the other." And Russell acknowledges his indebtedness to Cantor, *Math. Annalen*, Vol. XLVI. § 6.

35. *STD.*, Vol. II, 358.
36. *Ibid.*, 358.
37. *Ibid.*, 358.
38. *Ibid.*, 358.
39. *Ibid.*, 358.
40. *Ibid.*, 359.
41. *Ibid.*, 360.
42. *Ibid.*, 362.
43. *Ibid.*, 362.
44. *Ibid.*, 363.
45. *Ibid.*, 364.
46. *Ibid.*, 364.

47. Anna Forbes Liddell, *Alexander's Space, Time and Deity* (Chapel Hill, N. C., The University of North Carolina, The Department of Philosophy, n.d.), 25.

48. *STD.*, Vol. II, 361.
49. *Ibid.*, 361.
50. *Ibid.*, 364.
51. *Ibid.*, 361.
52. *Ibid.*, 365.
53. *Ibid.*, 366.
54. *Ibid.*, 365.
55. *Ibid.*, 365.
56. *Ibid.*, 366.
57. *Ibid.*, 366.

58. C. Lloyd Morgan, *Emergent Evolution* (New York, Henry Holt and Company, 1923), 11.

59. *Ibid.*, 10. Alexander is modest in expressing his differences with Morgan in *STD*, Vol. II, 46, note 2: "I fear I cannot assume that I should have Mr. Lloyd Morgan with me in all that I say in detail, especially as concerns secondary qualities of matter." He could have added his concep-

NOTES PART I

tion of the successive phases of deity, as well as his differences from Morgan's conception of God as Divine Activity. We shall return to some of these differences in the critical part of this work.

60. *STD.*, Vol. II, 367.
61. *Ibid.*, 368.
62. *Ibid.*, 368.
63. *Ibid.*, 368.
64. *Ibid.*, 368.
65. "Artistic Creation and Cosmic Creation," *PLP*, 269.
66. *STD.*, Vol. II, 369.
67. *Ibid.*, 368.
68. *Ibid.*, 368.
69. *Ibid.*, 368.
70. *Ibid.*, 368.
71. *Ibid.*, 369. This discussion of the Absolute is in part already covered on pages 45-47.
72. *Ibid.*, 369.
73. *STD.*, Vol. I, 346.
74. *Ibid.*, 347.
75. *STD.*, Vol. II, 369.
76. *Ibid.*, 370.
77. *Ibid.*, 370.
78. *Ibid.*, 370.
79. *Ibid.*, 371.
80. *Ibid.*, 371,
81. *Ibid.*, 370.
82. *Ibid.*, 371.
83. *Ibid.*, 371.
84. *Ibid.*, 371.
85. It is worthy of note that Alexander's objections to the submergence of finites is also found in A. S. Pringle-Pattison, *The Idea of God, op. cit.,* Lecture XIV, "The Absolute and the Finite Individual."
86. *STD.*, Vol. II, 368.
87. Philippe Devaux, *op. cit.*, 106.
88. *Ibid.*, 106, n. 1.
89. *STD.*, Vol. II, 368.
90. *Ibid.*, 370.
91. *Ibid.*, 368.
92. *Ibid.*, 365.
93. *Ibid.*, 367.
94. *Ibid.*, 353.
95. *Ibid.*, 364.
96. "Artistic Creation and Cosmic Creation," *PLP*, 273.

Chapter III

1. Samuel Alexander, "Theism and Pantheism," *PLP*, 317.
2. *STD.*, Vol. II, 373.

NOTES PART I

3. *Ibid.*, 375.
4. *Ibid.*, 375.
5. *Ibid.*, 375.
6. *Ibid.*, 376. Alexander indicates the source as *"Varieties of Religious Experience,* p. 515," but the source is page 505 of the Modern Library Edition, 1902.
7. W. James, *op. cit.*, 515.
8. *STD.*, Vol. II, 376.
9. *Ibid.*, 376.
10. *Ibid.*, 377.
11. *Ibid.*, 377.
12. *Ibid.*, 377. It is a moot point in Alexander's philospohy whether the whole of reality is characterized by the nisus or whether the nisus is a movement within a changeless reality. This inquiry belongs to the critical part of the thesis where we shall consider whether the Real is characterized by change, or whether changes take place within a changeless Real.
13. *Ibid.*, 377. In this connection, Alexander seems to consider the nisus as playing a role subsidiary to Time. We prefer a modification of Alexander's system in which Time is equal in rank with Space.
14. *Ibid.*, 377.
15. *Ibid.*, 377.
16. *Ibid.*, 377.
17. *Ibid.*, 377.
18. *Ibid.*, 382.
19. A. E. Taylor, *The Faith of a Moralist* (London, Macmillan and Company, Limited, 1930), Volume I, 2.
20. *Ibid.*, 2.
21. *STD.*, Vol. II, 378.
22. *Ibid.*, 378.
23. *Ibid.*, 379.
24. *Ibid.*, 379.
25. *Ibid.*, 379-380. At this point Alexander introduces the experience of the clairvoyant perceiving the future to indicate the plausibility of his conception of the emotional tone of deity as a future existent. We feel this is a rather unfortunate comparison in view of the charlatanism present among many clairvoyants.
26. *Ibid.*, 381.
27. *Ibid.*, 380.
28. *Ibid.*, 381. While this may seem an advanced conception of prayer, it is substantiated by James B. Pratt, *The Religious Consciousness* (New York, The Macmillan Company, 1946), 327: "With temperaments of the more philosophic type, the prayer of communion takes on a more cosmic aspect. It is the moment of larger views, the vision of the Whole of things in their cosmic setting, the means of gaining the true perspective in which small things that had loomed large resume their appropriate and petty place, and hence it is a way of liberation from the tyranny of little worries. With the more mystical, it is a conscious union with the All."
29. *Ibid.*, 382. It is interesting to note that at this point in his exposition, Alexander has some remarks to make on the "tedious and obsolete"

NOTES PART I

controversy of science and religion, "as if in the end a just conception of what is true about one element in the universe could be at variance with a just conception about what is true of another element in it." *Ibid.,* 383.

30. See Edgar Sheffield Brightman, *A Philosophy of Religion* (New York, Prentice-Hall, Inc., 1940), Chapter X, "Is God Finite?" 305-341.
31. *STD.,* Vol. II, 382.
32. *STD.,* Vol. II, 383.
33. Peter A. Bertocci, *Introduction to the Philosophy of Religion* (New York, Prentice Hall, Inc., 1951), 313.
34. *STD.,* Vol. II, 383.
35. *Ibid.,* 383.
36. *Ibid.,* 384.
37. See pages 47-51.
38. *STD.,* Vol. I, 343.
39. *STD.,* Vol. II, 384.
40. *Ibid.,* 384.
41. *Ibid.,* 384. In the exposition worked out above, it would appear that deity is never one being, but is fragmented in an infinity of beings higher than man. If, however, we postulate (through excessive extrapolation) a pervasive mystical sense in these higher beings, they might well feel mystically one, all united in "deity."
42. "Natural Piety," *PLP., op. cit.,* 313.
43. *STD.,* Vol. II, 384.
44. *Ibid.,* 384.
45. *Ibid.,* 385.
46. *Ibid.,* 385.
47. Höffding, *Philosophy of Religion,* 115, as quoted in *STD,* Vol. II, 386.
48. *STD.,* Vol. II, 386.
49. *Ibid.,* 386. Alexander was apparently not aware of the attitude of the Mohammedan Sufis which approaches the divine absorption found in Brahmanism: See Evelyn Underhill, *Mysticism* (London, Methuen and Co., Ltd.) 12th ed., 1930, page 132: "The Valley of Annihilation of Self: the supreme degree of union, or theopathetic state, in which the self is utterly merged 'like a fish in the sea' in the ocean of Divine Love."
50. *STD.,* Vol. II, 387.
51. Alexander seems to lack depth in speaking in the same sentence of goodness or a ritual as being pleasing to God. It is strange that a Jewish philosopher should ignore the contrast between ritualistic religion and prophetic religion which Old Testament prophets brought forth. But perhaps Alexander's condensed style prevents a full discussion of this subject.
52. *STD.,* Vol. II, 388. By "modern conceptions of God" with which Alexander's stress on mutuality is in agreement, we refer to Brightman's view of a finite God co-operating with his creatures, and better still to A. S. Pringle-Pattison, *The Idea of God, op. cit.,* p. 411: "No God, or Absolute, existing in solitary bliss and perfection, but a God who lives in the perpetual giving of himself, who shares the life of his finite creatures."
53. *Ibid.,* 388.
54. *Ibid.,* 388-389.
55. *Ibid.,* 389.

NOTES PART I

56. *Ibid.*, 389.
57. "Theism and Pantheism," *PLP.*, 322.
58. *Appearance and Reality*, 448, as quoted in *STD*, Vol. II, 389.
59. "Theism and Pantheism," *PLP*, 320.
60. *Ibid.*, 321.
61. *STD.*, Vol. II, 390.
62. *Ibid.*, 390. Two other doctrines of divine transcendence which Alexander could not mention since they arose after his Gifford lectures on *Space, Time and Deity* are the following: 1. E. S. Brightman's concept of God: "the power of his will is limited by The Given . . . The Given, with its purposeless processes, constitutes so great an obstacle to divine willing that the utmost endeavors of God lead to a blind alley and temporary defeat." (Brightman, *A Philosophy of Religion*, 337-338); 2. The resurgence of an extreme divine transcendence in Neo-orthodoxy.
63. *STD.*, Vol. II, 390.
64. R. G. Collingwood, *Religion and Philosophy* (London, Macmillan, 1916), 71.
65. *STD.*, Vol. II, 390.
66. *Ibid.*, 390.
67. R. G. Collingwood, *op. cit.*, 70.
68. *STD.*, Vol. II, 391.
69. "Theism and Pantheism," *PLP*, 323.
70. *Ibid.*, 323-4.
71. It is interesting to note that in some types of theology, the metaphysical distance between man and God is not even bridged by the Incarnation. For instance, note Baillie's criticism of Kierkegaard: "If no revelation of the nature of God were to be found in the incarnate life, what would be the gain of believing that God therein became man? If the 'divine incognito' remains in this extreme form, what saving virtue is there in the dogma of the Incarnation?"—D. M. Baillie, *God was in Christ* (New York, Charles Scribner's Sons, 1948), 49.
72. *STD*, Vol. II, 391. For a criticism of the incarnation which Alexander would probably favor, see Shirley Jackson Case, "The Lure of Christology," *The Journal of Religion*, Vol. XXV, No. 3 (July, 1945), 157-167.
73. *STD.*, Vol. II, 392.
74. *The Idea of God, op. cit.*, 407-408.
75. "Theism and Pantheism," *PLP*, 326.
76. *Ibid.*, 327.
77. *Ibid.*, 327.
78. *Ibid.*, 327.
79. *Ibid.*, 327.
80. Peter A. Bertocci, *An Introduction to the Philosophy of Religion* (New York, Prentice Hall, Inc., 1951), 450.
81. "Theism and Pantheism," *PLP*, 327-328.
82. Peter A. Bertocci, *op. cit.*, 451.
83. *STD.*, Vol. II, 392.
84. *Ibid.*, 392.
85. *Ibid.*, 393.
86. *Ibid.*, 393.

NOTES PART I

87. *Ibid.*, 393.
88. *Ibid.*, 393.
89. *Ibid.*, 394.
90. *Ibid.*, 394.
91. *Ibid.*, 394.
92. *Ibid.*, 394.
93. See above, page 65.
94. *STD.*, Vol. II, 395.
95. *Ibid.*, 395.
96. *Ibid.*, 395.
97. *Ibid.*, 395.
98. *Ibid.*, 395.
99. For a somewhat similar conception see A. S. Pringle-Pattison, *The Idea of God, op. cit.*, page 212: "The organism is developed and its powers perfected as an instrument of Nature's purpose of self-revelation."
100. *Ibid.*, 395.
101. *Ibid.*, 395.
102. *Ibid.*, 396. Alexander could have developed a third aspect of his philosophy of religion, that which we described as "infra-pantheistic" but he demurred: "If immanence means simply working in some department of creation, as in human values, this is not immanence in the natural sense which pantheism attaches to the conception, that of working in every part of creation." *Ibid.*, 388 n.
103. *Ibid.*, 396.
104. *Ibid.*, 396.
105. *Ibid.*, 396.
106. *Ibid.*, 397.
107. *Ibid.*, 397.
108. *Ibid.*, 397. Alexander's treatment of the problem of immortality will be discussed in the following chapter.
109. *Ibid.*, 397.
110. *Ibid.*, 397.
111. *Ibid.*, 397.
112. *Ibid.*, 397-398.
113. *Ibid.*, 398.
114. *Ibid.*, 398.
115. *Ibid.*, 398.
116. *Ibid.*, 398.
117. *Ibid.*, 398.
118. *Ibid.*, 398.
119. *Ibid.*, 398.
120. *Ibid.*, 399.
121. *Ibid.*, 399.
122. *Ibid.*, 399.
123. "Theism and Pantheism," *PLP*, 329-330.
124. *STD.*, Vol. II, 399.
125. "Theism and Pantheism," *PLP*, 331.
126. *Ibid.*, 331.
127. *Ibid.*, 331.

NOTES PART I

128. *STD.*, Vol. II, 399.
129. *Ibid.*, 399.
130. *Ibid.*, 400.
131. *Ibid.*, 400.
132. *Ibid.*, 400.
133. *Ibid.*, 400. This discussion of the problem of evil as conceived by Alexander is necessarily sketchy. It will be resumed in the following chapter.
134. *Ibid.*, 401.
135. *Ibid.*, 401.
136. *Ibid.*, 398.
137. *Ibid.*, 395.

Chapter IV

1. *Ibid.*, 402.
2. *Ibid.*, 402.
3. *Ibid.*, 403.
4. *Ibid.*, 404.
5. *Ibid.*, 404.
6. *Ibid.*, 405. Alexander quotes Johnson: "A wicked fellow is the most pious when he takes to it. He'll beat you all at piety." Alexander does not seem to give full weight to the fact that this is a deceptive piety assumed for the occasion.
7. Harald Höffding. *The Philosophy of Religion* (London, Macmillan and Company, 1906), 113. Part of this quotation is given by Alexander in *STD*, Vol. II, 405. Höffding holds to a conception of intrinsic value apart from what man himself may hold to be value. Alexander does not.
8. Bradley, *Appearance and Reality*, 438, as quoted in *STD*, Vol. II, 406.
9. *Varieties of Religious Experience*, 47, 48, as quoted in *STD*, Vol. II, 407.
10. *STD.*, Vol. II, 407, n 2.
11. Felix Adler, *Our Part in this World* (New York, King's Crown Press, 1946), 65-66.
12. *STD.*, Vol. II, 408.
13. *Ibid.*, 408.
14. *Ibid.*, 409.
15. Samuel Alexander, *Beauty and Other Forms of Value* (London, Macmillan and Co., Limited, 1933), 292.
16. *Ibid.*, 293.
17. *Ibid.*, 293-294.
18. A. E. Taylor, *The Faith of a Moralist, op. cit.*, 31-32.
19. *STD.*, Vol. II, 238.
20. *Ibid.*, 244-245.
21. Samuel Alexander, *Beauty and Other Forms of Value, op. cit.*, 30.
22. *Ibid.*, 33.
23. *Ibid.*, 20.
24. William Temple, *Nature, Man and God* (London, Macmillan and

NOTES PART I

Company, Ltd., 1934), 215. For a similar dissent from Alexander at this point, see C. Lloyd Morgan, *Emergent Evolution* (New York, Henry Holt and Company, 1923), Vol. I, 225.

25. *STD.*, Vol. II, 249.
26. *Ibid.*, 249.
27. *Ibid.*, 251.
28. *Ibid.*, 252.
29. Samuel Alexander, *Beauty and Other Forms of Value*, 227.
30. *STD.*, Vol. II, 252-253.
31. *Ibid.*, 258.
32. *Ibid.*, 277.
33. *Ibid.*, 280. It is interesting to note that Alexander is so fond of referring to Adam Smith. In his work, *Beauty and Other Forms of Value*, he again mentions Smith on page 249, after mentioning R. H. Tawney, *Religion and Capitalism* (this is an error, the correct title being *Religion and the Rise of Capitalism*) on page 246. One would never learn from Alexander that there is any conflict of ethical and social theory between Tawney and Adam Smith!
34. *Beauty and Other Forms of Value*, 260.
35. *STD.*, Vol. II, 302.
36. *Ibid.*, 304.
37. *Ibid.*, 304.
38. Samuel Alexander, *Beauty and Other Forms of Value*, 299.
39. *STD.*, Vol. II, 308. We reserve criticism of this theory of adaptation in the second part of this work.
40. *Ibid.*, 413.
41. *Ibid.*, 413.
42. This vindication of the role of the nisus is one of the points on which we differ from Alexander, and we shall return to this difference in the critical part of this work.
43. *STD.*, Vol. II, 413.
44. *Ibid.*, 416.
45. *Ibid.*, 416.
46. *Ibid.*, 417.
47. Samuel Alexander *et al.*, *Science and Religion*, (New York, Charles Scribner's Sons, 1931), 138.
48. *STD.*, Vol. II, 417.
49. *Ibid.*, 418.
50. *Ibid.*, 418.
51. *Ibid.*, 418.
52. *Ibid.*, 418.
53. *Ibid.*, 400.
54. *Ibid.*, 309.
55. *Ibid.*, 418.
56. *Ibid.*, 418.
57. *Ibid.*, 418.
58. *Ibid.*, 418.
59. *Ibid.*, 419.
60. *Ibid.*, 419.

NOTES PART I

61. We shall return to these qualities of the supremely great individual in the critical part of this work in considering what possible meaning the symbol of the "incarnation" might be given in Alexander's system. It would be, of course, not incarnation as a total embodiment of the divine, but as a culmination of a creative process.
62. *STD.*, Vol. II, 414.
63. *Ibid.*, 414.
64. *Ibid.*, 414.
65. *Ibid.*, 414.
66. *Ibid.*, 415.
67. *Ibid.*, 419.
68. *Ibid.*, 415.
69. *Ibid.*, 414.
70. *Ibid.*, 415.
71. This is one of many examples of the smoothness of style of Alexander, a deceiving lucidity which tells us nothing about the precise meaning of a permanent mental life in deity. How can this be when on page 414 Alexander tells us: "deity is a tendency rather than an achievement."
72. *Ibid.*, 415.
73. *Ibid.*, 415.
74. *Ibid.*, 419.
75. *Ibid.*, 419-420. Quoted from Browning's poem, *The Ring and the Book.*
76. *Ibid.*, 420.
77. *Ibid.*, 420.
78. *Ibid.*, 420.
79. *Ibid.*, 420.
80. *Ibid.*, 420-421.
81. *Ibid.*, 384. See pages 103-107 of this work.
82. *Ibid.*, 421.
83. *Ibid.*, 421.
84. *Ibid.*, 421. But note John Wild, *op. cit.*, 183: "The whole is simply all the parts grasped indistinctly and implicitly."
85. *Ibid.*, 420.
86. *Ibid.*, 399.
87. *Ibid.*, 421.
88. *Ibid.*, 421.
89. *Ibid.*, 422.
90. *Beauty and Other forms of Value*, 160.
91. *STD.*, Vol. II, 422.
92. *Ibid.*, 422.
93. *Ibid.*, 422.
94. *Ibid.*, 422.
95. *Ibid.*, 423.
96. *Ibid.*, 423.
97. *Ibid.*, 423.
98. *Ibid.*, 423.
99. *Ibid.*, 423.
100. *Ibid.*, 423.

NOTES PART I

101. *Ibid.*, 424.
102. *Ibid.*, 424.
103. *Ibid.*, 424.
104. *Ibid.*, 424.
105. *Ibid.*, 424.
106. *Ibid.*, 424-425.
107. *Ibid.*, 425.
108. *Ibid.*, 425. Italics are Alexander's.
109. *Ibid.*, 425.
110. *Ibid.*, 427.
111. *Ibid.*, 427.
112. *Ibid.*, 426.
113. *Ibid.*, 426.
114. *Ibid.*, 364.
115. *Ibid.*, 427.
116. *Ibid.*, 428.
117. *Ibid.*, 428.

418

NOTES PART II

Chapter I

1. John Elof Boodin, *Cosmic Evolution* (New York, The Macmillan Company, 1925), 87.
2. *Ibid.*, 89-90.
3. J. E. Turner, *A Theory of Direct Realism* (London, George Allen & Unwin, Ltd., 1925), 224-225.
4. *STD.*, Vol. I, 59.
5. *Ibid.*, 152.
6. *Ibid.*, 162.
7. Henri Bergson, *Creative Evolution* (New York, The Modern Library, 1944), 367-368.
8. Samuel Alexander, "Some Explanations," *Mind*, N. S. Vol. XXX, No. 4 (October, 1921), 413.
9. J. E. Turner, *op. cit.*, 208.
10. James M. Cork, *Radioactivity and Nuclear Physics* (New York, D. Van Nostrand Co., 1950), 29, 31, 33.
11. *Ibid.*, 25. In the equation, λ is a probability constant, and e is a mathematical constant often used in equations of growth and decay. The only variable is time t in the exponent, so that the number N of particles is directly proportional to the time, t. Recent medical investigations have shown the great value of using isotope atoms as tracers in detecting their presence in chemicals of diseased tissue. Radioactive atoms retain their radioactivity whether they are independent atoms or are united in chemical compounds. This bears out the metaphysical principle to the effect that when parts unite to form various wholes, the parts do not change radically, but it is their "organization," their "integration" which matters.
12. G. Dawes Hicks, review of S. Alexander, "Space, Time, and Deity," *The Hibbert Journal*, Vol. XIX, No. 3 (April, 1921), 578.
13. Fred Hoyle, *The Nature of the Universe* (New York, Harper & Brothers, 1950), 110-111.
14. C. Lloyd Morgan, *Emergent Evolution, op. cit.*, 23-24.
15. Fred Hoyle, *op. cit.*, 122, 123, 124, 125, 131-2. The theory of the creation of matter was also mentioned by Professor Karl Popper when delivering the William James Lectures at Harvard University, Spring 1950.
16. Viscount Samuel, "A Criticism of Present-Day Physics," *Philosophy*, Vol. XXVII (January, 1952), 55.
17. *Ibid.*, 56.

NOTES PART II

18. *Supra*, 45-47.
19. *STD.*, Vol. I, 74.
20. *Ibid.*, 67.
21. For instance, Donald Williams asserts that he has derived his metaphysics from both Alexander and Bosanquet: "anyone who will amalgamate the larger metaphysical opinions of Alexander and Bosanquet will have a pretty fair approximation to what I deem the truth" in "a total philosophical system." "Scientific Evidence and Action Patterns," *The Philosophical Review*, Vol. LV, No. 5 (September, 1946), 580. But if Williams amalgamates Alexander to Bosanquet, is he not bound to misinterpret Alexander's completely historical Space-Time in terms of Bosanquet's changeless Whole?
22. S. Alexander, "The Historicity of Things," *Philosophy and History*, eds. Raymond Klibanski and H. J. Paton (Oxford, Clarendon Press, 1936), 11.
23. *STD.*, Vol. I, 67.
24. *Ibid.*, 44.
25. Henri Bergson, *op. cit.*, 26-27.
26. Wilbur Urban, *The Intelligible World* (New York, The Macmillan Company, 1929), 322.
27. *Ibid.*, 323.
28. *Ibid.*, 324.
29. *Ibid.*, 256.
30. *Ibid.*, 259.
31. Henri Bergson, *op. cit.*, 347.
32. Wilbur Urban, *op. cit.*, 268.
33. Henri Bergson, *op. cit.*, 344.
34. *Ibid.*, 393-394.
35. Bernard Bosanquet, *The Meeting of Extremes in Philosophy* (London, Macmillan and Company, 1921), 192.
36. *Ibid.*, 213.
37. John Laird, *Theism and Cosmology* (London, George Allen and Unwin, 1940), 136-137.
38. W. T. Stace, *Religion and the Modern Mind* (Philadelphia and New York, J. B. Lippincott Company, 1952), 243-244.
39. John Wild, *op. cit.*, 284.
40. H. N. Wieman, *The Source of Human Good* (Chicago, University of Chicago Press, 1946), 298.
41. Joseph Alexander Leighton. *Man and the Cosmos* (New York, D. Appleton and Company, 1922), 236, 237.
42. "Natural Piety," *PLP*, 308.
43. "Naturalism and Value," *PLP*, 281.
44. For a general consideration of Process philosophies, see W. H. Sheldon, *God and Polarity*, Yale University Press, 1954.
45. G. P. Conger, *Epitomization* (Minneapolis, University of Minnesota Library, 1949).
46. John Wild, *Plato's Modern Enemies and the Theory of Natural Law* (Chicago, The University of Chicago Press, 1953), Chapter VII.
47. J. C. Smuts, *Holism and Evolution* (New York, The Macmillan Company, 1926), 10.
48. *Ibid.*, 329.

NOTES PART II

49. H. N. Wieman, *The Source of Human Good* (Chicago, The University of Chicago Press, 1946), 190-191.
50. John Wild, *op. cit.*, 197. A slight addition may be in order. Inorganic things do not merely move to new positions but may form highly organized patterns, such as the chemical formation of glucose in photosynthesis from simple carbon dioxide and water—a process still defying the skill of modern laboratories.
51. Edmund W. Sinnott, *Cell and Psyche* (Chapel Hill, The University of North Carolina Press, 1950), 22.
52. *Ibid.*, 89.
53. Joseph Needham, *Order and Life* (New Haven, Yale University Press, 1936), 110.
54. J. E. Turner, *The Philosophic Basis of Moral Obligation* (London, Macmillan and Co., 1924), 69-70.
55. *STD.*, Vol. II, 67.
56. Roy Wood Sellars, *Evolutionary Naturalism* (Chicago, The Open Court Publishing Company, 1922), 331.
57. A. S. Pringle-Pattison, *The Idea of God in the Light of Recent Philosophy* (Oxford, at the Clarendon Press, 1917), 209-210.
58. J. A. Leighton, *op. cit.*, 237.
59. A. S. Pringle-Pattison, *op. cit.*, 211.
60. *STD.*, Vol. II, 395.
61. William Temple, *Nature, Man, and God* (London, Macmillan and Company, 1934), 487. The very fact that the italics are in the original indicates how important Archbishop Temple felt this conception to be.
62. *Ibid.*, 489.
63. William Pepperell Montague, *The Ways of Things* (New York, Prentice-Hall Inc., 1940), 438.
64. "Natural Piety," *PLP*, 313.
65. *STD.*, Vol. II, 327.
66. *Ibid.*, 327.
67. W. P. Montague, *op. cit.*, 428-429.
68. *Ibid.*, 428.
69. C. D. Broad, *The Mind and Its Place in Nature* (London, Routledge and Kegan Paul Limited, 1949), 62-63.
70. *Ibid.*, 63.
71. *Ibid.*, 64.
72. *Ibid.*, 65.
73. *STD.*, Vol. II, 329.

Chapter II

1. *STD.*, Vol. II, 353.
2. John W. McCarthy, *The Naturalism of Samuel Alexander* (New York, King's Crown Press, 1948), 103.
3. *STD.*, Vol. II, 361.
4. *Ibid.*, 361.
5. *Ibid.*, 363.

NOTES PART II

6. *Ibid.*, 365.
7. *Ibid.*, 347.
8. *Ibid.*, 364.
9. *Ibid.*, 353.
10. Peter A. Bertocci, *op. cit.*, 307.
11. *STD.*, Vol. II, 38-39.
12. "Theaetetus," *The Dialogues of Plato (Jowett Translation), op. cit.*, par. 152, p. 153.
13. *STD.*, Vol. II, 39.
14. Charles Hartshorne, *Beyond Humanism* (Chicago, Willett, Clark & Company, 1937), 244.
15. Dorothy Emmet, "Time is the Mind of Space," *Philosophy*, Vol. XXV, No. 94 (July, 1950), 229.
16. *STD.*, Vol. II, 384.
17. *Supra*, 103-107.
18. *STD.*, Vol. II, 384.
19. *Ibid.*, 384.
20. *Ibid.*, 384.
21. *Ibid.*, 361.
22. Charles Hartshorne and William L. Reese, *Philosophers Speak of God* (Chicago, The University of Chicago Press, 1953), 366.
23. *Ibid.*, xiii.
24. *STD.*, Vol. II., 400.
25. Hartshorne and Reese, *op. cit.*, xiii.
26. We have discussed extensively this question; See, *supra*, 111-126.
27. *STD.*, Vol. II, 388.
28. *Ibid.*, 391.
29. Varieties of theism, orthodox and liberal, may be found in Henry Nelson Wieman and Bernard Eugene Meland, *American Philosophies of Religion* (Chicago, Willett, Clark & Company, 1936).
30. "Theism and Pantheism," *PLP*, 330-331.
31. *STD.*, Vol. II, 395.
32. William Temple, *Nature, Man, and God, op. cit.*, 269.
33. *STD.*, Vol. II, 397.
34. Rudolf Metz, *A Hundred Years of British Philosophy* (London, George Allen and Unwin Ltd., 1950), 650.
35. Cornelia Geer Le Boutillier, *Religious Values in the Philosophy of Emergent Evolution*, (New York, Columbia University, Ph.D. thesis, 1936), 87.
36. *Ibid.*, 98.
37. Hartshorne and Reese, *op. cit.*, 371.
38. Le Boutillier, *op. cit.*, 53.
39. John Laird, "Samuel Alexander's Theism," *The Hibbert Journal*, Vol. XL, No. 2 (January, 1942), 146.
40. *Ibid.*, 149.
41. *Ibid.*, 149.
42. *Ibid.*, 150.
43. *Ibid.*, 150.
44. *Ibid.*, 150.

NOTES PART II

45. *Ibid.*, 151.
46. *Ibid.*, 151.
47. *Ibid.*, 151.
48. *STD.*, Vol. II, 365.
49. John Laird, *op. cit.*, 151.
50. *Ibid.*, 151.
51. *Ibid.*, 151.

52. *Ibid.*, 151. It is difficult to keep this speculation as to what the universe may bring forth from being somewhat humorous. For instance, Edmund W. Sinnot, *op. cit.*, p. 93: "But the universe is a remarkable and often unpredictable place, and unexpected things keep coming out of it." Also, H. S. Jennings, *The Universe and Life* (New Haven, Yale University Press, 1933), 59: "Super-cats, super-elephants, equal to or beyond present mankind in mind and social organization are possibilities of evolution." J. E. Turner, however, takes future possibilities very seriously: "it becomes in my opinion, perfectly reasonable to conceive of the evolutionary process being continued as far beyond the intellect of a Newton or Einstein, or the genius of a Shakespeare or Beethoven, as these transcend, not merely the infant mind, but the consciousness of an amoeba; it is indeed extremely probable that posterity will produce a super-Newton or super-Shakespeare." *The Nature of Deity* (London, George Allen & Unwin Ltd., 1927), 49. But George Gaylord Simpson in his latest work is more somber: "evolution can run into blind alleys, from which there is no turning back, and . . . perhaps some day all will end in a blind alley." *The Major Features of Evolution* (New York, Columbia University Press, 1953), 312.

53. *Ibid.*, 151.
54. *Ibid.*, 152.

55. We are here using Alexander's view of infinite Time for eternity, being aware that this is not the meaning used in traditional theology.

56. John Laird, *op. cit.*, 152.
57. *Ibid.*, 152.
58. *Ibid.*, 152.
59. *STD.*, Vol. II, 356.
60. John Laird, *op. cit.*, 152.
61. *STD.*, Vol. II, 417. The italics are John Laird's.
62. G. Dawes Hicks, review of S. Alexander's "Space, Time, and Deity," *The Hibbert Journal*, Vol. XIX, No. 3 (April, 1921), 580-581.
63. *STD.*, Vol. II, 348.
64. G. Dawes Hicks, *op. cit.*, 581.
65. John Laird, *op. cit.*, 153.
66. John Elof Boodin, *God* (New York, The Macmillan Company, 1934), 39.

67. William Ralph Inge, *God and the Astronomers* (New York, Longmans, Green and Company, 1933), 9-10. Dean Inge uses capital letters to refer to the "Second Law of Thermodynamics" for to him it is a supreme cosmic principle able to slay Alexander's God. That the second law of thermodynamics need not be taken with the rigidity of Dean Inge's ardor for it may be observed from a recent article by P. W. Bridgman, "Reflections on Thermodynamics," *American Scientist*, Vol. 41, No. 4 (October,

NOTES PART II

1945), 549: "it would . . . not be surprising if the logical foundation on which thermodynamics rests is less satisfactory than the superstructure." Also, that there is a tendency toward disorganization does not necessarily nullify the tendency toward organization, as is indicated by Dean Edmund W. Sinnott: "The significant fact seems to be that at every level the tendency toward order and organization is opposed by one toward *disorder* and *dis*organization. . . . Nevertheless, this age-old opposition of order to disorder, of progress to degeneration, of cosmos to chaos, perhaps can tell us something about the ultimate meaning of things. One wonders whether this may not be a part of some great fact or purpose in the universe, of something germinative there; manifest most simply in biological organization and evolutionary progress, then in the inherent purposiveness of vital activities, then in our own conscious purposes, and finally, perhaps, even in the grand design of nature itself." *Two Roads to Truth* (New York, The Viking Press, 1953), 132. Similar arguments based on the inherent creativity of the Universe may be found in H. F. Hallet, *Aeternitas, A Spinozistic Study* (Oxford, Clarendon Press, 1930), 216: "scientists generally are excusably amused when an unwary philosopher suggests the possibility of suspending the operation of the second law of thermodynamics; and yet . . . I venture to ask, what is it that the living bodies of the scientist and the philosopher, together with all other organic bodies down to the most primitive protozoa, are doing throughout the whole course of their lives, if it is not partly suspending that law by organizing energy within their contours?" Also, "Our life, indeed our power of retarding the increase of entropy within our own contours, and even in our context, is an imperfect reproduction, within corporeal nature, of the eternal self-creation of the whole. It involves the irruption of no psychical or quasi-psychical entity within extended reality . . . in the Real is eternal creation." *Ibid.*, 218.

68. R. G. Collingwood, *The Idea of Nature* (Oxford, at the Clarendon Press, 1945), 27.
69. *STD.*, Vol. I, 127.
70. *STD.*, Vol. II, 379.
71. *Ibid.*, 379.
72. *Ibid.*, 379-380.
73. *STD.*, Vol. I, 71-72.
74. *Ibid.*, 69.
75. *Ibid.*, 75.
76. *STD.*, Vol. II, 337.
77. Anna Forbes Liddell, *Alexander's Space, Time, and Deity* (Chapel Hill, N. C., The University of North Carolina, The Department of Philosophy, n. d.), 42.
78. *STD.*, Vol. I, 63.
79. *Ibid.*, 61. The question of these immovable points has brought serious objection from G. Dawes Hicks, *op. cit.*, 578: "what one vainly seeks to learn is how point-instants, whose points do *not* move in the system of points, are conceived to generate, when in some way they cohere together in groups, existents (electrons, atoms, things, etc.) whose points *do* move in the system of points, and which successively 'occupy' different space-times." The answer which Alexander might make is that objects are actually waves

NOTES PART II

which, through time and nisus, animate the points to bear qualities in the flow of Time. However, this topic would take us beyond our present interest in deity.

80. *STD.*, Vol. II, 337.
81. *Ibid.*, 348.
82. Charles D. Tenney, "The Romance of Emergence," *Studies in Philosophical Naturalism*, ed. H. G. Townsend, University of Oregon Publications, The Humanities Series, Vol. 1, No. 1 (March, 1931), 24.
83. *STD.*, Vol. II, 346.
84. Henri Bergson, *Creative Evolution* (New York, The Modern Library, 1944), 7.
85. *Ibid.*, 52.
86. *STD.*, Vol. II, 364.
87. *Ibid.*, 358.
88. *Ibid.*, 362.
89. *Ibid.*, 370.
90. *Ibid.*, 400.
91. "Artistic Creation and Cosmic Creation," *PLP.*, 273.
92. This is not the place to elaborate on the differences between Alexander and Bergson, some of which have already been mentioned. But a criticism of Collingwood deserves to be made: "What is wrong with Bergson's philosophy, regarded as a cosmology, is not the fact that he takes life seriously but the fact that he takes nothing else seriously. . . . The inanimate world of the physicist is a dead weight on Bergson's metaphysics; he can do nothing with it except try to digest it in the stomach of his life-process; but it proves indigestible. . . . This is the vicious circle of Bergson's cosmology: ostensibly he regards matter as a by-product of life, but actually he cannot explain how that or any other special by-product can arise without presupposing, alongside of and indeed prior to life, matter itself." *The Idea of Nature*, (Oxford, at the Clarendon Press, 1945), 140, 141. It is interesting to note that the idealist Collingwood objects to Bergson because he does not make enough of matter; but we have observed that the idealist Leighton objects to Alexander because he makes too much of matter!
93. "Artistic Creation and Cosmic Creation," *PLP*, 273.
94. E. W. Sinnott, *Cell and Psyche, op. cit.*, 22.
95. "Artistic Creation and Cosmic Creation," *PLP*, 274.
96. *Ibid.*, 274.
97. *Ibid.*, 274.
98. *Ibid.*, 273.
99. Dorothy Emmet, "Time is the Mind of Space," *Philosophy*, Vol. XXV, No. 94 (July, 1950), 232.
100. *Ibid.*, 233.
101. *Ibid.*, 233.
102. Bergson, *Creative Evolution, op. cit.*, 290.
103. *Ibid.*, 274.
104. A. N. Whitehead, *Adventures of Ideas* (New York, The Macmillan Company, 1933), 303.
105. A. N. Whitehead, *Process and Reality* (New York, The Macmillan Company, 1929), 344.

NOTES PART II

106. Paul Weiss, *Reality* (New York, Peter Smith, 1949), 207-209.
107. C. Lloyd Morgan, *Emergent Evolution* (New York, Henry Holt and Company, 1923), 36.

Chapter III

1. *STD.*, Vol. II, 302.
2. Samuel Alexander, "Truth, Goodness, and Beauty," *The Hibbert Journal*, Vol. XXVIII, No. 4 (July, 1930), 622. It is true Alexander attempts to overcome this subjectivity when he asserts: "The meaning which the artist infuses into his material is ultimately got from his experience of the universe." *Ibid.*, 628. But we do not feel that this qualification changes our discussion.
3. *STD.*, Vol. II, 279.
4. *Ibid.*, 280.
5. *Ibid.*, 280.
6. *Ibid.*, 258.
7. Samuel Alexander, *Beauty and Other Forms of Value* (London, Macmillan and Company, 1933), 260.
8. *STD.*, Vol. II, 310.
9. *Ibid.*, 308-309.
10. Theodore Meyer Greene, *The Arts and the Art of Criticism* (Princeton, Princeton University Press, 1947), 4.
11. *Ibid.*, 4.
12. Note the apt description of Eliseo Vivas: "a truculent army of verbosophers seeks to legislate their limited interests into universal laws." "The Nature of Aesthetics," John Wild (ed.), *The Return to Reason* (Chicago, Henry Regnery Company, 1953), 217.
13. *Ibid.*, 206, 207.
14. Paul Weiss, *Man's Freedom* (New Haven, Yale University Press, 1950), 105.
15. T. M. Greene, *op. cit.*, 6.
16. G. E. Moore, *Principia Ethica* (Cambridge, University Press, 1951), 15.
17. The analysis of Moore and Greene which we have given is all too brief to do justice to the thought of these two important thinkers in value theory, and we regret that our primary discussion of deity did not warrant a fuller discussion of the objectivity of values. A basic position of value realism had to be established, however, prior to a discussion of deity's relation to value. What may appear as an all too brief summary of Greene's aesthetic theory is warranted by the fact that Alexander's interest in the latter years of his life was concentrated on problems of aesthetics, as is indicated by his work, *Beauty and Other Forms of Value*. This entire work, however, is governed by what appears to be a subjective theory of aesthetics, and it was necessary to indicate a rival theory consistent with our thoroughgoing realistic philosophic approach to the whole philosophy of Alexander. See also James K. Feibleman, *Aesthetics* (New York,, Sloan and Pearce, 1949) for an objective theory quite opposed to that of Alexander.
18. T. M. Greene, *op. cit.*, 269.
19. *Ibid.*, 271.

NOTES PART II

20. *Ibid.*, 271.
21. *Ibid.*, 272.
22. *Ibid.*, 284.
23. *Ibid.*, 284. For an objective criticism of Kant's aesthetic theory by Greene, see "A Reassessment of Kant's Aesthetic Theory," in *The Heritage of Kant*, eds. G. T. Whitney and D. F. Bowers (Princeton, Princeton University Press, 1939), 323-356.
24. Milton R. Konvitz, *On The Nature of Value* (New York, King's Crown Press, 1946), 37.
25. G. E. Moore, *op. cit.*, 190.
26. *Ibid.*, 190.
27. *STD.*, Vol. II, 280.
28. *Beauty and Other Forms of Value*, 244.
29. *Ibid.*, 245.
30. Milton R. Konvitz, *op. cit.*, 98.
31. *Ibid.*, 98.
32. Raphael Demos, "Moral Value as Irreducible, Objective, and Cognizable," *Philosophy and Phenomenological Research*, Vol. VI, No. 2 (December, 1945), 177-178.
33. Samuel Alexander, *Beauty and Other Forms of Value, op. cit.*, 245.
34. James Bissett Pratt, *Can We Keep the Faith?* (New Haven, Yale University Press, 1941), 138.
35. Samuel Alexander, *Beauty and Other Forms of Value*, 257-258.
36. *Ibid.*, 260.
37. John Wild, *Introduction to Realistic Philosophy* (New York, Harper & Brothers Publishers, 1948), 191.
38. *STD.*, Vol. II, 258.
39. Milton R. Konvitz, *op. cit.*, 108.
40. Samuel Alexander, *Beauty and Other Forms of Value*, 219.
41. *Ibid.*, 234.
42. Alfred North Whitehead, *Adventure of Ideas* (New York, The Macmillan Company, 1933), 321.
43. John Wild, "The Present Relevance of Catholic Theology," Edward D. Myers, ed., *Christianity and Reason* (New York, Oxford University Press, 1951), 27.
44. Eliseo Vivas, *The Moral Life and the Ethical Life* (Chicago, The University of Chicago Press, 1950), 63.
45. John Wild, *Plato's Modern Enemies and the Theory of Natural Law* (Chicago, The University of Chicago Press, 1953), 191. We are indebted to John Wild for pointing out the deficiencies of Moore's value theory. We are not quite convinced that Moore may be completely discarded, however, and we are attempting to supplement Moore by means of the realistic philosophy of natural law.
46. *Ibid.*, 194.
47. *Ibid.*, 194.
48. *Ibid.*, 194.
49. *Ibid.*, 107.
50. *Ibid.*, 104-5.
51. *Ibid.*, 69.
52. George Gaylord Simpson. *The Meaning of Evolution* (New Haven,

NOTES PART II

Yale University Press, 1950), 268: "In the Darwinian system, natural selection was elimination, death, of the unfit and survival of the fit in a struggle for existence, a process included in natural selection as it is now known but not forming all or even the major part of that process." Also to be noted are Simpson's affirmations of the unique character of man's evolution: "It is still false to conclude that man is *nothing but* the most progressvie product of organic evolution. He is also a fundamentally new sort of animal and one in which, although organic evolution continues on its way, a fundamentally new sort of evolution has also appeared. The basis of this new sort of evolution is a new sort of heredity, the inheritance of learning. This sort of heredity appears modestly in other mammals and even lower in the animal kingdom, but in man it has incomparable fuller development and it combines with man's other characteristics unique in degree with a result that cannot be considered unique only in degree but must also be considered unique in kind." *Ibid.*, 286.

53. J. H. Woodger, *Biological Principles* (New York, Harcourt, Brace and Company, 1929), 413.
54. *Ibid.*, 416.
55. Richard Hofstadter, *Social Darwinism in American Thought* 1860-1915 (Philadelphia, University of Pennsylvania Press, 1945), 176.
56. G. E. Moore, *op. cit.*, 48.
57. *STD.*, Vol. II, 417-418.
58. *Ibid.*, 416.
59. *Ibid.*, 416.
60. *Ibid.*, 416.
61. Samuel Alexander, *Beauty and Other Forms of Value, op. cit.*, 177.
62. *STD.*, Vol. II, 414.
63. *Ibid.*, 414.
64. *Ibid.*, 415.
65. *Ibid.*, 415.
66. *Ibid.*, 415.
67. *Ibid.*, 419.
68. Raphael Demos, *op. cit.*, 181, 183. A puzzling phrase in the enumeration quoted is "the moral evil of sacrifice." I presume Professor Demos means useless sacrifice, for sacrifice may sometimes be required and may be of great moral value. Incidentally, his list of errors indicates that an intuitionist theory of ethics makes room for errors, just as much as does a theory of epistemological realism make room for errors. On this point, see John Wild, *Introduction to Realistic Philosophy, op. cit.*, 430-436.
69. A. S. Pringle-Pattison, *The Idea of God in the Light of Recent Philosophy* (Oxford, at the Clarendon Press, 1917), 414.
70. Psalm 46:1.
71. *STD.*, Vol. II, 400.
72. *Ibid.*, 400.
73. Henri Bergson, *The Two Sources of Morality and Religion* (New York, Henry Holt and Company, 1935), 203-204.
74. A. S. Pringle-Pattison, *op. cit.*, 415-416.
75. *STD.*, Vol. II, 402.
76. *Ibid.*, 408.

NOTES PART II

77. *Ibid.*, 377.
78. *Ibid.*, 406.
79. *Ibid.*, 406.
80. Rudolf Otto, *The Idea of the Holy* (London, Oxford University Press, 1923), 25.
81. Samuel Alexander, *et al, Science and Religion, A Symposium* (New York, Charles Scribner's Sons, 1931), 133.
82. Joachim Wach, *Types of Religious Experience Christian and non-Christian* (Chicago, The University of Chicago Press, 1951), 32, 33.
83. *STD.*, Vol. II, 405.
84. *Ibid.*, 396.
85. Joachim Wach, *op. cit.*, 35.
86. Paul Tillich, *Systematic Theology* (Chicago, The University of Chicago Press, 1951), Vol. I, 43.
87. *STD.*, Vol. II, 424.
88. William Ralph Inge, *God and the Astronomers* (London, Longmans, Green and Co., 1933), 275.
89. *Ibid.*, 297.
90. *Ibid.*, 298.
91. A. S. Pringle-Pattison, *The Idea of Immortality* (Oxford, at Clarendon Press, 1922), 205-206.
92. *Ibid.*, 166.
93. Wilbur Urban, *The Intelligible World* (New York, The Macmillan Company, 1929), 247, 248.
94. Raphael Demos, *op. cit.*, 168.
95. *Ibid.*, 167-8. On this problem see John Wild, *Plato's Modern Enemies and the Theory of Natural Law*, 105-107.
96. Raphael Demos, *op. cit.*, 173.
97. A. C. Ewing, *The Definition of Good* (New York, The Macmillan Company, 1947), 1.
98. *Ibid.*, 15.
99. Note A. E. Taylor, *The Faith of a Moralist, op. cit.*, 61-62: "What confronts us in actual life is neither facts without value nor values attached to no facts, but fact revealing value, and dependent, for the wealth of its content, on its character as thus revelatory, and values which are realities and not arbitrary fancies, precisely because they are embedded in fact and give it its meaning."
100. This idealistic interpretation of Plato is challenged by John Wild, *Plato's Theory of Man* (Cambridge, Harvard University Press, 1946), 13: "Idealistic philosophy . . . has encouraged a tendency to produce such misinterpretation of Plato along the lines of speculative German idealism. . . . Plato was looked upon primarily as the author of an idealistic epistemology, or theory of ideas."
101. Henry Veatch, "Aristotelianism," Vergilius Ferm (ed.), *A History of Philosophical Systems* (New York, the Philosophical Library, 1950), 108.
102. Gregory Vlastos, *Christian Faith and Democracy* (New York, Association Press, 1939), 64.
103. John Wild, *Introduction to Realistic Philosophy*, 47.
104. *Ibid.*, 47.

NOTES PART II

105. Natural law is given some recognition in Morris Raphael Cohen, *Reason and Law* (Glencoe, The Free Press, 1950), 86: "Where inequality of privilege exists, natural law demands its abolition"; also 190: "the doctrine has not only a great past but is significant for today and for tomorrow."

106. For comparison of physical laws and moral laws, see Henry Veatch, "Concerning the Distinction Between Descriptive and Normative Sciences," *Philosophy and Phenomenological Research*, Vol. VI, No. 2 (December, 1945), 284-306.

107. Alexander's system implies the doctrine of law as immanent rather than doctrine of law as imposed. See, A. N. Whitehead, *Adventure of Ideas, op. cit.*, 142 ff.

108. G. E. Moore, *op. cit.*, 31.

109. J. C. Smuts, *Holism and Evolution* (New York, The Macmillan Company, 1926), 104, 105. The crucial difference between a philosophy of emergence and one of Holism is indicated in the important footnote where Smuts differentiates his theory from that of C. Lloyd Morgan. He might as well have mentioned Alexander: "To him emergence of the new in the evolution of the universe is the essential fact; to me there is something more fundamental—the character of the wholeness, the tendency to wholes, ever more intensive and effective wholes, which is basic to the universe, and of which emergence or creativeness is but one feature, however important it is in other respects." *Ibid.*, 321, n. 1.

110. *Ibid.*, 56.

111. Wilbur M. Urban, *The Intelligible World*, 50-51.

112. J. C. Smuts, *Holism and Evolution*, 142, 144.

113. Bergson, *Creative Evolution*, 51.

114. A. N. Whitehead, *Process and Reality* (New York, The Macmillan Company, 1929), 31-32.

115. We are indebted to Professor William A. Christian, Associate Professor of Religion, Yale Divinity School, for suggesting a very instructive article on the relationships of Bergson, Alexander, and Whitehead: Victor Lowe, "The Influence of Bergson, James, and Alexander on Whitehead," *The Journal of the History of Ideas*, Vol. X, No. 2 (April, 1949), 267-296. Space did not permit utilization of this material. A question may be raised as to why we did not use Whitehead's well-known doctrines, such as the primordial order of God, the consequent order of God, the eternal objects, etc., in order to correct Alexander, rather than the very general notion of Creativity. The reason is that we are not convinced of the relevance of these admittedly important elements of Whitehead's philosophy for our present purpose. We agree with H. N. Wieman's criticisms of Whitehead in *The Source of Human Good* (Chicago, The University of Chicago Press, 1946), 189-195; and we also find pertinent the chapter, "Whitehead's Philosophy of Organism," in James Feibleman, *The Revival of Realism* (Chapel Hill, The University of North Carolina Press, 1946), 46-83. On the other hand, W. T. Stace may be too severe: "But Whitehead has had up to date almost no influence on the thought of our time." *Religion and the Modern Mind, op. cit.*, 207.

116. John Wild, *Introduction to Realistic Philosophy* (New York, Harper

NOTES PART II

& Brothers, 1948), 287.

117. *STD.*, Vol. I, 341.

118. Alexander, "Artistic Creation and Cosmic Creation," *PLP,* 271.

119. John Wild, *Plato's Modern Enemies and the Theory of Natural Law, op. cit.,* 194, 195. That a philosophy of hylomorphism may be intimately connected with a study of evolutionary forms of life is readily perceived from D'Arcy Wentworth Thompson's *On Growth and Form* (New York, The Macmillan Company, 1948).

120. Henry Nelson Wieman, *The Source of Human Good* (Chicago, The University of Chicago Press, 1946), 192.

121. *Ibid.,* 192.

122. John Wild, "Western Realism and Oriental Thought," Charles A. Moore, (ed.), *Essays in East-West Philosophy* (Honolulu, University of Hawaii Press, 1951), 265-266.

123. Henry Nelson Wieman and Walter Marshall Horton, *The Growth of Religion* (Chicago, Willett, Clark & Company, 1938), 326.

124. Henry Nelson Wieman, "Faith and Knowledge," *Christendom,* Vol. I, No. 5 (Fall, 1936), 777.

125. *Ibid.,* 778.

126. *STD.,* Vol. I, 338.

127. Wieman and Horton, *op. cit.,* 346.

128. *Ibid.,* 480.

129. *STD.,* Vol. II, 377.

130. H. N. Wieman, *The Source of Human Good,* 194-195.

131. Wieman and Horton, *op. cit.,* 319.

132. *Ibid.,* 321.

133. Rudolf Otto, *The Idea of the Holy,* tr. John W. Harvey (London, Humphrey Milford, Oxford University Press, 1924), 31.

134. A very interesting account of the attachment which God the Son has won rather than God the Father is found in B. H. Streeter, "The Suffering of God," *The Hibbert Journal,* Vol. XII, No. 3 (April, 1914), 605: "The Christian *Creed* acknowledges but one God and one quality of Godhead—so far Athanasius won his cause; but the Christian *imagination* has been driven by this postulate of the impassibility of God to worship two. Side by side sit throned in Heaven God the Father omnipotent, unchangeable, impassible, and on His right hand God the Son, 'passus, crucifixus, mortuus, resurrectus.' What is this but Arianism, routed in the field of intellectual definition, triumphing in the more important sphere of the imaginative presentation of the object of the belief?"

135. *STD.,* Vol. II, 418.

136. Robert Ulich, *Conditions of Civilized Living* (New York, E. P. Dutton & Co., Inc., 1946), 234, 235.

137. Samuel Alexander, *Beauty and Other Forms of Value, op. cit.,* 147.

138. Shailer Mathews, *Is God Emeritus?* (New York, the Macmillan Company, 1940), 84.

139. Radoslav A. Tsanoff, *The Ways of Genius* (New York, Harper & Brothers Publishers, 1949), 258.

140. J. E. Turner, *Essentials in the Development of Religion* (New York, The Macmillan Company, 1934), 155.

NOTES PART II

141. A. A. Bowman, *A Sacramental Universe* (Princeton, Princeton University Press, 1939), 371. Note also: "The originality of a prophet lies commonly in his ability to fuse into a white heat combustible material which is there, to express and to appear to meet the half-formed prayers of some at least of his contemporaries." A. D. Nock, *Conversion* (London, Oxford University Press, 1933), 9. In contrast with the insights of Bowman and Nock, compare the indictment of much of modern religion by Whitehead: "Religion is tending to degenerate into a decent formula wherewith to embellish a comfortable life." *Science and the Modern World* (New York, The Macmillan Company, 1950), 269-270.

Chapter IV

1. Milton R. Konvitz, *On the Nature of Value* (New York, King's Crown Press, 1946), 111.
2. F. E. England, *The Validity of Religious Experience* (New York and London, Harper & Brothers Publishers, 1938), 84. I am indebted to Professor John E. Smith, Department of Philosophy, Yale University, for a reference to this work.
3. H. N. Wieman, *The Source of Human Good*, 170, 171.
4. *Ibid.*, 176.
5. Julian Huxley, *Evolution in Action* (New York, Harper & Brothers, 1953), 2.
6. *Ibid.*, 150.
7. Talcott Parsons, *The Social System* (Glencoe, The Free Press, 1951), 349.
8. *Ibid.*, 358.
9. John Laird, "The Philosophy of Incarnation," *The Harvard Theological Review*, Vol. XXXIII, No. 2 (April, 1940), 148.
10. *Ibid.*, 148-149.
11. *Ibid.*, 149.
12. Compare Etienne Gilson, *Being and Some Philosophers* (Toronto, Canada, Pontifical Institute of Mediaeval Studies, 1949), x: "Bearing in mind possible brethren in metaphysical misery, it is the public confession of what has actually been a wandering quest of truth."
13. There are courses in epistemology which stress merely knowledge of sensations and predictions from these sensations. The moment a student inquires whether these sensations are not really apprehensions of an independent object, such inquiry is ruled out of the course in epistemology, for it implies metaphysics, a totally different kind of inquiry not covered by the course. . . . To suggest in such courses that knowledge in any real sense is knowledge of the external world is almost to commit the "unpardonable sin." But in opposition to this general tendency the words of an Idealist whose epistemology is that of direct Realism are worthy of note: "Against this general standpoint it must be maintained, in accordance with the Idealism common to Plato and Hegel, that human thought and knowledge are always concerned directly with the real universe." J. E. Turner, *The Nature of Deity* (London, George Allen & Unwin Ltd, 1927), 45.

NOTES PART II

14. *STD.*, Vol. I, 2.
15. R. G. Collingwood, *The Idea of Nature* (Oxford, at the Clarendon Press, 1945), 158.
15a. Raphael Demos, Review of *Science and Common Sense* by James B. Conant, *The Journal of Philosophy*, Vol. XLIX, No. 1 (January 3, 1952) 16-17.
16. *Ibid.*, 18.
17. John Wild, *Introduction to Realistic Philosophy, op. cit.*, 32.
18. Brand Blanshard et al., *Philosophy in American Education*, (New York, Harper & Brothers Publishers, 1945), 32. Another quotation from Blanshard which bears on this issue is: "When they (philosophers) are looking for a man who can speak to puzzled youth with some sense and sanity on ultimate things, they are not wholly reassured by finding that the chief claim of a given candidate is that he has constructed a symbolic mechanism which facilitates the manipulation of a four-valued logic or that he is an expert in analyzing the sentences—meaningless sentences, he explains —in which metaphysics and ethics are now seen to consist. And they ask with some concern whether the river of philosophic reflection that has been fertilizing and humanizing men's minds from Plato's day on down is to sink away in sands like these. . . . As the culmination of this tendency comes the positivism that would quietly dispossess philosophy of its kingdom and bestow its ancient name upon the hermeneutics of scientific sentences." "The Escape from Philosophical Futility," in *Freedom and Experience, Essays Presented to Horace M. Kallen*, Sidney Hook and Milton R. Konvitz (eds.), (Ithaca and New York, Cornell University Press, 1947), 195, 201.
19. Donald Williams, "Naturalism and the Nature of Things," *The Philosophical Review*, Vol. LIII, No. 5 (September, 1944), 419-420.
20. Roy Wood Sellars, *The Philosophy of Physical Realism* (New York, The Macmillan Company, 1932), vii.
21. W. P. Montague, *Great Visions of Philosophy* (La Salle, The Open Court Publishing Company, 1950), xii-xiii. We do not wish to give the impression, however, that all semanticists and symbolic logicians are unaware of the reality of ontological problems. Note Frederic B. Fitch, "On God and Immortality," *Philosophy and Phenomenological Research*, Vol. VIII, No. 4 (June 1948), 688-693.
22. W. T. Stace, *Religion and the Modern Mind, op. cit.*, 172.
23. *Ibid.*, 172.
24. Note Viscount Samuel, *Essay in Physics* (Oxford, Basil Blackwell, 1951), 4: "The grin of the Cheshire cat in *Alice in Wonderland*, which remained some time after the rest of the cat had vanished, is hardly a defensible conception in metaphysics."
25. Paul Weiss, *Reality* (New York, Peter Smith, 1949), 20.
26. R. G. Collingwood, *The Idea of Nature*, 163.
27. Etienne Gilson, *The Unity of Philosophical Experience* (New York, Charles Scribner's Sons, 1937), 317-318.
28. Paul Tillich, *Systematic Theology* (Chicago, The University of Chicago Press, 1951), 163.
29. *Ibid.*, 20.
30. A. N. Whitehead, *Science and the Modern World* (New York, The

NOTES PART II

Macmillan Company, 1939), 80.

31. A. S. Pringle-Pattison, *The Idea of God in the Light of Recent Philosophy* (Oxford, at the Clarendon Press, 1917), 127.

32. J. C. Smuts, *Holism and Evolution, op. cit.*, 2. The justification of Alexander in terms of a metaphysics of emergent levels and wholes is further substantiated by the affirmation of an eminent biologist: "The future historian of our times will note as a remarkable phenomenon that, since the time of the First World War, similar conceptions about nature, mind, life, and society arose independently, not only in different sciences but also in different countries. Everywhere we find the same leading motifs: the concepts of organization showing new characteristics and laws at each level, those of the dynamic nature of, and the antitheses within reality." Finding similarities in the views of Nicolai Hartmann, Woodger, Driesch, J. B. S. Haldane, Smuts, Meyer-Abich, Marx and Engels, Ludwig von Bertalanffy concludes: "The fact that from absolutely different and even diametrically opposed starting-points, from the most varied fields of scientific research, from idealistic and materialistic philosophies, in different countries and social environments, essentially similar conceptions have evolved, shows their intrinsic necessity. It can mean nothing less than that these common general concepts are essentially true and unavoidable." *Problems of Life* (New York, John Wiley & Sons, Inc., 1952), 194, 198-199. We are indebted to Professor Charles W. Hendel for calling to our attention the relevant chapters in *The Problem of Knowledge* bearing on such topics as "Developmental History," "Darwinism," and Vitalism." The increasing importance of "holism" is indicated: "The development of scientific biology in the nineteenth century may be generally characterized by the fact that it has accorded the 'idea of the whole' an ever greater significance." Ernst Cassirer, *The Problem of Knowledge*, translated by William H. Woglom and Charles W. Hendel (New Haven, Yale University Press, 1950), 212.

33. *Ibid.*, 3.

34. Moritz Schlick, *Philosophy of Nature*, tr. Amethe von Zeppelin (New York, Philosophical Library, 1949), 111.

35. Lincoln Barnett, *The Universe and Dr. Einstein* (New York, William Sloan Associates, 1948), 11. Note, however the *New York Times* report, July 30, 1953, entitled "Einstein Cosmos Equations Solved," to the effect that Professor Vaclav Hlavaty, The Graduate Institute for Applied Mathematics, University of Indiana, "has achieved solutions to the equations in Professor Einstein's 1953 mathematical model of the universe." These are multi-dimensional equations relating electromagnetism and gravitation. But no sooner are the equations discovered than objective tests are sought: "The solutions, Professor Hlavaty said, lend themselves to physical interpretation, and this opens the possibility at least to devise experiments for testing Professor Einstein's latest Unified Field Theory, which Professor Einstein admitted he had so far been unable to do." The point is that a physical interpretation definitely implies that the discoveries of Einstein and Hlavaty are not merely mental constructions but are apprehensions of an objective structure in the universe. Surely such familiar elements of Einstein's universe as the curvature of space, the bending of light rays, the increase of mass with acceleration, and the unity of electromagnetism and gravitation

NOTES PART II

are objective structures of the spatial-temporal universe. Is it not nonsense to imagine that electromagnetic and gravitational forces of the universe become unified only when Professor Hlavaty works out his equations? They were unified as objective structures of the world long before there was any mind on earth. The glory of Einstein's discoveries does not lie in merely subjectivist equations but in the fact that by means of these equations the mind of man apprehends the structure of Reality. Our interpretation is, thus, quite opposed to that of Barnett. Note also the view of an eminent Realist: "In the determination of the nature and true value of physico-mathematical science, the place, the part and the bearing of its explications, metaphysics not only maintains order in the system of our forms of knowledge, but renders to physico-mathematics the essential service of protecting it against otherwise almost inevitable deformations, above all, against the pernicious illusion that it is itself called on to be a philosophy of nature and the belief that things only begin to exist when submitted to the measurement of our instruments." Jacques Maritain, *The Degrees of Knowledge* (London, Geoffrey Bles: The Centenary Press, 1937), 80.

36. A. A. Bowman, *op. cit.*, "Appendix B—Berkeley and Contemporary Philosophy," 213. See also Norman Kemp Smith, *Prolegomena to an Idealist Theory of Knowledge*, (London Macmillan and Company, 1924), "Berkeley's Perverse Procedure," 54-58. This is not the place to engage in a polemic of Realism over against Subjective Idealism, but important statements by distinguished idealists bearing on the shortcomings of Subjectivism cannot be ignored: "Subjective Idealism has rightly fallen into discredit. It will not stand as a theory of Reality; and it affords no foundation for a sane theory of knowledge or of conduct. It fails when it takes the consistent form of Solipsism; and it fails equally when it assumes the half-hearted form of a spiritual pluralism. Neither I myself and my psychical states, nor an assemblage of finite selves each wrapped up in his own ideas, can constitute the ultimate reality." Harold H. Joachim, *The Nature of Truth* (Oxford, at the Clarendon Press, 1906), 61. Also, "What realism desires is more valid objectivity, substantiality in the world beyond self. It is the latter want, I venture to say, which chiefly limits the effectiveness of idealism in religion: to satisfy the pragmatic test, idealism must become more realistic: for idealism in religion does not give sufficient credence to the authoritative Object, shows, so far, no adequate comprehension of the attitude of *worship*." W. E. Hocking, *The Meaning of God in Human Experience* (New Haven, Yale University Press, 1912), xi. The sharp separation between Idealism and Realism is again indicated by Etienne Gilson: "The most tempting of all the false first principles is: that *thought*, not *being*, is involved in all my representations. Here lies the initial option between idealism and realism. . . . Man is not a mind that thinks, but a being who knows other beings as true, who loves them as good, and who enjoys them as beautiful. For all that which is, down to the humblest form of existence, exhibits the inseparable privileges of being, which are truth, goodness and beauty." *The Unity of Philosophical Experience* (New York, Charles Scribner's Sons, 1937), 316, 317. We venture the opinion that a Subjective Idealism whose chief emphasis is the denial of an independent external world of structured objects for a coherent system of inter-subjective

NOTES PART II

thought characterized by logical necessity has nothing to do with Realism. On the contrary, it is closely allied to a Positivism whose chief emphasis is also the denial of an independent world for a coherent system of intersubjective sentences characterized by logical necessity.

To return to Berkeley as the *bête noire* of our reflections, we shall add as concluding note the forthright rejection of James Edwin Creighton: "Idealists . . . ought not to allow their affection for 'the good Berkeley' to deter them from repudiating all alliance with his philosophical doctrines. Moreover, if this speculative idealism is to be defended and developed, it must rid itself of the ambiguities and restrictions that have resulted from its association with "mentalism," and that seem to make it a doctrine remote from the movements of science and the interests of practical life." "Two Types of Idealism," in W. G. Muelder and L. Sears, eds., *The Development of American Philosophy* (Boston, Houghton Mifflin Co., 1940), 292.

37. William Ralph Inge, *God and the Astronomers, op. cit.*, 41.

38. *Ibid.*, 41. There would seem to be no such thing as *"the* philosophy of science" but many philosophies of science informed by various metaphysical positions, idealism, materialism, Thomism, Process philosophy, and positivism which implies the metaphysical position that the structure of the universe is such that it can have no ontology whatever! "What the positivists have done is to hold on to experimentation, and thus as they see it to empiricism, at the cost of denying reality to the scientific subject-matter itself. They have saved the method only by sacrificing the existence of that which the method studies." Julius W. Friend and James Feibleman, *What Science Really Means* (London, George Allen and Unwin, 1937), 20. Note also Emile Meyerson, *Identity and Reality* (New York, The Macmillan Company, 1930), 21: "We must still add that in spite of the celebrity of Comte's work and the prestige which his writings enjoy, no scientist, in the course of his studies, has ever tried to follow the principles laid down by positivism. . . . Never has any scientist worthy of the name doubted that nature, even in its most intimate recesses, was entirely subject to law. A single doubt in this respect would have been sufficient . . . to put a stop to all research." And even more forcibly, Meyerson states on page 384: "Science is *not* positive and does not even contain positive data in the precise meaning which August Comte and his adherents have given to this term—that is, data 'stripped of all ontology.' Ontology is of a piece with science itself and cannot be separated from it. . . . The positivist plan is, therefore, truly chimerical."

39. *Ibid.*, viii.

40. We are grateful to Professor H. N. Wieman for a cogent objection raised to our provisional definition of religion as "man's whole response to the whole universe." The following pages are an attempt to clarify this problem in a manner enlightened by Alexander's philosophy and by our "reconstructed Alexandrian system."

41. Edgar Sheffield Brightman, *Nature and Values* (New York, Abingdon-Cokesbury Press, 1945), 89.

42. J. H. Woodger, *Biological Principles, op. cit.*, 106. For a comparison between Alexander and Morgan, with comments favorable to Morgan, see H. F. Hallett, *Aeternitas, op. cit.*, 276. Another comparison between Alex-

NOTES PART II

ander and Morgan is found in S. Eldridge, *The Organization of Life* (New York, Thomas Y. Crowell Company, 1925), 206.

43. The Wieman tradition at the Divinity School of the University of Chicago seems to be continued by the present Dean, Bernard M. Loomer; see his articles, "Neo-Naturalism and Neo-Orthodoxy," *The Journal of Religion*, Vol. XXVIII, No. 2 (April, 1948), 79-91; "Christian Faith and Process Philosophy," *The Journal of Religion*, Vol. XXIX, No. 3 (July, 1949), 181-203.

44. D. C. Macintosh (ed.), *Religious Realism* (New York, The Macmillan Company, 1931), 393-394.

45. *STD.*, Vol. II, 376-7.

46. *Ibid.*, 377.

47. *Ibid.*, 377.

48. S. Alexander, *Beauty and Other Forms of Value*, 299.

49. S. Alexander et al., *Science and Religion*, 133.

50. "Spinoza and Time," *PLP*, 377.

51. Otto, *The Idea of the Holy*, 7.

52. *Ibid.*, 6.

53. *Ibid.*, 10.

54. *Ibid.*, 13.

55. Smuts's conception of a "holistic" principle must not be confused with the "holy" in Otto. Smuts simply means the pervasive tendency of the evolutionary process to form organic unities or wholes at any level of emergence, from electron to cell to organism to man himself. Otto by the "holy" means the numinous impact of Reality in its tremendous, aweful, mysterious, fascinating aspects.

It would appear, however, as the result of our analysis that Alexander is justified philosophically by his theory of levels of emergence closely allied to the Holism of Smuts; he is justified religiously by his espousal of the "numinous" as presented by Otto. It is significant that an eminent sociologist, Pitirim A. Sorokin, also finds in Otto's sense of the "holy" the ultimate characterization of religion "The ultimate nature of the values [of religion] is another term for what others call God. It embraces values which are styled *"sacred"* or "holy" or *"mysterium tremendum et fascinosum!"* It points out the inexhaustible and basic character of the religious values as the matrix from which all other values, including the differentiated categories of the Good, the True and the Beautiful are derived. . . . If a person does not have any system of ultimate values and views them all as quite relative, he does not have a religion." *Society, Culture, and Personality* (New York and London, Harper & Brothers Publishers, 1947), 225-226.

56. Otto, *op. cit.*, 24.

57. Willard L. Sperry, "Liberalism and Neo-Orthodoxy," *Religion in Life*, Vol. XVI, No. 3 (Summer, 1947), 323-335.

58. Otto, *op. cit.*, 31.

59. *Ibid.*, 31.

60. *Ibid.*, 31.

61. *Ibid.*, 33.

62. Henri Bergson, *The Two Sources of Morality and Religion*, 214.

NOTES PART II

63. Robert J. Hutcheon, *Frankness in Religion* (New York, The Macmillan Company, 1929), 255. Professor Hutcheon speaks of that rare type of religious humanism which has kept alive an orientation to the universe, not of the type which frustrates itself in pragmatism, positivism, and semanticism.

64. F. E. England, *The Validity of Religious Experience*, 141.

65. It is significant to note that John H. Dietrich, one of the pioneers of religious humanism in America, had a remarkable change of mind as to this cosmic orientation: "[humanism] is a dated philosophy—a philosophy too narrow in its conception of great cosmic schemes, about which we know so little, and concerning which we should be less dogmatic and arrogant. It in no wise reflects the humility which becomes the real seeker after truth. But that is the kind of fellows we were in those days. In fact, I was one of the chief offenders, and I confess it now in all humility. I see now that my utter reliance upon science and reason and my contempt for any intuitive insights and intangible values, which are the very essence of art and religion, was a great mistake." "Comments on the Humanist Manifesto," *The Humanist*, Vol. XIII, No. 3 (May-June 1953), 137.

66. Willard L. Sperry, *Reality in Worship* (New York, The Macmillan Company, 1939), 93.

67. George P. Conger, *The Ideologies of Religion* (New York, Round Table Press, 1940), 193-194.

ACKNOWLEDGMENTS

I am grateful to the following publishers for permission to quote from their copyrighted works:

The Clarendon Press, Oxford, for excerpts from R. G. Collingwood, *The Idea of Nature,* and A. Seth Pringle-Pattison, *The Idea of God in the Light of Recent Philosophy.*

Columbia University Press for excerpts from Milton R. Konvitz, *On the Nature of Value.*

Harper & Brothers for excerpts from Fred Hoyle, *The Nature of the Universe,* Henry N. Wieman and Walter M. Horton, *The Growth of Religion,* and John Wild, *Introduction to Realistic Philosophy.*

Henry Holt and Company, Incorporated, for brief excerpts from Henri Bergson, *Creative Evolution.*

Dr. L. A. Garrad, Editor, *The Hibbert Journal,* for excerpts from two articles: G. Dawes Hicks, review of Samuel Alexander, *Space, Time, and Deity,* Vol. XIV, No. 3 (April 1924), and John Laird, "Samuel Alexander's Theism," Vol. XL, No. 2 (January 1942).

The J. B. Lippincott Company for excerpts from W. T. Stace, *Religion and the Modern Mind.*

Longmans, Green & Co., Limited, London, England, for excerpts from William Ralph Inge, *God and the Astronomers.*

The Macmillan Company for excerpts from Jan C. Smuts, *Holism and Evolution,* and Wilbur M. Urban, *The Intelligible World.*

Oxford University Press, London, England, for excerpts from Samuel Alexander, "The Basis of Realism," *Proceedings of the British Academy,* 1913-1914.

ACKNOWLEDGMENTS

Professor Marvin Farber, Editor, *Philosophy and Phenomenological Research,* The University of Buffalo, and Professor Raphael Demos, for excerpts from the latter's article, "Moral Values as Irreducible, Objective, and Cognizable," Vol. VI, No. 2 (December 1945).

Prentice-Hall, Inc., for excerpts from Peter A. Bertocci, *Introduction to the Philosophy of Religion,* copyright 1951.

Routledge and Kegan Paul Ltd., London, England, for excerpts from C. D. Broad, *The Mind and Its Place in Nature.*

The Royal Institute of Philosophy, London, England, and Professor Dorothy Emmet for several excerpts from Dr. Emmet's article, "Time is the Mind of Space," *Philosophy* Vol. XXV, No. 94 (July 1950).

St. Martin's Press, Incorporated, New York, and Macmillan and Company, Limited, London, England, for numerous quotations from the following works of Samuel Alexander, *Beauty and Other Forms of Value, Philosophical and Literary Pieces,* and *Space, Time, and Deity.* I am particularly indebted to the generosity of these publishers.

St. Martin's Press, Incorporated, New York, Macmillan and Company, Limited, London, England, and Mrs. William Temple, for excerpts from William Temple, *Nature, Man and God.*

The University of Chicago Press for excerpts from Henry Nelson Wieman, *The Source of Human Good,* copyright 1946; and John Wild, *Plato's Modern Enemies and the Theory of Natural Law,* copyright 1953.

Williams and Norgate, London, England, for a reproduction of the diagram on page 11 of Lloyd Morgan, *Emergent Evolution.*

A. P. S.

INDEX

A

Aaron, R. I., xxiii
Absolute, 45-47, 80-85, 88, 112, 121, 202, 210, 268, 396, 398, 410, 412
Absolutism, 84
Abt Vogler (Browning), 33
Active Tendency, 207, 212, 215-216, 311, 313, 320, 367
Adaptation, 157, 174, 183, 293, 314-315, 317-318, 416
Adler, Felix, 143, 415
Adventure of Ideas (Whitehead), 425, 427, 430
Aesthetics, 141, 148, 217, 291, 295, 297-298, 330, 360, 362, 393, 426-427
Aesthetics (Feibleman), 426
Aeternitas (Hallet), 424, 437
Agnosticism, 171, 288, 323
Alexander's Space, Time, and Deity (Liddell), 409, 424
Alice in Wonderland, 378
American Philosophies of Religion (Wieman and Meland), 422
American Scientist, 423
Analogy, 55, 63, 86, 91, 158, 238-239, 264, 350
Angel, 61, 67, 70, 72-73, 75-76, 123, 138, 179, 187, 232-233, 242, 254-255, 260, 263, 273, 352, 365
Anthropomorphism, 235-236, 239, 244, 253
Appearance, 84, 112, 380
Appearance and Reality (Bradley), 413, 415
Aristotle, 3, 111, 154, 181, 331, 339-340, 349-351, 372, 374, 376
Arnold, Matthew, 181
Art, 142, 149-150, 166, 212, 291, 297-299, 325, 344-345, 360-361, 366, 376, 381, 401-402, 426, 431, 438
Arts and the Art of Criticism, The (Greene), 426
Astronomy, 194, 196, 309, 385
Atomic Theory, 33
Avenarius, Richard, 386
Awareness, 6, 60, 239, 255, 268, 295, 356
Axiology, 337

B

Baillie, D. M., 413
Barnett, Lincoln, 386-387, 434-435
Barth, Karl, xvi, 252-253
Basis of Realism, The (Alexander), 4
Beauty, 1, 109, 140, 142, 145, 150, 156-157, 161, 181, 231, 290-291, 293-294, 296-297, 299, 309, 320, 325-326, 330, 333-334, 338-339, 344-345, 358, 365-366, 381-382, 392, 397-399, 426, 435, 437
Beauty and Other Forms of Value (Alexander), 407, 415-417, 426-428, 437
Becoming, 182, 187, 204-206, 208
Being, xii, 27, 90, 110, 118-119, 248, 250, 312, 339, 373, 378, 380, 435; as changeless, 204-205; as determinate, 26, 215; as future, xvii, 271; as historical, 376; as infinite, 55; as perfect, 55, 142; as potential, 349; as ultimate, 336, 350, 401; attributes of, 3, 372; highest, 145, 362; primordial, xvii; timeless, xi-xii, 376, 398

441

INDEX

Being and Some Philosophers (Gilson), 432
Beliefs, 292, 307, 431
Bergson, Henri, 1, 12, 19, 42-43, 91, 191-192, 201, 203-205, 212, 227, 248-249, 278, 280, 285, 287, 305, 324, 345-346, 348, 365, 371, 381-383, 398, 419-420, 425, 428, 430, 438
Berkeley, George, 6-7, 386-387, 436
Bertalanffy, von, Ludwig, 434
Bertocci, P. A., 119, 412-413, 422
Beyond Humanism (Hartshorne), 422
Bible, 48
Biological Principles (Woodger), 428, 436
Biology, 215-216, 281-282, 287, 315-316, 321-322, 343, 345, 352, 368, 370, 385, 424, 434
Blanshard, Brand, xxiii, 433
Boodin, J. E., 35, 188-191, 201, 263, 407, 419, 423
Bosanquet, Bernard, xxiii, 3, 11, 24, 47, 204-206, 228, 381, 406, 420
Bowers, D. F., 427
Bowman, A. A., 363, 384, 386, 432, 435
Bradley, F. H., 2-3, 46-47, 112, 142, 206-207, 404, 413, 415
Brahmanism, 108
Bridgman, P. W., 423
Brightman, E. S., 412-413, 436
Broad, C. D., 224-227, 229, 421
Browning, Robert, 33, 406, 417
Bruno, 307
Buddha, x, 399
Buddhism, xi, 207

C

Calkins, Mary Whiton, 45, 407
Can We Keep the Faith? (Pratt), 427
Case, S. J., 413
Cassirer, Ernst, 434
Categories, 3, 12-28, 34, 39-41, 44, 56, 65-66, 87, 181, 188, 208, 347-348, 351, 353, 370, 394, 399
Causality, 27, 374
Cell and Psyche (Sinnott), 421, 425

Change, 46-47, 101, 200-202, 205-209, 310, 312, 340, 349, 372, 381
Christ, 370
Christendom, 431
Christian, W. A., 430
Christian Faith and Democracy (Vlastos), 429
Christianity, xi, 48-49, 51, 102, 113-116, 165, 394
Christianity and Reason (Wild), 427
Christians, xiv, xv
Christology, 361, 413
Church, 312
Cognition, 96, 98, 100, 391, 393
Cohen, Morris R., 430
Collingwood, R. G., 115, 265, 372, 413, 424-425, 433
Color, 25, 34, 38, 50-51, 148, 161, 217, 261, 288, 297, 338; of the universe, 57. 79, 87, 188, 316
Common Sense, 356, 387
Communion, 93-94, 331-333, 359, 361, 390, 399, 411
Community, 109, 141, 292, 303-304, 307, 334
Competition, 157, 293, 319
Compresence, 5-6, 64, 107, 125, 148
Comte, Auguste, xix, 436
Conant, James B., 373, 433
Conation, 95, 130, 142, 390
Conditions of Civilized Living (Ulich), 431
Conformity, 154, 292
Confucius, x
Conger, G. P., 212, 402, 420, 438
Conscience, 304
Consciousness, 6, 25, 50-51, 81, 105, 180, 191, 196, 209, 220-221, 239, 243, 262, 265, 293, 383, 386, 389, 396
Contextualism, 208-209
Contingency, 315, 382
Conversion (Nock), 432
Cork, James M., 419
Cosmic Evolution (Boodin), 407, 419
Cosmology, xxi, 195-196, 228, 265, 367, 425
Cosmos, 143, 253-255, 257, 264, 296, 352, 370, 395, 398, 402, 424, **434**, 438

INDEX

Creation, 41, 113-114, 118-120, 197, 198, 265, 280, 285, 346, 410, 425
Creative Evolution (Bergson), 419, 425, 430
Creative impetus, 398
Creativity, 91, 100, 130-131, 133, 137, 183, 209, 212, 282, 285-289, 330, 343-348, 352-353, 356, 360; as universal of universals, 347
Creighton, J. E., 436

D

Darwin, Charles, 280, 293
Darwinism, 30, 163, 183, 280, 293, 314-316, 428, 434
Definition of Good, The (Ewing), 429
Degrees of Knowledge, The (Maritain), 435
Deism, 112-113
Deity, xvii, xxi-xxiii, 1, 11-12, 32, 38, 52, 59-60, 187, 219-220, 228; and God, 53, 91, 229; and goodness, 144-146, 239; and religious consciousness, 92-139; and value, 140-183, 188, 290-363; as futuristic, 248-250, 254, 257, 260, 263, 265, 268, 272-273, 277-279, 287-289, 294, 316, 319, 321-325, 359-360, 364, 389-390, 411; as ideal, 60; as next empirical quality, 57-58, 68-71, 73, 75, 78, 80, 82, 123, 145, 228, 230-232, 252-253, 259-261, 318; as nisus, 66, 85-91; as realized, 79-80, 87-88, 98, 103-104, 165, 188, 232-234, 242, 251, 258-259, 317; as soul of God, 123; as Spirit, 58-59; knowledge possessed by deity, 102-106, 171, 239-244; successive phases of deity, 73-78, 82-83, 85, 88-90, 98, 104, 123-124, 128, 138, 145, 231-235, 240, 242, 256, 270, 273, 277, 365
Demos, Raphael, 303, 322, 335-337, 374, 407, 427-429, 433
Descartes, René, 201, 208, 311
Determinism, 227
Development of American Philosophy, The (Creighton), 436

Devaux, Philippe, 25, 40, 86, 404, 406-407, 410
Devolution, 368
Dewey, John, 356-357
Dialogues of Plato, The, 407, 422
Dietrich, John H., 438
Ditheism, 289
Driesch, Hans, 37, 434
du Noüy, Lecomte, 346
Dualism, 277
Durée réelle, 12
Duty, 132

E

Eddington, Sir Arthur S., 228, 265
Education, 324, 359
Einstein, Albert, 13, 385-386, 399, 434-435
Elan vital, 91, 249, 280, 342, 345-346, 348, 382, 388
Eldridge, S., 437
Emergence, 28, 45, 51, 52, *passim;* and the numinous, 393-399, histories of, 368
Emergent Evolution (Morgan), 407, 409, 416, 419, 426
Emerson, R. W., 280
Emmet, Dorothy, 238, 283-284, 422, 425
Empiricism, 436
Empiricists, 295-296
Energy, 198, 213-214, 311, 367, 386, 390, 396, 398, 402, 424
England, F. E., 365, 432, 438
Enlightenment, 329, 398
Entelechy, 37
Epistemology, 1, 296, 371-372, 376, 378, 432; Alexander's 5-13, 34-35, 146, 294
Epitomization, 212
Epitomization (Conger), 420
Error, 145, 151, 153, 159, 170, 173, 178, 231, 269, 292, 297, 307, 322, 428
Essay in Physics (Samuel), 433
Essay on Man (Pope), 78

443

INDEX

Essays in East-West Philosophy (Wild), 431
Essence, 351
Essentialism, 310-311
Essentials in the Development of Religion (Turner), 405, 431
Eternal object, 50-51, 287, 430
Eternity, 30, 47-52, 59, 63, 102, 115, 206-207, 249, 257-258, 331-332, 353, 358, 395
Ether, 194, 367
Ethical Culture, 143
Ethics, 76, 110, 112, 137, 143-144, 302, 305, 328, 330, 337, 360, 369, 373, 376, 393, 433
Event, 16, 21, 44, 46, 196, 200, 209, 267, 275-276, 282-283, 353, 366; creative, 214, 352; future, 267-271
Evil, x-xi, 121, 135, 158-159, 181, 188, 214, 231, 303, 353, 363, 402; problem of, 135, 166-179, 320-324, 368, 415
Evolution, 30, 43-44, 75, 78, 91, 98, 133, 166, 171, 196, 199, 201-202, 206, 208, 211-213, 218, 256, 263, 265, 280, 282-283, 288, 310, 314-315, 342-346, 351, 358-359, 362, 368, 371, 381, 388-389, 395, 397, 406, 428, 430
Evolution in Action (Huxley), 432
Evolutionary Naturalism (Sellars), 32, 421
Ewing, A. C., 429
Existence, 3, 19, 26-27, 30, 43, 98, 112, 142, 144, 147, 159, 162, 170, 174, 180, 205, 210, 217-218, 256, 267, 269, 280, 319, 323, 335-336, 356, 358, 360, 372, 378-379, 435
Experience, 6-9, 12, 60, 63, 89, 99, 173, 192, 311, 336, 357, 379, 389, 400
Extension, 136

F

Faith of a Moralist, The (Taylor), 411, 415, 429
Fasti (Ovid), 97
Feibleman, J. K., 426, 436

Finalism, 346, 348
Finite deities, 63, 75, 254, 260, 288, 319, 388
Finite gods, 62-63, 67, 70, 72, 75-76, 77, 119, 123, 138, 179-180; 187, 232-233, 242, 254, 260, 273, 277, 288, 319, 352, 365
Fitch, F. B., 433
Flammarion, Camille, 401
Forms, 150, 158-159, 168, 170, 173-174, 199, 204-205, 211-212, 236, 241, 267, 334, 346, 349; artistic, 291, 366; evolutionary, 237, 257, 280, 287, 293, 314, 321, 345, 368, 389-390, 395, 397, 401, 431
Frankness in Religion (Hutcheon), 438
Freedom, 315, 362
Freedom and Experience (Blanshard), 433
Friend, J. W., 436
Future, The, 16-19, 25, 43-45, 59, 66, 74, 98-99, 102, 124, 227-228, 232-235, 239, 242-243, 249, 266, 278, 289, 391; as ideal, xvii; as real, 267, 269, 271-274

G

Galileo, 295-296, 307
Gandhi, x
Genius, 359, 362-363, 372, 402
Gifford Lectures, 1, 134, 413
Gilson, Etienne, 379, 432-433, 435
God, xii, xvi, xxii, 1, 45, 48-49, 53-55, 141, 174, 182, 229, 274, 279, 305, 318-319, 358, 382; as Creator, 48, 107, 111, 113-115, 118-119, 126-133, 137-138, 200, 208, 247, 282, 285-286, 362; as eternal, 63, 102, 137, 181, 206, 257-258, 286, 381; as first Cause, 55, 118, 351; as ground of world, 118; as Mind, 354-355; as Father, 130-131, 431; as ideal, 66, 68-70, 75, 79, 87-88, 135, 179, 233; as Other, 326, 330, 396; as personal, 101, 119, 131, 135, 137, 187, 236, 246, 282; as principle of conservation of value, 144, 160; as

444

INDEX

Son, 431; as sovereign, 134; as Substance, 230; as temporal, 243, 265-266; as ultimate, 253; as universe possessing deity, 59-66, 90, 171, 230, 235; as universe tending to deity, 76, 88, 95, 111, 122, 128, 132-133, 135, 157, 165, 220, 231, 234, 240, 246, 248-249, 261, 278, 354, 389; as unknown, 57, 356; as value, 144-147, 358; body of, 58, 62-63, 65-66, 69, 71-73, 76-77, 83, 85, 90, 95, 101, 103-104, 106, 108, 111, 114, 122, 125, 128-134, 138-139, 156-157, 166-167, 169-172, 179, 230-231, 235-244, 246, 249-250, 261-263, 264, 287-289, 321, 354, 364-365; definitions of, 53, 298, 355; goodness of, 102-103, 107-108, 115, 134, 156, 172; love of, 54, 109, 117, 121, 132, 137, 161; mind of, 59, 62-63, 65-66, 85, 90, 95, 123, 179, 230, 235-244, 246, 250, 263, 288-289, 354, 364; omnipotent, 102, 119, 135; omnipresent, 63; omniscient, 102-103, 107-108, 135, 137; of religion, 92-94, 97, 99, 100, 112, 244, 323-324, 333, 352-353, 363, 400-401, 403, 410, 413, 430, 437; religious criteria for concept of, 100-111, 137-138; timelessness of, 133-136, 231; Wieman's conception of, 352-358; will of, 116, 134; wisdom of, 117; word of, 114, 118

God (Boodin), 423

God-man, 116-117

God and Polarity (Sheldon), xxiii, 420

God and the Astronomers (Inge), 423, 429, 436

God was in Christ (Baillie), 413

Good, the, 121, 141, 146-148, 154, 157-159, 166, 169-173, 175, 181, 188, 214, 221, 231, 292, 297, 299, 301, 303-307, 309, 316, 337, 353, 435, 437; coherence theory of, 292, 302; common, 307, 316; indefinable, 300, 313; intrinsic, 155, 312

Goodness, 1, 109-110, 121, 140, 142, 144-147, 153-157, 159, 161-162, 168, 174, 181, 291-294, 297, 299-300, 309, 320, 323-324, 326, 333-335, 338-339, 345-346, 358, 360, 365-366, 382, 392-393, 397, 426

Gravitation, 36-37, 342, 434-435

Great Visions of Philosophy (Montague), 433

Green, T. H., 108

Greene, Theodore M., xxiii, 294-295, 297-298, 337, 366, 426-427

Growth, 310, 321, 353-355, 360

Growth of Religion, The (Wieman and Horton), 431

H

Haldane, J. B. S., 434
Hallet, H. F., 424, 437
Happiness, 301-302
Hartmann, Nicolai, 434
Hartshorne, Charles, 238, 243, 249, 422
Harvard Theological Review, The, 432
Hazelton, Roger, 48, 407
Heaven, 48-49, 302, 331
Hegel, G. W. F., 111, 432
Hendel, C. W., 434
Heraclitus, 307
Heresy, 153, 292, 304, 306-307
Heritage of Kant, The (Whitney and Bowers), 427
Hibbert Journal, The, 407-408, 419, 422-423, 426, 431
Hicks, G. Dawes, 194-196, 261-262, 288, 419, 423-424
Hierarchy: of existents, 71, 74, 86, 92, 100, 107-108, 125, 136, 158, 163, 165, 170, 180, 182, 187, 263, 273, 277, 310; of forms, 32, 158; of levels, 38, 216-217, 265-266; of qualities, 32, 78, 80, 85, 87-88, 90-91, 104-105, 123-124, 162, 240, 320, 343; of values, 320; of wholes, 344
Hinduism, 206-207
History of Philosophical Systems, A (Veatch), 429
Hitler, 302
Hlavaty, Vaclav, 434-435

INDEX

Hocking, W. E., 329, 435
Hoernlé, R. F. Alfred, xix-xx
Höffding, H., 109, 141-142, 144, 156, 160, 392, 412, 415
Hofstadter, Richard, 315, 428
Holism, 212-213, 342-346, 348, 351, 354, 367, 370, 382-383, 388, 392, 395, 401, 430, 434, 437
Holism and Evolution (Smuts), 342, 383, 420, 430, 434
Holy, the, 393, 437
Horton, W. M., 431
Hoyle, Fred, 194-198, 265, 367, 419
Humanism, 315, 400-401, 438
Humanist, The, 438
Hume, David, 7, 27, 207
Hundred Years of British Philosophy, A (Metz), 404, 422
Hutcheon, R. J., 399, 438
Huxley, Julian, 368, 432
Hylomorphism, 348-351, 431
Hyle, 23
Hymn to Colour (Meredith), 235, 408

I

Idea of God in the Light of Recent Philosophy, The (Pringle-Pattison), 404-405, 410, 412, 414, 421, 428, 434
Idea of Immortality, The (Pringle-Pattison), 429
Idea of Nature (Collingwood), 424-425, 433
Idea of the Holy (Otto), 429, 431, 437
Idealism, xix-xxi, 3-4, 45, 47, 200, 204, 206-207, 213, 376, 403-404, 432, 434, 436; Absolute, 3, 52, 80-85, 108, 112, 182; Berkeleyan, 387; ethical, 305; German, 429; in Platonism, 340; subjective, 371, 435
Idealists, xiv, 212-213, 228, 335, 374, 432, 435-436
Ideals, 304-306, 325, 344
Identity, 26-28
Identity and Reality (Meyerson), 436

Ideologies of Religion, The (Conger), 438
Ideology, 369, 374
Illusion, 151, 206-207, 214, 265-266, 270, 275, 296, 391, 435
Immanence, 36, 55, 90, 111-112, 114-120, 125, 220, 245-249, 285-287, 289, 313, 338, 342, 346, 348, 353, 396, 414, 430
Immortality, 127, 175-179, 330-333, 357, 368
Incarnation, 117, 298-299, 358-359, 361-363, 370, 384-385, 397, 399, 401-402, 413, 417
Individuality, 36, 113, 121-122, 125, 156, 216
Individuation, 351
Infinity, 44-45, 63-66, 89, 102, 133
Infra-pantheism, 91, 138, 235, 283, 355, 414
Inge, William Ralph, 45, 49, 264-266, 288, 331-332, 386-387, 407, 423, 429, 436
Inquiry, process of, 356-357, 366, 378, 396
Instinct, 325-326, 366
Integration, 32, 57, 71, 210, 219, 419
Intellect, 330, 360, 389, 391
Intelligible World (Urban), 420, 429-430
Internal rearrangements, 46, 63, 69, 71-74, 92, 128
Introduction to Realistic Philosophy (Wild), 404, 427-430, 433
Introduction to the Philosophy of Religion (Bertocci), 412-413
Intuition, 60, 203-204, 305, 314, 438
Irving, John A., xxiv
Is God Emeritus? (Mathews), 431
Isotopes, 193
Israel, 118

J

Jahve, 118
James, William, 94, 142, 411, 430
Jeans, Sir James, 228, 265
Jennings, H. S., 423
Jesus, x-xii, xv, 132, 165, 399

446

INDEX

Joachim, M. H., 435
Johnson, Samuel, 415
Journal of Philosophy, The, 433
Journal of Religion, The, 407, 413, 437
Journal of The History of Ideas, The, 430
Journal of the History of Ideas, The, 430
Judaism, 112
Justice, 301

K

Kant, Immanuel, 26, 114, 118, 396, 401, 427
Keats, John, 149, 395
Kierkegaard, S., 413
Klibanski, R., 407, 420
Knowledge, 106-107, 375, 383, 400, 432, 434-435
Konvitz, Milton R., xxii, 299, 302, 365, 427, 432

L

Laird, John, 2, 205, 208, 211, 250-263, 288, 370, 404, 420, 422-423, 432
Laplace, Pierre Simon de, 106, 222, 227, 269
Laws, of nature, 36, 100, 225-226, 266, 288, 308, 342, 377, 430, 436
Le Boutillier, Cornelia Geer, 248, 250, 252, 422
Le Système d'Alexander (Devaux), 404
Leibniz, G. W., 60, 116, 204, 379
Leighton, J. A., 209-211, 213, 218-220, 420-421
Levels of Existence, 30-33, 35-36, 39, 42, 56-59, 63-64, 68, 70, 72, 78, 80, 89, 91, 99, 106, 145, 157-158, 160, 162, 171, 178, 179, 187-188, 196, 199, 207, 210-211, 213-216, 218-219, 222-223, 233, 237, 256, 260, 264, 277, 284, 293, 317, 342, 350, 352-355, 364, 368, 378, 382-385, 388-389, 392, 395, 408, 434, 437

Liddell, Anna Forbes, 66, 271, 409, 424
Life: and physico-chemical processes, 33, 35-38, 50, 58, 210, 217, 220-223, 228, 255-256, 280-281, 370; as wave, 285; eternal, 357-358; future, 177, 331; mental, 168-170, 321-322, 417
Lincoln, Abraham, 301
Lines of advance, 15-18, 41-43, 75
Locke John 7, 9
Logic, 203, 372, 376, 433
Loomer, Bernard H., 437
Love, 142, 305, 307, 345, 358, 412
Lowe, Victor, 430

M

McCarthy, John W., 231, 421
Mach, Ernst, 386
Macintosh, D. C., 389, 437
McTaggart, J. M. E. 2
Major Features of Evolution, The (Simpson), 423
Man, 24, 44, 72, 83, 85, 121-122, 134-135, 137, 144, 156, 168, 172, 196, 205, 239, 241, 243, 246, 250, 260, 280, 293, 296, 311, 314, 376; as dependent on God, 108-109, 120, 130; as measure of all things, 237; as pattern of all things, 237, 287; continuous with God, 113, 400; greatness of, 163-166, 360, 382; obedience to God, 110; organic to nature, 219, 343, 345, 367, 395, 428; response to universe, 11, 143, 325 327, 358, 360, 362, 436
Man and the Cosmos (Leighton), 420
Man's Freedom (Weiss), 426
Maritain, Jacques, 252-253, 435
Materialism, 4, 209-221, 375-377, 386-387, 434, 436; mechanical, 212-213, 216, 218, 228, 360; reductive, 37, 207, 217, 385
Materiality, 25, 35, 38, 57-58, 61-62, 72, 74, 194-195, 197, 199, 228, 238, 252, 254-255, 261-262, 266, 364, 368, 384

INDEX

Math. Annalen., 409
Mathematics, 187-192, 197, 199, 201, 223, 309, 387, 409, 419, 434-435
Mathematics and the Imagination (Kasner and Newman), 409
Mathews, Shailer, 431
Matter, 32-34, 37-38, 61, 70, 72, 74, 85, 115, 119, 145, 192-193, 196-197, 199, 211-214, 216-217, 221-222, 237-238, 261, 265, 270, 273, 280, 290, 295, 311, 338, 344, 355, 360, 364, 371-372, 379, 383-386, 408, 425; prime, 349-351
Maya, 206
Meaning of Evolution, The (Simpson), 428
Meaning of God in Human Experience, The (Hocking), 435
Mechanism, 37, 210-211, 227-228, 344, 346, 348, 370
Meeting of Extremes in Contemporary Philosophy, The (Bosanquet), 406, 420
Meland, B. E., 422
Memory, 6, 63-64, 238, 267
Mental, the, 6, 105, 258-259
Mentalism, 308, 372, 385-386, 434, 436
Meredith, George, 131, 235, 408
Metabolism, 36
Metaphysics, xii, xvi, xxi, 1-4, 19, 24, 26, 28, 33, 41, 53-54, 58-60, 64, 72, 75-77, 80, 82, 84, 86-87, 90-93, 95, 99, 106, 108, 111-112, 122, 125, 127, 130-131, 133, 136-137, 166, 176, 179, 182, 188-189, 198, 202, 209, 211-212, 214, 219-220, 225, 253, 258, 260, 265, 286, 310, 337, 343, 355, 370-372, 383-384, 425, 432-433, 435; as meaningless, 373; schools of, 373-381
Metz, Rudolf, 1, 247, 249, 404, 406, 422
Meyer-Abich, 434
Meyerson, Emile, 387, 436
Microcosm, 154, 370
Mill, J. S., xiv
Mind: and brain, 236; and physical-chemical processes, 81, 124, 176, 217, 220, 262; and works of art, 291-299; cosmic, 348; creativity of, 357, 360; enjoyment of, 5-6, 10, 124, 209, 242-243, 254; of lower level, 237-239, 264
Mind, 405, 419
Mind and its Place in Nature, The (Broad), 421
Minds, other, 99, 156
Minkowski, H., 13
Monads, 116
Monism, 81
Monotheism, 76, 102
Montague, W. P., 221-224, 226-227, 229, 375-376, 404, 421, 433
Moore, G. E., 294-295, 297, 299-300, 310, 313-314, 343, 366, 426-428, 430
Moral Life and the Ethical Life, The (Vivas), 427
Morality, 121, 141-143, 155, 175, 243, 290, 292, 303, 305, 313, 322, 328, 366, 377
Morgan, C. Lloyd, 74-75, 196, 212, 287, 345, 348, 386, 388-389, 407, 409-410, 416, 419, 426, 430, 436
Motion, 25, 27-28, 34-36, 40-41, 43, 72, 81, 87, 105, 212, 217, 223, 405
Mysterium tremendum, xxiii, 326, 358, 395-397, 437
Mystery, 143, 325-326, 358, 361, 379, 392, 397-398
Mysticism, 109, 120, 161, 206, 305, 361, 393, 397-398, **411-412**
Mysticism (Underhill), 412
Mysticism in Religion (Inge), 407
Mythology, 117, 127, 233, 242

N

Natural law, 212, 312-314, 341-342, 344, 348, 366-367, 427, 430
Natural piety, 107, 222-223, 226-227, 229, 351, 363, 406
Natural selection, 164, 293, 314-315, 428
Naturalism, xix-xx, 207, 211, 214, 288, 316, 403, 433; evolutionary,

INDEX

212, 375-376; higher, 218-219; lower, 218-219; theistic, 357-358, 371
Naturalism of Samuel Alexander, The (McCarthy), 421
Naturalistic fallacy, 297
Nature, 57, 113, 117, 121, 140, 142-143, 149-150, 174, 178, 198, 205-207, 212, 214, 219, 248-249, 266, 296, 298, 308, 312, 324, 360-361, 363, 382, 414; as qualitied, 380; as sublime, 381; dynamism of, 216, 340, 349, 351, 367, 388, 395, 401, 434; history of, 31-32, 215; human, 177, 305-306, 341-342; inorganic, 344
Nature and Values (Brightman), 436
Nature, Man and God (Temple), 415, 421-422
Nature of Deity, The (Turner), 423, 432
Nature of the Universe, The (Hoyle), 419
Nature of Truth, The (Joachim), 435
Needham, Joseph, 421
Neo-Realism, xix, xx, 2, 9
Neo-Thomism, xxiii, 2, 7
New York Times, 434
Nirvana, xi
Nisus, xvi, 56-60, 63, 66-67, 71, 74, 77-80, 85-91, 95-98, 100, 105, 107, 123, 128, 131, 133, 136-138, 140, 157, 159, 162-166, 173, 175, 177, 179, 181-183, 187-188, 203, 207-208, 212, 216, 218, 220, 359-360, 394, 396; and God and Deity, 230-289; and value, 288, 339, 346, 392; as creative, 275-280, 282-289, 320, 325, 328, 339, 342, 344-345, 348, 352-355, 358, 361, 369, 382, 388-392, 398, 411, 416, 425; as law, 266; as spontaneous, 347
Nock, A. D., 432
Nontheism, 312
Norms, 312-314, 341, 344, 348, 367
Noumenalism, 9-10
Nows, as perishing, 16, 200
Numinous, the, 326-327, 329, 392-396, 399, 402, 437

O

Object, 146, 155, 214, 240, 300, 336, 339; artistic, 149, 290-291, 299; as contemplated; 5-6, 10, 242, 254; as independent, 9-10, 295, 344, 380, 432
Objectivity, 295, 306, 334-335, 337-338, 366, 377, 435
On Growth and Form (Thompson), 431
On the Nature of Value (Konvitz), xxii, 427, 432
One and the Many, 42, 81
Ontology, xxiii, 198, 311-312, 334, 375, 378-380, 383, 386, 433, 436
Order and Life (Needham), 421
Organic Unities, 310, 313-314, 338, 343-344, 437
Organic Whole, 297, 299, 313, 338, 343-344
Organisms, 32, 36, 38, 81, 83, 94, 124, 159, 167-169, 211, 215-216, 220-221, 282, 311, 313-315, 321-322, 330, 342-343, 345, 354, 367, 369, 377, 384, 388, 414, 424, 437
Organization, 32, 37, 215-218, 280, 282, 284, 287, 302, 315, 318, 339, 343, 345, 347, 360, 395, 419, 424, 434
Organization of Life, The (Eldridge), 437
Orthodoxy, 100, 116, 120, 245
Otto, Rudolf, xxiii, 326, 329, 392-399, 429, 431, 437
Our Part in this World (Adler), 415
Ovid, 97

P

Paganism, 324
Palágyi, 24
Panpsychism, 29
Pantheism, xiv, xvii, 91, 101, 108, 111-126, 136, 138, 166, 172-173, 230-231, 244, 250, 253, 263, 265, 277, 282, 287-288, 321, 355, 410, 414
Paradise Lost (Milton), 179
Parmenides, 207

INDEX

Parsons, Talcott, 369, 432
Past, the, 16-19, 21, 25, 43-45, 52, 102, 267-269, 271-276, 278, 365
Paton, H. J., 407, 420
Pearson, Karl, 386
Perception, 6, 9-10
Perfection, 144-145, 156, 165, 170, 181, 205, 256, 326, 359
Pericles, 97
Perry, Ralph Barton, xix
Persistent Problems of Philosophy, The (Calkins), 407
Personalism, 375
Personality, 36, 93, 95-96, 113, 178, 348, 359-363, 384, 389, 392, 399
Persons, 141, 154, 178, 236-237, 290-363, 380, 401
Phenomenalism, 9, 373, 375, 378, 388
Philosophers Speak of God (Hartshorne and Reese), 422
Philosophic Basis of Moral Obligation, The (Turner), 421
Philosophical and Literary Pieces, (Alexander), 404
Philosophical Review, The, 420, 433
Philosophy, 2, 136, 141, 203, 328-329, 334, 340, 357, 375; evolutionary, 212-213, 229, 351, 361, 371, 406; modern, 207, 295, 373, 386; modernist; 202; of nature, 434-435; of organism, 287; of science, 436; Realistic, 295, 427
Philosophy, 419, 422, 425
Philosophy and History (Klibanski and Paton), 407, 420
Philosophy and Phenomenological Research, 427, 430, 433
Philosophy in American Education (Blanshard), 433
Philosophy of Nature (Schlick), 434
Philosophy of Physical Realism, The (Sellars), 405, 433
Philosophy of Religion, A (Brightman), 412-413
Philosopohy of Religion (Höffding), 412, 415
Plato, 4, 26, 48-49, 114, 206, 432-433
Platonism, 48, 50-51, 102, 340, 373, 376

Plato's Modern Enemies and the Theory of Natural Law (Wild), 420, 427, 429, 431
Pltato's Theory of Man (Wild), 429
Pluralism, 81, 435
Point-instants, 13-14, 17, 19, 29, 41, 63, 71, 77, 194, 270, 272-273, 276-277, 284, 289, 350, 391, 424
Point-instant-values, 338, 345, 347
Polytheism, 61, 76, 101, 233, 263, 288, 365
Pope, Alexander, 78
Popper, Karl, 419
Positivism, 206-207, 295, 341, 371, 373-376, 384, 386, 388, 433, 436, 438
Potentiality, 39-40, 98, 250, 310-312, 332, 339, 360, 382
Pragmatism, 188, 371, 375, 402, 435, 438
Pratt, J. B., 305, 411, 427
Prediction, 221-227, 267-268, 373, 380, 432
Present, the, 17-18, 25, 44-45, 98, 267-268, 271, 274-275, 280, 365, 381
Present Philosophic Tendencies (Perry), xx
Principia Ethica (Moore), 426
Principles of Mathematics, The (Russell), 409
Pringle-Pattison, A. S., 11, 117, 218-220, 228, 264, 323-324, 332-333, 380, 404-405, 407, 410, 412, 414, 421, 428-429, 434
Problem of Knowledge, The (Cassirer), 434
Problems of Life (Bertalanffy), 434
Proceedings of the British Academy, 404
Process, 134, 137, 160, 187, 198-199, 208, 210-211, 214, 217-219, 232, 251, 256, 265-266, 280, 285, 323, 342-343, 354, 385, 389-390, 397, 401, 437
Process: Philosophy, xxiii, 39, 207, 212-213, 216, 381, 383, 385, 387-388, 436-437; as co-eternal with universe, 256-258
Process and Reality (Whitehead), 408, 425, 430

450

INDEX

Progress, 252, 256-257, 424
Prolegomena to an Idealistic Theory of Knowledge (N. K. Smith), 435
Prometheus, 103, 240, 255
Prophets, xi, 132, 302-307, 399, 412, 432
Propositions, 151-153, 155
Protagoras, 237
Protoplasm, 215
Providence, 135, 172, 353
Psychical research, 177
Psychoid, 37
Psychologism, 327, 391
Purpose, 175, 296, 308, 321-323, 362, 377, 424

Q

Qualities, 27, 29-33, 37, 39-42, 50, 62-63, 90, 163, 166, 181-182, 187, 208-210, 224, 240, 262, 266, 268, 277, 284, 288, 292, 317, 332, 342, 366-368; aesthetic, 36, 211, 294-295; mental, 386; objective, 294-295, 313, 345; primary, 7-8, 33, 35-36, 38, 147, 156, 237, 261, 290, 295, 297, 336-338; secondary, 7-8, 11, 25-26, 34-36, 38, 51, 147-148, 156, 209, 237, 290, 294-295, 297, 320, 333, 336-338, 380-381, 409; spiritual, 36, 211-212, 298, 359; tertiary, 1, 147-148, 155, 157, 161, 290, 294-295, 297, 320, 333, 336-338, 359 380-381, 392

R

Radioactivity and Nuclear Physics (Cork), 419
Real, the, 4, 147, 168, 411, 424
Realism, xx, 9, 11, 35, 213, 357, 387-389, 404, 435; Alexander's, 1-52, 96, 146, 182, 290, 336, 378-381, 383; Anglo-American, 375; critical, 9-10, 380, 405-406; direct, xxi, 7-8, 34, 371, 380, 406, 428, 432; emergent, 375; ethical, 309, 312, metaphysics of, xxi, 146, 294, 378-381; modern, 407; religious, 437; Scholastic, xxi; schools of, 7, 34; value, 294, 366, 381, 426
Realists, 8, 10, 34, 312, 335, 388, 403, 435
Reality, 16, 33, 49, 55, 67, 81, 94-95, 97-98, 137, 144, 151-153, 156, 169, 187, 190, 199, 210, 217, 219, 292, 295, 308-309, 311, 325, 368, 380, 382-385, 390, 399; as becoming, 381; as duration, 203; as eternal, 206, 411; as objective, xiii, 52, 356, 385, 435; as physical, 9; as ultimate, xvi, 19, 327, 340-341, 379, 387, 435, 437; creativeness of, 205, 211, 333, 362; religious view of, 11, 329
Reality (Weiss), 426, 433
Reality in Worship (Sperry), 438
Reason, 323, 341, 352, 396, 407, 426, 430, 438
Reason and Law (Cohen), 430
Redemption, 169-170, 257-258, 322
Reese, William L., 243, 249, 422
Relations, 298; cognitive, 6; external, 311; logical, 203-204; physical, 221
Relativity, theory of, 189-190, 198, 385, 434-435
Religion, 53-54, 60-61, 81, 130, 135 141-144, 146-147, 162, 165-166, 206-207, 212, 218, 233, 242, 258, 328, 330, 402-403; as illusion, 96; as irrational, 353, 396; as subjective, 137; definitions of, 11, 325, 359, 385, 391, 405, 436-437; Moslem, 326; natural, 107; of humanity, xix; philosophy of, xviii-xxi, 94, 111, 121, 126, 231, 244-245, 352, 376, 382, 388, 393, 398, 402-403, 414, 435; primary concern of, ix-xvii, 377, 382, 388, 400, 438; sociology of, 97; supreme exemplars of, 369-370, 382, 402
Religion and Philosophy (Collingwood), 413
Religion and the Modern Mind (Stace), 206, 384, 420, 433
Religion and the Rise of Capitalism (Tawney), 416
Religion in Life, 437

451

INDEX

Religions, 76, 110, 141, 164, 323
Religious: consciousness, 92-139, 233, 328, 356, 401-402; emotion, 54, 93-95, 99-100, 126, 137, 156, 298, 325, 328, 330, 390, 394; experience, xi, xiii, 92, 99, 122, 126, 268, 298, 327-329, 382; faith, 61, 144, 352, 356, 400, 437; giants, 165, 358, 360, 363, 385, 400-401; object, 146, 156, 391-392, 396, 435; passion, 54, 325-326; sentiment, 53-54, 92-98, 127, 130, 136-137, 140-144, 161, 176-177, 205, 250, 267, 325-334, 371, 391; thought, ix, xvi, xviii, 162, 377
Religions Consciousness, The (Pratt), 411
Religious Realism, (Macintosh), 437
Religious Values in the Philosophy of Emergent Evolution (Le Boutillier), 422
Return to Reason, The (Wild), 407, 426
Right, 154, 291-292, 300
Righteousness, 181, 399
Roads to Truth, Two (Sinnott), 424
Russell, Bertrand, 386, 404, 409

S

Sacramental Universe, A. (Bowman), 384, 432
Sacrifice, 134, 174, 323-324, 353, 363, 428
St. Augustine, 49
St. Chrysostom, 400
St. Paul, x-xi
Samuel, Herbert, Viscount, 197-199, 367, 385, 419, 433
Schleiermacher, F. E. D., 109, 331
Schlick, Moritz, 384, 434
Scholasticism, 62
Science, 2, 141, 151-153, 194, 201, 206, 212, 223, 226, 265, 280, 308, 315-316, 328-329, 359, 373-375, 385-387, 389, 401-402, 408, 412, 436, 438
Science and Common Sense (Conant), 433

Science and Religion (Alexander), 416, 429, 437
Science and the Modern World (Whitehead), 432-433
Self-Creativity, 286, 424
Self-Realization, 313-314, 339, 367
Sellars, Roy Wood, 9, 32, 212, 217, 371, 375, 405-406, 421, 433
Semanticism, 371, 375-376, 433, 438
Sensation, 6-8, 140, 377, 432
Sensum, 7
Sheldon, W. H., xxiii, 420
Simpson, G. G., 314, 423, 427-428
Sinnott, Edmund W., 421, 424-425
Skepticism, 207
Smith, Adam, 154, 416
Smith John E., 435
Smith, Norman Kemp, 435
Smuts, J. C., 212, 215-216, 287, 342-346, 348, 354, 371, 381-384, 388, 395, 420, 430, 434, 437
Social Darwinism in American Thought (Hofstadter), 428
Social System, The (Parsons), 432
Society, 168, 292, 300, 303-306, 315, 321
Society, Culture, and Personality (Sorokin), 437
Sociology, 369
Socrates, 171
Solipsism, 435
Sophistes (Plato), 26
Sorokin, Pitirim A., 437
Soul, 38-39, 127, 170, 396, 398, 400
Source of Human Good, The (Wieman), 420-421, 431-432
Space, 71, 85, 159, 169, 172, 189, 271, 321, 338; as full of memory, 21; as total, 29, 230, 275; as whole of parts, 13-14, 42, 167, 196-197, 236, 272; Bergson's doctrine of, 19; dimensions of, 12-13, 190; union with Time, 13-17, 20, 23, 28, 187, 189, 192-199
Space-Time: and categories, 12-28, 231; as Absolute, 45-52, 80-85; as actual, 78-79, 318; as animated, 39; as historical, 23, 44-45, 51-52, 59, 71, 82, 88, 90, 123-124,

INDEX

130, 166, 175, 199-209, 255, 257, 267, 270, 310, 367, 420; as infinite becoming, 41, 45, 47, 182, 187, 199, 355; as mathematical, 187-191, 367; as pattern of body and mind, 236-239; as phenomenal, 334-335; as *plenum*, 23, 189-190, 194, 196-198, 367; as potential, 349; as primordial, 33, 35, 38-41, 57 ff., 187, 193-194, 196, 210-211, 219, 230, 238, 266, 283, 332, 345, 348-350; as stuff, 24, 33, 37, 59-60, 349-350; as whole, 14, 42 ff., 172, 199-209, 228, 230-231, 240, 247, 249-250, 275, 277-278, 280, 284-285, 287, 317, 320, 335, 340, 342, 395, 420; formula for, 28-45; total, 21-23, 166, 188, 350

Space, Time, and Deity (S. Alexander), xxi, 1-2, 28, 56, 85, 221, 326, 404

Space-Time-Value, 332, 334-348, 367

Sperry, Willard L., 396, 437-438

Spinoza, 54, 118, 121, 136-137, 204, 206, 230, 244, 279, 408, 437

Spinozism, 204

Spirit, xx, 58-59, 70, 75, 112, 212, 236, 330, 400; Absolute, 80-85

Spiritualism, 331

Spirituality, 359, 363, 371

Stace, W. T., 206-207, 377, 384, 386, 420, 433

Stevenson, C. L., 337

Stiernotte, Alfred P., ix, xiii-xiv, xvii, xxiv

Stirling, J. H., 11

Streeter, B. H., 431

Studies in Philosophic Naturalism (Tenney), 425

Subjectivism, 8-9, 96, 146, 291, 295-297, 308-309, 313, 334-337, 357, 372-374, 376-377, 380, 383-386, 396, 426, 435

Subsistence, 27

Substance, 24, 27, 136, 212, 349, 351, 386

Suffering, 134, 323, 400

Symbolic logic, 373, 433

Symbols, 131, 135, 334-335, 359, 396, 400

Swedenborg, Emanuel, 236

Syntheses, 214-215, 226, 239, 282-285, 310, 320, 347, 354

Systematic Theology (Tillich), 429, 433

T

Tawney, R. H., 416

Taylor, A. E., 97, 147, 411, 415, 429

Temple, William, archbishop, 220-221, 228, 247, 415, 421-422

Tenney, Charles D., 425

Theism, xiv, xvii, 11, 101, 107-108, 111-126, 135-138, 165-166, 172-173, 176, 218, 220, 228, 231, 235, 244-254, 258, 285, 287, 298, 312, 323, 410, 414; Christian, 264, 353, 358; empirical, 138, 243, 320, 352, 389; evolutionary, 227; temporalistic 243

Theism and Cosmology (Laird), 420

Theology, 22, 55, 93, 108, 116-117, 119-120, 127, 131, 139, 235-236, 238-239, 244, 247, 253, 264, 274, 327, 329, 361, 363, 369; Buddhist, 92; Christian, 92, 114-155, 127, 386, 389; civil, 97; empirical, xxii, 358; Jewish, 92; natural, 97; Neo-orthodox, 305, 437

Theory of Direct Realism, A (Turner), 405, 419

Thermodynamics, second law of, 264-266, 288, 423-424

Thomism, 436

Thompson, D'A. W., 431

Thought, 6-7, 129, 134, 136, 140-141, 161, 239, 269, 313; and being, 379, 435; laws of, 26

Tillich, Paul xvi, 329, 379, 402, 429, 433

Timaeus, (Plato), 48, 114

Time, 60, 63, 68, 73, 128, 133-134, 163, 166, 170-171, 208, 240, 242, 244, 250, 256-258, 265-266, 288, 333, 338; as created, 48, 114; as duration, 44, 49, 191, 339, 391; as mathematical, 47, 52, 191-192, 201; as

453

INDEX

mind or soul of Space, 28-29, 38, 56, 77, 79-80, 85-88, 136, 212, 236, 284-285; as real, 16, 45, 52, 201-202, 204-205, 207, 211, 218, 232-234, 269, 271-272, 310, 342, 365, 381; as spatial, 19, 272-274; as total, 29; as unreal, 202-203, 227, 275, 382; as whole of parts, 13-14, 16, 42-43, 45, 63, 236, 249; characters of, 12, 30, 200, 267-268, 283, 350; creativity of, 48, 56, 271, 283
Time-coefficients, 17-19, 21-23, 45, 272, 274, 350, 405
Totum simul, 22, 45
Transcedence, 90, 111-120, 123, 125, 232-233, 245-248, 330
Troelstsch, Ernest, 333
Truth, 1, 109, 113, 140, 142, 146-148, 151-152, 156-157, 159, 161, 181, 231, 290, 293-294, 307-309, 320, 326, 333-334, 346, 358, 360, 382, 392, 397, 401, 426, 435, 437; as antecedent, 366; coherence theory of, 151-154, 292, 308, 365; correspondence theory of, 151-153, 308
Tsanoff, Radoslav A., 431
Turner, J. E., 8, 10, 189, 192, 217, 362, 405, 419, 423, 431-432
Turner, William, 149
Two Sources of Morality and Religion (Bergson), 428, 438
Types of Religious Experience Christian and Non-Christian (Wach), 429

U

Ulich, Robert, 360, 431
Undeity, 145
Underhill, Evelyn, 412
Unity of Philosophical Experience, The (Gilson), 433, 435
Universality, 27
Universals, 27, 44, 66, 140, 297-298, 339, 347-348, 361, 402
Universe, 5, 11-12, 16-17, 20, 42-43, *passim.;* as historical, 22, 46-48, 59, 239, 255-256; as mental, 371; as mysterious, 325-327, 330, 361, 382, 395-396, 399-401; as non-mental, 212, 374, 435; as running down, 265-266; creativity of, 330, 360-363, 398-399, 401-403, 424, 430; origin of, 355-356. *See* Creation
Universe and Dr. Einstein, The (Barnett), 386, 434-435
Universe and Life, The (Jennings), 423
Unmind, 145
Unvalue, 145, 170, 293, 317
Urban, Wilbur, 202, 204, 206, 228, 334, 420, 429-430

V

Validity of Religious Experience, The (England), 432, 438
Value, 109, 135, 140, 161, 178, 253, 296, 361, 369, 399, 401-402; and deity, 140-183, 290-363, 408, 426; aesthetic, 291, 299-300, 309; as human inventions, 144-147, 151, 156, 290, 310, 312, 317, 365-366, 368, 392; as interest, 337, 342; conservation of, 142, 144, 156, 160, 178, 318-320, 328, 362-363, 392; criticism of Alexander's theory of, 290-316, 325, 329, 334, 365-366; economic, 181; ethical, 299, 309, 330; in nature, 296, 385; intrinsic, 291, 300, 309, 415; objective, xxi, 146, 156, 291, 295, 298-299, 309-310, 313, 320, 327, 333-348, 367, 392, 402, 426, 429, 437; relative, 301, 437; spiritual, 332, 334, 438; subjective, xxi, 148, 291, 295, 334-335, 337, 426; survival, 158-159, 182, 293, 314, 316-317
Varieties of Religious Experience (James), 94, 411, 415
Veatch, Henry, 429-430
Vivas, Eliseo, 426-427
Vitalism, 37, 434
Vlastos, Gregory, 341, 429

W

Wach, Joachim, 327-328, 429

INDEX

Ways of Genius, The (Tsanoff), 431
Ways of Things, (Montague), 404, 421
Weiss, Paul, 296, 378, 426, 433
Welldon, 49
What Science Really Means (Friend and Feibleman), 436
Whitehead, A. N., 1-2, 49-51, 95, 284-287, 308, 329, 345, 347-348, 351-352, 371-372, 380, 382-383, 388, 404, 408, 425, 427, 430, 432-433
Whitney, G. T., 427
Whole, 3, 47, 121, 153, 199-209, 216-217, 225, 268, 282, 303, 344, 346, 348, 350, 367, 381, 395, 401, 411; and parts, 343, 347, 354, 388, 417, 419, 430
Wieman, Henry Nelson, xxiii, 36, 139, 208, 243-244, 320, 329, 351-358, 366-367, 383, 388-389, 396, 420-422, 431-432, 436-437
Wild, John, xxiii, 8, 34-35, 207, 306, 311-312, 351, 353, 366, 404, 407, 417, 420-421, 427-431, 433
Will, 154-155, 168, 172, 174, 292, 300-302, 304
Williams, Donald, xxiii, 376, 420, 433
Woodger, J. H., 216, 314, 388, 428, 434, 436

Wordsworth, William, 149
World, 2-3, 5, 53, 55, 59, 61-62, 90, 94, 101, 105, 111, 117-118, 134-135, 161, 164, 171, 175, 209, 237, 243, 264, 323, 357, 376-377, 380, 391; as appearance, 206; as external, 432, 436; as historical, 20, 44-46, 106, 200, 268; as illusion, 206-207, 378; as material, 112, 115, 118, 295-296, 389; as temporal, 51, 203; as tendency to deity, 96-99, 123, 135, 162, 175, 187, 232, 261-263, 269, 278, 280, 282; creative advance into novelty, 278, 347; origigin of, *see* Creation; permeated with values, 296, 341, 355
World War I, 134, 323, 434
World-soul, 29, 77-80, 82, 87-88
Worship, xvii, 53, 60-61, 100, 109, 113, 117-118, 120-121, 130, 136, 141, 147, 161, 362, 402, 435, 438

Y

Yale University, xxix

Z

Zeus, 103, 240

To Bro James Pond
with Best wish-
Alex P Kleinic